ESSAYS ON

Renaissance Poetry

*The Greek Anthology in France and in the Latin Writers
of the Netherlands to the Year 1800*

The Greek Anthology in Italy to the Year 1800

ESSAYS ON
Renaissance Poetry

JAMES HUTTON

EDITED BY *Rita Guerlac*

FOREWORD BY *D. P. Walker*

Cornell University Press

ITHACA AND LONDON

PN 1181
H 88

THIS BOOK HAS BEEN PUBLISHED WITH THE AID
OF A GRANT FROM THE HULL MEMORIAL PUBLICATION FUND OF CORNELL UNIVERSITY

The photograph on page 240 is © S.P.A.D.E.M., Paris/V.A.G.A., New York, 1980.

First published 1980 by Cornell University Press.
Published in the United Kingdom by Cornell University Press Ltd.,
2–4 Brook Street, London W1Y 1AA.

International Standard Book Number 0-8014-1253-6
Library of Congress Catalog Card Number 80-66898
Printed in the United States of America
*Librarians: Library of Congress cataloging information appears
on the last page of the book.*

Foreword

The practice of collecting and publishing the articles, dispersed in many periodicals, of eminent scholars needs, I think, no justification. All serious students of the Renaissance know how valuable such collections are—those of P. O. Kristeller, Eugenio Garin, or E. H. Gombrich for example—and how much time they save. In the case of James Hutton, the need for such a volume is particularly urgent because, since his two monumental studies on the Greek Anthology were published in 1937 and 1946, all his work has appeared in the form of articles. It is of great importance that this work should be made accessible to present-day students. For he is a scholar of a kind that has always been rare and is likely soon to become rarer still: a thoroughly trained classicist who has spent most of his life studying Renaissance literature, both vernacular and Latin.

Now, as he himself wrote in the preface to his first book, "the effect of Greek and Roman literature upon the modern literature of Europe is . . . a theme that must be endlessly worked out by those who profess to make the modern literatures the object of serious study." This work can be done only by someone who is both thoroughly familiar with the ancient models and able to read neo-Latin texts swiftly and surely. This last ability, also very rare nowadays, is essential because, again to quote Hutton, one must regard "the Latin culture of the Middle Ages and of the Renaissance as the matrix of the major ideas and intentions carried over into the vernacular."

But of course the task of tracing the survival and transformations of literary themes over many centuries demands far more than linguistic competence and a sound classical education. This kind of work badly done results merely in a modern poem's being disintegrated into a miscellaneous lot of possible sources; our understand-

5

ing of it is not deepened, and our appreciation may be spoiled. But if this work is done with the sensitivity to poetic beauty and the breadth of historical knowledge possessed by James Hutton, then we realize that to know in great detail the tradition in which a poet is writing does not diminish our appreciation by lessening his originality, but on the contrary increases our awareness of all he has brought to that tradition by omissions and additions, by subtle changes of emphasis and tone. In any art variations are understandable, or indeed perceptible, only if the model or models are precisely known.

I must of course leave these essays to speak for themselves; but I cannot forbear pointing out a couple of examples of the way in which they combine profound erudition with the imaginative ability to see unexpected and illuminating connections. Both examples come from the wonderful first, long essay, in which the author gives a masterly history of the literary tradition of the Praise of Music. Look at page 42, where in Puritan England the unmusical man, "the man that hath no music in himself," "arose from the *laudes musicae* and seemed to walk the earth as an English reality"; and then at page 48, where, discussing Lorenzo's speech in *The Merchant of Venice,* he suggests that "in Lorenzo's cherubins, sung to by the stars, the fanciful poet has fleetingly assimilated the traditional angels to the equally traditional infants that for a millennium and a half had invariably been lulled by nurses' singing in the *laudes musicae.*"

I end this foreword, as Montaigne ended his *Essais,* by wishing this fine scholar, who has honored me with his friendship, what Horace asked of Apollo:

> Frui paratis et valido mihi,
> Latoë, dones et, precor, integra
> Cum mente, nec turpem senectam
> Degere, nec cythara carentem.

D. P. WALKER

Warburg Institute, London

Acknowledgments

It is a pleasure to thank the friends of Professor Hutton who have helped me in the preparation of this book: William and Elizabeth Austin, Mary Fuertes Boynton, Kevin Clinton, Jane Dieckmann, Henry Guerlac, Bernhard Kendler, Helen North, Dorothy Wirtz Tyler, and D. P. Walker, and to list with them editors Marilyn Sale and Kay Scheuer of Cornell University Press. Very special thanks are due to Carol Kaske. The staff of Cornell's John M. Olin Library has been characteristically helpful. Finally I should like to thank the Hull Fund Publication Committee of Cornell University for its generous support.

R.G.

7

Contents

9

Illustrations

Preface

The permeation of Renaissance poetry by the poetry and thought of classical antiquity has engaged James Hutton throughout his scholarly career. Of the essays presented here, "Some English Poems in Praise of Music" and "Spenser's 'Adamantine Chains'" he intended to develop into books. Several of the essays grew out of materials gathered casually in the course of working on his two books about the Greek Anthology in Italy and in France. Six of the later ones were offshoots of a large work on the peace poetry of the Renaissance still in progress. And three have not been previously published.

Students, colleagues, and admirers of James Hutton in Renaissance studies are aware that the intended books might have been completed, and the work on peace poetry would doubtless be in print, were it not for the uncommon generosity of their author. No one has ever approached James Hutton with a manuscript (however rough or presumably polished, however slight or voluminous) and not been the beneficiary of a careful reading, meticulous corrections, and illuminating suggestions, delivered with courtesy and, if possible, a word of praise. No one knows how many substantial books on classical and Renaissance literature are the better for his perusal of the manuscripts.

At Cornell in the 1920s James Hutton was a student of Lane Cooper, a pioneer in the field now generally called comparative literature (a term he disliked). Professor Cooper's philological, historical, and comparative approach to the study and teaching of Western literature created a *seminarium* in which a gifted student could grow and develop his own critical and creative powers. In 1927 Professor Cooper formed the first separate department in the country for the comparative study of literature, and it was this department that lured James Hutton back to Cornell from his first teaching post at Columbia University. But, as often happens in

11

universities, hoped-for funds to enlarge the new department never materialized, and it continued as a one-man operation. While Mr. Hutton maintained a foothold in it with two memorable courses, Modern Writers on Art and, somewhat later, Humanism in the Renaissance, he accepted a post in Cornell's Department of Classics.

Professor Hutton taught classics at Cornell for nearly fifty years and, as one distinguished classicist remembers him, "he was thorough, demanding, sensitive to the deficiencies of the class, witty and amusing, and from beginning to end gave the impression of a command of his subject so vast that even as freshmen we were awed by the sense that there would never be time enough to find out all he knew."

But while he was teaching classics, James Hutton was writing on the Renaissance. His two splendid volumes on the Greek Anthology in Italy and in France earned him the admiration of Renaissance scholars everywhere, as did a succession of learned and elegant essays, a number of which have been selected for this volume. Many in the Cornell academic community were unaware that their colleague in classics had a distinguished reputation in Renaissance literature, and that the name of James Hutton was in some ways better known outside Cornell than on the campus.

One man who foresaw Hutton's eminence was the noted Spenser scholar Charles Grosvenor Osgood of Princeton, a Yale classmate of Lane Cooper and his lifelong friend. The Cooper papers in the Cornell archives contain letters, which Mr. Hutton has never seen, expressing Professor Osgood's admiration for the younger man. "His learning is something to wonder at," he wrote Cooper in 1951. "But he carries it so easily, with a touch of fun here and there, and with the air of having a royal good time with it . . . that it is made proof against any of the 'awkward ostentation' of pedantry." Another letter was exclamatory: "What a scholar!" he wrote. "If I were his coeval, he would afflict me with the Scholar's melancholy."

It is safe to say that James Hutton has never afflicted anyone with melancholy. His is that "serener, saner, more cheerful strain"— melancholy's opposite—which perhaps like Ronsard he drew from the Greeks. His company is a delight. He observes the *comédie humaine* with insight, wisdom, and a sense of the absurd that gleams in irony through these pages. And to borrow once more his words about Ronsard, he makes the reader feel that in contemplating these themes of peace, music, and poetry, "he is moving in high places where it is good for him to be."

RITA GUERLAC

Ithaca, New York

ESSAYS ON

Renaissance Poetry

Some English Poems
in Praise of Music

I

The finest poems and poetical passages on the subject of music in any language are to be found in the writings of the English poets of the sixteenth and seventeenth centuries. So it has been observed, and the observation may well be true. At least, I could not name, in any other literature known to me, poems *de laudibus musicae* that hold anything like the place held in English literature by Lorenzo's speech in *The Merchant of Venice*, by Milton's *At a Solemn Music*, and by Dryden's *Alexander's Feast* and *A Song for St. Cecilia's Day*. And these are only the greatest, or the best known, among a very large number of attractive and interesting poems on music that range from broadside ballads and occasional verses to the musical passages of *Paradise Lost*. This rather remarkable output no doubt can readily be explained by the fact that the English throughout this period were a musical nation; but that may not be the whole story, and the subject will bear some further scrutiny. Here, however, our object will be, not so much to explain why these poems were written (though we return to that question), as to trace the background of the ideas on which some, if not all, of them are based. In a general way, these ideas are familiar enough to students of the history of music; but it has not perhaps been firmly grasped that at the center there is a literary theme on which the transmission largely depends. One has only to turn over the current editions of the English, and not only the English, poets to see how insensitive the commentators generally are to an area of thought and feeling that once was universally understood.

Much has been written, for example, about Lorenzo's almost too

From *English Miscellany* 2 (1951) 1–63.

familiar lines (*M.V.* 5.1. 55–88) on the music of the stars and of the soul, and the muddy vesture of decay. Everyone recognizes that the topics are traditional, but, if I am not mistaken, it is always assumed that Shakespeare himself has brought them together. A stumbling-block has been that commentators easily recognize the music of the spheres as traditional, and are detained by that topic, not realizing that it is but one item of a thematic complex that extends through the unmusical man of lines 83–88. Thus the late John Burnet, in an arresting article, discovers that "Shakespeare has given us the finest of Greek Philosophy," and thinks it "no great marvel that the creator of Hamlet and Falstaff could also recreate Pythagoras from stray hints tradition had preserved."[1] He suggests that Shakespeare may have picked up the doctrine of the relation of the human soul to the world-soul from some morality play that echoed the Platonism of the School of Chartres—not a very likely guess. Earlier, H. J. Conrat, lighting on the other end of the passage, had opined that Shakespeare, a reader of Plutarch's *Lives,* took his idea of the moral value of music, and hence his scorn of the unmusical man, from Plutarch's *De Musica*—again, it would seem, without considering the tradition that brought the *laudes musicae* to Shakespeare's door.[2] More recent writers have done better, and have recognized that the music of the spheres and one or two other topics of Lorenzo's speech are traditional points commonly brought forward when music is discussed;[3] but it has not, I think, been made clear that this speech not only contains traditional topics, but that the arrangement is traditional and one part implies the presence of the others—in short, that we have here to do with a coherent literary theme that Shakespeare has taken bodily into his play.

Before viewing this theme more at large, let us glance at its appearance in some earlier authors, chosen partly because I am quite sure that none of them is Shakespeare's "source." Thus the

---

[1]"Shakespeare and Greek Philosophy" in *A Book of Homage to Shakespeare* (London, 1916); reprinted in Burnet's posthumous *Essays and Addresses* (London, 1929), pp. 163–68.

[2]"La Musica in Shakespeare" in *Rivista musicale italiana* 10 (1903) 655–62.

[3]Leo Spitzer, "Classical and Christian Ideas of World Harmony: Prolegomena to an Interpretation of the Word 'Stimmung'" in *Traditio* 2 (1944) 409–64 and 3 (1945) 307–64; Gretchen L. Finney, "Ecstasy and Music in Seventeenth-century England," in *Journal of the History of Ideas* 8 (1947) 153–86, and "'Organical Music' and Ecstasy,'" *ibid.*, pp. 273–92. I am much indebted both to Professor Spitzer and to Mrs. Finney.

18

following topics occur in this order (though I have severely compressed them) in Martianus Capella's discussion of music (9.922): Harmonia, created by divine effulgence, accompanies the motions of the stars, and places souls in their earthly tenements, governing them and giving them rhythm; she teaches the use of instruments, and the use of music in divine worship; music has its place in war, to which even horses are incited by trumpets, and in peace; it cures perturbations of mind and body; the very animals respond to it, and also, as Orpheus showed, inanimate things. The following topics appear in this order, though much expanded, in Gioseffo Zarlino's *Institutioni harmoniche* 1.2-4 (1558): The Pythagoreans said that the world is musically composed, the heavens produce harmony, and that the human soul, formed on the same principle, is moved and vivifies its virtue by music; music is an important ingredient in the other arts and disciplines—Theology, for example, ranges the angelic hosts in singing hierarchies—and is the only art practiced in Paradise; the earth is full of natural music; man the microcosm should respond to music, since even insensible things do so, and Linus and Orpheus tamed beasts and birds, moved rocks, and checked streams; the Pythagoreans and others cured ills of mind and body with music; one who does not delight in it must be of base character, and nature has failed to provide him with the organ that judges of harmony. Ronsard, from whom I only quote two sentences, begins with Zarlino's last point (*Préface sur la Musique*, 1562): "The ancients used music as a touchstone to distinguish magnanimous souls—such as have not lost their original essence—from those that are bastardized in this mortal body, and have forgotten the celestial harmony, as the companions of Ulysses forgot being men when turned into swine by Circe. The man who, on hearing a sweet accord of instruments or the sweetness of the natural voice, is not delighted and is not moved and does not tremble from head to foot, sweetly ravished and transported, gives proof thereby that he has a crooked, vicious, and depraved soul, and is to be guarded against as one not happily born." It is as one more of these *laudes musicae* that an Elizabethan audience would hear Lorenzo's familiar words:

> How sweet the moonlight sleeps upon this bank!
> Here will we sit, and let the sounds of music
> Creep in our ears; soft stillness and the night

Become the touches of sweet harmony.
Sit, Jessica; look how the floor of heaven
Is thick inlaid with patines of bright gold;
There's not the smallest orb which thou behold'st
But in his motion like an angel sings,
Still quiring to the young-eyed cherubins;
Such harmony is in immortal souls;
But whilst this muddy vesture of decay
Doth grossly close it in, we cannot hear it.

(Enter musicians)

Come, ho! and wake Diana with a hymn:
With sweetest touches pierce your mistress' ear,
And draw her home with music.
Jessica. I am never merry when I hear sweet music.
Lorenzo. The reason is, your spirits are attentive:
For do but note a wild and wanton herd,
Or race of youthful and unhandled colts,
Fetching mad bounds, bellowing and neighing loud,
Which is the hot condition of their blood;
If they but hear perchance a trumpet sound,
Or any air of music touch their ears,
You shall perceive them make a mutual stand,

Their savage eyes turn'd to a modest gaze
By the sweet power of music: therefore the poet
Did feign that Orpheus drew trees, stones, and floods,
Since nought so stockish, hard, and full of rage,
But music for the time doth change his nature:
The man that hath no music in himself,
Nor is not moved with concord of sweet sounds,
Is fit for treasons, stratagems, and spoils;
The motions of his spirit are dull as night,
And his affections dark as Erebus:
Let no such man be trusted.

The topics—world-music and soul-music; the effects of music upon human beings (Portia, Jessica); and upon animals and inanimate things; and at the end a remark on the unmusical man—all are evidently the regular parts of a coherent theme. So familiar a theme, indeed, that Shakespeare permits himself to treat it in a kind of shorthand. It was all intelligible enough to his contemporaries, but when we approach his text analytically, we puzzle ourselves to know what it is "we cannot hear"—sphere-music or soul-music; and may think it odd reasoning to say that Jessica is affected by music because ('for') wild herds and colts are tamed by it. When, however, we look at the passage as a shorthand version of a theme with many analogues, there is no difficulty in seeing that it is always the celestial music that is unheard; and that the *a fortiori* transition, "rational man should be moved, since even brute beasts respond to music," is so intimate a part of the topic that it is often glibly telescoped, especially, as we shall see, in the English versions. Again, the analytical student, imagining that Shakespeare like a modern scholar kept the classics carefully in mind, exerts himself to discover who 'the poet' of line 79 may be. Does Shakespeare refer to Ovid or to Virgil or perhaps to Horace?[4] Our study of the tradition will suggest an answer which the analyst could not have suspected. A study of the tradition followed by Shakespeare may also save us from seeing significance in verbal similarities when actually there is none; the topics of the thematic complex necessarily find expression in similar language. Hence, surprisingly close as it is, Shakespeare's conclusion about the unmusical man: "Let no such man be trusted," is not likely to be a translation of Ronsard's "du quel il faut se donner garde." Some real relationships, however, we may hope to find.[5]

II

As an organized topic the Praise of Music belongs primarily to the school-tradition of the liberal arts. This tradition achieved its form, or nearly so, in the Hellenistic period, and perhaps we have some right to infer not only that the technical content of the several arts was then established in its main outlines, but that at the same

[4]Thus Robert K. Root, *Classical Mythology in Shakespeare* (New York, 1903), thinks that "the poet probably is Ovid" (*Met.* 10–11), but disturbed at finding "floods" neither in Ovid's account of Orpheus nor in Virgil's, resorts for this item to Horace, *Carm.* 1,12.7–10. But we see "floods" already in the complex of the *encomium musicae* in Zarlino's list of Orpheus' feats; and Zarlino depends on Martianus Capella in a passage omitted from the summary given above.

[5]Under the name of *Ethoslehre* or the like, the general subject here treated is, as aforesaid, familiar to historians of music, and I have gladly availed myself of the well-known books of Hermann Abert and Théodore Gérold and of others less well known. The present study, however, is based on the collection and comparison of texts, with the object of establishing relationships among them and of thus sharpening our focus on the English examples.

time there were prepared for textbooks of the arts protreptic introductions which did not lose their essential identity until quite recent times. At all events, it is significant that in later antiquity such a protreptic Introduction to the art of music regularly appears in its fullest form in close relation to the arts tradition—in Quintilian's review of the liberal arts, in Sextus Empiricus, or in writers of handbooks *de musica*. Its main contentions were based on the position given to music by Plato—and hence ultimately by the Pythagoreans—and by Aristotle; that is to say, on the metaphysical meaning of music in the construction of the universe and of man (*Republic* x, 617; *Timaeus* 36, 47), and on its moral and political value in the education of a citizen (*Republic* iii, 398–99; *Laws* ii and vii; Aristotle, *Politics* viii). Heraclides Ponticus, Theophrastus, and others had further extended the subject; and the whole was reduced by the Hellenistic schoolmen to simple statements illuminated by suitable *exempla*. An ideal outline of this Proem (including, however, some later developments) may be sketched somewhat as follows:

> Music, the science rather than the practice, is one of the liberal arts, perhaps the chief of them. Music has been esteemed from of old, and was invented by Linus or Orpheus; it was valued by great men: Socrates in old age learned to play the lyre, Epaminondas was a musician. Plato and the Pythagoreans teach us that the universe is musically constructed, and that the human soul is similarly formed. Hence music governs the motions of the soul and can cure its distempers: it cures lust, as when Pythagoras restrained a drunken youth by having a spondaic rhythm played on the lyre; it rouses courage for war, whence the Spartans and Cretans marched to the sound of lyre and flute and the Amazons to the pipes; Timotheus was able to stir and then subdue the martial spirits of Alexander; Asclepiades cured a madman. It can also cure bodily ills: Terpander, Arion, and Thaletas drove out plagues by music; Ismenias cured sciatica. It is useful in civil life: Lycurgus approved of it; Terpander repressed a sedition with music. It lightens labor, as witness the singing of rowers in the galleys. It is natural, since even infants are lulled by nurses' singing, and the very beasts respond to it: flocks follow piping, horses at Sybaris were taught to dance, and fishes in an Alexandrian pool rose when music was played. It is used to praise the Gods; and at sacrifices; at banquets; at funerals; and has had a place in education ever since Chiron taught Achilles. The unmusical were accounted uneducated: Themistocles, for example, who could not play the lyre. All these excellent effects, however, are those of the old music; modern music is degen-

erate and disturbing: the Spartans banned Timotheus for adding a string to the lyre.

From the beginning the recklessness of epideictic rhetoric made itself felt in this *thema* of praise, and evoked the criticism of the more positive Epicureans. Thus perhaps the earliest evidence for the existence of our theme is in the polemic of Philodemus' *De Musica;* and polemic, present throughout its history, often makes the "defense" a more appropriate designation than the "praise" of music. Nevertheless, though marked by paradox, the early representatives are sober compared with the claims advanced for music as the tradition passed through the climate of Neopythagoreanism and Neoplatonism, and of Christianity. Yet here is the road we must traverse, rapidly, in the direction of Shakespeare's "muddy vesture of decay" and "cherubins."

The coherent theme emerges toward the end of the first century at once in Latin with Quintilian and in Greek with Plutarch (if Plutarch's *De Musica* is genuine). In Latin, the tradition was probably fixed by Varro in the treatise *De Musica* forming part of his series on the liberal arts, and Quintilian may depend on him. The following is a skeleton of the theme as Quintilian presents it (*Inst. orat.* 1.10.9-33):

[Music is part of the *enkuklios paideia.*] . . . It was venerated and studied in ancient times; Orpheus and Linus were at once musicians, poets, and philosophers. The Pythagoreans taught that the universe is constructed on the principle of the lyre, and attributed sound to the motions of the celestial bodies; see Plato's *Timaeus.* Socrates learned to play the lyre; and generals as well as philosophers honor music; the Spartan armies used the lyre as the Romans now use the trumpet. Plato required music of his ideal statesman, and the Stoics require it of their wise man. Lycurgus approved of it. Nature gave music to lighten labor; rowers in the galleys chant in unison, and solitary workers also are solaced by artless song. Formerly the art of music and the art of letters were united, some even subordinating grammar to music. The lyre, too, was passed round at banquets, and Themistocles was deemed uneducated when he declined his turn. Music is useful to the orator, and necessary in reading poetry. It has been important in education ever since Chiron taught Achilles; but it is the old music that should be taught, not modern music depraved by the theatre. Pythagoras with a spondaic measure calmed a youth bent on outrage; Chrysippus selects tunes by which nurses may lull infants to sleep.

23

While the general complex persists, usually in some relation to the liberal-arts tradition, individual motives and examples may not appear in each and every version; and yet these too have a remarkable vitality. For instance, Quintilian exemplifies the naturalness of music by rowers in the galleys singing in unison and by the uncouth singing (*rudi modulatione*) of solitary workers (*singulorum fatigatio solatur*). Since the rowers reappear not only in the Latin versions of Censorinus and Isidore of Seville, but also in Sextus Empiricus and in Aristides Quintilianus in Greek, we must regard them as belonging to the tradition and not specifically to Quintilian. It is fair then to inquire who Quintilian's "solitary workers" are, since the phrase is an obvious *et cetera;* and here Ovid perhaps supplies an answer. In a passage (*Tristia* 4.1.5–16) that may well reflect a writer *de musica,* he names ditchers, canal-boatmen, rowers, shepherds, women spinning. These beguile their labors (*labor decipitur*) by singing *indocili numero,* as Quintilian's workers sing *rudi modulatione.*[6] A list not unlike Ovid's is drawn, surely from the same arts tradition, by St. John Chrysostom (on Psalm 41): rowers, wayfarers, farmers, women knitting.[7] To look still farther forward, in mediaeval and Renaissance versions Quintilian's sentence is often taken over intact, but quite as often filled out. Thus Castiglione, in a general paraphrase of Quintilian (*Cortegiano* 1.47.55–64), cites: "Duri lavoratori de' campi (col rozzo ed agreste cantare); la inculta contadinella che . . . a filare o a tessere si lieva; miseri marinari; stanchi peregrini; prigionieri." Commentators assemble various parallels, but miss the right one, which is St. John Chrysostom. Prisoners, to be sure, are missing from his list; but presently he remarks that Paul and Silas sang in prison (not a common example in the *laudes*), and Castiglione has included this item with the rest.[8]

Though Plutarch (*De Musica* 26 and 40) emphasizes with Plato the moral effects of music—as, "good music makes a man harmonious in acts and judgment"—his topics often coincide with those of Quintilian. Compare Quintilian: "The Spartan armies used the lyre as the Romans now use the trumpet," and Plutarch: "The Spartans marched to the flute, the Cretans to the lyre, while today we use trumpets." Neither Quintilian nor Plutarch employs

---

[6]The equivalent of this phrase is nearly all that remains of the motive in Boethius (*De Musica* 1,1), who says: "Qui suaviter canere non potest, sibi tamen aliquid canit."
[7]Still under the topic "music is natural," and like Quintilian, Chrysostom distinguishes between singing in company and singing alone.
[8]Chrysostom's *Exposit. in Ps. 41* is often cited by writers on music.

the topic, "animals also are affected," but that it was already present in the complex is suggested by Sextus Empiricus (second century), who does not fail to ridicule it in his attack on the "effects" of music. Plutarch introduces the item "music of the spheres" at the end of his discussion, Quintilian near the beginning of his, but neither relates it to the topic "nature of the soul," as Shakespeare does. That connection, implying the relation of macrocosm and microcosm, had to wait for Neoplatonism; and when under that influence the connection is made in the form "harmonious structure of the universe reflected in the human soul," this combination regularly appears near the beginning, and the topic "music of the spheres" is treated separately at the end. The two are distinct, the one philosophical and the other "scientific." The first topic is used to suggest that we respond to music because we "recollect" the divine music, or having "forgotten" the divine music because of mixture with body are reminded of it by earthly music; while the sphere-music is said to be unheard by us because of the physical incapacity of our ears.

So Censorinus (third century), in an influential embodiment of our theme (*De Die natali* 12–3), first says (c. 12): "Music shares in the divine and powerfully moves souls; divine, it pleases the gods, and human minds (*pace* Epicurus), being themselves divine, recognize their nature through song; sailors use song to lighten labor; . . . Asclepiades cured madmen," [etc.]; and then later (c. 13): "Pythagoras declares that the universe is built on a musical principle, and that the seven planets (which control our birth) produce concordant sounds, making a melody which we, however, cannot hear because the sound is too great for the narrowness (*angustiae*) of our ears." The *angustiae aurium* is the common explanation of our inability to hear the physical sphere-music.[9] Aristides Quintilianus (probably third century), in the most elaborate treatise *de musica* that has come down from antiquity, gathers up most of our topics, including the effect on animals.[10] A Platonist, he too recog-

[9]So Cicero, *Somn. Scip.* 5: ". . . tantus sonitus, ut aures capere non possint"; and he illustrates by the deafening effect of the Nile cataract upon the natives ("ea gens . . . sensu audiendi caret"). The illustration seems rather to belong to an alternative explanation, namely that we fail to hear the sphere-music because it has always been with us: so copper-smiths cease to be aware of the din in their shops (Aristotle, *De Caelo* 2.9).

[10]Since Aristides' work was only published by Meibom in 1652, it had no influence on the Renaissance, save possibly through Franchino Gafori (below), who had a translation of it made for his private use; see Paul Oskar Kristeller in *Journ. Ren. and Baroque Music* 1 (1946) 268.

nizes the parallel structure of universe and soul (1.3) and the soul's "forgetfulness" (2.2); but coming at the end (3.20) to the sphere-music, says that we fail to hear it "because of the distance and our turbid mixture with body" (ἐκ τε τῆς πολλῆς ἀποστάσεως καὶ τῆς πρὸς τὸ σῶμα κράσεως θολερωτέρας). Choice spirits, however, can hear it; and the allusion is doubtless to Pythagoras, who is said to have heard this music.[11] Even here, despite their similarity or even identity, the two topics remain distinct: (1) In the bonds of the body we forget our relation to heaven, and (2) In the bonds of the body most of us cannot hear the sphere-music.

In order to see our topic completely immersed in a Neoplatonic atmosphere, we advance rapidly to Macrobius' fifth-century Commentary on the *Somnium Scipionis* of Cicero. The passage (*Comm.* 2.3–4) here outlined had an effect on the tradition that can hardly be exaggerated:

3. Plato's Sirens on the spheres denote music, since *siren* means one singing to God; by the nine Muses theologians indicate the sounds of the eight spheres plus the harmony of all. . . . Because heaven sings, music is employed at sacrifices (strophe and antistrophe in hymns signify the movement of the heavens); and at funerals, because the soul is returning to heaven, the source of music. It captivates every living soul, however barbaric, inspiring to virtue or softening to plea-sure, because the soul brings to the body a memory of the celestial music; and thus no breast is so savage and hard (*nullum tam immite, tam asperum pectus*) as not to delight in it. Thence comes the fable of Orpheus drawing (*trahere*) animals and Amphion rocks, for they first attracted by song peoples who were barbarous and irrational or stolid like rocks. In short, states of mind are governed by music; in war advance and retreat are sounded by music; it brings and dispels sleep and cares, stirs wrath, persuades to mercy. It also cures bodily ills. And what wonder if it controls men, when even birds, as nightingales and swans, practise music, and some are lured into snares by it, while flocks are quieted by piping? No wonder, since they share in the world-soul, which also gives motion and sound to the spheres. . . .
4. Explanation of the music of the spheres. Of the three musical *genera*, enharmonic, diatonic, and chromatic, the diatonic is best and assigned by Plato to the world-harmony. We cannot hear this harmony because of the incapacity (*angustiae*) of our ears.

[11]Iamblichus, *Vita Pyth.* 15(65).

Though we are physically incapable of hearing the sphere-music, we respond to music in general because of our memory of the celestial harmony; and the lower animals also respond, since they share in the world-soul. Macrobius here omits the obverse of memory, namely our forgetfulness of the celestial music, a point stressed, for example, by Chalcidius (*In Timaeum* 47A): "The original modulation of the soul is lost through association with the body (*ob consortium corporis*) and forgotten, and hence the souls of the majority are inharmonious. The cure is music; not, however, vulgar music, but divine intelligible music, which recalls the straying soul to its pristine harmony. The best harmony in our moral nature is justice."

For Shakespeare, too, our birth is a forgetting, though apparently without a latent memory of the divine music. Yet something from Macrobius may be present in the Shakespearean passage, where the expression "nought so stockish, hard, and full of rage" might pass for an Elizabethan translation of *nullum tam immite, tam asperum pectus,* and is similarly joined with the fable of Orpheus. We return to these points later. Meanwhile we have to account not only for the relation of the human soul to the divine music, but also for the constitution of the divine music itself. In Shakespeare, it is the stars quiring to the Cherubim. Thus far we have found only the stars, or rather the spheres, singing alone; but Macrobius' Muses perhaps open other possibilities.

Muses on the spheres in place of Plato's Sirens seem to have been a commonplace of Neoplatonism; and the idea was to re-emerge conspicuously in the Platonism of the Renaissance.[12] Besides Macrobius, our chief witnesses are Plutarch (*Symp.* 9.14.6), Porphyry (*Vit. Pythag.* 31), and Martianus Capella (*De Nupt.* 1,27–9); but possibly the form given to the idea by Proclus is more suggestive. He rejects the simple assignment of the Muses to the spheres (*In Rem publ.* 2.237.17 Kroll); the Muses, being close to Apollo Musagetes, who is the source of harmony in the universe (*op. cit.* 2.4), are in control of the Sirens, who produce a *corporeal* harmony, while the Muses themselves bestow the *intelligible* harmony (*op. cit.* 2.239). Human music, at a further remove, also is the gift of the Muses and "their ultimate image" (*In Alc. pr.*, p. 205 Creuzer). Now it will be recalled that, besides the harmony of the Sirens on the

[12]A connection between Muses and Sirens was very old (Preller-Robert 1.615).

spheres, Plato imagines "round about at equal intervals" another band, namely the Fates, "who accompany with their voices the harmony of the Sirens." (One of the speakers in Plutarch identifies *this* band with the Muses.) For Proclus the relation of the Fates to the Sirens is comparable to that of the Muses, though less direct; "the Muses provide the cosmos with the Form of harmony, the Fates with the Form of order" (*In Rem publ.* 2.241 Kroll). At all events, in the relation of the Sirens to the Muses or to the Fates, there lies the possibility of the concert between the corporeal music of the spheres and the superior music of some higher order.[13]

In a Christian setting, such a higher order would naturally be the angels.[14] It seems impossible, however, to find any early Christian writer who imagines such a relation between the angels and the singing spheres. Yet Philo long before had anticipated this notion (*De Somniis* 1.6.35; 7.37); I paraphrase:

> Heaven is always singing, as the heavenly bodies in their motion make perfect melody. Could this sound reach our ears, we should in utter ecstasy leave off mortal sustenance and live on this music alone, as did Moses in the wilderness. Heaven is the archetype of musical instruments, and was tuned to make musical accompaniment to the hymns sung in honor of the Father of all.

The last sentence requires only to be expanded in a Christian setting, and then adjusted to the Dionysian hierarchies, to account for the motive as known to Shakespeare and Milton; but the step was not easily taken. To be sure, a number of Biblical texts might suggest it—"the heavens declare the glory of God"; and the angels were sometimes regarded as having the heavens in their charge;[15] but this is far from a definite concept of a concert of spheres and angels. Origen, for whom (*c. Cels.* 5.10) the stars are animated and "praise the Lord," and other (Philastrius, Theodore of Mopsuestia,

---

[13]Proclus' views on these matters were accessible in the Renaissance even to the general public; thus G. F. Algarotti sets forth the doctrine of *In. Alc.* in the Preface to his *Secondo libro de' madrigali* (1567); see Alfred Einstein, *The Italian Madrigal* (Princeton, 1949), 1,217.

[14]It is possible to think of the universe as an instrument played directly by God; so Dorylaus in Censorinus 13, and perhaps the Pythagorean world-lyre was so played; but late theology, pagan and Christian, was committed to the employment of intermediate agents (cf. E. R. Dodds, *Proclus, The Elements of Theology*, p. 294).

[15]Athenagoras, *Pro Christianis*, c. 10 (Fr. Andres, *Die Engellehre der Gr. Apologeten* [Paderborn, 1914], p. 67, n. 1).

Cosmas Indicopleustes), who thought the stars ensouled and impelled by angels, perhaps were ready for this Neoplatonic notion; but orthodoxy did not encourage the thought.[16] At this time the *encomium musicae* finds its home in commentaries on the Psalms, where its topics were available in the defense of congregational singing—for example, in St. Basil, Gregory of Nyssa, and St. John Chrysostom; but these too know nothing of the concert. Was the idea existent but purposely ignored? For the West, Ambrose is of prime importance in this connection. In the following paraphrase (*Explanatio Psalmorum XII, init.*), not only are the topics of our theme felt throughout, but the unexplained juxtaposition of angelic singing and sphere-music possibly betrays that Ambrose knew a version in which they were united:

> God made the enjoyment of future bliss a chief incentive to virtue; the devil devised enjoyment as a spur to sin; Adam proves both statements. Angels praise the Lord, Powers harp to Him, and before the beginning of the world Cherubim and Seraphim sang "Holy, Holy, Holy." The heavens are said to revolve with harmony heard at the ends of the earth where the secrets of nature are. Pleasure is natural; even beasts and birds delight in pleasant places and well-tuned voices, and infants ... are pleased by caresses. David, seeking to repair man's fallen estate, introduced psalmody as a kind of celestial converse.... God delights to be praised, and also to be reconciled by song.... In the Psalms is the medicine of salvation, a remedy of human passion.... David expelled Saul's evil spirit.... The Psalms are a benediction, a praise of God, ... allay wrath, and free us from care and grief. The Psalter, played by the prophet, makes the sweetness of celestial music re-echo on earth. As lyre-players are said to sing internally, so we should sing the Psalms.

Besides the addition of the singing angels to the celestial music, a number of other developments were made in our theme by Christian thought. The topic "music honored from earliest times" grew into "the inventors of music," among whom Linus and Orpheus are flanked by the Biblical Jubal. The superiority of theoretical to practical music, a point stressed by Boethius, combines with the Platonic concept that true music is philosophy and the ordering of the soul to produce the important extension, already made by Philo (*De Plantatione*, c. 30,126), that "internal singing" is more valuable than

---

[16]Ferdinand Piper, *Mythologie der Christlichen Kunst* (Weimar, 1851), 2.203–76.

audible music. The Psalm-commentaries regularly advert to this topic, and it is the point, for example, of the legend of St. Cecilia; at her wedding, while the instruments sounded, she sang internally to God alone (*cantantibus organis illa in corde suo soli Domino decantabat*). Close to this idea, but developed from the Neoplatonic idea of the purgative value of music, is the topic of musical ecstasy, "music raises the soul to God." So St. John Chrysostom: "Nothing so raises the soul and gives it wings and frees it from the earth, nothing so frees it from the bonds of the flesh and makes it philosophize, . . . as music and the rhythm of divine song" (*Exposit. in Ps. 41*); and Cassiodorus, in an influential passage of his Psalm-commentary (Preface), maintains that psalmody makes us "return" to God, and that "we mingle our praises with those of God's angels, whom we cannot hear." The topic "music given by Nature" (Quintilian) returns to its Platonic form, "music given by God" (*Laws* ii, 653 d). The idea that "music is natural to man" is stressed by the Christian writers, who delight in the analogy between the human body and a musical instrument (e.g., Gregory of Nyssa). That music was originally used in the worship of the gods (Plutarch, Censorinus) is of course replaced by "music used in Christian rites" (Cassiodorus), and in mediaeval treatises on music this topic develops into a discussion of music in the Church. That modern and theatrical music are bad as compared with the simple ancient music (Plutarch, Boethius) gives way to "modern and theatrical music are bad (even devilish) as compared with sacred music, especially that of the Psalms" (so, for example, St. John Chrysostom). Among the cures effected by music, David restoring Saul becomes a fixture beside Asclepiades curing the madman; and from this example (coupled with timeless superstition) grew the important topic that devils fear music and are driven off by it (*musica diabolum fugat*).[17]

Yet these developments did not take effect at once in the academic treatment of our theme. After Martianus Capella, the important authorities are Boethius, *De Musica;* Cassiodorus, *Institutio;* and Isidore of Seville, *Etymologiae;* all dealing with music as one of the liberal arts, and hence not concerned to stress the Christian modifications, though these are to some extent present in Cas-

---

[17]Convenient tags for the "effects" are found in the *Complexus viginti effectuum musicae* of Joannes Tinctoris (d. 1511), though this sixteenth-century work was first printed by Coussemaker (*Scriptores musici* 4.191).

siodorus and Isidore. Boethius (I,1–2) offers an *encomium musicae* not unlike that of Quintilian in form but in content much indebted to the musical passage in Cicero's *Leges* 2.15.38–9. Where the topic "relation of the soul to celestial harmony" must be mentioned near the beginning of the complex, he is discreet and not Neoplatonic: "Plato rightly said that the world-soul is compact of harmony; and our reception and enjoyment of musical sounds suggest that we are similarly constituted." Then, after dilating with Cicero on the political importance of good music, he proceeds through the usual topics and examples. We have seen that it was customary, at the end of the *laudes* proper, to add something more "scientific" on the music of the spheres. Boethius gives this appendix a remarkable extension, under the heads *musica mundana, humana,* and *instrumentalis—* terms which he fixed permanently upon the tradition. "World-music" is the music of the Spheres, the combining of the four Elements, and the succession of the Seasons.[18] "Human music" is the juncture of soul and body and the harmony of the tripartite soul. "Instrumental music" is what the words suggest. In this appendix, *musica mundana* and *humana* are, as it were, scientific footnotes to the key-sentence, "celestial harmony and soul-harmony," in the core of the theme.

A word must be spared for Cassiodorus' influence on our topic, which was exercised less perhaps by his *Institutio* or even his Psalm-commentary than by his rhetorical letter to Boethius (*Variae* 2.40). A few of the phrases here coined by him, and endlessly repeated by later writers, may be briefly noted:

Music enters our ears and alters our spirits (*mutat animos*), and as queen of the senses (*regina sensuum*) drives out other thoughts. It cheers sadness, soothes rage, softens cruelty, banishes sloth, ... [a rhetorical "summation passage" such as appears in nearly all the *laudes musicae;* compare Macrobius and Ambrose, above]. It expels troubles of mind (*expellit animi passiones*). The lyre was placed by astronomers among the constellations to suggest that music is heavenly (*coelestem esse musicam*). The harmony of heaven is presented by reason to the mind, not by nature to the ear; but we are told that celestial Beatitude enjoys it for ever, and it never fades.

---

[18]The object is to complete the music of the spheres, since the elements exist in spheres below and continuous with the sphere of the Moon, and the seasons have to do with the central Earth.

It must be left for a more extended treatment of the subject to trace the very considerable fortunes of our theme in the Middle Ages. Here it will be sufficient, as background for the English poets, to note the external form in which the topic is generally presented, and to touch on the development of one or two of the major items of the complex. In doing so, we shall find it convenient in each case to make the transition into the Renaissance.

The mediaeval bent for classification led to the isolation of certain motives in separate chapters. Thus "music venerated in early times" (cf. Quintilian) turns into a chapter *de inventoribus*. These divisions, introduced by Isidore, become more elaborate as time advances, but usually take some such form as: (1) Definition of Music; (2) Derivation of terms; (3) Inventors; (4) The Use (or Power) of Music; etc. Here the center of our theme evidently falls in Chapter 4. A typical instance may be summarized from the *Summa Musicae* of Joannes de Muris (early fourteenth century):

1. Definition; derivations; inventors. 2. The Use of Music; the theorist superior to the practician; music cures diseases, especially those arising from melancholy. It comforts travelers, scares away robbers, fortifies the timid in war; by music Pythagoras restored a youth to continence. Some music expels *luxuria,* some induces it; some puts one to sleep, some awakens one, music mitigates wrath, cheers the sad, drives out evil spirits, as when David cured Saul. No wonder if rational man is affected, since herds, birds, and fishes seem to be charmed by music. 3. Place of music in church; Scriptural authority for its acceptance. 4. Music is "natural" and "instrumental": under "natural" come *musica mundana* and *musica humana,* [etc.].

These divisions, variously modified, persist in the Renaissance writers on music, from Franchino Gafori (1480) to John Case (1586), and beyond. What distinguishes the Renaissance treatises is a new fulness of content. Broadly speaking, the mediaeval writers draw their material from Martianus Capella, Boethius, Cassiodorus, and Isidore, with hints from the Psalm-commentaries, and later, with new light from Aristotle (as from *De Caelo* 2.9, against the music of the spheres) and from the Arabs. The Renaissance writers, beginning with Tinctoris and Gafori, aim with some success at gathering up all that antiquity had to say upon the subject; and scattered fragments of the theme were thus replaced, so to speak, in the complex. Or again, this fulness of research coupled with the mediaeval divisions will produce an impressive chapter on the inventors of music and its parts in Polydore Vergil's *De rerum Inventoribus* (1499).

Another mark of the Renaissance is the ubiquity of the theme. Its home is in the treatises on music and on the liberal arts, but it is found everywhere. That is partly because so much of the characteristic writing of the Renaissance is in some way involved in the tradition of the liberal arts. Thus our theme receives full organic treatment in Castiglione's *Cortegiano* (1.47), where Quintilian's version is largely followed, for the *Cortegiano* is a sort of adaptation of the *Education of an Orator* to modern conditions. It occurs in Maurice Scève's *Microcosme* (Book 2, end) in a review of the liberal arts, and in a similar review in Du Bartas' *Semaines* ("Les Colomnes"). But its use goes far beyond this central realm. It is, for example, associated with the Renaissance belief in the poet-musician, and in connection with this topic finds full treatment in an important academic oration by the elder Filippo Beroaldo (*In Tusculanas et Horatium*, 1491), which was often copied, and in L. G. Giraldi's *De Poetis* (1545).

Most important for the spread of our topic is the lively interest that the Renaissance took in the "effects" of music.[19] If ancient music cured madmen, the empirical Renaissance desired a modern music that should be equally successful. Antiquity was to be rivaled in every realm. Such views were the inspiration of Baïf's Académie de Poésie et de Musique founded in 1570, and of the Florentine Camerata dei Bardi. Montaigne's father, taking the "effects" to heart, had his son put to sleep and awakened by music; like the ancient Pythagoreans he was to have the harmony of body and soul restored at night after the distractions of the day, and again in the morning after the heaviness of sleep. The wish being father to the thought, it was found that, sometimes, modern music really had these effects; so our theme gets some new *exempla:* the warlike passions of the Court of Denmark once were roused and again allayed by music; the lutenist Francesco di Milano similarly reduced a dinner party first to melancholy, then to ecstasy, and, changing

---

[19]See D. P. Walker, "Musical Humanism in the Sixteenth and Early Seventeenth Centuries" in *Musical Review* (1941–42): and "The Aims of Baïf's Académie de poésie et de musique" in *Journ. Ren. and Baroque Music* 1 (1946) 91–100.

the measure, restored them; the cure by music of the tarantula's bite was "a fact known to all."[20]

The explanation of these effects calls for special notice. They are due to the "penetration" of music, which is effected by agency of the internal "spirits" universally postulated by psychological theory from antiquity through the Renaissance. These spirits, commonly divided into natural, vital, and animal, are subtle vapors arising in the blood from nourishment, and are the instruments of every activity of the soul.[21] In particular they carry sensations from the sense-organs to the *sensus communis* or *phantasia,* which in turn forms them into concepts for presentation to the reason. The spirits therefore are the bond between soul and body, and the *phantasia* or imagination itself thus mediates between the higher and the lower parts of the soul. Plato already describes how, in hearing, sound "passes through the ears, and is transmitted by means of air, the brain, and the blood, to the soul" (*Timaeus* 67A), and it is commonly in a Platonic context that writers on music resort to the topic of penetration; for example, John of Salisbury in his defense of music (*Policraticus* 1.6). Ficino, in his commentary on the Platonic passage, explains at length:

> Music (*concentus*), by setting the air in motion, moves the body; by purified air it stirs the aërial spirit which is the bond of soul and body; by signification it acts on the mind; in short, by the motion of the subtle air it penetrates vehemently; by contemperation it sweetly flows over us (*lambit*); by its conforming quality it floods with marvelous delight both the spiritual and the corporeal nature, and at once ravishes and appropriates the whole man.[22]

This passage found its way into certain writers *de musica,* and thus lived an independent life in the Renaissance. Gregor Reisch

[20]The case of the Court of Denmark is perhaps first cited from Saxo Grammaticus in the context of our theme by Cornelius Agrippa, *De occulta Philosophia,* 1510; for Francesco di Milano, Pontus de Tyard (*Le Solitaire second ou prose de la musique,* 1555) relies on the witness of Jacques de Vintimille; the tarantula appears as early as Ficino, *De Vita coelitus comp.,* c. 21.

[21]Albertus Magnus, *De Somno et vigilia,* 1.1.7: "In corpore omnis animalis est corpus subtile quod vocatur spiritus. . . . Est autem evaporatio quae fit ab humiditate cibi. . . . Fit autem haec evaporatio per calorem naturalem, cuius primus et principalis fons est cor. . . . Est igitur instrumentum animae ad omnes operationes eius et ideo movetur sursum et deorsum et ad latera."

[22]*Opera omnia* (Basel, 1561), p. 1453. Ficino sometimes distinguishes between a lower *imaginatio* and a higher *phantasia;* see Paul Oskar Kristeller, *The Philosophy of Marsilio Ficino* (New York, 1943), p. 235.

quotes it in his popular handbook of the liberal arts *Margarita philosophica* 5.1 (1503), whence, for example, it passed into Maurice Scève's *Microcosme*;[23] and it still figures in the musical section of Robert Fludd's *Utriusque cosmi majoris historia* (1617). Cornelius Agrippa, in a very elaborate account of music (*De occulta Philosophia* 2.25); takes a similar, and somewhat clearer, statement of the same thought from Ficino's *Epistulae,* and makes it explicit that the harmony or song originates in the mind and phantasy of the artist, and by penetration "moves emotion with emotion, and affects phantasy by phantasy, mind by mind."[24]

Music has, moreover, a special power of fixing the attention of the soul and its spirits; it "ravishes and appropriates the whole man." Cassiodorus already knows that "music enters our ears and alters our spirits, and as queen of the senses drives out other thoughts." So Dante: "Music draws to itself the human spirits which are, as it were, mainly vapors of the heart, so that they almost cease from action of their own, so undivided is the soul when it listens to music; and the virtue of all the spirits is, as it were, concentrated in the spirit of sense which receives the sound.[25] And accordingly the effect of Casella's singing in *Purg.* 2.116–19 is that all present "appeared so content, that nothing else might touch the mind of any":

> parevan sì contenti,
> come a nessun toccasse altro la mente.
> Noi eravam tutti fissi e attenti
> alle sue note.

It is thus that Jessica's spirits are said to be attentive.[26] Finally, in the heightened Platonism of the Renaissance, "penetration" and "attention" open the way for an influx of the divine in musical ecstasy; for the intelligible music creates the sense-music, and the musician and hearer may pass upward from sense-music to the divine intellectual music (Plotinus, *Enn.* 1.3; 5.8).

[23]V.-L. Saulnier, *Maurice Scève* (Paris, 1949), 1.474, 480; 2.230. Perhaps Ronsard (above) echoes the last part of Ficino's sentence.
[24]Ficino, *Op. om.*, p. 651; Kristeller, *op. cit.*, p. 307. The words quoted above are Agrippa's addition.
[25]*Convivio* II, xiii. 24 (tr. by W. W. Jackson, p. 110). Busnelli and Vandelli illustrate this sentence with the passage of Albertus which I have borrowed from them, and by passages of Thomas Aquinas on "attention."
[26]The lower animals, be it noted, also have spirits, and a lower kind of phantasy; cf. Albertus (n. 21 above).

Such are the ways of music with the microcosm. The music of the macrocosm also enjoyed a development in the theories of the Middle Ages and the Renaissance. We left this item of the theme with Ambrose, who was able only to juxtapose the music of the angels and the music of the spheres. Thus too most mediaeval writers on music, from Aurelian of Réomé onwards, are content to leave it.[27] Evidently, however, the universal acceptance in the Middle Ages of the ancient idea of Intelligences as motors of the spheres kept the way open for the concert of angels and spheres, since the Intelligences were "vulgarly" (so Albertus and Dante say) understood to be angels, and angels now implied the Dionysian hierarchies. St. Thomas Aquinas indeed once suggests that, among the hierarchies, it is the Virtues that govern the spheres (*Sum. c. Gent.* 3.80). There is still no concert. One may suppose, however, that it must have been conceived before Dante, who introduces it quite casually. On entering the Earthly Paradise (*Purg.* 30, 92–3), he hears the angels "who always sing following the notes of the eternal spheres" (*che notan sempre Dietro alle note delli etterni giri*). Furthermore, Dante, as is well known, has a complete system of correspondences between the nine orders of the angels and the nine spheres (*Convivio* II, vi; *Par.* 28), and recognizes that the spheres are moved by angels of the corresponding angelic orders. For this distribution of the spheres among the Dionysian hierarchies, commentators on Dante appear to have found no parallel.[28] The correspondence, never given fully by Dante, is as follows: Seraphim: Primum Mobile; Cherubim: Starry Heaven; Thrones: Saturn; Dominions: Jupiter; Virtues: Mars; Powers: Sun; Principalities: Venus; Archangels: Mercury; Angels: Moon.[29] Whatever may be the history of this correspondence, we find it again in Ficino (*De Christ. relig.*, c. 14): "Empireum stabilitati lucique Trinitatis recte accomodatur, novem reliqui [caeli] novem ordinibus angelorum; sunt enim quemadmodum Dionysio Areopagitae placet hierarchiae tres," [etc.]. Nor is

---

[27]Aurelian (9th century) in Gerbert, *Scriptores de musica medii aevi* 1.30: "There is music in Paradise; and music is pleasing to God, since by it we imitate the angelic choruses who ceaselessly praise him; the universe has a harmonic structure, extending to the seasons; and man is made for music, having vocal organs," [etc.].

[28]E. G. Gardner, *Dante's Ten Heavens* (London, 1900), p. 23, seems to regard this refinement as the invention of Dante. See also Bruno Nardi, *Dante e la cultura medievale* (Bari [Laterza], 1942), p. 239 and n. 6.

[29]In *Conv.* II, vi, following Gregory the Great instead of Dionysius on the Orders, he interchanges the Principalities and the Thrones.

the idea far from his thoughts in a chapter (12) of his *De Sole et lumine* where he compares the hierarchies with the planets surrounding the Sun, and goes on to speak of the Neoplatonic Muses on the spheres and even of spirits "gradatim stellis singulis dedicatos, quos Proculus etiam angelos et Iamblichus insuper archangelos principatusque cognominant." "Of these, such as are particularly 'solar' were called by the ancients 'Muses,' as presiding over the several sciences."[30]

It is in the ambience of Ficino's Neoplatonism that we first find this strict union of spheres and angels introduced within the context of the *laudes musicae*. This occurs in Gafori's *Theorica Musicae* already cited. Gafori, however, unlike Dante and Ficino, gives the following correspondences: Angels: the Earth or sphere of the Elements; Archangels: Moon; Virtues: Mercury; Powers: Venus; Principalities: Sun; Dominions: Mars; Thrones: Jupiter; Cherubim: Saturn; Seraphim: Starry Heaven. "The Primum Mobile is the abode of God, and embraces the melody of the lower spheres; and hence some poets have placed there the Heavenly Muse."[31] The hierarchies are offered as a "correction" of the Platonic Sirens, and are regarded as actually present on the spheres. The whole thought, together with some of the phrasing, is derived from Macrobius, whose sphere-Muses are replaced by the angels, except for the Heavenly Muse. That Macrobius' Muses are close to the surface is further confessed by an illustration in the edition of 1496 which shows the Muses, and not the angels, attached to the spheres.[32] This concept also passed into the writers on music; for instance, Beroaldo takes it directly from Macrobius, and in Cornelius Agrippa's chapters

---

[30]Dante in the passage of the *Convivio* cited above proceeds to distribute the spheres among the liberal arts. Such correspondences no doubt were made freely in the mediaeval and the Renaissance periods, but a more immediate Neoplatonic background may be suspected for Dante as for Ficino. L. G. Giraldi, *De Musis syntagma* (*Op. om.*, 1580, 1.533), may refer to Ficino when he says: "Nec defuerunt qui novem Musas novem beatorum animorum choros, hoc est, angelos designari crederent."

[31]This passage appears to depend upon the unpublished treatise *De Harmonia* of Giorgio Anselmo, which Gafori quotes. Gafori's manuscript copy of this work exists in the Ambrosian Library at Milan (G. Cesari, ed. of *Theorica Musicae* [Rome 1934], p. 19). The first part, explicitly cited by Gafori, is entitled "De harmonia coelesti."

[32]Reproduced by Jean Seznec, *La Survivance des dieux antiques* (London, 1940), pl. xxiv. On Gafori's interest in Ficino see Otto Kinkeldey, "Franchino Gafori and Marsilio Ficino" in *Harvard Library Bulletin* 1 (1947) 379–82, and Paul Oskar Kristeller, "Music and Learning in the Early Italian Renaissance" in *Journ. Ren. and Baroque Music* 1 (1946) 255–74.

on music (*De occulta Philosophia* 2.26) correspondences are elaborated between Muses, spheres, and the musical modes.[33]

These views about the angels and the spheres were available, then, in the sixteenth century, but remained perhaps rather esoteric.[34] Still that would not render them less accessible to the poets, who are especially sensitive to the Platonic elements in contemporary thought. And one cannot fail to be attracted by the suggestion of E. M. W. Tillyard that in the lines,

> There's not the smallest orb which thou behold'st
> But in his motion like an angel sings,
> Still quiring to the young-eyed cherubins,

Shakespeare alludes, not to the spheres in general, but to the eighth sphere or Starry Firmament, as governed specifically by the Cherubim.[35] Tillyard seems to think that this correspondence was in the main mediaeval tradition, and speaks as if it appeared in pseudo-Dionysius. My own findings, which are, however, incomplete, do not confirm this view, and rather suggest that beginning about the time of Dante, or actually with Dante, this rather fanciful

---

[33]So also in Thomas Morley, *A plaine and easy Introduction to practicall Musicke* (1597), Annot. An interesting variation on the idea is found in Vida's *Poetica* 1.515-29, where Prometheus, visiting the gods in heaven, sees the spheres harmoniously revolved each by its own Muse
> (argutos aetheris orbes,
> Quos sua quemque cient vario discrimine Musae),
and forthwith steals the Muses and brings them to mankind as a gift second only to fire in value. As a result, though the gods yielded the Muses, they chained Prometheus, and men did not venture to approach the Muses for many generations. Quite possibly the young Milton recalled this passage of Vida in his *De Sphaerarum concentu*, where "the audacity of the thievish Prometheus" is made the reason why we are denied the ability to hear the sphere-music. The Muses of the spheres had appeared sporadically in the Middle Ages in the wake of Macrobius and Martianus Capella; see E. R. Curtius, "Die Musen im Mittelalter," in *Zeitschrift für Romanische Philologie* 59 (1939) 128-88, and F. Piper, *Mythol.* 2.253, 269.

[34]Thus L. G. Giraldi (*De Poetis*, Dial. 1) knows these things, but passes them by: "Nonne, ut ad coelestes transeam, et novem ipsos angelorum choros nos et credimus et perinde colimus, qui assidue ad maiestatis eius solium concentus auribus mortalium inauditos edunt? Ut hic vobis mittam gentilium philosophorum coelestes quas vocant Musas, et agentes coeli sphaeras et globos Sirenas, abiunctasque quas vocant a materia substantias ceteraque id genus."

[35]*The Elizabethan World Picture* (London, 1948), pp. 38-39. Piper (*Mythol.* 2.276) apparently had the same thought, but did not develop it; more specific than Tillyard, however, he refers to Dante; but he starts from the German Shakespeare, which is here inexact ("singt Zum Chor der Hellgeaugten Cherubim").

correspondence flourished in the atmosphere of Renaissance Platonism. Even for this I have few texts to offer. Tillyard offers none. It is possible, however, to quote one which, though later than Shakespeare, comes from his environment. The correspondence between hierarchies and spheres is a principal topic of the fifth Tractate—"The Vertues"—of Thomas Heywood's *Hierarchie of the Blessed Angels* (1635), and is summed up in the following lines:

> The Primum Mobile doth first begin
> To chime unto the holy Seraphim.
> The Cherubim doth make concordance even
> With the eighth sphere, namely the Starry Heaven,
> The Thrones with Saturne. The like modulations
> Hath Jupiter with the high Dominations.
> The Vertues have with Mars a consonance sweet;
> The Potestates with Sol in symptores meet,
> The Principates with Venus best agree;
> Th' Archangels with the Planet Mercurie;
> The Angels with the Moone, which melodie
> Hosanna sing to Him that sits on high.[36]

Certainly the usual form of this motive is less specific, and contemplates only a general "concent" between the spheres and the heavenly hosts. Such is the impression left by Du Bartas' brief treatment, introduced at the proper point in the *encomium musicae* that forms part of his review of the liberal arts (*Les Colomnes* 691–96):

> La Voix souveraine
> Logea dans chaque ciel une douce Syrene
> Comme surintendente: à fin que ces bas cors [the spheres]
> Empruntassent des hauts leurs plus parfaits accors,
> Et qu' un chœur aime-bal avec le chœur des anges
> Dans sa chapelle ardente entonnast ses louanges.

If correspondence is here intended, compression has rendered it obscure; but the Platonic background is evident. Finally, Campanella, in a poem that is at once a *tour de force* and one of the most pleasing that our theme has inspired, leaves the impression only of

---

[36]The same correspondence is given by Athanasius Kircher at the end of his *Musurgia* (Rome, 1650), 2.458.

a general concert of instrumental spheres and singing hierarchies.[37] His reason for our not hearing the music of the stars also deserves notice.

Dal ciel la gloria del gran Dio rimbomba.
Egli è sonora tromba a pregi tanti;
I lumi stanti e que' ch' errando vanno
　　　　Musica fanno.

Musica fanno per ogni confino,
Dove il calor divino il ciel dispiega,
Ed amor lega tante luci, e muove
　　　　Altronde altrove.

Altronde altrove tutti van correndo,
Te, Dio, benedicendo e predicando,
Dolce sonando, ch' ogni moto è suono,
　　　　Come io ragiono.

Così io ragiono. Aimè! ch' udir non posso;
Ch' innato rumor grosso è, che m'occúpa
L'orecchia cupa, ed un molino vivo
　　　　Me ne fa privo.

Se mi fa privo, voi, spiriti eletti,
Che non siete soggetti a corpo sordo,
Fate un accordo al suon di tai strumenti
　　　　Co' vostri accenti.

Co' vostri accenti, sacri, intellettuali,
D'una spiegando l'ali in altra stella,
Vostra favella, "Santo, Santo, Santo,"
　　　　Dicete intanto.

Dicete intanto, ardenti Serafini,
Sagaci Cherubini, e giusti Troni,
Dominazioni, Virtú e Potestati
　　　　E Principati;

[37]"Salmodia che invita il cielo e le sue parti ed abitatori a lodar Dio benedetto" in *Scelta d'alcune poesie filosofiche* (1622), Giovanni Gentile, ed. (Bari; Laterza, 1915), p. 175. I have altered the punctuation in the passage quoted.

Principati, Arcangeli, e seguite,
Angeli, che venite a darmi aiuto.
Da voi, perduto il corpo, in cielo accolte
Son l'alme sciolte. . . .

III

In England the Praise of Music had a continuous tradition throughout the later Middle Ages, and is found not only in professional writers on music such as John Cotton, Walter of Evesham, and Simon Tunsted, but also, for example, in the encyclopedist Bartholomaeus Anglicus (thirteenth century), whose *De Proprietatibus rerum,* as translated into English by Trevisa, was printed by Wynken de Worde in 1495, and reprinted in 1535 and again, with additions by Stephen Batman, in 1582. In verse, the topic appears as part of a review of the liberal arts in *Reson and Sensuallyte,* formerly ascribed to Lydgate. Again in a review of the liberal arts, but now in direct contact with Italian humanism, it figures in Richard Pace's *De Fructu* (1518), in a passage in part transcribed from Beroaldo's oration already mentioned. Henceforward the English examples regularly shine with a light borrowed from the continental Renaissance or from the ancient authors that the Renaissance brought forward. Thus recent writers who have been citing John Case's *Praise of Musicke* (1586) as the expression of his personal observations should take note that the work is largely a compilation, and that the chapter dealing with the center of our theme (Ch. 6, "The Suavitie of Musicke") is an unacknowledged translation from L. G. Giraldi's *De Poetis.* In a series of poems on his mistress singing, Thomas Watson contrives one sonnet—"Esclepiad did cure with trumpets sound"—directly out of Martianus Capella, while Ben Jonson's verses in praise of Alfonso Ferrabosco the Younger again depend on the useful Beroaldo. Examples could be multiplied.

But if English writers thus draw the substance of their praise of music from continental and ancient sources, the spirit of their productions has a nearer and more domestic origin. We may boldly say that out of domestic controversy there came the impulse for the praise or rather defense of music that led to the unique florescence of the musical poem in England. What was a fairly academic topic elsewhere, possessed immediacy for the English, who were at once a musical nation and a Protestant nation verging toward Puritanism. Percy Scholes long ago convinced us in a lively book that the Puritans as such—he writes principally of the seventeenth century—were far from being the declared enemies of music, and that, on the contrary, they shared in the musical culture of their time.[38] Doubtless he is right; but mainly concerned with correcting modern errors about the Puritans, he has given less attention to the objections of their non-Puritan contemporaries, which ought to be taken into account, however prejudiced they may have been. To put it briefly, the objections of the Puritans to elaborate, and especially instrumental, music in divine service (to which Scholes devotes a chapter), and the known strictness of their views in general, provided a handle to the facile grasp of those who disliked them, and the unmusical man, "the man that hath no music in himself," arose from the *laudes musicae* and seemed to walk the earth as an English reality, especially in the eyes of those who were close to the theater. As Scholes himself points out, the objection to elaborate and instrumental music in church has been alive in all Christian centuries. It is found combining with our theme in the earliest Psalm-commentaries, and goes back to the topic "old music best," coupled with the objection to "theater music" in Plutarch and other pre-Christian writers, and so finally to Plato's distinction between "severe" and "vulgar" music. The Puritan controversy made this topic prominent in England. Hooker, for example, in defending music in the Church quite properly adduces the authority of St. Basil and Rabanus Maurus on the Psalms.

An obvious way in which to conduct the controversy was to appeal from one side of the tradition to the other. Thus Stephen Gosson, in attacking music and the theater, turns to Boethius and Chalcidius and exalts "unheard music"—*musica mundana* and *humana*—in his *School of Abuse* (1579):

> Pythagoras... condemns them for fools that judge Musicke by sounde and eare. If you will be good scholars, and profite well in the Art of Musicke, shutte your Fidels in their cases, and looke up to heaven: the order of the Spheres, the unfallible motion of the Planets, the... variety of Seasons, the concorde of the Elements.... The politike Lawes... the love of the King... this is right Musicke.

[38] *The Puritans and Music in England and New England* (London: Oxford University Press, 1934).

42

And in answering him Thomas Lodge (*A Defence of Poetry, Music, and Stage Plays*, 1579), simply brings out a larger selection from the store of the *laudes musicae*, from the harmony of the heavens to the rhythm of the pulse and Arion charming the dolphin.

It is in this atmosphere that the first English poems in praise of music begin to appear. The beginning is very humble indeed, the first such poem known to me being a broadside ballad by one Nicholas Whight, entered in the Stationer's Register under the year 1562–63: *A Commendation of Musicke and a Confutation of them which Disprayse it*.[39] The chief point of the commendation is the antiquity of music, which is demonstrated through a long list of inventors including some very strange names. There is no trouble, on the basis of our collections, in discovering that Whight has simply versified the musical sections of Polydore Vergil's *De Inventoribus*. The opening lines will be sample enough of his doggerel:

When first within the corps of man dame Nature built her bower,
She saw what troubles eke and thral was bent them to devower;
To whome she gave as in reward a pleasaunt note or sound,
Their carkes and cares to dryve away, whereby much ease was found.
Whereof in children proof is had, whome nurses have in charge:
How soone they stop and stay their cry when she doeth sound at large.

Vergilius: "Itaque Natura inde a principio mortalibus musicam velut muneri dedisse videtur,[40] quando ad tolerandos humanae vitae labores plurimum valet. Siquidem homo statim natus cum in cunabulis vagire incipit, continuo nutriculae cantitantis voce sopitus dormitat." Whight's tone throughout is that of one reasoning with an opponent, and he ends with a defiance of the enemy of music (not found in Vergilius):

This have I doen in Musickes cause; my pen now wyll I rest,
Syth that I have that worthy science as famouse once profest.
And who that seekes the losse of it—needes must I speake my mynd—
A great disprayse is to his wit, his wordes are coumpted wynd.

---

[39]In the same year 1563 Thomas Churchyard registered a ballad with the same title, *The Commendation of Music*, which is known only from the Stationer's Register, and may not have appeared (Hyder Rollins, ed. of *Paradise of Dainty Devices*, p. 227).
[40]From Quintilian (above).

43

Of about the same date are the better, and indeed famous, verses of Richard Edwards (d. 1566), *In Commendation of Musick,* published in the *Paradise of Dainty Devices* (1576), and employed by Shakespeare in *Romeo and Juliet* (4.5.128), and by other dramatists:

> Where gripying grief the hart would wound
> And dolful domps the minde oppresse,
> There Musick with her silver sound,
> Is wont with spede to give redresse.
> Of troubled minde for every sore,
> Swete Musick hath a salve therefore.
>
> In joye it makes our mirth abound,
> In grief it chers our heavy sprights,
> The carefull head release hath found
> By Musicks plesant swete delights.
> Our sences, what should I saie more,
> Are subject unto Musicks lore.
>
> The Godds by Musick hath their praie,
> The foule therein doth joye,
> For as the Romaine Poets saie,
> In seas whom Pirats would destroye,
> A Dolphin saved from death most sharpe,
> Arion playing on his harpe.
>
> A heavenly gift, that turnes the minde,
> Like as the sterne doth rule the ship,
> Musick whom the Gods assignde
> To comfort man, whom cares would nip,
> Sith thou both man and beast doest move,
> What wise man then will thee reprove?

Though no immediate source can be proposed for these verses, every phrase is traditional. Thus "our senses are subject" recalls Cassiodorus' "regina sensuum"; "whom the gods assigned to comfort man" is the equivalent of "Natura . . . solatia laboribus subministrat hominibus" (Giraldi, after Quintilian); "in joy it makes our mirth abound, In grief it cheers our heavy sprites" represents "moerentibus adimit moerorem, hilares efficit hilariores" (Beroaldo). In the third stanza, Edwards outdoes Shakespeare in the shorthand treatment of a familiar topic: The gods are praised by

44

music, and birds delight in it—obviously, for a dolphin saved Arion.[41]

Not to comment on every musical poem of the period, we may mention Humphrey Gifford's verses *In Praise of Music*, in his *Posie of Gilloflowers* (1580), as reflecting the Gosson-Lodge controversy then progressing, since to the story of Orpheus and Eurydice (emphasized by Lodge) Gifford appends the topics of celestial, moral, and political "music" stressed by both authors. He somewhat mildly deems "that man bereft of wits, which Music will not love"; but Thomas Watson, in some verses on Case's *Praise of Musicke,* is vehement enough.[42]

> Then may the solemn stoicke finde
> That Momus and himself are blynde, . . .
> Whiles will and witless ears are bent
> Against Apollo's sweet concent,
> The nursse of good, the scourge of ill. . . .

Many of Shakespeare's allusions to music fall within our theme—for instance (*Richard II* 5.5.42–63):

> How sour sweet music is
> When time is broke and no proportion kept!
> So is it in the music of men's lives. . . .
> This music mads me: let it sound no more;
> For though it have holp madmen to their wits,
> In me it seems it will make wise men mad.

Therein we catch the allusion to Asclepiades' madman and to Saul. In *Twelfth Night* (2.4.1) occurs the topic "old music is best":

> Now, good Cesario, but that piece of song,
> That old and antique song we heard last night,
> Methought it did relieve my passion much,
> More than light airs and recollected terms
> Of these most brisk and giddy-paced times.

---

[41]Rollins is clearly astray in saying (ed. of *Paradise of Dainty Devices,* p. 227): "Undoubtedly . . . in place of *praie* and *foule,* we should read *praise* and *soul*" [!]. With the same honest intent, but to no happier effect, some early editions replace "foule" with "fish."

[42]*Poems,* Arber, ed. (London, 1870), p. 10.

Old music is best for the relief of the passions. We may glance obliquely at Ronsard's use of the topic in the Preface already cited: "Ce livre de *Mellanges* . . . est composé des plus vielles chansons qui se puissent trouver aujourd'huy, pource qu' on a tousjours estimé la musique des anciens estre la plus divine, d'autant qu'elle a esté composée en un siècle plus heureux et moins entaché des vices qui regnent en ce dernier age de fer." Who are these "ancients"? And what was the happy age in which these old French songs were written? Or is Ronsard only rather irresponsibly reproducing a traditional *topos?*

A few remarks may here be added concerning Lorenzo's speech with which we began. That behind it there is an *encomium musicae* of a traditional type is evident; it begins with the music of the heavens and of the human soul, and proceeds to the effects through the usual reasoning that man should respond to music since even the beasts do so. Some difficulty arises from the fact that in Shakespeare's shorthand the concert of spheres and angels and the music of the human soul are rather huddled together, and the transitions are abrupt. What Lorenzo here seems to say is that every visible star in its motion sings, quiring to the Cherubim, and that a harmony like that of the stars is in our immortal souls, but inaudible while we are in the flesh. He cannot mean that; for it is grotesque to speak of hearing the harmony of our own souls, whether in the flesh or out of the flesh. His words are only hints, to be understood from the tradition to mean: A harmony like that of the heavens is in our immortal souls, but is lost to us while we are sunk in the flesh, and hence we do not respond to or hear the related celestial music.[43] The word "whilst" is weighted; upon release from the flesh, realizing our immortality, we shall hear it—when, in the words of Macrobius, "we return to heaven, the source of music." So Queen Katherine in *Henry VIII* (4.2.78-80):

> Play me that sad note
> I named my knell, whilst I sat meditating
> On that celestial harmony I go to.

[43] A bold attempt to save the sense of Lorenzo's words is made by Quiller-Couch and Wilson (eds. of *Merchant, ad loc.*), who remove the human soul entirely from the passage by printing an exclamation point ("Such harmony is in immortal souls!") making the line refer only to the Cherubim. But does it not rather make it refer to

Shakespeare thus knew our theme in a Platonic or Neoplatonic form, as was indeed almost inevitable in the Renaissance. His source is therefore the more likely to have included the exact correspondence of the Starry Heaven with the Cherubim, as Tillyard suggests; but even this concept is distorted, since not the stars, but the sphere should "in his motion" chime with the angels. Lorenzo's language is controlled by the poet's realization of the scene and of his characters, and is suited to the naïve view of the star-studded sky actually in sight (despite the flooding moonlight!) and to the understanding of Jessica. The words "quiring to" the cherubim are generally understood, in accordance with the tradition, to mean that the chorus of stars accompanies the chorus of the cherubim; and that certainly is what Shakespeare's source gave him. They may, however, quite simply mean that the stars sing as a choir to the young-eyed cherubim, who merely listen. Why the epithet "young-eyed," when every one knew that the Cherubim signify "plenitude of knowledge?"[44] That information indeed might have held little interest for Jessica; and theology is far from Shakespeare's thoughts. What came into his head with the word "cherubin" is revealed by *Othello* 4.2.64: "Patience, thou young and rose-lipped cherubin" (to Desdemona), and by *Tempest* 1.2.152–3: "O a cherubin thou wast, that did preserve me! Thou didst smile" (Prospero recalling Miranda's infancy). These youthful or infantine cherubs belong, not to the literary tradition, which is faithful to *plenitudo scientiae*, but to the world of Renaissance painting, where angels are generally young, and cherubim are infants' bodiless heads surrounded with wings. Lorenzo's epithet, for example, exactly suits the cherubs of Perugino's *Assumption of the Virgin*, in

---

the stars, which are hardly immortal souls for Shakespeare? And they must understand "close it in" two lines below as "close it out." In any event, the testimony of the *laudes* is unanimous for the topic "world-harmony reflected in the human soul" at this point in the complex. The word "immortal" perhaps represents something like Censorinus' "Nostraeque mentes, ipsae divinae, suam naturam per cantus agnoscunt"; and it may carry the connotation "disembodied."

[44]Pseudo-Dionysius, Gregory the Great *(plenitudo scientiae)*, Thomas Aquinas, and so down to Florio's *World of Words*. On the authority of Ezechiel 10.12, Athanasius and others call them "many-eyed." Their knowledge thus depends on their contemplation of God, and hence they also signify "contemplation" (ps.-Dion., *Coel. Hier.* 7); cf. Milton, *Pens.* 54: "bring...the Cherub Contemplation."

whose young eyes there sleeps a wonderful light of contemplation. It is as though, in Lorenzo's cherubins, sung to by the stars, the fanciful poet has fleetingly assimilated the traditional angels to the equally traditional infants that for a millenium and a half had invariably been lulled by nurses' singing in the *laudes musicae*.

While in the bonds of the flesh, we cannot hear the celestial music. And Lorenzo, having cut himself off, so to speak, from explaining our response to earthly music by "recollection," turns abruptly (at the entrance of the earthly musicians) to earthly music by calling for a "hymn" to Diana—possibly a reminiscence of the topic "music in the worship of the gods"; and compare Macrobius on hymns, above. He then alludes to the penetration of music: "With sweetest touches pierce your mistress' ear"; and penetration is a topic that in the atmosphere of Renaissance Platonism often has associations of magic (it appeals to persons like Cornelius Agrippa and Robert Fludd), which here seems to be hinted at in "draw her home with music". Is there not an echo of the familiar Virgilian incantation (*Ecl.* 8): "Ducite ab urbe domum, mea carmina, ducite Daphnim?" Lorenzo is thus concerned, as is proper at this point in the theme, with the explanation of our response to earthly music, and when Jessica has volunteered, "I am never merry when I hear sweet music," his answer arises from the penetration-theory: "The reason is, your spirits are attentive." That is to say, music, having penetrated to the animal spirits, holds them attentive and excludes all other thoughts. This explanation prevailed in Shakespeare's environment; so Burton: "Scaliger *Exercit.* 302, gives a reason for these effects [of music] 'because the spirits about the heart take in that trembling and dancing air into the body, are moved together, and stirred up by it'"; and Hooker: "The very harmony of sounds being framed in due sort, and carried from the ear to the spiritual faculties of our souls, is, by a native puissance and efficacy, greatly available to bring to a perfect temper whatever there is troubled, apt to quicken the spirits as to allay that which is too eager, sovereign against melancholy and despair, . . . able both to move and to moderate all affections."[45]

[45]Burton, *Anatomy of Melancholy* 2.133-34 (Shilleto); Hooker, *Eccl. Pol.* 5.38. Hooker is paraphrasing Cassiodorus' letter to Boethius. Compare also *Cymbeline* 2.3.11-35. That the spirits of women are especially susceptible to the penetration of music is a topic as old as Gregory of Nyssa (*Tract. in Ps. Insc., c.* 3); cf. Castiglione, *Cortegiano* 1.47: ". . . donne, gli animi delle quali, teneri e molli, facilmente sono dall'armonia penetrati."

In breaking away from the topic "world-harmony and soul-harmony" to seek a psychological explanation of our response to music, Shakespeare is not out of line with the *laudes musicae*. In the majority of the examples known to me, the topic "world- and soul-harmony" is thus mentioned and dropped, and there follows a list of "effects," within the reflection, "man certainly, since also the animals."[46] This is the way even of writers who, like Macrobius, explain the effects by "recollection," and of course "recollection" and "penetration" are not mutually exclusive—both indeed are Platonic. Actually this whole second part of Lorenzo's speech—on earthly music—forms a single statement, which we may paraphrase as follows: Music puts you into a sober frame of mind because it controls your spirits, as most certainly it does, since it similarly controls and calms irrational animals; and that is why the poet represents Orpheus as "drawing" not only irrational beasts but even inanimate things, meaning that no nature is so stubborn as to resist music; but if there is such a person, he is a public menace and not to be trusted. Now this train of thought, and not only the phrase "nought so stockish, hard, and full of rage," is plainly a transfer from the following words of Macrobius:

So captivated is [the soul] by the soothing properties of music that there is no breast so rude or fierce that it is not susceptible to such delights. In this principle, I think, originated the tale of Orpheus or Amphion, the one drawing irrational animals by songs, the other even rocks, since they first, perhaps, by singing drew to a sense of pleasure peoples who either were barbarians without rational culture or were insensible to emotion like rocks.[47]

---

[46]Shakespeare's colts are, rather curiously, tamed by the trumpet, which, according to the tradition (which accounts for the trumpet), should instead inspirit them for battle. Taming, however, is also a traditional effect; we may compare Shakespeare's "herd" with Macrobius' flocks quieted by piping, and may quote Zarlino on the equally traditional stags (they are from Aristotle by way of Martianus Capella): "Et per non mi distendere più sopra di questo, solamente dirò di conoscere alcuni i quali hanno veduto dei Cervi, che fermando il corso se ne stavano attenti ad ascoltare il suono della lira et del leuto" (*Ist. Harm.*, p. 7).

[47]Ita delinimentis canticis [anima] occupatur, ut nullum sit tam immite, tam asperum pectus, quod non oblectamentorum talium teneatur affectu. Hinc aestimo et Orphei vel Amphionis fabulam, quorum alter animalia rationae carentia, alter saxa quoque trahere cantibus referebantur, sumpsisse principium, quia primi forte gentes vel sine rationis cultu barbaras vel saxi instar nullo affectu mobiles ad sensum voluptatis canendo traxerunt *(Comm. in Som. Scip.* 2.3).

Shakespeare's immediate source, then, embodied this passage from Macrobius, but had perhaps already introduced a change of emphasis that makes Lorenzo seem slightly illogical. If there is "nought" so stockish but music doth change his nature, how is there room for the man who "is not moved"? It is in fact hyperbole. This man whose spirits are dull as night and affections dark as Erebus is below the beasts, and is no man but a devil. This will be clearer as we go on. Meanwhile we note that "the poet" in the Shakespearean passage need not be sought in the *Corpus Poetarum Latinorum,* but is only the shadow of Macrobius' *fabula.*

The link between Shakespeare and Macrobius finds a curious parallel in the praises of music as developed by Shakespeare's contemporary Sir John Davies, to whose *Hymne in Prayse of Musicke* we briefly turn:[48]

> Prayse, Pleasure, Profit, is that three-fold band,
> Which ties men's minds more fast then Gordions knot.
> Each one some drawes, al three none can withstand,
> Of force conjoyn'd, Conquest is hardly got.
>   Then Musicke may of harts a Monarcke bee,
>   Wherein Prayse, Pleasure, Profit so agree.

> Praise-worthy Musicke is, for God it prayseth,
> And pleasant, for brute beasts therein delight:
> Great profit from it flowes, for why it raiseth
> The mind ouerwhelmèd with rude passions might:
>   When against reason passions fond rebell,
>   Musicke doth that confirme, and these expell.

> If Musicke did not merit endlesse prayse,
> Would heav'nly Spheres delight in silver round?
> If joyous pleasure were not in sweet layes
> Would they in Court and Country so abound?
>   And profitable needs we must that call,
>   Which pleasure linkt with praise doth bring to al.

> Heroicke minds with praises most incited,
> Seeke praise in Musicke, and therein excell:
> God, man, beasts, birds, with Musicke are delighted;

---

[48]These stanzas, originally appearing in Davison's *Poetical Rhapsody* (1602) over the initials "I. D.," have by some been assigned to John Donne, but more plausibly by others to Davies; see Hyder Rollins, ed., *A Poetical Rhapsody* (Cambridge, Mass., 1931–32), 2.176.

And pleasant 'tis, which pleaseth all so well:
    No greater profit is then selfe content,
    And this doth Musick bring, and care prevent.

When antique Poets Musicks praises tell,
They say it beasts did please, and stones did move:
To prove more dull then stones, then beasts more fel,
Those men, which pleasing Musicke did not love;
    They fain'd it Cities built, and States defended,
    To shew that profit great on it depended.

Sweet birds (poore mens Musitians) never slake
To sing sweet Musicks prayses day and night:
The dying Swans in Musicke pleasure take,
To shew that it the dying can delight:
    In sickness, health, peace, war, we do it need,
    Which proves sweet Musicks profit doth exceed.

But I by niggard praysing do disprayse
Prayse-worthy Musicke in my worthles Ryme:
Ne can the pleasing profit of sweet layes,
Any save learned Muses well define:
    Yet all by these rude lines may clearly see,
    Prayse, Pleasure, Profit in sweet Musicke bee.

Under the heads "praise, pleasure, profit," Davies neatly contrives to weave together a good many of the commonplaces of our
theme, and nothing but these commonplaces. Even the common
ellipse, "pleasant, for brute beasts therein delight," occurs in the
second stanza. In the fifth stanza, we cannot fail to recognize again
Macrobius' allegory of Orpheus and Amphion, and with the same
alteration in its point that we have found in Shakespeare, but more
clearly revealing its origin. Macrobius: "The fable of Orpheus and
Amphion means that these singers moved men who were as irrational as beasts or as insensible as stones." Davies: "Antique poets
tell that music pleased beasts and moved stones, to prove that men
who do not love music are more dull than stones and than beasts
more fell." Whoever made the alteration was influenced by the
wish to score a point against the unmusical (Puritan) man, and
Shakespeare has brought out this point and elaborated it ("the man
that hath no music . . . is fit for treasons, . . . dull as night"). Macrobius' *fabula*, we note, is represented in Davies as "the antique
poets," as by "the poet" in Shakespeare. In Davies' next stanza

perhaps we may trace Macrobius' emphasis on the music of birds (above, p. 26), and his special mention of the nightingale and the swan.[49]

While our attention rests on the prominence of Macrobius in the background of these English poems, we must glance at a rather curious *encomium musicae* imbedded in Samuel Rowley's historical play *When You See Me, You Know Me* (1605). The celebrated musician Dr. Christopher Tye is thus represented as addressing Prince Edward:

> But would your Grace awhile be patient,
> In Musicke's praise, thus will I better it:
> Music is heavenly, for in Heaven is musicke,
> For there the Seraphim do sing continually;
> And when the best was born that ever was man,
> A quire of angels sang for joy of it;
> What of celestial was revealed to man
> Was much of musicke: 'tis said the beasts did worship
> And sang before the deitie supernall;
> The kingly prophet sang before the arke,
> And with his musicke charm'd the heart of Saul:
> *And if the poet fail us not, my lord,*
> *The dulcet tongue of musicke made the stones*
> *To move, irrational beasts and birds to dance.*
> And last the trumpet's musicke shall awake the dead,
> And clothe their naked bones in coates of flesh
> T' appeare in that high house of parliament,
> When those that gnash their teeth at musicke's sound
> Shall make that place where musicke nere was found.

---

[49] A part of this passage from Macrobius is quoted by Gafori, *Theor. Mus.*, Cesari, ed. sig. Aii. I note in passing that Macrobius' brief allegory, which evidently had so considerable a fortune, is the original of a sentence in the *Convivio* of Dante. This is the well-known passage (II,i,3) on the several senses of interpretation: "L'altro [senso] si chiama allegorico, e questo è quello che si nasconde sotto il manto di queste favole . . . : sì come quando dice Ovidio che Orfeo facea con la cetera mansuete le fiere, e li arbori e le pietre a sé muovere: che vuol dire che lo savio uomo con lo strumento de la sua voce fa mansuescere e umiliare li crudeli cuori, e fa muovere a la sua volontade *coloro che non hanno vita di scienza e d'arte: e coloro che non hanno vita ragionevole alcuna sono quasi come pietre.*" With these last expressions compare: "gentes vel sine rationis cultu barbaras vel saxi instar." For Dante, *fabula* has become the poet Ovid, who indeed doubtless also came to Shakespeare's mind. Even if we suspect that Dante had this bit of Macrobius at second hand, it suggests revising the statement of Edmund G. Gardner that he "does not seem to have been acquainted with the Commentary of Macrobius on Cicero's *Somnium Scipionis*" (*Dante and the Mystics* [London, 1913], p. 82).

The form of the *laudes* is here not wholly lost. Rowley begins, as is customary, with the celestial music, and the line "Music is heavenly, for in heaven is music" might have been transcribed from Cassiodorus' *coelestem esse musicam*. In due course the animals are mentioned. He has elected, however, probably in keeping with the devout character of Dr. Tye, to take from the tradition only the religious *exempla* (Seraphim, angels of the Nativity, beasts of the Apocalypse, David before the ark and curing Saul, the Last Trumpet)—with one exception, the fable of Amphion (stones) and Orpheus (beasts), which interrupts the series like an interpolation. And here is "the poet" again. Rowley might simply be influenced by Shakespeare, but he gives no other evidence of that, and our review of the theme suggests that this motive is inserted in obedience to the traditional form of the *laudes,* and that Rowley knew the same version (in which Macrobius' *fabula* had become "the poet") that was known to Shakespeare and to Davies.

Similarly, as Shakespeare proceeds to condemn the unmusical man, of "affections dark as Erebus," so Rowley contemplates a Last Judgment,

> When those that gnash their teeth at musicke's sound,
> Shall make that place where musicke nere was found.

That these were "Puritans" seems clear from an anonymous *Songe in Praise of Musique,* apparently written two years before, soon after the accession of James I in 1603:

> Sweete musique mournes, and hath donne longe—
> These fortie yeares and almost five—
> God knowes it hath the greater wronge
> By Puritanes that are alive,
> Whose hautie, proude, disdainfull myndes
> Much fault agaynst poore musique findes. . . .
>
> They doe abhorre, as devilles doe all,
> The pleasant noyse of musique's sounde. . . .[50]

The ballad proceeds to mention, much as Rowley does, King David, the angels, the Nativity, and the custom of the ancient Church. But possibly the most emphatic statement of this condemnation is

[50]Hyder Rollins, *Old English Ballads 1553–1625* (Cambridge, 1920), pp. 142–46.

found in the well-argued stanzas *In the most just Praise of Musicke* contributed some years later by John Davies of Hereford to Ravenscroft's *Briefe Discourse* (1614).[51] Like the anonymous balladist, Davies says outright what Shakespeare only implies:

> The tenfold Orbes of Heaven are said to move
> By Musicke; for they make Harmonious din:
> And all the Powers subordinate above
> Spend time, nay, spend Æternity therein.

> If Musicke, then, move all that All doth move,
> That's not compriz'd in All, that spights her state:
> If not in All, it's nought; which who doth love
> Is worse than nought, to love what Heav'n doth hate. . . .

> But no man is so ill that hath no good;
> So, no man in the Abstract can be nought:
> Then 'tis no man that hates sweete Musickes moode,
> But something worse than all that can be thought.

> A Beast? O no! A Monster? Neither. Then
> Is it a Devill? Nothing lesse; for these
> Have Beings with an Angell or a Man,
> But that exists not, that sweete Notes displease. . . .

> For had they soules produc'd in Harmony,
> Or rather Art itself (some wise avouch),
> They would be ravisht with her Suavity,
> And turn'd Coelestial with her Heavenly touch. . . .

The succession of English poems on music reaches its high point, though by no means its end, in the poetry of Milton. Milton's practical experience with music doubtless contributed to the warmth of his utterance on this subject, but as a poet he discloses his technical knowledge discreetly and sparingly, while his more striking elaborations are derived, as is natural in a literary man, from the literary tradition. Within that tradition, his attitude no doubt is first defined by the Puritan or intensified Protestant environment of his youth; it is in the line of the Psalm-commentaries, of Hooker, or of

---

[51]Davies, *Complete Works*, Grosart, ed., 1878, Part 2, p. 9. Compare Davies' sonnet, p. 56, "The motion of the ninefold sacred quire."

Wither's *A Preparation to the Psalter* (1619), and nearer to the attitude of Gosson's "looke up to heaven" than to that of Lodge and the theater. It is thus that, with broader culture, he is drawn principally to the Pythagorean or Platonic side of the theme, and dwells, so to speak, on the first half of Lorenzo's speech and not on the second. The true music is philosophy; instrumental sounds without the *logos* of speech are imperfect music; and Milton holds with personal intensity to the Renaissance belief that poetry and music are intimately allied. With critical care, he integrated the tradition of music into a total view of things which gives life to his every allusion; but he relies on our knowing the tradition if we are to be alive to the lights and shading of his thought.

This thought is already surprisingly complete in his college exercise *De Sphaerarum concentu* (c. 1626). Here the sphere-music, which is said to hold the universe together, is defended against Aristotle with playful seriousness. Pythagoras alone is said to have heard this music (he being one sent from heaven to fill men with sacred learning and recall them to virtue), but mankind in general have had little perception of this harmony since the sin of Prometheus deprived them of it and caused them to sink toward the violence and lust of brutes. If our hearts became as pure and chaste as Pythagoras', we should hear again the music of the stars, and "all things would immediately return as if to that golden age."[52] Here the Neoplatonic theme, that we have lost the celestial music *ob consortium corporis,* is transposed to the realm of "history" and settled on the sin of Prometheus, while the overtones faintly suggest that Prometheus represents Adam and Pythagoras Christ.

The same order of ideas informs the musical passages of the *Hymn on the Morning of Christ's Nativity* (1629). Here, however, we witness a miraculous moment in history. The angelic choruses had sounded on earth at the Creation (Stanza 12), but never again after the sin of Adam. Heard now beneath the sphere of the moon, the angelic music (voice and strings) takes the souls of the shepherds "in blissful rapture," and almost persuades Nature that "her part is done," for "such harmony alone Could hold all Heav'n and Earth in happier union." We know that now the *musica mundana,* primarily sphere-music, holds the universe together; but it is itself an imperfect copy of the music of the angels or the heavenly Muses. At

---

[52]Tr. by S. G. Spaeth, *Milton's Knowledge of Music* (Princeton, 1913), p. 136.

the moment of Christ's birth, the true music seems about to replace the copy. And the physical sphere-music is summoned (Stanza 13) to be heard and to be in perfect accord with the *prima musica:*

> Ring out, ye Crystal spheres,
> Once bless our human ears
>   (If ye have power to touch our senses so)...
> And with your ninefold harmony
> Make up full consort to th' Angelic symphony.
>
> For if such holy Song
> Enwrap our fancy long,
>   Time will run back, and fetch the age of gold.

If this perfection is attained, and the angels' song enwraps our phantasy in prolonged "attention," both the physical universe and human nature (as the next lines make clear) will have returned to their primitive accord with heaven. With an allusion to Virgil's fourth *Eclogue* ("*gens aurea*"), we are reminded of the Platonic "great year" (*tempus recurret*), when the universe will return to its prime perfection (*Timaeus* 39). That time has not yet come, as the poet presently explains (Stanza 16); and hence, though the angels' singing is really heard, the spheres are only bidden to be in perfect accord with them—a command or wish that is not fulfilled.

A year or two later the poet selected from the tradition for *L'Allegro* and *Il Penseroso* parallel motives to suit the contrasting moods of the two poems, and placed the main elaboration of the musical motives in each case near the end, perhaps to suggest as one meaning of his twin songs the ambivalent power of music, so often insisted on—"vel ad ardorem virtuis animantur, vel ad mollitiem voluptatis resolvuntur,... nec non curas et immittit et retrahit" (Macrobius). In *L'Allegro:*

> And ever against eating Cares,
> Lap me in soft Lydian airs,
> Married to immortal verse,
> Such as the meeting soul may pierce....
> Such strains as would have won the ear
> Of Pluto, to have quite set free
> His [Orpheus'] half-regain'd Eurydice.

The commentators inform us that Milton dissents from Plato's condemnation of the Lydian mode; but that is beside the point. Milton is merely reproducing Cassiodorus, who in reviewing the effects of the modes decides that "the Dorian bestows chastity ... the Ionian sharpens the intellect and turns the desires heavenward ... the Lydian restores us with relaxation and delight, being invented against excessive cares and worries (*contra nimias curas animaeque taedia repertus*)." Joined with immortal verse, these Lydian airs will perform their effect by penetration, the soul of the singer being met by the soul of the hearer (compare Agrippa, above). We shall again meet with Milton's conviction that a mingling of words and music is most effective for penetration. Here the effect is powerful enough to cause Pluto to set Eurydice wholly free—an old *exemplum* from the *laudes musicae*, renewed by hyperbole.[53] To balance this fanciful pagan miracle of music, suitable to *L'Allegro*, Milton placed near the end of *Il Penseroso* the chief traditional miracle of solemn or religious music—the musical ecstasy:

> There let the pealing Organ blow
> To the full voic'd choir below,
> In Service high and Anthems clear,
> As may with sweetness, through mine ear,
> Dissolve me into ecstasies,
> And bring all Heav'n before mine eyes.

Again the instrumental music must be joined with the words of the choir; "through mine ear" is a stock phrase, shorthand therefore, for penetration; and ecstasy ensues. The process will be clearer when we see these lines elaborated in *At a Solemn Music*.

These effects are selected from another part of the tradition than that which inspired the second *Prolusion* and the Nativity *Hymn*. Indeed, after the Nativity *Hymn* Milton in his verse never returned unequivocally to the concert between the spheres and the angels. In *Arcades* 61–78, he returns, as the subject requires, to the view of the second *Prolusion:* it is merely the sphere-music of *Republic* x that the semi-divine Genius can hear when "drowsiness Hath lock'd up

[53]The motive is not entirely new; Orpheus' singing induces Pluto to set Eurydice finally free at the end of Ottavio Rinuccini's opera *Euridice* (1600); see Luigi Marrone, "Il mito di Orfeo nella drammatica italiana," in *Stud. di Lett. ital.* 12 (1922) 119–59.

mortal sense," this music being thus audible to him, but quite inaudible to all 'of human mould with gross unpurgèd ear'. But for his full thought at this time (1633) we must read *At a Solemn Music:*

> Blest pair of Sirens, pledges of Heav'n's joy,
> Sphere-born harmonious Sisters, Voice and Verse,
> Wed your divine sounds, and mixt power employ
> Dead things with inbreath'd sense able to pierce,
> And to our high-rais'd phantasy present
> That undisturbèd Song of pure concent,
> Aye sung before the sapphire-color'd throne
> To him that sits thereon,
> With Saintly shout, and solemn Jubilee,
> Where the bright Seraphim in burning row
> Their loud up-lifted Angel-trumpets blow,
> And the Cherubic host in thousand quires
> Touch their immortal Harps of golden wires,
> With those just Spirits that wear victorious Palms,
> Hymns devout and holy Psalms
> Singing everlastingly;
> That we on Earth with undiscording voice
> May rightly answer that melodious noise;
> As once we did, till disproportion'd sin
> Jarr'd against nature's chime, and with harsh din
> Broke the fair music that all creatures made
> To their great Lord, whose love their motion sway'd
> In perfect Diapason, whilst they stood
> In first obedience, and their state of good.
> O may we soon again renew that Song,
> And keep in tune with Heav'n, till God ere long
> To his celestial consort us unite,
> To live with him, and sing in endless morn of light.

It is solemn or religious music, and certainly not "theater music," that turns the desires heavenward, and may dissolve us into ecstasies. Milton's insistence on the Renaissance canon of the poet-musician (a revival, of course, from antiquity) usually, as here, has the emphasis that instrumental sounds are weak without the *logos* of speech—Voice without Verse. Puritan and humanist agree. Music and poetry are *consanguinei* (Chalcidius, *In Tim.*, p. 287 Wroebel), brother and sister in Barnfield's well-known sonnet, simply identical, "une mesme chose," for Jean Lemaire, *cognatae artes* in Milton's *Ad Patrem*, married in *L'Allegro,* and sisters here. When these sisters "wed their divine sounds," the "mix'd power" resulting is supremely efficacious for penetration. This principle was well understood; Zarlino says: "Harmony alone gives pleasure; harmony with number suddenly has great power to move the soul; but join speech to these two, and it is impossible to say what force they have."[54] They have force, says Milton, to pierce dead things with inbreath'd sense—presumably an allusion to Orpheus moving inanimate things.[55]

These sisters are Sirens, but not the "celestial Sirens" of *Arcades* 63, being not on the spheres but "sphere-born," just as Echo in *Comus* 241 is "daughter of the sphere." They are earthly music, thrice removed from the archetypal music of the heavenly host: celestial music > sphere-music > earthly music; or as Proclus says, "the ultimate image" of the heavenly Muses. As such, however, they are "pledges of Heav'n's joy" because we return to heaven the source of music (Macrobius), and penetrating us they may present as a true image to our high-rais'd phantasy the heavenly music of their ultimate origin. By this cathartic process, just as Proclus' Sirens (*Plat. Theol.* 7.36) bring their followers back to the appropriate god, these Sirens are asked to bring us back into tune with the celestial music as we were before the Fall. (Once more Milton assimilates the "historical" fall of Adam with the Neoplatonic descent into the flesh). May we then, recovering, or converted to, our true nature through music in the highest sense (Chalcidius), continue thus until we are united with the celestial choirs (St. John Chrysostom; Gafori).

The Neoplatonism is Christian; we do not "recollect" from an earlier existence, but the "divine sounds" bring to our souls an image of heaven. The key to the poem is the expression "high-rais'd phantasy." Penetrating to the aërial spirit, the *nodus* of soul and body, the harmonious *logos* reaches the phantasy or imagina-

---

[54]*Ist. Harm.*, p. 71; here quoted from Mrs. Finney's first article mentioned above (n. 3), to which I am much indebted for all that relates to musical ecstasy. Compare Cornelius Agrippa, *op. cit.* 2.25, on penetration: "Cantus quam instrumentalis sonus plus potest."

[55]Certainly not a way of speaking of the flesh, which is not dead. This expression is therefore the usual shorthand for the *a fortiori* argument: Men are penetrable, since even the animals and inanimate things are.

tive faculty that offers true opinion to the intellect.[56] Phantasy, intermediate between sense and reason, according to *PL* 5.100–08, may sink to the one or rise to the other, as it does when in a good or "dry" state (Synesius). Solemn music puts it into a good state, and the adjective 'high-rais'd' is proleptic (= raise and present); but it is also not proleptic (= that has raised itself); it responds to the divinity in the music. The cathartic process is educative, and requires the cooperation of the will.[57] "Present the celestial music to our imagination, that we may rightly answer it, as we (man) did before the Fall: O may we soon renew that Song." The moments of heightened contemplation induced by music are rare; music only for a time doth change our nature. The end is a prayer. The whole poem is an invocation in the imperative mood; though ecstasy is psychologically possible, the sober poet does not assert that anything has happened.

The concept that in the Golden Age before the Fall celestial music was heard on earth, and was lost after the Fall, is not in the tradition of the *laudes musicae*. Nor does it seem to figure in the hexaëmeral tradition, though the music of the spheres finds a place there in the acts of the fourth day. It had a tradition, however, or could be readily improvised. Thus Dante on entering the Earthly Paradise (*Purg.* 29.22) hears a sweet melody, the singing of the heavenly hosts: "Whereupon a righteous zeal made me reproach the hardihood of Eve," for had she remained obedient, "I should have tasted those ineffable delights before, and for a longer time."[58] The topic deserves more exploration than we can now give it; but we may rest assured that no one had seized upon it more eagerly than the young Milton, who repeats it so often. Meanwhile it can be cited—only as a metaphor, to be sure, but a striking one—

[56]This phantasy is for us, according to Synesius (*De Somniis* 1292B), the only source of concepts.

[57]Cf. Synesius. *De Somniis* 1292–96 (transl. by Fitzgerald 2.335–37); and see Murray Wright Bundy, *The Theory of the Imagination in Classical and Mediaeval Thought* (Urbana, 1927), p. 150.

[58]Commentaries on Dante do not recognize a traditional idea here. Oddly enough, both Spitzer (*op. cit.*, 1945, p. 345) and Tillyard (*op. cit.*, p. 45) assume that the concept is traditional, but offer delusive proofs—Spitzer, a misinterpretation of Luis de Leon's poem *La Musica, A Francisco Salinas*, and Tillyard, a passage from Sidney's *Defense of Poesy* that does not mention music. The poem of Luis de Leon is an exact description of the conventional musical ecstasy, emphasizing "attention": "La alma . . . en él asi se anega, / que ningún accidente / extraño ó peregrino oye e siente."

from a poet who certainly came within Milton's early reading. Du Bartas describes the affinities that even today hold the world together as

> but a spark or shadow of that love
> Which at the first in everything did move,
> When as th' Earth's Muses with harmonious sound
> To heaven's sweet music humbly did resound.
> But Adam, being chief of all the strings
> Of this large lute, o'er reachèd, quickly brings
> All out of tune.[59]

Three years after *At a Solemn Music* was written, Milton inserted an *encomium musicae* of a more conventional type into his poem *Ad Patrem*—a fact that has escaped the editors of his Latin poems. It too turns on his understanding of true music as "voice and verse," for which he here has the convenient Latin word *carmen*. Without pausing to analyze these lines, we may note that they embody the familiar topics (vv. 17–55): Song not to be despised; Song of heavenly origin; Used at sacrifices; In heaven we shall sing songs to which the stars will echo, and even now a fiery spirit sings in the spheres; Song at the banquets of kings in the heroic age; By song, and not by a mere *vocis modulamen inane*, Orpheus performed his miracles.

In view of the important role of these musical ideas in Milton's early poems, it is of interest to see what becomes of them in the mature framework of *Paradise Lost*. Celestial, that is angelic, music is duly heard by Adam and Even before the Fall (*PL* 4.682–88):

> Celestial voices to the midnight air. . . .
> With Heav'nly touch of instrumental sounds
> In full harmonic number join'd, thir songs
> Divide the night, and lift our thoughts to heaven.

(Hardly any of our writers fails to mention the effect: *Mentum ad caelum elevat*). Hearing celestial music is insisted on when Raphael reminds Adam of the sixth day of Creation (*PL* 7.557–64):

> Up he [the Creator] rode
> Follow'd with acclamation and the sound

---

[59]Sylvester's translation of *Seconde Semaine: Les Furies* 37–43; quoted by Merritt Y. Hughes in his ed. of *Paradise Lost* (New York, 1935), p. xxv.

Symphonious of ten thousand Harps that tun'd
Angelic harmonies: the Earth, the Air
Resounded, (*thou remember'st, for thou heard'st*)
The Heavens and all the Constellations rung,
The Planets in thir stations list'ning stood,
While the bright Pomp ascended jubilant.

Here (almost in defiance of Job 38.7) there is no concert of the heavens and the angels; the heavens echo, as in *Ad Patrem,* and the planets listen. The concert is not so sure a doctrine that Milton will express it boldly in *Paradise Lost.* Yet he suggests it, darkly. In a subtle passage (*PL* 5.619–27), the angels dance about the sacred Hill (like Hesiodic Muses as in *Il Pens.* 47–48, but now they are Neoplatonic Muses, which are archetypes) in a "mystical dance" which the sphere of the heavens "resembles nearest." The heavens imitate the pattern of the angelic hierarchies. Yet here too, as in the account of Raphael, only the angels sing:

And in thir motions harmony Divine
So smooths her charming tones, that God's own ear
Listens delighted.

(*Musica Deum delectat* is seldom forgotten in the *laudes musicae;* and compare Ambrose, above.)

Nevertheless the heavens do sing, and the concert is hinted at; for we are doubtless intended to link the "mystical dance" of the Angel-Muses with an earlier passage of this musical Fifth Book, at which we now glance. The Morning Hymn of Adam and Eve (*PL* 5.153–208) is enriched in Milton's manner with several layers of thought and allusion. Like St. Francis' Canticle of the Creatures, it is mainly founded on Psalm 148, and calls upon the universe—the angelic choruses; the starry spheres; the elements; mists and exhalations, winds, fountains, birds, creatures of the waters and the earth—to praise the Creator. It thus generally follows the psalm, but with unbiblical elaborations, as:

And yee five other wandr'ing Fires that move
In mystic Dance not without Song, resound
His praise.

And before the mists and winds which represent the fire, hail, and snow of the psalm—"elements" in one sense—Milton interpolates:

> Ye Elements the eldest birth
> Of Nature's Womb, that in quaternion run
> Perpetual Circle, multiform; and mix
> And nourish all things.

One object is to revise the universe of the psalmist in conformity with the Christian Ptolemaic system, in which the spheres of the Elements lie next below the sphere of the Moon; but the main object is to invoke a sounding, musical universe, and Milton is well aware that this brings him within the scope of the Boethian *musica mundana*, the canon of which is: Heavenly spheres; Elements; Seasons.[60] But Boethius too is corrected; in the "perfect Diapason" that thus sounds before the Fall, there are no Seasons—there were none:

> till disproportioned sin
> Jarr'd against nature's chime, and with harsh din
> Broke the fair music that all creatures made
> To their great Lord.

When that had happened, the seasons are a result of the consequent dislocation of nature (*PL* 10.677–87). The Morning Hymn ends with a prayer:

> Hail universal Lord, be bounteous still
> To give us only good; and if the night
> Have gathered aught of evil or conceal'd,
> Disperse it, as now light dispels the dark.

The "evil" is primarily the baleful dream which had visited Eve, the psychological causes of which Adam has rashly dismissed as lying in her "mimic fancy" (5.100–19), while the reader has reason to fear that her true phantasy has been affected by Satan working on her

---

[60]St. Francis, under similar influences (Psalm-commentaries?), also replaces the terms of the psalm with the four elements, earth, air, fire, and water. Compare also Tasso, *Il Mondo creato*, 7th Day, 131–43 (p. 279 in the critical edition by Giorgio Petroechi, Florence [Le Monnier, 1951]). Conversely, Ps. 148 has influenced the topics of *musica mundana* in a number of mediaeval writers *de musica*.

"animal spirits that from pure blood arise" (4.805). The Morning Hymn may, then, in its close express its own "purgative" value ("gathered . . . disperse"), and carry an allusion to the Pythagorean use of morning music to restore the soul.[61] Editors have seen a parallel between these lines and the well-known verses quoted in Plato's *Alcibiades II* (142 E): "O Zeus, give us good things, whether we pray for them or not, and deliver us from all evil things even though we pray for them," and these verses are recognized as "Pythagorean."[62] However, since "The Morning Hymn" is Milton's own title for this piece, he may very well also have thought of the best-known of morning hymns, those of St. Ambrose; for example, *Hymn* 7.9–12):

> Quo fraude quicquid daemonum
> In noctibus deliquimus,
> Abstergat illud coelitus
> Tuae potestas gloriae.

That at least would suit the present case.[63]

The prevalence of celestial music in *Paradise Lost,* Book 5, might lead one to expect later an overt reference to its loss after the Fall, but there is none. In the last books we are simply left to feel the absence of this celestial music, when, after the departure of the

---

[61]Boethius, *De Mus.* 1.1: "Experrecti [Pythagorici] aliis quibusdam modis stuporem confusionemque purgabant, id nimirum scientes quod tota nostrae animae corporisque compago musica coaptatione coniuncta sit." Tyard *(Second Solitaire,* f. 125ʳ) makes it explicit that Pythagoras was calling back the scattered parts of the soul, and makes him say that by music after sleep: "Ie rappelle les Muses eslognées de moy par ce corporel exercice." The end of *Samson Agonistes* similarly calls attention to its own purgative value ("in calm of mind, all passion spent").

[62]So Jowett on the Platonic passage; cf. Diog. Laert. 8.9.

[63]Among the unbiblical elaborations of the Morning Hymn is the address to the birds: "Ye birds, / That singing up to Heaven Gate ascend, / Bear on your wings and in your notes his praise." This surely is an echo of Milton's *De Concentu:* "What say you to the belief that the very lark at day-break flies directly into the clouds, and that the nightingale passes the whole solitude of night in song, that they may order their melodies according to the harmonic relations of the heavens, to which they attentively listen?" (tr. by Spaeth, p. 134). I do not know how widespread this "belief" was; conceivably Milton may depend on Francis Pilkington, *The First Set of Madrigals,* 1614: "[God] instructeth the early Larke to warble forth his praise; who (as some hould) learneth his layes from the musical motions of the heavenly Spheares." Quite possibly this association lay in Shakespeare's mind when with insistence on the special "penetration" of morning music—"I am advised to give her music o'mornings: they say it will penetrate"—he introduces as his morning song, "Hark! hark! the lark at heaven's gate sings" (*Cymbeline* 2.3.11–35).

angels, no longer "Cherubic Songs by night from neighboring Hills Aerial music send" (*PL* 5.547–48). Only in Adam's vision of the doubtful doom of human kind (*PL* 11.558–63) some beautiful lines mark the invention of earthly music by Jubal.[64]

We have remarked that Milton's chief concern is, so to speak, with the first part of Lorenzo's theme, the celestial music, and not with the second, the traditional "effects." This part of the *laudes* does, however, once make its appearance in *Paradise Lost*—in Hell, that home of lost causes. The passage is often admired, but perhaps not often scrutinized. Satan's standard is raised (*PL* 1.531–65) to "the warlike sound Of Trumpets loud and Clarions":

> All the while
> Sonorous metal blowing martial sounds:
> At which the universal Host upsent
> A shout that tore Hell's Concave, and beyond
> Frighted the Reign of Chaos and old Night. . . .
>   Anon they move
> In perfect Phalanx to the Dorian mood
> Of Flutes and soft Recorders; such as rais'd
> To highth of noblest temper Heroes old
> Arming to Battle, and instead of rage
> Deliberate valour breath'd, firm and unmov'd
> With dread of death to flight or foul retreat,
> Nor wanting power to mitigate and swage
> With solemn touches, troubl'd thoughts, and chase
> Anguish and doubt and fear and sorrow and pain
> From mortal or immortal minds. Thus they
> Breathing united force with fixèd thought
> Mov'd on in silence to soft Pipes that charm'd
> Thir painful steps o'er the burnt soil; and now
> Advanc't in view they stand, a horrid front
> Of dreadful length and dazzling Arms, in guise
> Of Warriors old with order'd Spear and Shield.

Roused by trumpets and clarions they shout aloud, and presently at the sound of flutes and recorders they march quietly and in order, going not, as one might expect, into battle, but only to assembly to hear their chief. The opposed effects of loud and soft music on their unstable spirits are not, however, the only point. Without

[64]For Jubal, editors refer to Du Bartas, but the item is in virtually all the versions of our theme from Isidore of Seville onwards.

needlessly inquiring whether recorders had a place in military bands in Milton's time, we may at once recognize in these demons the Spartans who march to the flute, the Cretans who march to the lyre, and the Amazons who march to the pipes in the *laudes musicae;* after mention of whom our writers, copying one another, commonly add: "As nowadays our legions march to the trumpet or drums" (Quintilian, Plutarch, L. G. Giraldi, Ronsard). In one aspect, the demons and their phalanx are out of date, "in guise of warriors old with order'd spear and shield." Commentators on this passage adduce Plato (*Rep.* III, 273–74) on the Dorian mode as suited to soldiers, Thucydides 5.70 on the Spartans marching to the flute, and *Iliad* 3.8–9; but these piecemeal parallels tell us nothing. Yet Milton's full intention perhaps first becomes clear when we consider the most likely source, a *locus classicus* on these effects, Gellius' *Noctes Atticae* 1.11. I paraphrase:

> Thucydides says that in battle the Spartans employed flutes instead of trumpets and clarions; not to rouse their courage, as trumpets and clarions do, but to make them calm and orderly. They thought that in meeting the enemy and entering battle, nothing was more conducive to confident valor than being soothed by gentle sounds, and not being immoderately enraged. And hence, when the army was drawn up, and about to advance against the enemy, flute-players began to play, and by this quiet, delightful, and even solemn prelude, the impetuosity of the soldiers was checked by a kind of musical discipline.... "The attack began. The Argives came on in a rage, but the Spartans moved slowly to the music of many flute-players" (Thucydides 5.70). The Cretans likewise went into battle preceded by the moderating music of the lyre.... But Homer says that the Achaeans joined battle relying not on the music of lyres and flutes but on a silent harmony and union of spirit (*Il.* 3.8–9):
>
> Οἱ δ'ἄρ' ἴσαν σιγῇ μένεα πνείοντες Ἀχαιοί,
> Ἐν θυμῷ μεμαῶτες ἀλεξέμεν ἀλλήλοισιν.
>
> "The Achaeans moved on in silence, breathing force, resolved in mind to defend one another." What, then, means the tremendous shout (*ardentissimus clamor*) of the Roman soldiers when they entered battle? Was it contrary to discipline? Or should not a quiet pace and silence be used when advancing against a visible but distant foe, but when it has almost come to blows, then they should be thrown back by an onrush and terrified by a shout?

This chapter of the *Noctes Atticae* has not just one, but two separate items in common with Milton's lines: (1) the Spartans and

Cretans (heroes old) marching without rage to the music of flute or lyre, and (2) the lines from Homer which Milton translates in part: "Thus they / Breathing united force with fixed throught / Moved on in silence." These two elements are not found elsewhere thus combined.

We no longer have to think of Milton picking up now a bit from Thucydides, and now a jewel from Homer, merely to adorn his poem. He is dealing with Gellius' theme of loud and soft in military music, and gladly takes Thucydides and Homer with the rest. The shout of the demons, when the foe is not even in view, frightens not the foe, as was the purpose of the Roman soldiers' shout, but the reign of Chaos and old Night—a splendid image of emptiness and futility. Yet the fallen angels of Book I have not attained the perfection, so to speak, of their evil; they still, like heroes old, can have their impetuosity checked by the discipline of the military music of flutes and recorders.

Into this thought from Gellius Milton has inserted a more general description of the effects of music: "Nor wanting power . . . immortal minds." Not strictly required by the context, it might represent an impulse shared by many of our writers on music, to fill out the theme once it has been entered upon; and the thought is not far from that to which Milton had given somewhat cautious assent in his tractate *Of Education* (1644) in speaking of "ditties, which, if wise men and prophets be not extremely out, have a great power over dispositions and manners, to smooth and make them gentle from rustic harshness and distempered passions." That careful sentence, however, is in some contrast to the rather reckless expansion here on the traditional *pellit curas*. Was Milton now satisfied that the music of soft recorders (not "ditties," which are voice and verse) could chase anguish and doubt and fear and sorrow and pain from the minds of mortals and immortals? The sentence represents the rhetorical "summation-sentence" that is a regular feature of the *laudes musicae*. Its exaggeration renders it suspect. At all events, the half-truths of Hell are corrected in Heaven. There, as the heavenly hosts march forth to battle (*PL* 6.59–66), not flutes and soft recorders, but only:

> the loud
> Etherial Trumpet from on high gan blow;
> At which command the Powers Militant
> That stood for Heav'n, in mighty Quadrate join'd

Of Union irresistible, mov'd on
In silence their bright Legions, to the sound
Of instrumental Harmony that breath'd
Heroic ardor to advent'rous deeds.

These legions will have the advantage of the phalanx with its outmoded methods. They march united, and move in silence even while the trumpet sounds, and will save their shouts until the first blows are struck, only then (*PL* 6.200) uttering their *ardentissimum clamorem*, their:

> shout,
> Presage of Victorie and fierce desire
> Of Battel.

The seductive description of the effects of music shown in Hell is of a piece with the seductive picture of Athens put into the mouth of Satan in *Paradise Regained* 4.236–84; the glimmer of truth in antiquity has been transcended in the dawn of the new dispensation. But that is by no means all. Milton insists on the classical music of the fallen angels. In *PL* 2.546–55 they retire like the heroes in Virgil's Elysian Fields to

> sing
> With notes Angelical to many a Harp
> Thir own Heroic deeds and hapless fall. . . .
> Thir song was partial, but the harmony
> (What could it less when Spirits immortal sing?)
> Suspended Hell, and took with ravishment
> The thronging audience.

Is there, then, music in Hell, and does Milton disagree with Samuel Rowley and Davies of Hereford? Not altogether. These demons have not yet lost all their original brightness; but presently, when Satan with Eve has compassed the Fall, angelic music ceases in Hell as it does in Eden. On earth, Jubal will restore its shadow in earthly music. In Hell it is replaced by the negation of music, a universal hiss. Satan's success is fatal to the demons. The effect of celestial music now would be that

Hell itself [would] pass away,
And leave her dolorous mansions to the peering day.

[*Nativity* 139–40]

Let us conclude with a rapid forward glance. Indeed with Milton we have already ceased dealing with the Praise of Music as an organized topic; to the seventeenth century it was now too familiar a subject to be set down at length in its simplicity. Moreover, in the course of the century, the discrediting of the old psychology and the old astronomy weakened its serious appeal. This change is reflected in Milton, even though for poetical purposes he retains the old psychology and astronomy. Yet, as we know, the theme was adaptable, and if the grosser effects seemed less probable, the subtler effects on manners and on the passions were still taken seriously. In any case, the topic remained among the common presuppositions, and its terms were the current coin of writers and their readers. Today we can hardly join in the startled response expected by Sir Thomas Browne for his monstrous paradox: "Even that vulgar and tavern music, which makes one man merry, and another mad, strikes in me a deep fit of devotion, and a profound contemplation of the First Composer." That is to fly in in the face ancient wisdom, and to do so too in a day when many were bent on casting instrumental music out of the Church as all too suggestive of tavern or theater.

Poems on music written in the second half of the century are accordingly apt to take up only some aspect of the theme. Such is William Strode's ode *In Commendation of Music* (1658), on the soul as a harmony, with its exquisite comparisons for music:

> Like snow on wool thy fallings are,
> Soft like a spirit's are thy feet.

In Andrew Marvell's *Music's Empire* we have the invention of music by Jubal; in Edward Benlowes' *Poetic Descant upon a private Music-meeting,* the subject is *musica mundana;* in Cowley's ode *The Resurrection* it is the effect of the sounding of the last trumpet; but in the same poet's *Davideis,* in connection with David's cure of Saul, for once the theme appears intact, with sphere-music and soul-music, and even bodily cures. From Cowley, Dryden drew some of the material of *A Song for St. Cecilia's Day,* which with *Alexander's Feast* makes him perhaps the most celebrated writer of musical poems in the language. For him St. Cecilia represents, not "inward singing" or unheard intellectual and celestial music, as was traditional, but the allied topic "religious music best, profane music inferior," which was a subject of contemporary interest. Besides, Dryden was

69

writing a libretto for the annual music exhibition of St. Cecilia's Day, and this circumstance made its claims on his topics. Inaugurated with this ode in 1683, the "music feasts" succeeded annually until 1703, and sporadically thereafter.

Other writers of the odes—for example, Congreve and Addison—sometimes gather up fragments of our theme, and Pope follows suit in his *Ode on St. Cecilia's Day* (1703)—for example:

> Music the fiercest grief can charm,
> And fate's severest rage disarm.
> Music can soften pain to ease,
> And make despair and madness please:
> Our joys below it can improve,
> And antedate the bliss above.

To these glib verses one might well prefer the expression of the same thought by old Wither in his hymn *For a Musician* (1641):

> Teach me the skill
>   Of him whose harp assuaged
> Those passions ill
>   Which oft afflicted Saul;
> Teach me the strain
>   Which calmeth minds enraged,
> And which from vain
>   Affections doth recall:
> So to the choir
>   Where angels music make,
> I may aspire
>   When I this life forsake.

Wither believed what he was saying; Pope did not. Already, among others, John Wallis, professor of mathematics at Oxford, had pronounced the "effects" fabulous in his report "On the Strange Effects of Music in former Times" (*Philosophical Transactions*, No. 243, p. 297, August, 1698). Nevertheless, the poet Collins persists in believing that at least for those former times the effects were real (*The Passions*, 1746):

> O Music! sphere-descended maid,
> Friend of Pleasure, Wisdom's aid!
> Why, Goddess, why, to us denied,

Lay'st thou thy ancient lyre aside? . . .
'Tis said, and I believe the tale,
Thy humblest reed could more prevail,
Had more of strength, diviner rage,
Than all which charms this laggard age. . . .
O bid our vain endeavours cease:
Revive the just designs of Greece:
Return in all thy simple state!
Confirm the tales her sons relate!

Hawkins, the historian of music (1776), on the whole decides against the "effects," though he argues for certain of the moral ones. Charles Burney will have none of them.

Still even in the nineteenth century—even today—fragments of our theme linger in the literary consciousness. So long a tradition is slow to die even when the view of the universe and of man, that suggested so many correspondences, has been profoundly altered. Echoes of the words *musica humana* may prompt a poet to strike out the phrase, "the still, sad music of humanity," and the same echoes make his readers accept it as intelligible, associated as it is with a kind of *musica mundana,* to which the poet professes himself to be abnormally sensitive. Again, having used the traditional title *Power of Music* for a minor effort, Wordsworth calls his chief poem on our theme *On the Power of Sound* (1828). It deserves study in the light of the traditional *laudes musicae,* of which it must be one of the latest examples. That the stanza (xii) that begins with the music of the spheres ends with the rhythm of the seasons, is evidence that Wordsworth was conscious of the Boethian *musica mundana.* Again—to quote the poet's own Argument—"The power of music, whence proceeding, exemplified in the idiot": this, in the language of Wordsworth, is what in the language of the gods had been, "For though it have holp madmen to their wits" [etc.]; and the stanza in question (vii) describes how "a solemn cadence" (? Pythagoras' spondaic rhythm) entering "the mouldy vaults of the dull idiot's brain" gradually affects him, "as at the world Of reason partially let in." Even the rowers in the galleys are here (Stanza iv):

For the tired slave, Song lifts the languid oar,
And bids it aptly fall.

One would be glad to know what Wordsworth read in preparing to write this poem. . . .

> Heard melodies are sweet, but those unheard
> Are sweeter; therefore, ye soft pipes, play on;
> Not to the sensual ear, but, more endear'd,
> Pipe to the spirit ditties of no tone.

The *musica intellectualis* never found finer expression than in these lines of Keats. From Plato's hint that the true music is philosophy to the Neoplatonic exaltation of celestial music (see Chalcidius, above) and the Christian preference for "inward singing," the idea had been continually kept alive. "Not to the sensual ear"—the phrase might be Gosson's—reflects the context in which the motive belongs. In the context of the *Grecian Urn*, with reference to the silent, sculptured pipers, we might think it a piece of wreckage tossed up by tradition and accepted in an altered sense. On the contrary, it allows the true subject of the poem, which is Time and Eternity, to pierce through the elaborate veil of the Grecian Urn— intellectual or celestial music is eternal, heard melodies are fleeting—and sets the Platonic theme that will break out again at the end in the Platonic "Beauty is truth, truth beauty". The image of an eternity that is not for us is suggested to the twenty-four-year-old Keats by the sculptured urn; the image of an eternity that we may enjoy is suggested to the twenty-four-year-old Milton by a solemn music. Milton's image has certainly the better tradition. Plotinus, at least (*Enn.* 5.9.11), places sculpture among the arts "born here below," while music, so far as it studies what is intelligible in rhythm, "is an image of the [celestial and intellectual] music."

But Plotinus accepts architecture also as having its principle "in the intelligible world" of numbers and proportion. And indeed it is a fixed item of the *laudes musicae* that "music enters into all the arts" (so, for example, Vitruvius, Isidore, Zarlino), while the more limited statement that it is necessary to the other liberal arts rests on the same principle of intelligible harmony or unheard music. One may wonder if those who endlessly quote the aphorism of Walter Pater ("All art," he says, "constantly aspires to the condition of music") are aware of its long tradition. Was he aware of it? Let it serve to bring us back—even if not "in perfect diapason"—to the origin of our theme in the Greek handbooks of the liberal arts, and so back to Plato and Pythagoras, of whose thought so many of these concepts are the "ultimate image."

[In Milton's lines *At a Solemn Music* (p. 58 above), I have read *sphere-born* with the printed editions, including that of 1645 which Milton presumably supervised. The autograph Cambridge manuscript, however, gives *sphere-borne*. Possibly only a change in spelling is involved. In any case, Voice and Verse are summoned to produce, not sphere-music, but earthly music audible to us and affecting our imagination. See *A Variorum Commentary on the Poems of John Milton*, Merrit T. Hughes, ed., vol. 2, *The Minor Poems*, A. S. P. Woodhouse and Douglas Bush, Part One (New York: Columbia University Press, 1972), pp. 175–91, esp. pp. 184–85.]

Amor Fugitivus: The First Idyl of Moschus in Imitations to the Year 1800

A striking thing about Alexandrian poetry is the vitality of its inventions. We do well to acknowledge the power that was capable of attracting a Catullus, a Propertius, a Virgil, and that, even in its fragments, commanded the genius of Ronsard, of Herrick, and was not without a part in forming the new romantic poetry from André Chénier and Shelley to Théodore de Banville.

In pastoral poetry the pervading influence of Theocritus has always to be reckoned with even when the poetic form is quite unlike that of his Idyls, or when the concept seems to spring directly from nature as in the poetry of William Barnes. Again, it would not be safe to say that any truly moving lament since composed is without a light from the Lament for Bion. In addition to the Lament for Bion, three other poems, ascribed to the somewhat uncertain authorship of Moschus, have won the same tribute of persistent imitation—the *Europa,* the epigram on Eros Turned Ploughman, and the Ἔρως Δραπέτης—Fugitive Love.

Like other notable inventions of its period, Ἔρως Δραπέτης is a happy combination of mythological lore with matter from daily life. Cypris has lost Eros, and makes advertisement for his return, offering a reward, as for a runaway slave. That calls for a description of the boy; and thereby the poet has provided himself with a fair chance for the display of an allegorical fancy that leaves no line without its telling point.[1]

Ἁ Κύπρις τὸν Ἔρωτα τὸν υἱέα μακρὸν ἐβώστρει·
'ὅστις ἐνὶ τριόδοισι πλανώμενον εἶδεν Ἔρωτα,
δραπετίδας ἐμός ἐστιν, ὁ μανύσας γέρας ἕξει·
μισθόν τοι τὸ φίλαμα τὸ Κύπριδος, ἢν δ᾽ ἀγάγηι νιν,

From the *American Journal of Philosophy* 49 (1928) 105–36. Copyright © 1928, The Johns Hopkins University Press.
[1]The text is that of Wilamowitz-Moellendorff, *Bucolici Graeci* (Oxford, 1905), p. 120, with omission of the last (spurious) line.

οὐ γυμνὸν τὸ φίλαμα, τὺ δ᾽ ὦ ξένε καὶ πλέον ἕξεις.　　　5
ἔστι δ᾽ ὁ παῖς περίσαμος· ἐν εἴκοσι πᾶσι μάθοις νιν.
χρῶτα μὲν οὐ λευκός, πυρὶ δ᾽ εἴκελος· ὄμματα δ᾽ αὐτῶι
δριμύλα καὶ φλογόεντα· κακαὶ φρένες, ἁδὺ λάλημα·
οὐ γὰρ ἴσον νοέει καὶ φθέγγεται· ὡς μέλι φωνά,
ὡς δὲ χολὰ νόος ἐστίν, ἀνάμερος, ἠπεροπευτάς,　　　10
οὐδὲν ἀλαθεύων, δόλιον βρέφος, ἄγρια παίσδων.
εὐπλόκαμον τὸ κάρανον, ἔχει δ᾽ ἰταμὸν τὸ μέτωπον.
μικύλα μὲν τήνωι τὰ χερύδρια, μακρὰ δὲ βάλλει,
βάλλει κεῖς Ἀχέροντα καὶ εἰς Ἀίδα βασίλεια.
γυμνὸς ὅλος τό γε σῶμα, νόος δέ οἱ εὖ πεπύκασται.　　　15
καὶ πτερόεις ὡς ὄρνις ἐφίπταται ἄλλον ἐπ᾽ ἄλλωι,
ἀνέρας ἠδὲ γυναῖκας, ἐπὶ σπλάγχνοις δὲ κάθηται.
τόξον ἔχει μάλα βαιόν, ὑπὲρ τόξῳ δὲ βέλεμνον,
τυτθὸν μὲν τὸ βέλεμνον, ἐς αἰθέρα δ᾽ἄχρι φορεῖται.
καὶ χρύσεον περὶ νῶτα φαρέτριον, ἔνδοθι δ᾽ ἐντί　　　20
τοὶ πικροὶ κάλαμοι, τοῖς πολλάκι κἀμὲ τιτρώσκει.
πάντα μὲν ἄγρια ταῦτα, πολὺ πλέον ἁ δαῖς αὐτῶι·
βαιὰ λαμπὰς ἐοῖσα τὸν Ἅλιον αὐτὸν ἀναίθει.
ἢν τύ γ᾽ ἕληις τῆνον, δήσας ἄγε μηδ᾽ ἐλεήσηις.
κἢν ποτίδηις κλαίοντα, φυλάσσεο μή σε πλανάσηι.　　　25
κἢν γελάηι, τύ νιν ἕλκε, καὶ ἢν ἐθέληι σε φιλᾶσαι,
φεῦγε· κακὸν τὸ φίλαμα, τὰ χείλεα φάρμακον ἐντί.
ἢν δὲ λέγηι "λάβε ταῦτα, χαρίζομαι ὅσσα μοι ὅπλα,"
μὴ τὺ θίγηις πλάνα δῶρα· τὰ γὰρ πυρὶ πάντα βέβαπται.᾽

In this paper my aim is to offer some evidence of the vitality of Moschus' theme, and, if possible, to retrace the principal channels through which its influence has passed.[2]

In Classical and Byzantine Writers

Seemingly not many years after Moschus' poem was written, the Gadarene poet Meleager took up the theme, reduced it by more than half so as to make it a true epigram—the concept was obviously epigrammatic material—and added a new conceit at the end:[3]

Κηρύσσω τὸν Ἔρωτα, τὸν ἄγριον· ἄρτι γὰρ ἄρτι
ὀρθρινὸς ἐκ κοίτας ᾤχετ᾽ ἀποπτάμενος.

---

[2]The materials that follow are excerpts from a study of the influence of the Greek Anthology, in which Moschus' poem is included, *AP* 9.440. Seventeen of the imitations here dealt with were listed by W. P. Mustard in "Later Echoes of the Greek Bucolic Poets," *AJP* 30.245.

[3]*AP* 5.177(176); cf. 178–80 by Meleager, and likewise indebted to Moschus 1.

Essays on Renaissance Poetry

ἔστι δ' ὁ παῖς γλυκύδακρυς, ἀείλαλος, ὠκύς, ἀθαμβής,
σιμὰ γελῶν, πτερόεις νῶτα, φαρετροφόρος.
πατρὸς δ' οὐκέτ' ἔχω φράζειν τίνος· οὔτε γὰρ Αἰθήρ,
οὐ Χθών φησι τεκεῖν τὸν θρασύν, οὐ Πέλαγος·
πάντῃ γὰρ καὶ πᾶσιν ἀπέχθεται. ἀλλ' ἐσορᾶτε
μή που νῦν ψυχαῖς ἄλλα τίθησι λίνα.
καίτοι κεῖνος, ἰδού, περὶ φωλεόν. Οὔ με λέληθας,
τοξότα, Ζηνοφίλας ὄμμασι κρυπτόμενος.

Where Moschus had ended with a warning for all to beware of
the blandishments of Eros, Meleager now finishes with the finding
of Love: "But wait! there he is near his nest!—You have not escaped me, Archer, by hiding in Zenophila's eyes!" In later variations of the theme, this conceit, added by Meleager, will more
than once appear.

A pleasing adaptation of Moschus' theme was made by Apuleius
(*Met.* 6.7–8). On this occasion Venus is in search of Psyche; Mercury is the crier:

Nec Mercurius omisit obsequium; nam per omnium ora populorum
passim discurrens sic mandatae praedicationis munus exsequebatur:
"Si quis a fuga retrahere vel occultam demonstrare poterit fugitivam
regis filiam, Veneris ancillam, nomine Psychen, conveniat retro metas
Murtias Mercurium praedicatorem, accepturus indicivae nomine ab
ipsa Venere septem savia suavia et unum blandientis appulsu linguae
longe mellitum."

This returns to follow more closely what was also the original of
Moschus' conceit—the customary form of proclamation for runaway slaves. Mercury stops with little more than the bare notice, and
gives no detailed description of Psyche, as Venus, in her earlier
proclamation, had given of Eros. Venus, however, seems to have
meant him to do so: "Fac ergo," she says to him, "mandatum ma-
tures meum et indicia, qui posset agnosci, manifeste designes.'⁴

Here is not the place to take account of the imitators of Apuleius,
so that adaptations of the theme that derive only from him shall not
detain us. Mention, however, must be made of La Fontaine's ver-

⁴With Moschus (14) compare also Apuleius, *Met.* 4.33:
        quo tremit ipse Iovis, quo numina terrificantur,
             flumina quem horrescunt et Stygiae tenebrae.
And with Moschus (21) compare *Met.* 5.30.

sion (*Psyché*, Book 2) which, since it is thrown into verse, draws us back to Moschus; the last line, in fact, is taken from Moschus, not from Apuleius.

> De par la reine de Cythère,
> Soient, dans l'un et l'autre hémisphère,
> Tous humains dûment avertis
> Qu'elle a perdu certaine esclave blonde,
> Se disant femme de son fils,
> Et qui court à présent le monde.
> Quiconque enseignera sa retraite à Vénus,
> Comme c'est chose qui la touche,
> Aura trois baisers de sa bouche;
> Qui la lui livrera, quelque chose de plus.[5]

In the *Drosilla and Charicles* of Nicetas Eugenianus (c. 1200), Clinias expresses his passion for his slave Drosilla in a song of Fugitive Love:[6]

> Ὦ πῶς, Δροσίλλα, πυρπολεῖς τὸν Κλεινίαν!
> ἡ Κύπρις εἰς Ἔρωτα τὸν ταύτης γόνον
> μέσαις ἀγυιαῖς ἐξεφώνει πρὶν μέγα,
> εἴ τις πλανηθὲν συλλάβῃ τὸ παιδίον,
> ἤ που στενωπῶν ἢ μέσαις ἐπ' ἀμφόδοις,
> τὸν δραπέτην Ἔρωτα, τὸν κακεργάτην,
> ὁ μηνυτής μοι λήψεται γέρας μέγα,
> τὸ Κύπριδος φίλημα μισθὸν ἁρπάσει.
> Ὦ πῶς, Δροσίλλα, πυρπολεῖς τὸν Κλεινίαν! κ. τ. λ.

In Neo-Latin Verse

Before being printed in the *editio princeps* of the Anthology, Florence, 1494, Moschus' First Idyl had appeared in the third edition of the Greek Grammar by Constantine Lascaris at Vicenza in 1489. It was thus one of the first pieces of Greek to be presented to the learner of the language. In 1496 it was again printed by Aldus in the first edition of the Bucolic Poets.

---

[5]See Apuleius, above, and, for the last four lines, Moschus (4–5).
[6]Nicetas 4.154ff. There are traits from Moschus in the ᾠδάριον ἐρωτικόν printed in Cramer's *Anecdota Par.* 4.380; compare also Propert. 2.12; Longus 2.4–5 owes something to this idyl.

77

Poliziano, whose Latin version is the first modern translation, knew the poem, and translated it, probably between 1470 and 1480. When sending a copy to Antonio Zeno some time later, he writes:[7] "Amorem fugitivum, quem paene puer adhuc e Graeco in Latinum converti, non sententiis modo sed numeris etiam servatis ac lineamentis paene omnibus, cupienti flagitantique diu tibi mitto tandem."

Poliziano's lines were first published in his *Opera*, Venice (Aldus), 1498, there accompanied by a good Italian rendering by Girolamo Benivieni: *Amor Fugitivo de Mosco poeta greco, tradotto in Latino de M. A. P. . . . e di Latino in lingua fiorentina.*[8] The Latin of Poliziano has nearly always been reprinted when a translation of the Greek has been required.[9]

Like most of his verses inspired by classical models, Sannazaro's *De Amore Fugitivo* has an original turn. He knew the Anthology; and it is possible that he is here aware of Meleager as well as of Moschus:

> Quaeritat huc illuc raptum sibi Cypria natum:
> Ille sed ad nostri pectoris ima latet.
> Me miserum, quid agam? durus puer, aspera mater;
> Et magnum in me ius altera, et alter habent.
> Si celem, video quantus deus ossa peruret;

---

[7] *Epistolae* 7.14.

[8] Benivieni's Italian may be seen with Poliziano's Latin in Poliziano's *Prose volgari . . . e poesie latine e greche*, Del Lungo, ed. (1867), p. 525.

[9] The fact that Poliziano's version became widely known makes it useful to notice some of its peculiarities:

(a) In the sixth line Poliziano translates: "*en omnia percipe signa!*" All MSS and most early edd. (e.g., Stephanus, 1566) have what Poliziano renders: ἐν εἰκόσι πᾶσι—the scholiast in M (Marcianus) explains: ἀντὶ τοῦ ἐν πάσαις ταῖς εἰκόσιν . . . ἢ ἐν πᾶσι τοῖς εἰκόσιν ἀντὶ σημείοις καὶ εἰκασμοῖς. Apuleius may have read εἰκόσι; cf. "*indicia,*" above. At present, reading εἴκοσι with Opsopœus (?), and then εἴκοσι παισὶ with Heinsius, we must translate, as Grotius: *viginti in pueris.* Wilamowitz reads εἴκοσι πᾶσι, and does not discuss εἰκόσι.

But this was not Poliziano's only attempt at rendering the line. His version, printed in Soter's *Epigrammata Graeca* (Cologne, 1525), has: "*totam ac cognosce figuram.*" (See also Del Lungo, *loc. cit.*) *Figuram* is an interpretation peculiar to Poliziano—see below, on Turbervile.

(b) In line 23 Poliziano has: "*seque ipsum multo quoque saevius angit;*" the reading behind this is also abandoned.

(c) Finally, for δαμάσας, line 24, the reading of M, he translates, "*verbere.*" No other direct translation shows this, the reading, in any case, having been promptly corrected to δάσας (now δήσας).

Sin prodam, merito durior hostis erit.
Adde, quod haec non est, quae natum ad flagra reposcat,
Sed quae de nostro bella cruore velit.[10]
Ergo istic, fugitive, late; sed parcius ure:
Haud alio poteris tutior esse loco.

Possibly the notion of Amor dwelling within the lover's breast and troubling it comes from the ever-popular Anacreontic verses ascribed to Julianus (*AP* 16.388). In any case Sannazaro's epigram henceforth becomes one of the principal sources of Amor Fugitivus.

Girolamo Angeriano published his Ἐρωτοπαίγνιον at Naples in 1520; it gained no small reputation, and was republished at Paris in 1542 with the poems of Marullus and Joannes Secundus.[11] Angeriano's *Amor Fugitivus,* though in the main a version of Moschus, takes its point from Sannazaro, and enforces it with a conceit from Paulus Silentiarius (*AP* 5.268.5–6); Angeriano is elsewhere deeply indebted to the Greek Anthology:[12]

Dum Venus in triviis errantem quaerit Amorem,
Huic loquor: "Errantis dic mihi signa dei. . . ."
Tunc ego, sublatis ridens clamoribus, inquam:
"Non procul hinc natus, Cypria diva, tuus;
Pectore sub nostro Deus hic affigitur: alas
Perdidit, et claudo stans pede, abire nequit."

A third Neapolitan, Pontano, in his *Eridana* (1518), has a free elegiac treatment of our theme: *De Venere Amorem quaerente, Ad Hieronymum Carbonem,* beginning:[13]

Dicite, Nereides (nam vos quoque procreat unda),
Anne aliquis vestris sit puer hospes aquis.

---

[10]Propert. 2.12.16: adsiduusque meo sanguine bella gerit.

[11]Reprinted in the *Carmina Illust. Poetarum Italorum* (Florence, 1719), 1.273. For Angeriano's influence on Barnabe Barnes, see Sidney Lee, *Elizabethan Sonnets* 1.lxxvii.

[12]With the last distich in the quotation compare Paulus: ἀστεμφής, ἀδόνητος ἐνέζεται, οὐδὲ μετέστη, εἰς ἐμὲ συζυγίην κειράμενος πτερύγων: "Within my breast Love remains fixed and immovable, and goes not hence; for on me he has shed his two feathered wings." Compare also Propert. 2.12.13–15.

[13][*Poemata*], Venice (Aldus), 1518, *fo.* 105.

It is a marine elegy. In her search, Venus falls in with Charybdis, who, returning the lost Eros, says:

> 'O dea—namque deam testantur singula—mecum est
> Ipse puer, lacrimis tu modo parce tuis. . . .
> Hunc tibi, diva parens, proles Jovis, author amandi,
> Restituo; tua me, te mea cura premat.
> Accepi infantem, blandum do, pro rude doctum,
> Proque fide fraudem, simplicitate dolum.
> Pro lacrimis risum docui, pro melle venenum.'

The moral of the allegory is addressed to Carbo:

> At tu Pieridum studiis cultissime Carbo,
> Namque et amas, facito sit tibi notus Amor.
> Sint notae maris insidiae, sit nota Charybdis
> Cincta sinum canibus, virginis ora ferens.

As befits the author of *De Amore Conjugali,* and of pleasing Latin cradle-songs,[14] Pontano is apparently the first definitely to abandon the proclamation for a runaway slave, and to picture instead a mother's distress for her strayed child. In this change he precedes Tasso, Baïf, Spenser, and most of the notable modern versions. Venus complains to the sea-nymphs:

> Matris vos miserae moveat dolor et labor, illum
> Anxia tam longa quae sequor usque via.
> Ipse puer nudusque abiit, nec cognitus ulli,
> Quique meo numquam cesserat ante sinu,
> Maternis fotum mammis, fotumque sub ulnis, . . .
> Effugit e gremio fallens. Ipsa excita somno
> Hinc nemora, et saltus, hinc loca culta peto.

Giraldi Cintio, author of the *Hecatommithi,* published his Latin poems at Ferrara in 1537; one of them, *Ad Venerem,* may be taken as an answer to Sannazaro's version of Fugitive Love. Sannazaro fears the consequences of restoring Cupid to his mother and to liberty; Giraldi would only too gladly be rid of him: "Call your boy

---

[14]See Monnier, *Le Quattrocento* (1920), 1.321, and Tallarigo, *Giovanni Pontano e i suoi tempi* (1874), p. 636.

hence, Cytherea; I ask for no kisses; reward enough for me if the
boy quits my heart!"[15]

> Ne gnatum in triviis fugitivum, Cypria, quaeras.
> Huc propera: in nostro pectore regnat Amor.
> Hicque furit latitans, agrum et crudeliter urit,
> Igni addens ignem; nec volat hinc, alio.
> Tu puerum hinc, Cytherea, voca: non basia posco;
> Sat mihi mercedis si puer hinc abeat.
> Sic tuus adsiduo tecum Mars igne calescat,
> Sic semper cedat Juno, Minerva, tibi!

Fabius Segnius, a Florentine living in the second half of the sixteenth century (Tiraboschi 3.4.25), who elsewhere gives evidence
of knowing the Anthology, recalls Meleager's version of the
theme:[16]

> Dum nemora et saltus omnes Venus alma peragrat
> Quaerens parvus ubi delituisset Amor,
> Replebat moestis terras atque astra querelis:
> Cernere erat lacrimis ora rigare deam.
> Spes ubi nulla fuit, latitantem protinus illum
> Luminibus vidit, diva Neaera, tuis.
> Tunc ait, Idalium valeat, valeatque Cythera,
> O nate! hic sedes nostra perennis erit.

Benedetto Lampridio's version, written in hendecasyllabics, is
related both to Moschus and to Meleager, as the closing lines will
show:[17]

> Cui tantas Cytherea proflat iras?
> Quid quaerit sibi? Maenas it furore
> Velut concita Bacchico; minatur
> Dextra, fert creperum altera flagellum.
> Natum quaerit, ais? puellulum ipse
> Vidi. . . .
>
> Teutonillam
> Post fanum Sophiae sacrum require,

---

[15] *Carmina Illus. Poet. Ital.* 5.385. In line 3 read *aegrum?*
[16] *Ibid.* 9.24.
[17] *Ibid.* 6.29; for a German imitation of Lampridio's version, see below.

81

Erronem invenies, modo e papillis
Modo e luminibus puellulae, immo
E tota iacere et facem et sagittam.

In the *Epigrammata Graeca*—selections from the Anthology with translations—published by Joannes Soter (?Heil), Cologne, 1525, the version of Moschus by Poliziano is printed, followed by an anonymous imitation in hexameters (of which we shall later need to take notice), and then the following verses by Caspar Ursinus Velius (Bernhardi):[18]

Basiolum merui Veneris, si frivola non sunt
  Verba deae, servat pollicitisque fidem.
Namque per immensum profugum dum quaeritat orbem
  Filiolum, et triviis errat in ambiguis,
Aequoreosque aditus rimatur, et ardua coeli
  Culmina, nec puerum repperit alma parens,
Inveni fugitivum in me sua tela novantem
  Intra formosae lumina Pasiphiles.
Prodere quem mens est, nostris namque ossibus ille
  Ignem lascivis implicat ex oculis.
Accenditque malis crudelis amoribus aegrum.
  Si prodo hunc, duplici commoditate fruar:
Suaviolum Cytherea dabit, me prensus et ille
  Desinet occulta perdere saevitia.
Quod si diva neget mortali basia, tanti
  Mi fuerit si det figere Pasiphilae.

Ursinus has plainly been reading Sannazaro's epigram, to which his poem, like Giraldi's, is in some sense a reply; the fourth couplet goes back to Meleager; but the end seems to be Ursinus' own, and will be repeated in later versions. Soter's book went through three editions (1525, 1528, 1544), and appears to have been widely used.

The foregoing translations or imitations are the work of persons who chose the theme for itself. The following also had their part in making the poem familiar to writers in the various vernaculars: Henri Estienne, *Moschi, Bionis, Theocriti . . . idyllia aliquot . . . latina facta. Eiusdem carmina non diversi ab illis argumenti.* Venice (Aldus), 1555; idem, *Theoc. aliorumque poetarum idyllia . . . omnia cum interp.*

[18]Soter, p. 53. Ursinus' Latin poems were published at Vienna in 1517; for his life see Allen, *Erasmi Epistolae* 2 (1910) 499.

lat. Paris, 1579; A. Mekerchus, [Greek title] *Moschi et Bionis idyllia . . . omnia latine . . . carmine reddita.* Bruges, 1565; Bonaventura Vulcanius, *Moschi . . . Bionis . . . idyllia . . . totidem numeris latine reddita.* Antwerp, 1584; Eoban Hess in *Theoc., Bionis, et Moschi carmina . . . latino carmine.* Leyden, 1799 (I cannot discover when Hess's version was first published—with his Theocritus in 1545? It is again reprinted in Valckenaer's ed. of the *Carmina bucolica,* Leyden 1810); David Whitford, *Musaei, Moschi, et Bionis quae extant omnia . . . latino carmine reddita.* London, 1659; Bernardo Zamagna, *Theocriti, Moschi, et Bionis idyllia omnia . . . latinis versibus expressa.* Parma, 1792.

Add to these the version made by Grotius between 1630 and 1635, but not regularly published until 1795 in the edition of the *Anth. Plan.* by De Bosch; it may be seen also in the Didot Anthology 2.91.

In Italian

After Benivieni's translation of Poliziano, the first allusion to Fugitive Love in the Italian vernacular seems to be an epigram by Girolamo Casio de' Medici (1465?–1531):[19]

> Vener, cercando il fugitivo Amore,
> Scontrò la donna mia, e in fra sè disse:
> "Se questa stata fusse a nostre risse,
> Dava a lei il pomo, e non a me, il Pastore!"

Firenzuola has a translation.[20] There is a version by Benedetto Varchi printed with the *Rime burlesche* of Agnolo Bronzino (Allori), Venice, 1810. In the *Versi et regole de la nuova poesia toscana,* Rome, 1539, an anonymous translator has put Sannazaro's Latin epigram into Italian elegiacs.[21] Luigi Alamanni, some time between 1539 and 1547, in France, made a good translation: *Amor fuggitivo da Teocrito.*[22]

---

[19]*L'Epigramma italiano,* L. De-Mauri (Ernesto Sarasino), ed. (1918), p. 29.
[20]*Opere,* Bianchi, ed. (1848), 2.284. Firenzuola translates Apuleius' version in the *Asino d'Oro, ibid.,* p. 114.
[21]Carducci, *La poesia barbara nei secoli xv e xvi* (1881), p. 256.
[22]*Versi e prose,* Raffaelli, ed. (1859), 2.137. The Life of Theocritus prefixed to his *Idyls* reports the supposed identification of him with Moschus.

83

A poem in *ottava rima* by Thomaso Castellani, freely treating the theme, was published at Venice in 1545.[23] The opening stanza has additions in common with the beginning of the Epilogue to Tasso's *Aminta:*

> Non tremi alcun mortal di maraviglia
> Che qua giù mira il mio divin' aspetto:
> Io son la Dea di Cipro, del mar figlia,
> Donna e splendor del terzo alto ricetto.
> Come materna cura mi consiglia,
> Il fuggitivo mio figliuol diletto
> Cercando vo: chi l'ha veduto il dica,
> Se Vener cerca a suoi desiri amica.

Likewise, with Tasso's Epilogue, 26 ff., may be compared the last stanza of Castellani, especially the lines:

> Donne, se mai materno Amor v' accese,
> S' alcuna l'ha di voi me lo reveli:
> Ne contra Vener sia tanto scortese,
> Che tolga le sue forze over le celi.

In Italian the best-known handling of Amor Fuggitivo is in Tasso's *Aminta*. Both the Prologue and the Epilogue should be noticed.[24] In the Prologue, Cupid, disguised as a shepherd, is seeking to hide from his mother, who would have him active only in princely courts; the Epilogue is spoken by Venus in quest of her son; the play, as Carducci observes, is inserted as an episode between the flight of Cupid and his pursuit by Venus.

Tasso does not depend solely on Moschus; he recalls for his purpose certain neo-Latin versions; probably he knows Castellani's poem; he adds a trait from an epigram attributed to Moschus; and he makes developments of his own. Thus in the Prologue Cupid says he has run away because Venus would confine him to courts

---

[23]Lodovico Domenichi, *Rime diverse di molti excel. auttori* (1545), 1.53.
[24]*Teatro,* Solerti, ed. (1895), pp. 5 ff., 29 ff. The Epilogue is sometimes printed as a separate piece.

(18); Venus in the Epilogue gives another reason, which, while reminiscent of Pontano and Castellani, is really new with Tasso:[25]

> Scesa dal terzo cielo,
> Io che sono di lui reina e dea,
> Cerco il mio figlio fuggitivo Amore:
> Il qual mentre sedea
> Ne'l mio grembo scherzando,
> O fosse elezione o fosse errore,
> Con un suo strale aurato,
> Mi punse il manco lato,
> E poi fuggì da me ratto volando
> Per non esser punito.

Less known is a sonnet by Tasso on the same theme. It will serve to illustrate the statement that "the sonnet is the Italian epigram," inasmuch as it is a fairly close version of Sannazaro's epigram quoted above.[26]

> Cercando va per questo e quel sentiero
> Venere il figlio; ed io mesto e dolente
> L' ascondo entro il mio petto onde la mente
> Tutta in dubbio rivolge il mio pensiero.
> Chè la madre è sdegnata e 'l figlio altiero,
> E l'una e l'altro in me puote egualmente:
> Se più l'ascondo son già tutto ardente,
> Se 'l manifesto ei diverrà più fiero.
> Oltre che so che castigare Amore
> Ella non vuol, nè il cerca a tale effetto,
> Ma sol perchè ne dia pena e dolore.
> Statti pur dunque ascoso entro 'l mio petto,
> Ma tempra alquanto il troppo immenso ardore,
> Chè più sicuro aver non puoi ricetto.

---

[25]With *Am.*, Ep. 60 ff., *E da gli omeri suoi Spiccate aver de' l'ali*, compare Angeriano, above; with l. 63, *E la faretra ancor deposta e l'arco* (and Pro. 45), compare the epigram by Moschus (?), *AP* 16.200, of which Tasso has elsewhere made a madrigal: *Amor l'arco e la face Depose*, etc. (*Rime*, Solerti, ed. 2.498); with 69–74, *Egli, ben che sia vecchio ... Picciolo è sì che ancor fanciullo ei sembra*, compare Longus 2.5 (Eros speaks): οὗτοι παῖς ἐγώ, καὶ εἰ δοκῶ παῖς, ἀλλὰ τοῦ Κρόνου πρεσβύτερος καὶ αὐτοῦ τοῦ παντὸς χρόνου; compare also Lucian, *Dial. Deor.* 2.

The *Aminta* made Moschus' theme everywhere familiar; for a list of translations see Solerti's edition, pp. cxi–cxx.

[26]*Rime* 2.411.

A graceful version of Moschus, ascribed to the "Abbate Nicolao de Oddis," is printed in the 1621 edition of Alciati's *Emblemata* (p. 659):[27]

> Con alti gridi un giorno
> Cercava il figlio Amore
> Venere, etc.

In a *Mascherata degli Amorini e di Venere*, Leonardo Salviati plays on the theme in the manner of Meleager:[28]

> Questa il suo figlio Amore,
> Ch' un tempo visse a lei lunge in disparte,
> Cercando in ogni parte,
> Ha visto alfin che nel gelato core,
> Nel dolce canto, e ne' begli occhi assiso,
> Nel vago riso, e nel sereno volto,
> L' avete, Donne, voi gran tempo accolto.

See also the following: Antonio Maria Salvini, *Teocrito*, [etc.] *volgarizzati*. Venice, 1718; 1726; 1744; Arezzo, 1754; Domenico Regolotto, *Teocrito, Mosco, Bione . . . volgarizzati*. Turin, 1728; Pompei, *Alcuni idilli di Mosco tradotti in versi italiani*. 1764; Anon., *Il Pseudolo . . . alcuni idilli di Mosco*. 1765; Il Conte C. Gaetani della Torre, *Le ode di Anacreonte e gli idilli ed epigrammi di Teocrito, Bione, e Mosco trad. in rime italiani*. 2 vols. Syracuse, 1776; L. A. Pagnini, *Teocrito*, [etc.] *volgarizzati*. 2 vols. Parma, 1780; G. B. Vicini, *Gl' idilli di Teocrito*, [etc.] *traslati in varj toscani metri*. Venice, 1781.

In French

It is unfortunate that in the modern editions of Clément Marot his two poems on Amor Fugitivus appear with no warning of their relationship in widely separated parts of his works, so that the opening lines of the second, *D'Amour Fugitif, Invention de Marot*, are quite unintelligible, depending as they do on the first poem,

---

[27]It is intended to illustrate Emb. 155: *Errabat socio Mors iuncta Cupidine*. This concept of Death and Love is common in the Renaissance poets; cf. Marot, *Chanson* 6. Alciati's Emb. 114, a description of Eros, may owe something to Moschus.
[28]*Rime*, Manzoni, ed. (1871), p. 65.

D'Amour Fugitif, de Lucien.[29] The two form a single piece, and were composed together between 1525 and 1527.[30]

D'Amour Fugitif, de Lucien is, as it purports to be, a translation; but why it is referred to Lucian is not easy to explain. As Marot was ignorant of the language, he was not translating the Greek, and seemingly had no clear idea of the original authorship of his poem.[31] What he was translating is surely the anonymous Latin imitation printed in Soter's *Epigrammata* (1525). This will be best demonstrated by a comparison of a few lines of the French and the Latin, with an eye to their divergences from the Greek of Moschus printed above.

> Advint un jour que Vénus Cytherée,
> Mére pour lors dolente et esplorée,
> Perdit son filz qui ça et là voloit:
> Et ainsi triste, en haste s'en alloit
> Par maint carroy, par maint canton et place,
> Pour le chercher: *puis sus quelque terrace,*
> *Ou sus un mont eslevé se plantoit,*
> Et devant tous à haulte voix chantoit
> Ce qui s'ensuyt: Quiconques de bon vueil
> M'enseignera, ou au doigt ou à l'œil,
> En quelle voye, ou devers quel costé,
> Mon Cupido fuyant s'est transporté:
> Pour son loyer (qui faire le sçaura)
> Un franc baiser de Vénus il aura;
> Et si quelc'un prisonnier le ramaine,
> La mère lors, envers luy plus humaine,
> Luy donnera (pour plus son cueur aiser)
> Quelque autre don par dessus le baiser.
>   Toy qui iras, affin que par tous lieux
> Ce faulx garson puisses congnoistre mieulx,
> Je t'en diray *vingt enseignes et taches,*[32]
> Que finement fault qu'en memoire caches: . . .

---

[29]*Œuvres complètes,* Jannet, ed. (1884), 2.82 and 3.143.
[30]Sidney Lee, *Eliz. Son.* 1. lxxviii, dates the (?) first part "about 1540"; but the second part depends on it and echoes it, and was surely done about 1527.
[31]See bracketed addition at the end of this essay.
[32]The anonymous translator leads Marot to render both εἴκοσι and εἰκόσι! (see above, n. 9[a]). Stadtmüller ascribes the correction to Opsopœus, i.e., to the year 1540 when O. published his Notes on the Anthology; but, as we see, it appears in a Latin translation in 1525.

Lors que dedans son grand char stygieux
Il amena Proserpine aux beaulx yeux ...[33]
Et si de franc et liberal visage
Il te promet des dons à son usage,
C'est asçavoir, fleches et arc *turquoys*[34]
La trousse paincte et le doré carquoys,
Fuy tous ces dons de nuysance et reproche:
Ilz vont bruslant tout ce qui d'eulx s'approche.

Perdiderat natum genitrix Cytherea vagantem,
  Anxia sollicito quem dum per compita passu
Quaerit, *ab excelso tales canit aggere voces:*
  Errabunda meus vestigia forte Cupido
Qua fugiens tulerit, quisquis monstrarit aperto
Indicio, huic merces Veneris libanda ferentur
Oscula. Captivum si quisquam adduxerit, illi
Mox aliquid gaudens ultra dabit oscula mater.
    Quo reperire queas puerum, *bis dena* dabuntur
Signa tibi, cautus memori quae mente recondes: ...
  Candida cum stygio rapta est Proserpina curru. ...
  Si vero facili promittet vulnera vultu,
Telaque *Gnosiacosque* arcus, pictamque pharetram,
Noxia dona time, quicquid tetigere perurunt.

If the translation is properly to be dated in or after 1525 when
Soter's book appeared, the second poem, *D'Amour Fugitif, Invention
de Marot*, seems to have been composed in or before 1527—the date
to which it is generally assigned; but it can not be earlier than the
translation of which it forms the sequel. In 1527 Marot edited the
Roman de la Rose; in October of the same year he was arrested, or
rearrested, for his Protestant sympathies. In the *Invention*, moved
by the present events of his own career, and inspired by the satirical
parts of the *Roman de la Rose*, he turns Moschus' theme to the uses
of religious satire against the friars—

un peuple à celluy resemblant
Que Jean de Mehun appelle Faulx-Semblant. [61–62]

---

[33]Proserpina is not mentioned in Moschus.
[34]This trait is from Propertius 2.12.10.

The opening lines connect the *Invention* with the preceding translation:

> Le propre jour que Vénus aux yeulx verts
> Parmy le monde alloit chanter *ces vers,*
> Desir de veoir et d'ouyr nouveauté
> Me feit courir après sa grand' beauté
> Jusque à Paris. Quand fut en plain carroy,
> Sus un hault lieu se meit en bel arroy,
> Monstrant en face avoir cueur assez triste,
> Ce néanmoins en habitz cointe et miste.
>   Lors d'une voix plus doulce et resonnante
> Que d'Orpheus la harpe bien sonnante
> Chanta les vers que dessus declairons, etc.

After her proclamation was made, he says, she departed in her car through the air; and, in the crowd that was left staring after her, one said to another: "Would that I could point him out, and win the reward!" or "Would that I had him bound, to win the greater prize!" But the poet is not concerned; all his pleasure is in Minerva. As he silently contemplates the people charmed by Venus, among them he marks a throng of men with heads bent—the friars. They are minded to win Venus' reward:

> Si vont querir libelles sophistiques,
> Corps enchassez et bulles papistiques,
> Et là dessus vouèrent tous à Dieu . . .
> De Cupido lyer, prendre, et estraindre . . .
> Aucuns d'iceulx par serment entrepris
> Portent sur eux des cordes à gros noudz
> Pour luy lier jambes, piedz, et genoulx.
>   Et sur ce poinct prendra repos ma muse, . . .
> En concluant que cestuy cy racompte,
> A qui aura bien compris mon traicté.
> Dont procéda le vœu de chasteté.

Amadis Jamyn adopts the theme for a sonnet, ending with a fresh turn:[35]

> "Fuyez tous ses baisers, ce disoit Cytherée,
> Ses baisers rendent l'âme ardente et alterée,

[35]*Œuvres poétiques,* Brunet, ed. (1878), p. 124.

Ilz sont pleins de venin, ilz sont pleins de poison."
Par toy je le connois, ô Nymphe sans pareille!
Depuis que j'ai baisé ta lèvre si vermeille,
Je brûle, je suis feu, j'ai perdu ma raison.

About 1570 Jean-Antoine de Baïf made a version of Moschus inscribed *A Madamoiselle Victoire*, introducing his translation with these words:[36]

Si de son fils Vénus étoit en queste,
Je lui criroy: "Mère d'Amour, arreste!
Je t'en diray la nouvelle bien seure:
Ou dans mon coeur trouveras sa demeure,
Ou dans le sein de la belle Victoire.
Victoire donc, ô des Graces la gloire
Et des Amours, quand à vous je dedie
Amour Fugitif, la raison je n'oublie.

The verses which follow the dedication, though doubtless written with Moschus at hand, show the influence of other reworkings of the theme, especially in the lines that explain how Cupid ran away, and how his mother searched for him before she made proclamation. The dedicatory lines themselves combine Sannazaro's conceit with something like that in Meleager's version.

Baïf was a friend of Philippe Desportes, who has directly translated Sannazaro's epigram: *Vénus cherche son fils, Vénus tout en colère,* etc.[37]

The *Bibliothèque Poétique*, Paris, 1745, contains a madrigal by Longepierre (Hilaire-Bernard de Requeleyne, Baron de Longepierre, 1659–1721) which, says the note appended, is a "traduction du Marini, qui l'a imité d'une idylle de Moschus."[38]

Vénus, je sçais qu'Amour fugitif et rebelle,
S'est sauvé de ton sein, et se cache à tes yeux;
Et que si l'on t'apprend l'endroit qui le recelle,

---

[36]*Œuvres*, Marty-Laveaux, ed. (1881–90), 2.276.
[37]*Œuvres*, Michaels, ed. (1852), p. 116.
[38]*Bibl. Poét.* 3.492. Marino's madrigal appears in Gilles Ménage's *Anti-Baillet* (1730), p. 373, followed by a Greek epigram on the same theme by Ménage, and following another Italian madrigal by Isabella Andreini, this last descending from Moschus through Giraldi Cintio. These, I regret, were not found in time for inclusion above in the proper places.

Tu promets de donner un baiser précieux
Pour prix de cet avis fidelle:
Donne-moi le baiser promis,
O Déesse! ou plutôt ordonne
Que ma maîtresse me le donne;
C'est dans ses beaux yeux qu'est ton fils.

Longepierre made also a strict translation of Moschus' idyl in *Les idylles de Bion et de Moschus, traduites . . . en vers*, Paris, 1686. I have been unable to consult either this or the reprint: *Bionis et Moschi idyllia . . . versiones metricae, Gallica Longapetraei et Latina Whitfordi*, Venice, 1746.

The spirit of Amor Fugitivus was at one with that of French society in the eighteenth century, before the Revolution; and I cannot suppose that I have noticed every appearance of it. The author of *L'Art d'Aimer*, Gentil-Bernard, with a pleasing wit, combines Moschus' theme as it derives through Sannazaro with a conceit common in Renaissance Latin (and vernacular) verse: Eros mistakes my lady for his mother:[39]

Le dieu d'amour a déserté Cythère,
Et dans mon cœur le transfuge s'est mis.
De par Vénus trois baisers sont promis
A qui rendra son fils à sa colère.
Le livrerai-je? en ferai-je mystère?
Vénus m'attend; ses baisers sont bien doux!
O vous! Daphné, qu'il prendroit pour sa mère,
Au même prix, dites: le voulez-vous?

The *Almanach des Muses* for 1766 (p. 109) contains an anonymous translation: "La Reine de Cythère un jour perdit son fils," etc.; and the same miscellany for 1776 (p. 182) offers an imitation by "M. D." Though strongly reminiscent of Longepierre's madrigal, it is not so apt. It is printed as "a translation from the Anthology"—but is hardly that.

L'Amour est égaré, Vénus se désespère:
Elle a fait publier à Paphos, à Cythère,
Qu'elle est prête à récompenser

[39] *Poésies choisies*, Drujon, ed. (1884), p. 283. Compare the Portuguese sonnet by Diniz, below, and Marot, *Epigramme* 103.

D'un baiser,
Celui qui le mettra dans les bras de sa mère.
O Vénus! calme ta douleur;
J'ai retrouvé ton fils: il étoit dans mon cœur.
Donne-moi le baiser promis pour récompense;
Ou plutôt (et le prix en sera plus flatteur)
Laisse-le-moi cueillir sur les lèvres d'Hortense.

Poinsinet de Sivry, usually a graceful translator, has a diffuse version of Moschus.[40]

Vénus avoit perdu son fils:
Triste, plaintive, et vagabonde,
Elle remplissoit de ses cris
Cythère et le reste du monde, etc.

The Idyls of Moschus also appear in an anonymous verse-translation in the *Bibliothèque Universelle des Dames*, Paris, 1785.[41]

In Spanish and Portuguese

Before Tasso, and long before Ben Jonson, the Portuguese Gil Vicente (c. 1465–1536?) had turned Amor Fugitivus to a dramatic purpose in his *Fragoa d'Amor*. This agreeable little *"tragicomedia"* was presented at the betrothal of João III and Queen Catherina of Portugal in 1525. Two pilgrims meet and discuss the recent capture of a noble castle (Catherina) by "el Capitan Cupido" who had run away from heaven for the purpose. As they converse, Venus enters: Vem a Deosa Venus, Rainha da Musica, e diz:[42]

No sé á quien perguntar
Por el mi hijo Cupido,
Vuestro Dios damor, perdido;
Y no sé en que lugar
Se me ha desparecido.

---

[40]*Anacréon, Sapho, Moschus . . . traduits en vers* (Nancy, 1758); 3d ed., *Les Muses grecques* (Paris, 1771), p. 235.
[41]I have not seen this, nor the prose translation by J. J. Moutonnet-Clairfons (Paris, 1773), nor J.-B. Gail, *Idylles . . . de Moschus, ibid.* (1796).
[42]*Obras de Gil Vicente*, Mendes dos Remedios, ed. (1912), 2.156.

At the end of her complaint, the pilgrims inquire what she will give them to reveal Love's hiding-place. Her promise is reminiscent of that made to Paris more than of the reward offered in Moschus:

> "Prometo de os hacer
> Que no ameis á muger,
> Que della no alcanceis
> Quanto vueso amor quisiere."

Moved by this they relate the business that Love has been engaged in—the service of Portugal, in uniting João and Catherina—whereupon Venus, recognizing the "signs" of her son, relents:

> "Y pues que anduvo ocupado
> En obras tan divinales,
> Tomo á bien el mal pasado."

Next, near the "Castello," is revealed the Furnace of Love where Cupid, assisted by the planets, Mercury, Jupiter, Saturn, Sol, his workmen, changes the natures of men to the better; and the remainder of the masque is occupied with the transformation of a negro, a justice, a friar, a fool, and others.

Amor Fugido, de Mosco is the title of Antonio Ferreira's (1528–69) seventh elegy. He handles the theme freely in *terza rima*, introducing it as follows:[43]

> Correndo os prados vay, correndo os montes
> Cabello solto ao vento, dos pés nua,
> Deixados os seus banhos, e suas fontes,
> Em busca de Cupido a triste sua
> Mãy, e cativa Venus, voz em grito,
> Suspira, e chora, e cansa, e geme, e sua.

The reward offered by Venus is mainly new, though partly reminiscent of Vicente:

> "As frias neves, as ardentes fragoas,
> Em que tremeis e ardeis, temperey;
> Doam-vos os que ouvís as minhas mágoas.

[43] *Poemas lusitanos* (Lisbon, 1829), 1.165.

Nimphas, por hum prazer, mil vos darey.
Faunos, eu pagarey vossos amores.
Tornay-me o Amor, que eu vo-lo tornarey.
Abri vossos choupanas, meus Pastores,
Descobri-me, se o tendes, meu thesouro,
Eu o farey piadoso a vossas dores."

The sonnet that follows, by the Arcadian Antonio Diniz (1731–99), perhaps depends directly on some French or Italian model; but it is descended from Moschus through Meleager:[44]

Da bella mae perdido Amor errava
Pelos campos que corta o Tejo brando,
E a todos quantos via suspirando
Sem descanço por ella procurava.
Os farpões lhe caíam da aurea aljava;
Mas elle de arco e settas não curando,
Mil glórias promettia, soluçando,
A quem á deusa o leve, que buscava.
Quando Jonia, que alli seu gado pasce,
Enxugando-lhe as lagrymas que chora,
A Venus lhe monstrar, leda, se offrece:
Mas Amor dando um vôo á linda face
Beijando-a lhe tornou: "Gentil pastora,
Quem os teus olhos ve, Venus esquece."

There is a respectable translation, sufficiently close to the Greek, by Bocage.[45]

In Spanish the only early version I have seen is that of Hernando de Acuña (1522?–1586?).[46] His *Venus Quaerens Filium*—fifteen stanzas in octaves—is, for the most part, as Crawford has shown, an expansion and, in places, a close translation, of the poem by Thomaso Castellani (above).[47] Acuña, however, assigns a new occasion for the loss of Cupid:

En caza de una fiera le he perdido,
Que otras veces así suele perderse, etc.

[44]*Parnaso lusitano* (Paris, 1827), 3.16.
[45]*Obras poeticas* (Porto, 1875), 5.25.
[46]There is a Spanish translation of Tasso's *Aminta* by Jauregui (1607); and of the epilogue alone by Alberto Lista, *Bibl. de Aut. Esp.* 67 (1875), 330.
[47]Acuña, *Varias poesías*, 2d ed. (Madrid, 1804; 1st ed. Salamanca, 1591), pp. 228–32. See J. P. W. Crawford, *Romanic Review* 7 (1916) 314, where Acuña's poem is referred to its original.

There is also a translation by Joseph Antonio Conde, *Poesías de Anacreón, Teócrito, Bion y Mosco*, Madrid, 1746.

In German

The Latin versions made by German humanists seem not to have been followed very early by translations into the vernacular. Daniel Morhof, author of a history of poetry, in a ballet and a masque for the birthday of the Prince of Schleswig-Holstein, February 3, 1668, represents Cupid searching for his lost mother.[48] The reversal of Moschus' theme betrays at least a consciousness of its existence.

The first clear echo of Amor Fugitivus that I have noticed in German verse is a sonnet printed under the initials "C. E." in the *Gedichte* of Hofmannswaldau and other poets of his school, Leipzig, 1697.[49] It is descended from Moschus and Meleager through the Latin poem of Lampridio (above) which it follows—in places, verbally:

Was will der heisse zorn? was das vergällte dräuen?
Und was die ruthe dort in deiner rechten hand?
Wo kommstu so verwirrt, so hitzig hergerant?
Wie? Venus, hörstu nicht? Sie schwieg; bald hört' ich schreyen:
Du abgefeimter dieb! lernstu dich noch nicht scheuen?
Ich habe dir vorlängst die ruthe zuerkannt;
Nun aber solt du seyn aus meiner gunst verbannt.
Halt schelm! halt bösewicht! es soll dir wohl gereuen!
Ich rieff ihr weiter zu: Was? suchstu deinen sohn?
Er baut bey Solimen gleich itzt den liebesthron,
Und mühet sich durch sie die hertzen zu entzünden:
Bald reitzt er durch ihr aug, bald wieder durch den mund.
Ach Venus! räche mich; er hat mich auch verwundt.
Lauff hin zur Solime, da da wirst du ihn finden.

Götz (the translator, with Uz, of Anacreon, 1746), in some verses on *Der Verlorene Amor*, shows a knowledge of the conceits of both Moschus and Meleager.[50] He is, however, translating the madrigal by Longepierre (above)—or, less probably, its Italian original:

Venus, O! mir sind deine Kümmernisse,
Dass dein holdes Kind dir entfloh, bekannt.

[48]*Unterricht v. der Teutschen Sprache*, etc. (Lübeck and Leipzig, 1718), p. 420.
[49]*Herrn v. Hoffmannswaldau u. andrer Deutschen auserlesener u. bissher ungedruckter Gedichte anderer Theil* (Leipzig, 1697), p. 31.
[50]*Vermischte Gedichte*, K. W. Ramler, ed. (Mannheim, 1785), 1.8.

95

Du versprachst dem einen deiner Küsse,
Der dir sicher saget, wo sich's hingewandt.
Ich will deines Grams izt dich überheben;
Gieb mir nur den Kuss, gieb den süssen Lohn;
Oder lass mir ihn durch Dorinden geben:
Wiss' in ihren Augen sizt dein schöner Sohn.

Hölty, the lyrical poet, made a translation of Moschus 1 into fine prose, about the year 1770.[51]

The following books should not be disregarded: S. H. Lieber-kühn, *Die Idyllen Theokrits, Moschus, und Bions, aus dem Griechischen übersetzt.* Berlin, 1757; K. A. Kütner, *Idyllen des Theokrit, Bion, Moschus, und Koluthus, aus dem Griechischen.* Mietau u. Leipzig, 1772; S. H. Catel, *Bion, Moschus, Anakreon, und Sappho, aus dem Gr. Übersetzung in Versen.* Berlin, 1787.[52]

In English

The first notice of Amor Fugitivus in English seems to be the rather weak translation by Turbervile (1576), *Of Ladie Venus.*[53] It is a translation, not from the Greek, but from Poliziano's Latin. Moschus begins with the statement 'Α Κύπρις τὸν Ἔρωτα ... ἐβώστρει; Poliziano begins: "Cum Venus intento natum clamore vo-caret"; and Turbervile: "What time the Ladie Venus sought her little sonne." He reproduces all the peculiarities of Poliziano.[54] For line 6 he renders the reading of Poliziano in Soter's *Epigrammata:* "totam ac cognosce figuram"—"Marke every lim And member"; for line 22 he takes Poliziano's "seque ipsum multo quoque saevius angit"—"But most of all the foolish fretting elfe In cruel wise doth cruelly torment himselfe"; finally, he even accepts Poliziano's peculiar "verbere" (line 24)—"Doe beate the Boy."

A second notice of Moschus—and of Poliziano—occurs in the Gloss to Spenser's *Shepheardes Calender* (1579). A third is the trans-lation by Barnabe Barnes, *The First Eidillion of Moschus, describing Love* (1593).[55] Sidney Lee believed that Barnes "doubtless owed

[51]L. C. H. Hölty, *Sämtliche Werke*, Michael, ed. 1 (1914) 273.
[52]The translation by J. H. Voss did not appear until 1808 (Tübingen); Fr. Jacobs, the editor of the Anthology, has an excellent version of Meleager's epigram, *Vermischte Schriften* (1824), 2.280, and of Moschus' idyl *ibid.*, p. 300, both in the original meters.
[53]Chalmers, *English Poets* (1810), 2.636.
[54]See n. 9, above.
[55]*Elizabethan Sonnets* (1904), 1.268.

more to the French adaptations than to the Greek original."[56] It is a
reasonable suspicion; but none of the French versions I have examined lends color to it; on the contrary, the lines seem to come directly
from the Greek.[57]

More noteworthy is the adaptation of Amor Fugitivus by
Spenser. In the third book of the *Faerie Queene* (3.6.11–26) Venus is
introduced searching for Cupid; in vain she visits Court, City, and
Country, till she comes upon Diana and her company in a wood.
Diana cruelly makes sport of her loss. A quarrel ensues, at the end
of which Diana and the nymphs join Venus in her search; but they
find Crysogone and her babes instead of Love.

This part of the *Faerie Queene* derives from Moschus, but can
hardly be regarded as a translation. In the Gloss to the March
Eclogue in the *Shepheardes Calender,* however, "E. K." seems to say
that Spenser had made a translation: "But who liste more at large
to behold Cupids colours and furniture, let him reade ether Propertius, or Moschus his Idyllion of wandering love, being now most
excellently translated into Latine by the singular learned man
Angelus Politianus: whych worke I have seene amongst other of
thys Poets doings, very wel translated also into Englishe Rymes."[58]

If Spenser made a translation from Moschus, and if later he used
it in the *Faerie Queene,* he there employed it mainly as a ground for
elaboration.[59] His stanzas are compounded of Moschus' theme, of
new elements which he has brought into relation with it—for
example, the search through Court, City, and Country—and of his
memory of other modern versions, for one, Tasso's in the *Aminta.*[60]

The following lines show how Spenser had dealt with the theme,
and wherein his version resembles other variations.

> 3.6.11.   It fortuned, faire Venus having lost
> Her little sonne, the winged god of love,
> Who for some light displeasure, which him crost,[61]

---

[56]*Ibid.,* lxxvii.

[57]Barnes twice departs slightly from the Greek: (l.6) "Thou shalt not only kiss, but
as guest stay"; and (l.13) "as any wasp he stingeth."

[58]Must "thys Poet" be Spenser? The sentence is not unambiguous.

[59]Yet see Buck, "Spenser's Lost Poems," *PMLA* 23 (1908) 94, and Miss Sandison,
"Spenser's 'Lost' Works and Their Probable Relation to his *Faerie Queene,*" ibid. 25
(1910) 134.

[60]Bruce, *MLN* 27 (1912) 183, suggests the connection with Tasso's Prologue. The
Epilogue should also be compared. But in no case are the verbal correspondences
striking.

[61]Cf. Tasso, *Aminta,* Pro. 13 ff.

Was from her fled, as flit as ayerie Dove,
And left her blisfull bowre of joy above,[62]
(So from her often he had fled away,[63]
When she for ought him sharpely did reprove,[64]
And wandred in the world in strange aray,
Disguiz'd in thousand shapes, that none might him bewray),[65]

12.   Him for to seeke, she left her heavenly hous,
      The house of goodly formes and faire aspects,
      Whence all the world derives the glorious
      Features of beautie. . . .[66]
      She promist kisses sweet, and sweeter things
      Unto the man that of him tydings to her brings.[67]

13.   First she him sought in Court, where most he used
      Whylome to haunt. . . .[68]
      Ladies and Lords she every where mote heare
      Complayning, how with his empoysned shot
      Their wofull harts he wounded had whyleare.[69]

Ben Jonson's masque now called *The Hue and Cry after Cupid* was performed at the marriage, at Court, of John, Lord Ramsay, and the Lady Elizabeth Ratcliffe, daughter of the Earl of Sussex, on Shrove-Tuesday night, 1608.[70] The scene was "a high, steep, red cliff, advancing itself into the clouds." Venus enters, with the Graces, and says:[71]

It is no common cause, ye will conceive,
My lovely Graces, makes your goddess leave
Her state in heaven to-night to visit earth.[72]

---

[62]Tasso, *Am.*, Epi. 1; cf. also Castellani, line 4, above.
[63]Cf. Tasso, *Am.*, Pro. 41: Onde sovente ella me cerca in vano; and Acuña: Que otras veces así suele perderse.
[64]Cf. Baïf: Contre son fils un jour Vénus . . . Se corrouça.
[65]Cf. Castellani: Et perchè in mille forme inganna altrui I segni udite da conoscer lui.
[66]Cf. Tasso, *Am.*, Epi. 1: Scesa dal terzo cielo. The Platonism is Spenser's addition.
[67]Somewhat nearer, as Bruce observes, to Tasso, *Am.*, Pro. 33–34 than to Moschus (5).
[68]Cf. Tasso, *Am.*, Pro. 18 ff.
[69]Moschus (27, 29).
[70]The title is Gifford's; earlier edd. have *The Description of the Masque*, etc.
[71]*Works*, Cunningham, ed. (1903), 3.36.
[72]Cf. Tasso, *Am.*, Epi. 1, and Spenser, *FQ* 3.6.12.1.

Amor Fugitivus

> Love late is fled away, my eldest birth,
> Cupid, whom I did joy to call my son;
> And whom long absent Venus is undone.

She bids the Graces make hue and cry; and, when they have done with describing him, Cupid enters, only to vanish again as Hymen appears. Hymen relates the business that Cupid has been engaged in—the union of Ramsay and the Lady Elizabeth—whereupon Venus relents: "My Cupid's absence I forgive and praise."

Next, Vulcan appears; the cliff parts in the midst, and discloses a sphere of silver, where, in a golden zodiac, twelve maskers, for the twelve signs, are placed. Vulcan describes the virtues of each, in "the heaven of marriage." And, at the end, the Epithalamion is sung alternately with dancing by the "twelve signs."

Is it impossible that, for the general course of the masque, Jonson may have taken a hint from Vicente's *Fragoa d'Amor*? He was well read in the modern literatures. Be that as it may, for his description of Cupid he has consulted not Moschus alone, but also the followers of Moschus; in his own words: "In this Love I express Cupid as he is *Veneris filius*, and owner of the following qualities ascribed to him by the antique and later poets." The passages that have to do with our present subject are these:

> *Ven.*   Stay, nymphs, we then will try
> A nearer way. Look all these ladies' eyes,
> And see if there he not concealed lies;[73]
> Or in their bosoms, 'twixt their swelling breasts;
> The wag affects to make himself such nests;[74]
> Perchance he hath got some simple heart to hide
> His subtle shape in;[75] I will have him cried,
> And all his virtues told![76] that, when they'd know
> What spright he is, she soon may let him go
> That guards him now, and think herself right blest,
> To be so timely rid of such a guest.[77]
> Begin, soft Graces, and proclaim reward
> To her that brings him in. Speak to be heard.

[73]Meleager 9–10; Segnius (above); Lampridio (above); Tasso, *Am.*, Epi. 26–28.
[74]Cf. Lampridio, Baïf, and Meleager 9: φωλεόν (?).
[75]Sannazaro, Angeriano, Giraldi Cintio, Baïf.
[76]Moschus (6).
[77]Giraldi Cintio 5–6.

1 Grace.

Beauties, have you seen this toy
Called Love, a little boy,
Almost naked,[78] wanton,[79] blind,
Cruel now, and then as kind?[80]
If he be amongst ye, say?
He is Venus' runaway.[81]

2 Grace.

She that will but now discover
Where the winged wag doth hover,
Shall to-night receive a kiss,[82]
How or where herself would wish;
But who brings him to his mother,
Shall have that kiss and another.[83]

3 Grace.

He hath marks about him plenty:
You shall know him among twenty.[84]
All his body is a fire....[85]

1 Grace.

At his sight, the sun hath turned,
Neptune in the waters burned;
Hell hath felt a greater heat;
Jove himself forsook his seat....[86]

2 Grace.

Wings he hath, which though ye clip,
He will leap from lip to lip
Over liver, lights, and heart....[87]

---

[78] Moschus (15).
[79] Moschus (10).
[80] Moschus (8-9).
[81] Ἔρως δραπέτης.
[82] Moschus (3-4).
[83] Moschus (4-5); Apuleius (above).
[84] Moschus (6).
[85] Moschus (7).
[86] Jonson refers to Lucian, *Dial. Deor.* (12), Claudian, *In raptu Proserp.*, and "Phil. Poe." (Philippus, *AP* 16.104). But these are only analogues (e.g., *De Rapt. Pro.* 1.26, qua lampade Ditem flexit Amor, and *ibid.* 1.227) to what is in reality an expansion of Moschus (14). Compare also Tasso, *Am.*, Pro. 6-9, Apuleius, *Met.* 4.33, and Ronsard, *Le Trophée d'Amour*, in *Œuvres*, Marty-Laveaux, ed. (1887), 3.466.
[87] Moschus (16-17); Spenser, *FQ* 3.6.24.9.

3 Grace.
>   He doth bear a golden bow,[88]
>   And a quiver hanging low,[89]
>   Full of arrows that outbrave
>   Dian's shafts; where, if he have
>   Any head more sharp than other,
>   With that first he strikes his mother....[90]

2 Grace.
>   Trust him not; his words, though sweet,
>   Seldom with his heart do meet.[91]
>   All his practice is deceit,[92]
>   Every gift it is a bait;
>   Not a kiss but poison bears;[93]
>   And most treason in his tears.[94]

3 Grace.
>   Idle minutes are his reign;
>   Then the straggler makes his gain,
>   By presenting maids with toys.[95]

There is a madrigal by Drummond of Hawthornden on this theme, *Love Vagabonding:*[96]

>   Sweet nymphes, if, as yee straye,
>   Yee finde the froth-borne Goddesse of the sea,
>   All blubbered, pale, undone,
>   Who seekes her giddie sone,
>   That litle God of Love,
>   Whose golden shafts your chastest bosomes prove,
>   Who, leaving all the heavens, hath runne away;
>   If she to him him findes will aught impart,
>   Her tell he nightlie lodgeth in my heart.

[88]Moschus (18).
[89]Moschus (20).
[90]Moschus (21).
[91]Moschus (8, 11).
[92]Moschus (11).
[93]Moschus (27).
[94]Moschus (25).
[95]Moschus (29).
[96]*Poetical Works*, Kastner, ed. (1913), 2.155. The fragments of George Peele's *Hunting of Cupid* in Drummond's *Commonplace Book* (see Malone Soc., *Collections*, Parts 4 and 5 (1911), pp. 307 ff.) betray no debt to Moschus. But compare "His dwellinge is in ladyes eyes" with the second line quoted above from Jonson. Peele's play appeared, it seems, in 1591.

The point is Sannazaro's; but, to judge from Drummond's habits, we should expect to find an immediate French or Italian original for these verses; yet none is known.

Shirley and Carew dispute the possession of a graceful transformation of Moschus' theme, called *The Hue and Cry*. It appears in Shirley's comedy *The Witty Fair One* (1628), with changes, among Carew's poems (1640), and in a third version among Shirley's poems (1646). Shirley has the better claim. A few lines from the beginning and the end will show how the theme was adapted:[97]

> In Love's name you are charged, oh, fly!
> And make a speedy hue and cry
> After a face which t'other day
> Stole my wandering heart away.
> To direct you, take in brief
> These few marks to know the thief.
> Her hair a net of beams would prove,
> Strong enough to imprison Jove, . . .
>   O straight surprise,
> And bring her into Love's assize;
> But lose no time, for fear that she
> Ruin all mankind, like me,
> Fate and philosophy control,
> And leave the world without a soul.

Crashaw has a translation, which, though recommended by its tripping measure, is hardly a favorable example of his rimes:[98]

> Love is lost, nor can his mother
> Her little fugitive discover, etc.

Thomas Stanley's version (1651, with his *Anacreon*) has the merit of being compact.[99] An anonymous version—"Love from his Mother-Goddess gone astray," etc.—is printed in *The Loves of Hero and Leander*, translated by James Sterling, London 1728, p. 67. Samuel Derrick calls his *Cupid Gone Astray* (1755) "A song imitated from Joannes Secundus." I cannot find that Secundus has anything

---

[97]The three versions are in Carew's *Poems*, Vincent, ed. (The Muses Library), pp. 179–81. Cf. also *The Dart, ibid.,* p. 154.
[98]"Out of the Greek. Cupid's Cryer" in *Poetical Works*, Martin, ed. (1927), p. 159.
[99]Reprinted in *The Greek Anthology* (1852), p. 150 (Bohn trans.).

on this theme. Derrick's song, whatever its immediate model, is a free handling of Moschus' conceit:[100]

> Tell me, lasses, have you seen,
> Lately wandering o'er the green
> Beauty's son, a little boy,
> Full of frolic, mirth, and joy? etc.

English verse-translations appear also in the following books: Thomas Cooke, *The idylliums of Moschus and Bion.* London, 1724; Francis Fawkes, *The works of Anacreon . . . the works of Moschus.* London, 1760 (published anonymously, as also again in 1789; with the name of the translator in 1793; reprinted by Chalmers, *English Poets*, London, 1810, 20.389); Richard Polwhele, *The idyllia, epigrams, and fragments of Theocritus, Bion, and Moschus . . . translated from the Greek into English verse.* 1 vol. Exeter, 1786; 2 vols. Bath, 1792; 2 vols. London, 1810;[101] E. Dubois, *The wreath.* London, 1799 (prose translation; I have not seen this).

Thus Fugitive Love, the invention of Moschus, has traveled from his cradle a long way; and doubtless a more persistent search would reveal other traces of his passage. His disguises have been many. In nothing more than in its adaptability has the vitality of the conceit been made manifest. As a conceit it has formed the substance of more than one epigram and sonnet; the dramatic character of the poem—Venus speaks directly in the first person—has suggested its use for court-masques to Gil Vicente, Tasso, and Ben Jonson; its connection with pastoral poetry has perhaps also recommended it to the attention of Tasso and Spenser; the witty allegorical portrait of Love has caught the fancy of erotic writers from Meleager, Apuleius, and Nicetas onward; allegory has inspired allegory to the length of Marot's satirical "invention." It is remarkable, too, that, while what is really clever in Moschus is his adaptation of an advertisement for runaway slaves to Aphrodite's search for Eros, modern writers, responding to a changed order of society, have generally, from Pontano onward, abandoned that idea, or suppressed it, and have pictured merely the mother's quest of a lost child.

[100]Reprinted in *The Shorter Poems of the Eighteenth Century*, Williams, ed. (1923), p. 357.
[101]Polwhele illustrates Amor Fugitivus by Canticles 3.2–3: I will rise now, and go about the city in the streets, and in the broad ways (τριόδοισι?) I will seek him whom my soul loveth.

Perhaps the greater part of literature is translation or, what is the same thing, *contaminatio*. While Moschus' conceit is hardly one of the major themes of poetry, its history supplies no bad example of the way in which translation in the larger sense proceeds. After the original, two adaptations hold a ruling place: that of Meleager who adds "that Love may be found in his mistress' eyes," and that of Sannazaro who adds "that Love may be found in his own heart." These two new combinations, together with the original, now forming partnership with one bit of fresh fancy, now with another, press on to become the possession of a *doctus poeta* like Ben Jonson, who digests almost the whole material.

Only when related pieces are seen together can their true connections be recognized—connections that in some cases the authors themselves may not have clearly understood; for by the end of the eighteenth century, to take Fugitive Love as an instance, the several variations were so generally diffused that a person might compose a "madrigal" on the theme without knowing whence came his version of the conceit, or even under the illusion that he was inventing it.

In the diffusion of the theme a factor deserving special attention is the part taken by the neo-Latin poets. Since the victory won by the various vernaculars in the sixteenth century, we have naturally forgotten that there was good reason for fighting. Among people who cared for letters, the Latin productions of the time were eagerly read everywhere. Even in the thick of the battle the cry was not "Belittle the ancients!"—that came later—but "Pillage the ancients for the good of the vernacular!"[102] The neo-Latin writers for some time had been pillaging the ancients for their own benefit. When a man turned to write in the vernacular, he necessarily took with him the ideas he had gained from reading Latin, whether classical or modern. Moreover, the neo-Latin writers were humanists, who stood in direct contact with the good things that all wished to obtain—a fact the vernacular poets were aware of.[103] For this reason the student of modern literature can scarcely afford to ignore the modern Latin poets.[104] In the case of Moschus' idyl, here is Sannazaro almost as much imitated as Meleager or the

---

[102]See Du Bellay, *Deffence,* Person, ed. (1878), p. 162 *et passim.*
[103]*Ibid.,* pp. 117–18; he urges the imitation of Sannazaro, Pontano, and Joannes Secundus.
[104]The whole matter is in need of particular study; see Chamard, *Les origines de la poésie française de la renaissance* (1920), p. 295.

original, here is Poliziano's version read everywhere, here again is the well-known version by Marot—in reality a faithful rendering of an anonymous Latin imitation. Marot knew no Greek, and only by going to translations could he secure this and other portions of Greek literature for the enrichment of his own. Doubtless the same is true of Turbervile, who for Greek epigrams goes to various neo-Latin translators, and, as we have seen, goes to Poliziano, not to the Greek, for the First Idyl of Moschus.[105]

[Two valuable supplements to the foregoing article were published by Professor Joseph G. Fucilla: "Additions to 'The First Idyl of Moschus in Imitations to the Year 1800,'" *AJP* 50 (1929) 190–93, and "Materials for the History of a Popular Classical Theme," *Classical Philology* 26 (1931) 135–52. Our efforts may serve to draw attention to the wide distribution of the *Amor Fugitivus* in European literature, but to control the very great number of existing translations and manipulations of this poem might well prove to be a hopeless undertaking. Poliziano's translation probably was not the first to be made in Latin in the fifteenth century; on translations by Battista Guarino and Francesco Guarnerio (or Francesco Maturanzio), see Ludwig Bertalot, "L'Antologia di Epigrammi di Lorenzo Abstemio nelle tre Edizioni Sonciniane," in *Miscellanea Giovanni Mercati* (Vatican City, 1946), (*Studi e Testi* 124) 4.305–26 (No. 52, pp. 321–22). See also Carlo Cordiè, "L'Humanista A. Pelotti, Traduttore dell'Amor Fugitivo di Mosco," in *Rendiconti dell'Istituto Lombardo di Scienze e Lettere* (classe lettere) 83 (1950) 425–38.

Bertalot's article allows us to recognize as Battista Guarino's translation the anonymous version in Soter's *Epigrammata* (above, p. 82) and the original of Clement Marot's *D'amour fugitif, de Lucien* (above, p. 87). It is included in Abstemius' miscellany with the superscription, *Carmen in Amorem fugitivum traductum ex graeco Luciano sive Moscho per Baptistam Guarinum* (Fano, Soncino, 1517). As for the ascription to Lucian (an obvious mistake), Bertalot shows that this translation had appeared anonymously at the end of certain Latin translations from Lucian printed in 1494 and reprinted repeatedly thereafter. Marot evidently depends on this tradition.]

[105]H. B. Lathrop's interesting article "Janus Cornarius's *Selecta Epigrammata Graeca* and the Early English Epigrammatists," in *MLN* 43 (1928), appeared when the present article was in proof. Lathrop shows that Turbervile was translating from the Latin versions in Cornarius' book.

To the neo-Latin imitations of Moschus 1, mentioned above, should be added those by Nicolas Bourbon, *Nugae* (Basel, 1540), pp. 45, 466.

Cupid and the Bee

" 'There's some herb that's good for everybody except for them that thinks they're sick when they ain't,' announced Mrs. Todd, with a truly professional air of finality. 'Come, William, let's have Sweet Home, an' then mother'll sing Cupid an' the Bee for us.' " Accuracy in detail is a merit that no one would deny to the work of Sarah Orne Jewett and hence some time ago, on reading the words just quoted from *The Country of the Pointed Firs*,[1] the present writer was puzzled at finding Cupid and the Bee linked with Sweet Home in a setting meant to call up nothing but the homely reality of Maine. The title suggested Theocritus (pseudo-Theocritus) or an Anacreon (pseudo-Anacreon) unlikely to be much on the mind of Mrs. Todd or her aged mother. Sweet Home is duly sung, but we hear no more of Cupid and the Bee. One only gathers that to Miss Jewett in 1896 it had the color of an old song suitable to the age of the singer. As I had long been noting down occurrences of the theme, I noted this one, thinking some time to make out what was meant. And now comes Professor Thompson, from whose recent book[2] it appears that Cupid and the Bee belongs to the "folklore" of the State of New York as well as to that of Maine. From the songs written down in the Orderly Books of the Fourth and Second New York Regiments in the American Revolution, Mr. Thompson gives us several, including *The Bee:*

> As Cupid midst the roses played,
> Transporting in the damask shade,

Reprinted by permission of the Modern Language Association of America from *PMLA* 56 (1941) 1036–58.
[1]Ch. xi, "The Old Singers."
[2]Harold W. Thompson, *Body, Boots, and Britches* (Philadelphia: Lippincott, 1940), p. 339.

Cupid and the Bee

A bee stepped unseen among
The silken leaves—his finger stung.

His beauteous cheeks with tears were drowned;
He stormed, he blew the burning wound,
Then nimbly running through the grove
Thus plaintive to the Queen of Love:

"I'm killed, Mamma; alas, I die!
A little serpent winged to fly
That's called the bee in yonder plain,
Has stung me, and I die with pain."

Venus smiling thus rejoining:
"My dear, if you such anguish find
From the resentment of a bee,
Think what they feel that's stung by thee."

If this was the song that Miss Jewett had in mind, then it was
"Anacreon" after all that William's mother sang, and in a familiar
version; for, with such changes as naturally attend on "folklore,"
this is the translation by John Addison, first published in 1735.[3]

As *Cupid* 'midst the Roses play'd,
Gay-sporting thro' the Damask Shade;
A Bee which slept unseen among
The Silken Leaves, his Finger stung.

In Tears his beauteous Cheeks were drown'd,
He storm'd, he blow'd the burning Wound;
Then running, flying thro' the Grove,
Thus plaintive to the Queen of Love:

I'm kill'd, Mama! Ah me, I die!
A little Serpent wing'd to fly,
That's call'd a Bee, on yonder Plain,
Has stung me; Oh, I die with Pain!

When *Venus*, smiling, thus rejoin'd,
My Dear, if you such Anguish find

[3] *The Works of Anacreon translated into English Verse* . . . by Mr. Addison, London.
The ambiguity of "Mr. Addison," which misled many readers, may have been intentional.

From the Resentment of a Bee,
Think what they feel who're stung by thee!

Finally, any doubt that this was the song known to Miss Jewett is dispelled by a glance into the songbooks of the late eighteenth and early nineteenth centuries. It appears, for example, with musical setting in *The American Musical Miscellany* (Northampton, 1798), and without music in *The Theatrical Songster and Musical Companion* (Boston, 1815).[4] As printed in these books the text is, if anything, more corrupt than the version known to the Revolutionary soldier:

As Cupid in a garden strayed,
Transported with the damask shade,
A little bee, unseen among
The silken weeds, his finger stung...
Then flying to a neighb'ring grove,
Thus plaintive told the Queen of Love:...
A little insect, wing'd to fly, etc.

In the corpus of the Greek Bucolic Poems there are two inventions, not perhaps much to present taste, that had, however, for our forefathers back to the Renaissance, an irresistible charm. The one is Moschus' Ἔρως δραπέτης, the second the Κηριοκλέπτης ascribed in the manuscripts to Theocritus, but now handed somewhat abruptly to Bion or Moschus. The devotion with which these two poems have been repeatedly translated and imitated in modern letters has almost the character of a special phenomenon, and hence at least a brief scrutiny of their influence is in order. This has already been accorded to the Ἔρως δραπέτης (*Amor Fugitivus*).[5] The notes that form the substance of the present paper on the Κηριοκλέπτης or Honey-Stealer, and on the related Anacreontic, have been somewhat casually assembled in a search through neo-Latin, Italian, French, and English books for other, but not dissimilar, matter. Accordingly no imitations in other languages are here

---

[4]In the first entitled *The Bee* and in the second (p. 188) *Cupid and a Bee*. For these references I am indebted to Professor Otto Kinkeldey of Cornell University and to the Music Division of the New York Public Library. I have at hand no facilities for tracing the song in English songbooks of the period. Music by Gossec for J. B. Gail's French version of the Anacreontic is printed at the end of Gail's *Odes d'Anacréon* (Paris, 1799).

[5]By the present writer, in the preceding essay, and by Professor J. G. Fucilla, in *AJP* 50 (1929) 190, and in *Classical Philology*, 26 (1931) 135.

offered. And the collection ends with the close of the eighteenth century.[6]

The Anacreontic, a translation of which we have just been considering, appears to be the only echo of the Κηριοκλέπτης in antiquity.[7] The substance of the two poems is so nearly identical that it is necessary to take up their influence together. Yet they have also certain divergent traits that make it usually easy to know which of them a modern imitator is following. Besides, while the Theocritean poem was first printed in the Aldine Theocritus of 1495, the Anacreontic was only discovered, with the other *Anacreontea*, by Henri Estienne in 1549 and published in his Anacreon of 1554, so that no version of the theme earlier than 1549 and probably none earlier than 1554 can very well have been derived from the Anacreontic.[8]

It will be enough for our purpose to begin with literal translations of the two poems. (The Theocritean poem is in eight hexameters, the Anacreontic in sixteen short "hemiambics," the familiar measure of Anacreon.)

"Theocritus" 19

Love the thief was once stung by a wicked bee, as he filched a honeycomb from the hive, and all his finger-tips were pricked. It hurt, and he blew on his hand, stamped the earth, and skipped about; and he showed his hurt to Aphrodite, complaining that the bee is but a tiny creature, but it causes such wounds. And his mother laughed: 'What! are you not like the bees, you who are also little, but cause such great wounds?'

[6]Of the modern versions of this theme, more than a hundred and thirty, that are mentioned below, nine have previously been listed by Fritzsche, *Theocriti Idyllia* (Leipzig, 1870), II, 103, eight others by Mustard, "Later Echoes of the Greek Bucolic Poets," *AJP* 30 (1909) 269, and ten of the English versions by Kerlin, *Theocritus in English Literature* (Lynchburg, 1910). I have been unable to consult R. Galos, "L'Amour et les abeilles," in *Irodalom-történeti közlemények* (Budapest, 1937).

[7]I find no real resemblance in the four Greek epigrams cited by Fritzsche, *op. cit.*, II, 102; there is more similarity in the epigram by Bianor (*AP* 9.548) compared with the Theocritean poem by Alciati (below), but it is accidental. Bullen, *Anacreon* (London, 1893), p. 219, speaks of "this favorite conceit, which we frequently find represented on gems"; but I find no justification for his statement. Bullen, indeed, reproduces on his cover a gem from the Poniatowski Collection, but this, as he says, is a modern fabrication. As such it is noteworthy for the modern influence of the theme. Before the Renaissance I know only the commonly cited paraphrase of the Anacreontic in the twelfth-century romance by the Byzantine Nicetas Eugenianus (IV, 313).

[8]Estienne communicated his discovery with several friends between 1549 and 1554; cf. Laumonier, *Ronsard poète lyrique*, 3d ed. (Paris, 1932), p. 121. But no version of Cupid and the Bee seems to be affected by this fact.

"Anacreon" 35 (40)
Love once failed to see among the roses a sleeping bee, and was stung.
His finger wounded, he bawled, and ran flying to lovely Cytherea:
'I'm done for, mother,' said he, 'done for, I'm dying! A little winged
serpent stuck me that the rustics call a bee.' But she said: 'If a bee's
sting hurts, what hurt think you they feel, Eros, whom you strike?'

For distinguishing marks, attention must be directed upon the following points. In the Theocritean poem (1) Love is stealing honey, (2) there is a lively account of his reaction ("He blew on his hand," etc.), and (3) Venus laughs. In the Anacreontic peculiarities are: (1) the phrase "among the roses," (2) direct address by Cupid to Venus, and (3) the naïve expression, "a little winged serpent." It will be noticed that Addison, in translating the Anacreontic, has borrowed from the other poem his line, "He storm'd, he blow'd the burning wound," and also "Venus smiling." Such crossing of the two originals, though perhaps less common than might be expected, will be found in several of the versions noted below.

In collecting modern variations on a theme of this kind, the aim is to bring to light relations among them. Too often the editors of modern poets have been content, and have had to be content, with recording that a given poem "comes from" such and such an ancient source, whereas it actually came from an earlier modern imitator. What we want, of course, in each case is the proximate source, and this will often reveal itself for several poets at once when an extensive collection is made of the variants of a given theme. In the present case, I regret that the casual manner in which the collection has grown has left me in some instances without complete copies, so that there are probably relationships among the poems I mention which I am now unable to detect.

Here it may not be out of place to repeat what is sometimes forgotten; namely, that a main purpose in discovering a poet's sources is to learn his methods of composition. You cannot tell how a poem was composed unless you know what it was composed of. In this connection I may perhaps be allowed to ask for attention to the remarks on Spenser given below.

Translations and imitations of "Theocritus" are placed first and followed by those of "Anacreon." Space permits little more than a bibliographical list with annotations.

Cupid and the Bee

"Theocritus" 19

Joannes Gazoldus. *Epigrammatum libellus,* Carpi, 1506 (?), f. 7^r: Saevus Amor dulces. Girolamo Angeriano. *Erotopaegnion,* Florence, 1512, f. 11^v: "De Caeliae Vulnere."[9] Ercole Strozzi. *Strozii Poetae pater et filius* [1513], Paris, 1530, f. 92^r.[10] Caspar Ursinus Velius. In Joannes Soter's *Epigrammata Graeca veterum,* Cologne, 1528, p. 58: Nuper apis furem.[11] Philip Melanchthon. *Ibid.:* E Parvo alveolo. Joachim Camerarius. *Ibid.:* Forte Favos. Jacobus Micyllus. *Ibid.:* Forte petiturus. Anonymous. *Ibid.:* Subdola apis.[12] Helius Eoban Hess: Four versions.[13] Andrea Alciati, *Emblemata,* Paris, 1534, Emb. 113.[14] Gilbert Ducher. *Epigrammatum libri duo,* Lyons, 1538,

[9] In the more accessible edition of Naples, 1520, sig. biiii^2. Angeriano's poems played a significant role in sixteenth-century lyric verse, since they were universally imitated by the vernacular poets. His method was to take a classical, usually a Greek theme, and give it a turn of his own. Thus his treatment of the present motive is typical:

Caelia dum fulgens per florea rura vagatur,
Saeva manum illius saeva momordit apes.
Unde has, inquit, habet volucris tam parva sagittas?
Illato ut tumeat vulnere nostra manus?
Tunc respondit Amor: Sum parvus et ipse tenerque,
Et iaculis (quae stant) mollio saxa meis.
Tu paulo maior quid non facis? ore pusillo
Atque oculis montes et maris uris aquas.

Cf. below, under Amboise and Scève. Angeriano has a second poem (sig. aiiii^7) on a bee slain by Caelia, happy to die by her hand, and buried by Love, who writes its epitaph. Cf. below, under Groto.

[10]
Dum Veneris puer alveolos furatur Hymetti,
Furanti digitum cuspide fixit apis.
Indoluit graviter, pueriliaque ora rigavit
Fletibus, et matri spicula questus, ait:
Unde hae tantillis vires animantibus? unde
Exili possunt laedere aculeolo?
Cui Dea subridens inquit, non tu quoque, nate,
Corpore non magno, vulnera magna facis?

[11] From Velius' *Poemata* (Basel, 1522). The Κηϱιοϰλέπτης is not in the first (1525) edition of Soter; in the third (1544) edition it appears on p. 65.

[12] Of these versions in Soter, all except the anonymous translation interpret the words χέϱ' ἐφύση ("he blew on his hand") as "his hand became swollen," e.g. Velius: *tumuerunt vulnere palmae.* Vernacular versions having this peculiarity can therefore be suspected of depending on one of these translations; but cf. Angeriano above, and also Alciati (*tumido ungue*). A second peculiarity in the translations by Melanchthon and Camerarius is that Love's fingers bleed: *digitos monstratque cruentos* (Mel.), *suffusum . . . cruorem* (Cam.).

[13] *Theocriti Idyllia* (Hagenau, 1530); Valckenaer's *Theocritus* (Leiden, 1810), p. 464.

[14] Alveolis dum mella legit, percussit Amorem

p. 44: (1) Furaturus erat [literal], (2) Dum furatur api [imitation]. Antoine de Gouvéa. *Epigrammaton libri duo,* Lyons, 1539, p. 9: Mella puer Veneris. Joannes Trimaninus. *Theocriti Opera,* Venice, 1539 [prose].[15] Georg Sabinus. *Emblemata.*[16] Gilbert Cousin, *Narrationum Sylva* [1547], Basel, 1567, p. 156: "De Cupidine fugitivo et melilego."[17] Andrea Dazzi. *Poemata,* Florence, 1549, pp. 126, 129: Nactus apes furax. Andreas Rapitius. *Facilioris Musae Carminum libri duo,* Venice, 1552, f. 13^r:

> Furacem mala apes, et summis spicula liquit
> In digitis: tumido gemit at puer anxius ungue,
> Et quatit errabundus humum, Venerique dolorem
> Indicat, et graviter queritur, quod apicula parvum
> Ipsa inferre animal tam noxia vulnera possit.
> Cui ridens Venus: Hanc imitaris tu quoque, dixit,
> Nate, feram, qui das tot noxia vulnera parvus.

The title of this emblem is "Fere simile ex Theocrito," because Emb. 112, entitled "Dulcia quandoque amara fieri," is on a child similarly stung by a bee (imitation of *AP* 9.548 in which the child is killed). The immense popularity of Alciati's *Emblems* is a main element in the spread of this theme. Here we may mention the French translations of Alciati by Jean Le Fèvre (Paris, 1536), by Barthélemy Aneau (Lyons, 1558), and by Claude Mignault (Paris, 1583); the English version by Geoffrey Whitney, *Choice of Emblems* (London, 1586); and German versions (after Le Fèvre) by Wolfgang Hunger in M. Rubensohn, *Griechische Epigramme und andere kleinere Dichtungen* (Weimar, 1897), pp. 11, 15. I give the Italian version by Giovanni Marquale, *Diverse Imprese . . . tratte da gli Emblemi dell' Alciato* (Lyons: Roville, 1549), p. 77:

> Lunge a la madre il pargoletto Amore
> Fura del mele, onde lo punse un' Ape.
> Così amaro dolor stringe e afferra
> Colui, che di dolcezza empie la terra.

Here the "moral," taken from Emb. 112, is combined with the fable; cf. Sabinus below.

[15] I have not seen this translation.

[16] Sabinus (Schuler) published his *Poemata* in 1544 and 1558 at Leipzig. I have seen neither of these books. The verses in question are given under Sabinus' name in Antonio Germano's *Giardino di Sentenze* (Rome, 1630), p. 296, and without his name in the Notes by Lorenzo Pignoria in *Andreae Alciati Emblemata* (Padua, 1621), p. 470. I quote Pignoria's remarks since they relate to the only Renaissance painting that I have seen mentioned as embodying this theme: "Tabella picta huius argumenti [Cupid and the Bee] extat apud Aloysium Corradinum Juris Consultum [?of Padua] et quidem manu periti artificis depicta, in qua leguntur hi versus:

> Dum puer alveolo furatur mella Cupido,
> Furanti digitum cuspide fixit apis.
> Sic etiam nobis brevis et peritura voluptas,
> Quam petimus tristi mixta dolore nocet."

Sabinus has affixed his "moral" to an adaptation of the first two verses of Strozzi's translation given above. See bracketed addition at the end of this essay.

[17] A prose fable combining Moschus I and Theoc. 1–19, with the "moral": "Voluptati dolor et calamitas plerumque comes est."

DVM PVER ALVEOLO FVRATVR MELLA CVPIDO.
FVRANTI DIGITVM SEDVLA PVNXIT APIS.
SIC ETIAM NOBIS BREVIS ET MORITVRA VOLVPE:
QVAM PETIMVS TRISTI MIXTA DOLORE NOCET

The Honey Stealer, Lucas Cranach. Courtesy of The Metropolitan Museum of Art, Robert Lehman Collection, 1975.

Caecus Amor quondam.   Andreas Divus. *Theocriti Idyllia*, Basel,
1554.[18]   Henri Estienne. *Moschi Bionis Theocriti Idyllia* Venice,
1555, sig. Bii: Improbe apis.   Fausto Sabeo. *Epigrammatum libri
quinque*, Rome, 1556: four translations, pp. 649, 823, 832, 835, and
an imitation (Amor pricked by a thorn), p. 136.   Fabio Segni. [In
Carmina quinque Hetruscorum poetarum, Florence, 1562] In *Carmina
Illustrium Poetarum Italorum*, Florence, 1719-26, IX, 18: Dum studio
raperet.   Anonymous. In J. A. Taygetus, *Carmina Praestantium
Poetarum*, Brescia, 1565, p. 91: Inventum reserat.   Johann
Stigel. In Gruter's *Delitiae CC Poetarum Germanorum*, Frankfort,
1612, VI, 555: Filius Idaliae.[19]   J. C. Scaliger. *Poemata* [1574],
Heidelberg, 1600, I, 149: Dum cellas vexat.[20]   Ippolito Capilupi.
Capiluporum Carmina, Rome, 1590, p. 127: Dum fur mel-
la.   Claude Mignault. *Alciati Emblemata* [1602] Padua, 1621,
p. 470: Noxia apis furacem.   Jacques Moisant de Brieux. *Poemata*,
Caen, 1663, p. 174: Praedantem Hyblaeo.   Samuel de Fermat.
Variorum Carminum libri quatuor, s. l., 1680, p. 92: Nuper cum
virides.   Anonymous. *Selecta ex poetis graecis*, Eton, 1762: Furem
quondam [prose].   Raimondo Cunich. In Zamagana's *Eco*,
Rome, 1764, p. 88: Furem olim.[21]   Bernardo Zamagna. *Theocriti
Moschi et Bionis*, etc., Siena, 1788.[22]

[18]I have not seen this translation.
[19]Stigel's poems were originally collected in 1566-69 and 1572, after his death. He
was a friend of Melanchthon, and his version of the present theme bears some
relation to those of Melanchthon and Camerarius in Soter's *Epigrammata*. Thus he
writes, "Figit apis cui dira manus digitosque tenellos": cf. Melanchthon, "Fixit apis
puerum Veneris digitosque tenellos"; again, "digitusque tumescit ab ictu": cf.
Camerarius, "digitusque tumebat ab ictu"; and, "Inque novo stimuli vulnere linquit
acum": cf. Camerarius, "stimulumque recenti in vulnere liquit." All these points
represent departures from the literal sense of the Greek.
[20]Scaliger ascribes the original to Moschus.
[21]Cunich's version also appears in his own *Anthologia* (Rome, 1771), p. 183, and
again in his *Theocriti Idyllia* (Parma, 1799).
[22]I have not seen this book; the translation of "Theocritus" 19 may be that of
Cunich.
As probable echoes of the Theocritean poem may be mentioned two epigrams by
Celio Calcagnini under the title, *Apes in pharetra Cupidinis* in *Jo. Baptistae Pignae
Carminum libri quatuor* (Venice, 1553), pp. 199-200, the first beginning:
> Pallantes excepit apes modo Cypride natus
> In pharetram, e pharetra nunc nova mella legit.
Love is then compared with the bee, and contrasted:
> Diversum hoc, sanabile apum, haud sanabile amoris
> Vulnus, apesque semel, non semel ille ferit.
(The text has *fuit*, an obvious misprint).

Cupid and the Bee

Bernardo Accolti. [*Verginia*, Florence, 1513] In L. De-Mauri, *L'Epigramma Italiano*, Milan, 1918, p. 34.[23]   Luigi Alamanni. [1555] in *Opere*, ed. by Raffaelli, Florence 1859, II, 141.[24]   Fabio Benvoglienti [In *Rime diverse di molti ecc. autori*, Venice, 1547]; Crescimbeni, *Volg. Poes.*, Rome, 1698, p. 76; Carducci. *Poes. Barb.*, Florence, 1881, p. 298: Mentre da dolci favi [Epigram in quantitative verse].   Lodovico Paterno, *Le Nuove Fiamme*, Venice, 1651, f. 39[r]: La bianca man [Strambotto].   Torquato Tasso. [1586] *Rime*, ed. by Solerti, Bologna, 1898, II, 341.[25]   Luigi Groto.

[23]   Da umil verme tra l'erbe remote
         Nella sinistra man fu punto Amore;
         E sentendo il dolor che lo percote
         Pallido, esangue, e perso ogni colore,
         Gridava: Citerea, or come pote
         Ferir breve animal con tal dolore?
         Disse Vener ridendo: Taci ormai;
         E tu che piccol sei, che piaghe fai?

[24]   Furando Amore il mele, un' ape ascosa
         Gli punge il dito irata e venenosa,
         Tal che forte piangente, e pien di duolo,
         In grembo a Citerea sen fugge a volo,
         Mostra il suo mal dicendo: Un animale
         Che così picciol sia fa piaga tale?
         Ella ridendo: E tu che picciol sei
         Che piaghe fai tra gli uomini e gli dei?

The form of this epigram, in distichs, suggests that Alamanni may have followed one of the Latin versions also in distichs. Like Strozzi he omits most of Love's lively reaction; but the extension in his last line, "among men and gods," not in the Greek, I find previously only in Ducher's imitation:

         Si potes ipse tuis contra coelum omnia telis,
         Qui fit ut in minimam sollicitemus apem?

In any case, Alamanni follows "Theocritus," and Raffaelli should not have printed the title "Da Anacreonte" for a poem probably written in 1547. It seems not to have been noticed that four "unedited" lines by Alamanni in Frati's *Rime inedite del cinquecento* (Bologna, 1918), p. 34, are the second half of this epigram.

[25]   Mentre in grembo a la madre Amore un giorno
         Dolcemente dormiva,
         Una zanzara zufolava intorno
         Per quella dolce riva,
         Disse allor, desto a quel susurro, Amore:
         Da sì picciola forma
         Com' esce sì gran voce e tal rumore
         Che sveglia ognun che dorma?
         Con maniere vezzose
         Lusingandogli il sonno col suo canto
         Venere gli rispose:
         E tu picciolo sei,
         Ma pur gli uomini in terra col tuo pianto
         E'n ciel desti gli dèi.

115

Rime [1577], Venice, 1587, p. 149.[26]   Giambattista Guarini. *Rime,* Venice, 1598, p. 94 (Mad. 73).[27]   Giovan Francesco Maia Materdona. *Rime,* Venice, 1629, p. 75: Mentre il garzone alato [Madrigal].   François-Séraphin Regnier Desmarais. [*Le Poesie d'Ana-*

Here the reappearance of the motive "men and gods" suggests, as do some other passages, that Tasso may have had Alamanni's version before him. The substitution of a gnat for the bee involves this madrigal in a whole series of amatory poems concerned with this creature. See Marcel Françon, "Un Motif de la Poésie Amoureuse," in *PMLA* 56 (1941) 307–36.

[26]Groto's madrigal is for the most part only a colorless reproduction of the theme: thus to represent the reaction of Cupid he has only the tame phrase "Sdegnato assai"; but his opening lines are unusual:

> Un tronco, ov' hebber gia le pecchie il nido
> Trovando Amor, cominciò trarne il mele
> Commisto con la cera.

The hollow bee-tree (*tronco*) may be simply a trait from nature, but as Groto is a bookish poet it is worth notice that the engraving for Alciati's Emb. 112 represents the bees as occupying such a *tronco.* On an earlier page (*Rime,* p. 113) Groto has a madrigal made from the epigram of Angeriano mentioned above, in which the bee is happy to die at the hand of the lady.

[27]Again a free handling of the theme:

> Punto da un' ape, a cui
> Rubava il mele il pargoletto Amore,
> Quel rubato licore
> Tutto pien d'ira e di vendetta pose
> Su le labra di rose
> A la mia Donna, e disse: In voi si serbe
> Memoria non mai spenta
> De le soavi mie rapine acerbe;
> E chi vi bacia senta
> De l'ape ch'io provai dolce e crudele
> L'ago nel core, e ne la bocca il mele.

A musical setting for this madrigal is perhaps to be found in *Madrigal a sei voci di Gioseffo Biffi* (Nuremberg, 1600) (cf. E. Vogel, *Bibliothek der gedruckten weltlichen Vocalmusik Italiens* [Berlin, 1892], I, 98: "Punto da un"); but, if so, it seems to have had no currency in this form. Yet it is hard to resist the impression that Guarini's madrigal is somehow behind the following song popular in England in the eighteenth century:

> To heal the wound a bee had made
> Upon my Kitty's face,
> Honey upon her cheek she laid,
> And bade me kiss the place.

> Pleased I obeyed, but from the wound,
> Imbibed both sweet and smart:
> The honey on my lips I found,
> The sting within my heart.

Two settings for this song are printed, and a third from the *Gentleman's Magazine* mentioned, in *English Songs of the Georgian Period,* A. Moffat and F. Kidson, eds. (London: Bayley and Ferguson, n.d.), pp. 194, 290.

creonte, Paris, 1693] *Poesie toscane*, Paris, 1708, p. 148: Ne' prati di Citera.[28]   Francesco de Lemene. *Dio. Sonetti ed inni*, Bologna, 1694, p. 337: Amor crudele [Lyric poem of 63 lines].   Biagio Garofali. *Considerazioni sulla poesia degli ebrei e de' greci* Rome, 1707, II, 73.[29]   Giambattista Pastorini. In Gobbi's *Rime d'alcuni illustri autori viventi*, 3rd ed., Venice, 1727, IV, 344: Stanco di tender l'arco [Sonnet].   Carlo Felici. *Epigrammi tratti dal greco*, Frascati, 1787, p. 95: Mentre vuol dall' alveare.   Gian Carlo Passeroni. *Rime*, Milan, 1789, III, 126: Mentre Amor ruba.   Carolo Roncalli-Parolino. *Epigrammi* [1792], Venice, 1801, p. 43: Mentre stava rubendo. Complete translations of Theocritus by Salvini ;(1717), Regolotti (1729), Della Torre (1775, Vicini (1781), and Pagnini (1786).

Eustorg de Beaulieu. *Les divers rapportz*, Lyons, 1537 f. 49: Ung iour advint.[30]   Michel d'Amboise. *Les cent Epigrammes*, Paris, 1532.[31]   Maurice Scève. *Délie* [1544], ed. by Parturier, Paris, 1916, p. 165 (Dizain 237): Cuydant ma Dame.[32]   Germain Colin

[28]A free imitation of "Theocritus" given in illustration of the Anacreontic. How free may be judged from what becomes of the expression, "he stamped and skipped about":

> E di flebili voci empiendo l'aria,
> I fior colti in mal' ora a terra batte.

Desmarais doubtless followed one of the Latin versions: Love's finger swells, and there is a reference at the end to the gods.

[29]Mentioned by Argelati, *Biblioteca degli volgarizzatori* (Milan, 1767), IV, 30. I have not seen this version.

[30]A professed translation of Melanchthon's Latin version. It is easily accessible in Miss Hélène Harvitt's dissertation, *Eustorg de Beaulieu, a disciple of Marot* (New York, 1918), p. 71. Beaulieu provides a setting: "En ung verger, ou des mouches à miel Avoient leur nidz," and extends the "point": "Veu que toy seul blesses toute nature."

[31]Most of D'Amboise's epigrams have neo-Latin sources, and this one is from Angeriano, as the reader may see by turning back to that writer:

> Ainsi qu'ung iour ma dame et ma maistresse
> Parmi les champs s'en alloit esbatant,
> Sa blanche main une mouche à miel blesse
> De son esquille: elle, le mal sentant,
> Dist: Comment peult si trespetite beste
> Si grant mal faire? Alors ne t'en enqueste,
> Respond Amours: plus beaucoup davantaige
> Ie peux, qui suis court et brief de corsaige,
> Car de mes dars ie rens les pierres molles,
> Et si faits tout selon mon appetit,
> Plus fort tu faitz: car de ton œil petit
> La mer, la terre, et le ciel tu affolles.

[32]As Parturier notes, Scève is dependent on D'Amboise, though he changes the point.

Bucher [d. 1545], *Poésies*, ed. by Denais, Paris, 1890, p. 129.[33]   Jacques Béreau, *Œuvres poétiques* [1565], ed. by Tranchère and Guyet, Paris, 1884, p. 208: Amour un jour [Sonnet].[34] Jean-Antoine de Baïf. *Passetems* [1573] in *Œuvres*, ed. by Marty-Laveaux, Paris, 1887, IV, 238: Le larron Amour,[35] and *Chansonetes* in *ed. cit.*, v, 380:Einski k'Amour.[36]   Jean Godard. *Œuvres poétiques*, Lyons, 1594, p. 189: Ce petit Cupidon [Sonnet].   Claude Garnier. *Amour victorieus*, Paris, 1609, f. 179ʳ: Amour, Amour, si la tendre [Sonnet].   Jean de La Fontaine. [1667] *Œuvres*, ed. by Regnier, Paris, 1892, IX, 407: Rien ne m'eût fait [Madrigal; allusion].   Samuel de Fermat. *Var. Carm.* [as above, Latin], p. 93: Amour déroboit de miel.   Madame Dacier. *Poésies d'Anacréon et de Sapho*, Paris, 1681,

[33]Bucher translates from Strozzi (above). Note, for example, Hymettus, pueriles lermettes, D'où vient, A quoy:

> Quand Cupido, cest enfant impudique,
> Sus Hymettus desroboit les avettes,
> Les desrobant, l'une tres fort le picque,
> Et de douleur luy faict playes aigrettes,
> Tant qu'il espand pueriles lermettes,
> Et se complaint durement à sa mere.
> —D'ou vient, dist il, que telles bestelettes
> Ont l'aguillon de picqueure si fiere?
> A quoy Venus en soubzriante chere
> Respond ainsy: Et toy, mon enfant doulx,
> Qui es petit, fais-tu pas playe amere,
> Blessure à mort, et non sanables coups?

With this last motive cf. Calcagnini above (note 22).

[34]The superscription, "Pris de Theocrite," is right, and the editors are mistaken in correcting it to Anacreon. The version is not literal, but I have not succeeded in detecting an intermediate source.

[35]Though composed in an anacreontic measure, this poem is from "Theocritus." The ending recalls Alamanni:

> Tu sois mingrelet,
> Tu ne vaux pas mieux:
> Voy quelle blessure
> Tu fais qu'on endure
> En terre et aux cieux.

As a whole, however, Baïf's poem, in the succession of motives and in certain phrases, recalls the Latin versions in Soter, and especially that of Melanchthon: cf. "ses tendres doigts" (*digitos tenellos*); "ses doigts s'en enflerent" (*intumuit manus*); "Dépit s'en courrouce, La terre repouce, Et d'un leger saut Il s'élance en haut, Et vole à mère" (*doloris Impatiens plodensque solum pernicibus alis Subvolat ad matrem*); "se prenant à rire" (*Mater ait ridens*: not *subridens*); "Tu ne vaux pas mieux" (*apibus non corpore praestas*).

[36]Augé-Chiquet, *J.-A. de Baïf* (Paris, 1909), p. 389 n, refers this unpublished poem to "Anacreon," but the initial words given by Marty-Laveaux suggest "Theocritus," and the fact that Baïf's earlier version is from this source supports my guess that here also "Theocritus" is the original.

Cupid and the Bee

p. 212: Un jour [prose]. Antoine-Louis Le Brun. *Epigrammes, madrigaux et chansons*, Paris, 1714, p. 225: L'Amour piqué. La Marquise de Simiane. *Porte-feuille de Madame****, Paris, 1715, p. 135: Un jour une jeune avete [imit.] Jean-François Dreux du Radier. *Les Heures de récréation*, Paris, 1740, p. 33: De mêmes yeux jamais [a fable]. Anonymous. In *Bibliothèque universelle des dames*, Paris, IX (1788), 98: Un jour une abeille [prose]. Complete French translations of Theocritus by Longepierre (1688), Chabanon (1775), Gin (1789), Gail (1792), Chateauneuf (1794), and Geoffroy (1800).

Timothy Kendall. *Flowers of Epigrammes: Trifles* [1577] London, 1874, p. 287: Cupido Venus dearling defte.[37] Thomas Watson. ΈΚΑΤΟΜΠΑΘΙΑ [1582] in *Poems*, ed. by Arber, London, 1874, p. 89: Where tender Love.[38] Edmund Spenser. *Amoretti* [1595] in *Poetical Works*, ed. by De Selincourt, London, 1921. p. 577:[39]

> Upon a day as love lay sweetly slumbring,
>   all in his mothers lap,
> A gentle Bee with his loud trumpet murm'ring,
>   about him flew by hap.
> Whereof when he was wakened with the noyse,
>   and saw the beast so small:
> Whats this (quoth he) that gives so great a voyce,
>   that wakens men withall?
> In angry wize he flyes about,
>   and threatens all with corage stout.
>
> To whom his mother closely smiling sayd,
>   twixt earnest and twixt game:
> See thou thy selfe likewise art lyttle made,

[37]"Translated out of Theocritus." Kendall's immediate source eludes me. It must have contained the trait from "Anacreon" which he reproduces:
  The Bee most vile and pestilent *hath kilde* Cupido thyne.
Hence it must be later than 1554 when the *Anacreontea* were first published.

[38]Watson's note is: "The two first partes of this sonnet are in imitation of certaine Greek verses of *Theocritus;* which verses as they are translated by many good Poets of later dayes, so moste aptlye and plainely by C. Ursinus Velius and his Epigrammes," and he quotes the first six lines of Ursinus' translation. The first nine lines of Watson's poem are from this source, the remaining nine, on Love's cure by Aesculapius, are his own invention.

[39]The list of versions, here broken off, is resumed below, following our remarks on Spenser.

119

if thou regard the same.
And yet thou suffrest neyther gods in sky,
    nor men in earth to rest:
But when thou art disposed cruelly,
    theyr sleepe thou doost molest.
Then eyther change thy cruelty,
    or give lyke leave unto the fly.

Nathlesse the cruell boy not so content,
    would needs the fly pursue:
And in his hand with heedlesse hardiment,
    him caught for to subdue.
But when on it he hasty hand did lay,
    the Bee him stung therefore:
Now out alasse (he cryde) and welaway,
    I wounded am full sore:
The fly that I so much did scorne
    hath hurt me with his little horne.

Unto his mother straight he weeping came,
    and of his griefe complayned:
Who could not chose but laugh at his fond game,
    though sad to see him pained.
Think now (quod she) my sonne how great the smart
    of those whom thou dost wound:
Full many hast thou pricked to the hart,
    that pitty never found:
Therefore henceforth some pitty take,
    when thou doest spoyle of lovers make.

She tooke him streight full pitiously lamenting,
    and wrapt him in her smock:
She wrapt him softly, all the while repenting,
    that he the fly did mock.
She drest his wound and it embaulmed wel
    with salve of soveraigne might:
And then she bath'd him in a dainty well
    the well of deare delight.
Who would not oft be stung as this,
    to be so bath'd in Venus blis?

The wanton boy was shortly wel recured,
    of that his malady:
But he soone after fresh againe enured,
    his former cruelty.

Cupid and the Bee

And since that time he wounded hath my selfe
  with his sharpe dart of love:
And now forgets the cruell carelesse elfe,
  his mothers heast to prove.
So now I languish, till he please
  my pining anguish to appease.

This poem with which Spenser ends his *Amoretti* is the most elaborate treatment of the theme that we have encountered. Its method of composition has not, I think, hitherto been understood, nor could it be understood before the sources were clearer than they have been. It seems not to have been observed, in the first place, that stanzas 1–2 are from Tasso's madrigal given above: Love disturbed by the humming of an insect, a gnat in Tasso, but by Spenser changed again into a bee.

Mentre in grembo a la madre Amore un giorno
Dolcemente dormiva.

Upon a day as love lay sweetly slumbring
  all in his mothers lap.

One could not ask for a closer translation. And the rhythm of Spenser's stanza is imitated from his original, from which, therefore, the initial idea of the whole poem arose.[40] Next, with stanza 3 Spenser reverts to the central theme of Cupid and the Bee, making the transition on a fancy that Love pursued and caught the "fly" that had disturbed his slumber, and so was stung. Finally, he adds two stanzas of new invention, containing Love's cure and his forgetting of his mother's admonition. The poem is thus made up of two stanzas from Tasso, two from the original theme of Cupid and the Bee, and two of new development, each part ending with its appropriate "moral."

Since Spenser, as the rhythm shows, took his start from Tasso, it will be difficult to determine the intermediate source of the middle part of his poem, for this is what Tasso's poem made him think of. It lay farther back in his mind, though he may have refreshed his memory by getting down a book. On analysis this part seems to belong more to the Anacreontic than to the Theocritean tradition: there is direct address by Cupid (though not to Venus); the naïve

---

[40]Yet within the translation Love's lively reaction ("in angry wize," etc.) is interpolated directly from Theocritus.

phrase of the Anacreontic, "little winged serpent," is represented by the naïveté,

> The fly that I so much did scorne
> hath hurt me with his little horne;

and finally, the admonition of Venus is rather that of "Anacreon" than that of "Theocritus":

> Think now (quod she) my sonne how great the smart
> of those whom thou dost wound.

Compare the endings of the two Greek poems as translated above. On the other hand, there are traits from "Theocritus," e.g., Venus "could not chose but laugh" and, less certain, the phrase "of his grief complayned" (μέμφετο). If, then, the poem behind Spenser in these two stanzas was a combination of "Anacreon" and "Theocritus," we first think of Ronsard (below), who mainly imitates "Anacreon," but has several points from the other poem. Ronsard's version has been considered by Sir Sidney Lee and by Professor Hughes,[41] wrongly as we see, to have been the original of Spenser's whole poem. No proof is offered save that Hughes says: "His [Lee's] suggestion that Spenser's trick of calling the bee a 'fly' is due to Ronsard's 'mouche à miel' is almost certainly correct." Strange proof—since Ronsard's poem, which Hughes has just quoted in full, nowhere employs the term *mouche à miel*. If that were proof, a better case could be made for Baïf's imitation of "Theocritus." Here we have not merely *mouche à miel* but actually *mouche* alone, and Spenser may have turned to Baïf, though I see no certainty of this. Compare however,

> Unto his mother straight he weeping came
> and of his grief complayned—

> Et vole à sa mère,
> L'orine Cytère,
> Avec triste pleur
> Montrer sa douleur,
> Et faire sa plainte.

[41]Merrit Y. Hughes, "Spenser and the Greek Pastoral Triad," *Studies in Philology* 20 (1923) 196–99.

Cupid and the Bee

In Ronsard Venus smiles ("se sourit"), in Baïf she begins to laugh ("se prenant à rire"), and in Spenser "could not chose but laugh." Nevertheless, these points are far from decisive, and the possibility remains that Spenser used Ronsard for this part. Note, for example, that in Ronsard as in Spenser Cupid's direct address on being stung is soliloquy and not spoken as in the Anacreontic to Venus.

The last two stanzas are Spenser's own development. The first of them, on Cupid's cure, is an exercise in amplification, and could have been suggested by Ronsard who has two lines on this subject; but, if any outside influence is felt here, it is that of Watson, who alone before Spenser elaborates this motive, giving it the second half of his poem. Watson's personal conclusion is also somewhat similar to Spenser's: the herbs that cured Love took force from the god, and

> By haplesse hap did breede my heartes decay:
> For there they fell, where long my hart had li'ne
> To wait for Love, and what he should assigne.

Compare:

> So now I languish, till he please
> my pining anguish to appease.

If, besides Tasso, Ronsard and Watson also are behind Spenser's poem, and if one contemplates the Renaissance versions behind them again, and so back to "Anacreon" and "Theocritus," one may well wonder at the amount of human wit, not forgetting Spenser's own, that has gone into the molding of this singular trifle.[42]

Just preceding this poem in the *Amoretti*, there is an epigram, *In youth before*, also employing the theme of love and the bee.

---

[42]The discovery that Spenser used Tasso for this poem might have been made by Francesco Viglione, if he had taken his own hint. See his recent book, *La Poesia lirica di Edmondo Spenser* (Genoa, 1937), p. 298. He believes that Spenser went directly to the Greek of "Anacreon," and having said so, throws out a suggestion nearer the truth than he knew: "Se poi doveva essere spinto da imitatori, egli aveva, più del Ronsard, familiare il Tasso, che fu dei primi a scrivere odicine sulle orme del lirico di Ceo" (*leg.* Teo). I note this "near miss" because it brings out the relative sureness of our method of collecting for inspection a large number of versions of a given theme.

William Drummond. *Poetical Works*, ed. by Kastner, II, 236: In-genious was that Bee.[43]   Thomas Creech. *The Idylliums of Theoc-ritus* [1681], Oxford 1784, p. 104: When wanton Love. Anonymous. In Dryden's *Miscellany*, London [1684–85], 1716, II, 230.[44]   Anonymous. In Mrs. Aphra Behn's *Miscellany*, London, 1685.[45]   John Elsum. *A Description of the Celebrated Pieces of Paintings*, etc., London, 1704, p. 106: The piece is live-ly. William Pattison. *Poetical Works* London, 1728, I, 83.[46]   Anonymous. In *Gentleman's Magazine*, 1733, p. 658: Cupid the errant'st knave alive.[47]   John Addison. *The Works of Anacreon*, London, 1735, p. 143: As Cupid robb'd.[48]   Anony-mous. In *The London Magazine*, 1741, p. 461: Cupid the sliest rogue alive[49]   James Scott, *Odes on Several Subjects*, London, 1761: Part of that honey.[50]   Francis Fawkes. *The Idylliums of Theocri-tus*, London, 1767: As Cupid the Slyest young wanton alive. Richard Polwhele. *The Idyllia*, etc., Exeter, 1786, p. 147: As Cupid once, the errant'st rogue alive.[51]   Anonymous. In *The*

---

[43]This madrigal is here noted only because Kastner regards it as condensed from Guarini's madrigal given above. I cannot see that it is related to Guarini's poem.

[44]Mentioned by Fritzsche, p. 103, and by Kerlin, p. 45; not seen by me.

[45]Not seen by me; mentioned by Kerlin, p. 46.

[46]Mentioned by Fritzsche and Kerlin. I have not seen this translation.

[47]This imitator has brought out a point, elsewhere, so far as I know, only made by Micyllus:

A bee enrag'd the thief to brand
Fix'd his keen sting upon his hand.

Micyllus: *signat cuspide furem.* The parallel seems to be only coincidence.

[48]In his comment on the Anacreontic. Addison's *Anacreon* is dependent on Madame Dacier's edition.

[49]Save for small textual differences, this anonymous poem, here referred to "Theocritus XIX," had figured in the same periodical for 1737 (p. 697) as an Imita-tion of Anacreon. It is, however, mainly from the Theocritean version, as witness,

He kick'd, he flung, he spurn'd the ground,
He blow'd and then he chafed the wound.

There may be an element of "Anacreon" in,

A little bird they call a bee;

but cf. Micyllus:

Vulnus, ait, faciat tam saevum parva volucris.

With the first line given above compare the first line of the anonymous version in *The Gentleman's Magazine* for 1733, quoted just before. The resemblance, however, goes no further, and the present translation is the better poem.

[50]Paraphrase in an ode *On Pleasure*, quoted in part by Kerlin, p. 72. Scott refers to Theoc. XIX. Not seen by me.

[51]Cf. the beginning of anon. in *Gent. Mag.* (1733), above, and also anon. in *Lond. Mag.* (1737, 1741), and Fawkes. The line coined by the anonymous imitator in 1733 seems to have rung in the ears of the eighteenth century; for surely this is not the only way of securing a rhyme for "hive."

Cupid and the Bee

Gentleman's Magazine, 1791, p. 1144: As Cupid once, a roguish boy. Edward Dubois. *The Wreath,* London, 1799, p. 20: A wicked bee [prose].

"Anacreon" 40 (35)

No attempt is here made to list the complete translations of the *Anacreontea,* though of course they always include this poem; a few, however, that seemed noteworthy have been mentioned.[52]

Henri Estienne. *Anacreontis Teij Odae,* Paris, 1554: Inter rosas Cupido. Elie André. *Anacreontis et aliorum lyricorum ... Odae* Paris, 1556: Apem rosas Cupido. Jean Morisot. *Liber Amatorius,* Lyons, 1558, p. 39: Dum legit pulchram [4 sapphic stanzas]. Flaminius Raius. [*ca.* 1560] In *Carmina Illustrium Poetarum Italorum,* Florence, 1719–26, VIII, 53: Inter purpureas rosas.[53] Joshua Barnes. *Anacreon Teius* [Cambridge, 1705], London 1734, p. 121: Cupido aliquando [prose].[54] Michael Maittaire. *Anacreontis editio altera,* London 1740 [first ed., 1725], pp. 91–4.[55] Noël Sanadon. *Carmina,* Paris, 1754, p. 80: Dum per vireta Cypri.

Carlos Maria Maggi. [*Rime,* Milan, 1668] in Sallengre, *Novus Thesaurus Antiquitatum,* Venice, 1735, III, 702: Punto d'ape [Sonnet]. Regnier Desmarais. [1693, as above] *Poesie toscane,* Paris, 1708, p. 147: Amor fiori un di. Antonio Conti. *Prose e poesie,* Venice, 1739, I, 269: Tra le rose Amor. Giambattista Mutinelli. In *Anno poetico ossia raccolta annuale,* Venice, 1793, I, 159: Di picciol' ape.

[52]Reference may be made to the bibliography in J. B. Gail's *Odes d'Anacréon* (Paris, 1799); pp. 197–202; to A. Delboulle, *Anacréon et les poèmes anacréontiques avec les traductions et imitations des poètes du xvie siècle* (Havre, 1891); to L. A. Michelangeli, *Anacreonte e la sua fortuna nei secoli, con una rassegna critica su gl'imitatori e i traduttori italiani delle anacreontee* (Bologna, 1922); and to Báraibar, Menéndez y Palayo, and others, *Poetas Liricos Griegos,* "Bibl. Class." (Madrid, 1898).
[53]Influenced by Estienne's version. Raius was a pupil of Pier Vettori to whom Estienne had communicated the *Anacreontea* soon after their discovery.
[54]To Barnes this ode is "omnium prima."
[55]Ten poems on this theme, in Greek and Latin, and in various metres: "Graeca et Latina aliquot variationis specimina, quae styli exercendi gratia Anonymus quidam in lepidissimam hanc fabellam lusit." These versions all frankly employ motives from "Theocritus" as well as from "Anacreon." Maittaire also quotes the Theocritean poem, with Estienne's translation. He gives two direct translations of the Anacreontic.

Pierre de Ronsard. [*Les Odes*, Paris, 1555] In *Œuvres complètes*, ed. by Laumonier, VII (Paris, 1934), 106: Le petit enfant Amour.[56]   Remy Belleau. [*Odes d'Anacréon*, Paris, 1556] In *Œuvres complètes*, ed. by Gouverneur, Paris, 1867, I, 43: Amour ne voyoit.[57]   Olivier de Magny. *Odes* [1559], ed. by Courbet, Paris, 1876, II, 139: Amour, Bizet, en pleurant.[58]   Jean Doublet.

[56]Laumonier, *Ronsard poète lyrique* (Paris, 1909), pp. 603–605, has successfully shown that this poem is a contamination of "Anacreon" and "Theocritus," together with some motives of Ronsard's invention. It may be possible to go further. For the Anacreontic Ronsard would naturally turn to Estienne's edition and translation just published. For the Theocritean poem he probably also employed one of the Latin versions. If so, he used one containing the mistranslation, "his hand swelled," for he has this motive; but my notes do not enable me to govern all the possibilities. Melanchthon's version has this point, and also *digitos tenellos* (Ronsard, "sa main tendrette"). I note also that Ducher's translation begins:

Furaturus lascivus mella Cupido
Inde, ubi parva casas aedificaret apis.

Compare:

Le petit enfant Amour
Cueilloit des fleurs, à l'entour
D'une ruche, où les avettes
Font leurs petites logettes.

I have at hand only these two lines of Ducher's version.

[57]Belleau followed the Greek, but helped himself somewhat by Estienne's Latin translation, and had, I think, Ronsard's version beside him. That he followed the Greek is shown at several points where he is slightly more faithful than Estienne, e.g., "Venus la belle" (καλὴν κυθήρην: Estienne, *candidam Cytheren*). That he looked at Estienne is clear from "Le mignon commence à se plaindre," where the Greek is ὠλόλυξε, and Estienne renders: *eiulare coepit* (Elie André, simply *eiulavit*). That he recalled Ronsard is suggested by motives occurring in Ronsard but not in "Anacreon" or his translators, e.g., the swollen hand:

Belleau: Voyant enfler sa blanche main.
Ronsard: Voyés quelle enflure.

Again:

Belleau: Voyez donc ma plaie cruelle.
Ronsard: Lui montra sa plaie amere.
Belleau: Entre les replis de la rose.
Ronsard: Dans le fond d'une fleurette.

This last is scarcely the natural translation of ἐν ῥόδοισι, for which Estienne has *Inter rosas*. André indeed has *Apem rosae insidentem*, but his version probably was not available to Ronsard. (See also Belleau's free imitation, *De la blessure d'Amour* in *Œuvres, ed. cit.* I, 149–51)

[58]An ode in eight eight-line stanzas, treating the theme freely, but proved to be from "Anacreon" (perhaps through Ronsard) by lines 9–13:

C'est cet oiselet . . .
Que le villageois appelle
Ce me semble mouche à miel.

Cf. Ronsard: "Les villageois . . . Le surnomment une avette." Perhaps by coincidence this version shows the extension, "men and gods," that we have found first in the imitations of "Theocritus" by Ducher and Alamanni, and this point becomes the chief motive of Magny's ode, being elaborated in the last five stanzas.

Cupid and the Bee

Elégies [1559], Paris, 1871, p. 122: Ce leger enfant.[59]   Jean
Godard. *Œuvres*, Lyons, 1594, p. 98: Amour un jour.[60]   Jean
Baudoin. *Recueil d'emblèmes divers*, Paris, 1638, pp. 19–34: Ce
folastre enfant.[61]   Claude Nicole. *Les Œuvres de Monsieur le Prés-
ident Nicole*, Paris, 1663, pp. 50–2: Amour couché sur des
roses.[62]   F.-S. Regnier Desmarais [1693] *Poésies françoises*, The
Hague, 1716, II, 387: Le tendre Amour cueillant.[63]   François
Gacon. *Anacréon*, Rotterdam, 1712, p. 254: L'Amour.
piqué.[64]   François-Charles Pannard. *Théâtre et œuvres diverses*,
Paris, 1763, IV, 19: Les bonbons et la friandise.   Julien-Jacques
Moutonnet-Clairfons. *Anacréon, Sapho, Bion et Moschus*, Paphos
[Paris], 1780, I, 56: L'Amour piqué [prose].   Mlle de Louven-
court. In *Bibliothèque universelle des dames: Mélanges* VIII (1787) 160–
162. Dans les jardins enchantés.[65]

Edmund Spenser.[66]   Thomas Lodge. In *England's Helicon*,
London, 1600, ed. by Rollins, Cambridge, Mass., 1935, I, 31: In
pride of youth.[67]   Thomas Bateson. [*Second Set of Madrigals,*

[59]A fairly close translation, but influenced by Ronsard: e.g., "Cueillant des roses,"
cf. Ronsard, "Cueilloit des fleurs" (not in "Anacreon"); "Venus souriant," cf. Ronsard, "Venus se sourit." The latter point Ronsard had from "Theocritus." Doublet's
line "Au bout d'un doit de la main" recalls "Theocritus," but is not represented by
Ronsard.
[60]A *chanson*, much indebted to Ronsard:
          Amour un iour ne vit point
          Une avette qui luy poingt
          Bien avant sa main tendrette
          En cueillant une fleurette.
Ronsard: "avette . . . sa main tendrette . . . cueillant . . . fleurette."
[61]A prose-emblem. The motto of this, the second, *Discours* is: "Que les choses
douces deviennent souvent amères," taken evidently from Alciati, Emb. 112.
Though the idea of making an emblem of this theme obviously came to Baudoin
from Alciati, he follows "Anacreon," whereas Alciati employed "Theocritus." The
Discours is preceded by a full-page engraving by Briot of Cupid and the Bee.
[62]A professed imitation of Anacreon, in seven stanzas. Note that Love is lying
(asleep) on the roses, a new motive in French imitations, but compare Bateson
below.
[63]Quoted, but wrongly ascribed to Mathurin Regnier, by Bullen, *Anacreon* (London, 1893), p. 220.
[64]This version is reprinted by Le Fort de La Morinière, *Bibliothèque poétique* (Paris,
1745), III, 498 (ascribed to G**.), and by Bruzen de La Martinière, *Passetemps
poétique* (Paris, 1757), II, 62 (anonymous).
[65]To judge from the opening lines, for I have not a complete copy, this looks like
an imitation of Regnier's or Sanadon's version of the theme.
[66]See above, under "Theocritus."
[67]Entitled *The Barginet* [pastoral] *of Antimachus*. This very free treatment of the
theme has been regularly claimed for "Theocritus," e.g., by Kerlin (p. 25) and by

1618] In *The English Madrigal School,* ed. by E. H. Fellowes, XXII (London, 1922), p. xi: Cupid in a bed of roses.[68]   Robert Herrick. *Hesperides* [1648] in *Poetical Works,* ed. by Moorman, London, 1921, p. 50: "the Wounded Cupid: Song."[69]   Thomas Stanley.

Rollins (II, 94); but on examination it turns irresistibly to the other tradition. The thread may be picked out thus: "Oft from her lap.... He leapt, and gathered sommer flowers, both violets and roses.... A bee that harbour'd hard thereby, Did sting his hand, and made him crye, Oh Mother, I am wounded.... the goddesse sayd, Who hath my Cupid so dismayd? He aunswered: Gentle Mother, The honyworker in the hive." Here Cupid gathers flowers (roses), not honey as in "Theocritus," and the direct address, "Oh Mother, I am wounded," is clearly from the Anacreontic. Further, the act of gathering flowers recalls Ronsard ("Cueilloit des fleurs"); and still other points suggest Ronsard as Lodge's source: as in Ronsard, Venus asks who wounded him ("Qui t'a, di moi, faus garson, Blessé de telle façon?"—"My little lad, the goddesse said, Who hath my Cupid so dismayd?"); she kisses him ("En le baisant le prit"—"She kist the lad"); she cures him ("Puis sa main lui a soufflée Pour guarir sa plaie enflée."—"She suckt the wound, and swag'd the sting"). None of these points is in either of the Greek originals. Lodge has developed an elaborate setting of his own, and at the end has made a new application of the fable.

[68]This excellent version seems to have been made directly from the Greek. It has, however, a peculiarity not found in earlier versions: "Cupid, in a bed of roses, sleeping," whereas in the original it is the bee that is sleeping among the roses. Cupid sleeping may be a reminiscence of Spenser, or of Watson's imitation of "Theocritus" which begins: "Where tender Love had laide him down to sleepe," but more likely it is a wilful variant. See below. The French had been able to sing Belleau's version to the music of Richard Renvoysy since 1559, and had had to wait until the end of the eighteenth century for Gossec's new musical setting for the translation by Gail (I know of no evidence that either of these was popular). Bateson's charming air deserves to have been popular, but whether it continued in favor until the eighteenth century began to sing John Addison's translation is doubtful.

[69]   Cupid, as he lay among
Roses, by a Bee was stung.
Whereupon in anger flying
To his Mother, said thus crying:
Help! O help! your Boy's a dying.
And why, my pretty Lad, said she?
Then blubbering, replyed he,
A winged Snake has bitten me,
Which Country people call a Bee.
At which she smil'd: then with her hairs
And kisses drying up his tears:
Alas! said she, my Wag! if this
Such a pernicious torment is,
Come tel me then, how great's the smart
Of those, thou woundest with they Dart.

Herrick's version seems to have been made from the Greek, but probably with Estienne's or André's Latin beside it (cf. André, *momordit:* "has bitten me"). The two Latin versions are both printed in the Plantin Lyric Poets, *Pindari Olympia,* etc.

Cupid and the Bee

[1649] In *Anacreon, with Thomas Stanley's Translation,* ed. by Bullen, London, 1893, p. 103.[70]   Anonymous. In *The Works of Anacreon and Sappho done from the Greek by several Hands,* London, 1713, p. 41.[71]   John Addison [1735, as above].   [Anon. In *The London Magazine,* 1737: see above, under "Theocritus"].   Francis Fawkes. [*Idylliums of Theocritus,* 1767] In Chalmers' *English Poets* xx, 217.[72]

We have here the familiar, but intricate, history of any Greek theme in modern literature. The Theocritean poem, first translated and imitated by the neo-Latin poets, is from them caught up by the poets of the several vernaculars. The tradition, in this instance, is complicated by the appearance in 1554 of a second Greek version, and we find contamination of the two. The early Latin translations of "Theocritus," though numerous, often have enough individuality to enable us to detect which of them a vernacular poet

---

(Antwerp, 1567). But the case for the intervening Latin is not here so plain as in Herrick's *The Cheat of Cupid* which Delattre has shown to be dependent on Estienne: Floris Delattre: *Robert Herrick* (Paris, 1912), p. 405. The first two lines are very likely a reminiscence of Bateson's song, while other departures from the original, in lines 6 and 10-11, are probably due to Herrick himself (but cf. Ronsard and Lodge). See the next note.

[70]
      Love, a Bee that lurk'd among
      Roses saw not, and was stung:
      Who for his hurt finger crying,
      Running sometimes, sometimes flying,
      Doth to his fair mother hie,
      And O help, cries he, I die;
      A wing'd snake hath bitten me,
      Call'd by countrymen a Bee:
      At which Venus, If such smart
      A Bee's little sting impart,
      How much greater is the pain,
      They, whom thou hast hurt, sustain?

Stanley has taken Herrick's poem of the year before, and corrected it to the Greek text, also regularizing the trochaic metre. It is very successfully done. Note that he retains the charming glide between verses one and two. In the Notes to his *Anacreon* (ed. of 1651, p. 106) Stanley alludes to Pignoria's report of a painting on the subject, and quotes Sabinus' verses.

[71]The tradition has now become fixed among the English, despite Stanley, that Cupid, not the bee, lay among the roses:

      As Cupid once with wanton play,
      Amidst the Rose-trees sporting lay, etc.

[72]
      Once as Cupid tir'd with play,
      On a bed of roses lay, etc.

followed.[73] Chief points in the tradition seem to be the free imitation by Angeriano, giving rise to the verses of D'Amboise and Scève; the German Latin versions included in Soter's widely known book; Alciati's Emblem with a strong influence of its own; the contaminated version of Ronsard which left its mark on his followers; and the free imitation of Tasso giving rise to the elaborate poem of Spenser. It is noteworthy that no French version seems traceable to an Italian intermediary. The earlier English imitators as usual are dependent on continental predecessors, but at the same time they show a determination to remake the theme in a degree hardly paralleled abroad. After the sixteenth century less interest attaches to the comparison of versions since the trade on foreign intermediaries dwindled, and that on neo-Latin intermediaries mostly came to an end. In the seventeenth and eighteenth centuries we find plenty of translations, but few attempts to work the theme off more or less as original composition. The convention regarding these things had wholly changed. For editors of the sixteenth-century poets, however, the rule stands: Never believe that your poet has gone directly to the original for any Greek theme; even if he says quite plainly "translated from the Greek," it very likely means only that his modern original was headed "E graeco," "Dal greco," or "Pris du grec."[74]

The "tabella picta" (p. 112 above) was presumably one of the paintings by Lucas Cranach. A version which hangs in the Villa Borghese in Rome correctly gives Sabinus' verses (see Charles W. Talbot, Jr., "An Interpretation of Two Paintings by Cranach in the Artist's Late Style," in *The National Gallery of Art, Report and Studies in the History of Art*, [Washington, D.C., 1967] pp. 67–88. Talbot

[73]Here once more the reader must be reminded of the shortcomings of my notes. It might repay someone to look again at the versions by Gazoldus, Ducher, Gouvéa, Rapitius, anon. in Taygetus, Capilupi, De Lemene, and Garnier, of which I have kept no copies, and also at those I note as not seen by me, though these are mostly late.

[74]The list of poems on Cupid and the Bee drawn up in the preceding pages no doubt could be indefinitely extended. Two further instances have recently come to my notice, too late for inclusion in the series. One, a sonnet by Amadis Jamyn (*Œuvres poétiques* [Paris, 1584], f. 35ʳ), having for its main subject a scratch received by the lady on her hand, employs the Greek theme as introduction, compressed into the first quatrain:

Amour fut autrefois picqué dedans la main
Par une mouche à miel volant à l'avanture.
Mais sa mère luy dist riant de sa pointure:
Ton trait blessant les cœurs est bien plus inhumain.

Cupid and the Bee

notes (p. 81) that Cranach's paintings were often accompanied by inscriptions). The theme of Venus and the Honey-Thief seems to have been a popular one among painters in Germany in the first half of the sixteenth century, treated by Dürer, the Cranachs, Hans Brosamer, Peter Flötner, and others (see Dieter Koepplin and Tilman Falk, *Lukas Cranach, Gemälde, Zeichnungen, Druckgraphik*, Vol. 2, Zur Ausstellung im Kunstmuseum Basel (1974) pp. 655–58). I am greatly indebted to Dr. George Szabo, Curator of the Robert Lehman Collection, The Metropolitan Museum of Art, for this information, as well as for permission to reproduce the Collection's own handsome Cranach. The reader will note that in the Lehman painting Cranach has misquoted three words of Sabinus' verse.

The *Honey-Thief* also figured prominently in the woodcut illustrations of emblem books, beginning with Alciati and continuing through the seventeenth century (see Mario Praz, *Studies in Seventeenth Century Imagery*, [London: The Warburg Institute, 1939–47]).

Finally, our theme appears at least once in sculpture. I owe to Jane Dieckmann notice of a marble statue of the "Honigschlecker" by Joseph Anton Feuchtmayer (1696–1770) in the Wallfahrtskirche at Neubirnau on the Bodensee.

Despite the compression, there remains one mark (*riant*) to show that Jamyn follows "Theocritus." Somewhat earlier, Claude Binet had turned out a *jeu d'esprit* on this theme as a contribution to *La Puce de Mlle des Roches* (1582) (*La Jeunesse d'Estienne Pasquier* [Paris, 1610], p. 622): Amour, flame in hand, approaches the lady, but is driven off and wounded by the *puce,* so that he runs to his mother—and the rest follows the original save for changes occasioned by the substitution of flea for bee, thus:

> C'est, dict-il, c'est un Serpenteau
> Qui va sautellant sur la peau,
> Puce est nommé par les Pucelles.

Clearly Binet's version is from "Anacreon." But it is also affected by the modern tradition so far as to show the extension "men and gods" (cf. Notes 24, 25, 28 , 35, 58 above):

> aux grans dieux
> Et aux humains dardant tes feux,
> Tu fais une plaie incurable.

Finally, for the iconography (cf. Notes 7, 16, 61 above) add a painting with this subject by Bon Boullongne (1649–1717) reported to be in the museum of Angers: see Denais' edition of Colin Bucher, p. 71n.

131

"That Most Justly Celebrated
of Modern Epigrams"

"Il est si rare de faire d'admirables Epigrammes, que c'est assez
d'en avoir fait une en sa vie." The observation is that of the
seventeenth-century critic René Rapin as reported by his contemporary Gilles Ménage.[1] In their time, when the epigram flourished
as a literary form, the point would seem worth making and would
easily be accepted. Today we do not have the same confidence in
epigrams. Nevertheless the critic's words are true. At least they
seem to be borne out by the remarkable fortune of a single epigram
written in the sixteenth century by the Latin poet Girolamo Amalteo. While Amalteo's other poems were not much read, and his
very name often forgotten, his one epigram on a beautiful one-
eyed boy and a beautiful one-eyed girl continued to be admired
almost universally for three centuries and more, sustained by a
literary sensibility that we have lost or outgrown:

> Lumine Acon dextro, capta est Leonilla sinistro,
> Et potis est forma vincere uterque deos.
> Blande puer, lumen quod habes concede puellae:
> Sic tu caecus Amor, sic erit illa Venus.

For today's reader the banality of Venus and Cupid perhaps is
hardly redeemed by the novelty of the theme, the wit (seasoned
with the absurd), the economy and precision of the language, and
the well-nigh perfect embodiment of epigram form. Yet with these
merits to recommend it the epigram continued to give pleasure
well into the nineteenth century. Henry Hallam, in his survey of
European literature (1837), quotes Amalteo's "famous lines,"

---

[1] *Menagiana* (1715 edition) 1.208.

though he doubts if this is necessary, since "most," he says, "know the lines by heart."[2]

Girolamo Amalteo belonged to the second generation of a literary family of Oderzo. The elder generation—three brothers, Paolo (c. 1450–1517), Marc-Antonio (1475–1558), and Francesco (married in 1503)—were all Latin poets of distinction; but their fame in this art was surpassed by the younger generation, also three brothers, sons of Francesco: Girolamo (1507–74), Giovanni Battista (1525–75), and Cornelio (c. 1530–1605). Girolamo was a physician. In 1532 he was appointed to lecture on Avicenna at Padua, where he had recently attained the doctorate, and in 1533 he became professor of moral philosophy. After a brief retirement at Oderzo, he took up the practice of medicine at Ceneda (1536–39), and later at Sarravalla, where he remained until 1558, having declined in 1542 the post of physician to the queen of Poland. He retired in 1558 to his native place, and died there on October 21, 1574.[3]

In noticing the poet's death De Thou alludes to a letter written by Antoine de Muret at Treviso to Denys Lambin, who was with the Cardinal de Tournon at Conegliano, for the purpose of introducing Amalteo to him. The letter is dated November 28, 1558.[4] "Since I have heard," he writes, "from him [Pagano, his host] that Girolamo Amalteo is to pass through here tomorrow on his way home, and as his plans call for a visit to Conegliano, I thought an opportunity had come my way of doing a favor to you all, and chiefly to the most renowned Cardinal. This is that Amalteo who, I have assured you, and more and more assure you, is the most eminent of all Italian poets now living, at least of all I am acquainted with. . . . And unless I am much mistaken, the Cardinal will himself take great pleasure in his conversation. In order to facilitate the matter, therefore, I have written this letter which will be given to Amalteo to bring with him." As evidence of the poet's contemporary reputation a letter of this kind must obviously be taken with reservations, but there can be no doubt that his fame was considerable.

While Amalteo's authorship of the epigram has not been seriously questioned, it is well to see on what grounds it is to be acknowledged as his, since for all his fame as a poet he did not

---

[2] *Introduction to the Literature of Europe* (London, 1843), 2.145 n.
[3] J. A. de Thou, *Hist.* 59.22; Niceron, *Mém.* 31.165.
[4] Muret, *Epistolae* (Leipzig [Tauchnitz, ed.], 1838), p. 374.

himself publish his poems. These were first collected in Giammateo Toscano's *Carmina Illustrium Poetarum Italorum* (Paris, 1576) and adequately published only in *Trium Fratrum Amaltheorum Carmina* (Venice, 1627), a volume edited by the younger Girolamo Aleandro. The epigram on Acon and Leonilla is included in both collections. It had, however, been printed before 1576. I find it first in 1563 when it appeared simultaneously at Milan in G. P. Ubaldini's *Carmina Poetarum Nobilium* (f. 29ᵛ) and at Venice in the *Opera* (p. 79 of *Epigram.*) of Publio Francesco Spinula. It may have been composed about that time, though one would have expected it to belong to an earlier period of the poet's life. Ubaldini ascribes it to Basilio Zanchi of Bergamo, but this ascription can hardly withstand the tradition that gives it to Amalteo;[5] Spinula entitles it, *De duobus geminis, Amalthei.* And finally, Amalteo has other epigrams employing the same theme, notably the following, entitled De Acone et Leonilla:[6]

> Ut fugeret fervorem aestu sub sidere cancri
> Nudus in algenti flumine natat Acon,
> Qui simul ac alto Leonillam in lettore vidit,
> Ah! miser in gelidis ferbuit ustus aquis.

The text of the first epigram printed above is that of Spinula and of the *Amaltheorum Carmina.* An early variant reading is *sorori* for *puellae* in line 3, and this is read by many of those who quote the epigram in France, as is natural since it is read by Toscano whose book first gave the epigram currency in that country.[7] The same conception had been expressed in Spinula's title; but it is plain from Amalteo's other epigram that he contemplates no blood-relationship between Acon and Leonilla. A second, but more recent, variation is *parenti,* evidently intended to press the parallel with Venus and Cupid. Italian writers have mostly preferred this form.[8] Other variants are *poterat* for *potis est,* and *parve puer* for *blande puer,* but these doubtless arise out of quotation from memory.

---

[5] It does not appear in Zanchi's *Poematum libri viii* (Rome, 1550).

[6] *Tr. Frat. Amal.,* p. 54; the first epigram precedes, on p. 52. In Toscano's *Carmina* (p. 17) the two epigrams appear together.

[7] Toscano's text was reprinted by Bottari, *Carmina Illustrium Poetarum Italorum* (Florence, 1719-26), 1.143.

[8] Following Crescimbeni, *Volgar Poesia* (Venice, 1731), 1.397, who cites as authority Emmanuele Tesauro, *Il Cannocchiale Aristotelico* (Turin, 1670), p. 408. Tesauro quotes only the last two lines.

The names Acon and Leonilla are obviously fictitious, and there is nothing to indicate what may have been the origin of these lines. A physician, Amalteo would be alive to physical peculiarities. It is worth noticing also that, if the epigram was written about 1550–60, such a subject as it embodies would easily suggest itself to an epigrammatist, since quite recently Italian poets had loosed a flood of epigrams and sonnets on the temporary blindness of Livia Colonna. In respect to her an allusion to Venus was obligatory, and one admirer, Francesco Franchini, a well-known poet, had written:[9]

> Ante alias forma pulcherrima Livia Nymphas,
>   Ipsa est in terris insidiosa Venus;
> Quod sit capta oculis, caveat sibi quisque: Cupido
>   Caecus erat tantum, nunc quoque caeca Venus.

It is easy to think that, whether or not Amalteo actually remembered this trifle of Franchini, his own is somehow linked with the epigrams on Livia Colonna.

To turn to the words of Joseph Warton that serve as title for this paper, whether justly or not, celebrated these Latin verses assuredly have been, probably beyond any other modern epigram. Their reputation seems to have begun in France following their publication at Paris in Toscano's collection. Hallam, indeed, in commenting on them in the first edition of his *Introduction to the Literature of Europe,* took them to be an abbreviated form of the following epigram by Jean Passerat, but he reversed this judgment in his second edition[10] on discovering that they had been printed by Toscano in 1576, whereas Passerat's verses only appeared in 1597. Passerat wrote:[11]

> Caetera formosi, dextro est orbatus ocello
>   Frater, et est laevo lumine capta soror.
> Frontibus adversis ambo si iungitis ora,
>   Bina quidem facies, vultus et unus erit.
> Sed tu, Carle, tuum lumen transmitte sorori,
>   Continuo ut vestrum fiat uterque deus:
> Plena haec fulgebit fraterna luce Diana,
>   Huius frater eris tu quoque caecus Amor.

[9]*Poemata* (Rome, 1554), p. 110.
[10]Hallam, *loc. cit.*
[11]In Janus Gruter, ed., *Delitiae C Poetarum Gallorum* (Frankfort, 1609), 3.141.

135

The neo-Latin poets seldom paraphrase one another, and when they do so, the second version is unlikely to be twice the length of the first. Such lengthening is rather a characteristic of vernacular imitations of Latin epigrams. For this and other reasons, there can be little doubt that Passerat's eight lines are a Latin translation of the French version of Amalteo made by Remy Belleau:[12]

> Carle est borgne d'un œil, sa soeur Isabeau
> Borgne d'un œil aussi, la plus belle brunette:
> Et luy, hors ce defaut, de beauté si parfaite
> Que rien ne se peut voir en ce monde plus beau.
> Carle, donne cet œil qui te reste à ta soeur
> Pour rendre à son beau front une grace immortelle:
> Ainsi vous serez Dieux—elle Venus la belle,
> Toy, ce Dieu qui sans yeux tire si droit au cœur.

Belleau's version was published in his *Œuvres* of 1578. Passerat in his last couplet has substituted a point of his own. He also knew the original epigram of Amalteo, however, since with it he specifies which eye was lost by each, a point passed over by Belleau.[13]

In the time of Belleau and Passerat, translations of Amalteo's epigram were published by Pierre Tamisier (1589),[14] Guillaume Bernard (1601),[15] Vauquelin de la Fresnaye who has two versions (1605),[16] and Etienne Pasquier (1610).[17] A little later we find the

---

[12]*Œuvres complètes*, Gouverneur, ed. (Paris, 1867), 1.221.

[13]This inference probably is correct, but another point should be mentioned. Rita Guerlac has brought to my attention the interesting fact that Passerat himself was a *borgne*, having lost an eye in his youth playing tennis. That this was his right eye is proved by his portrait in profile (*aet.* 64) reproduced by Gruter (see n. 11 above), which shows the left side of his face and conceals the right side.

[14]*Anthologie ou recueil des plus beaux épigrammes grecs . . . mis en vers françois sur la version de plusieurs doctes personnages* (Lyons, 1589), p. 159. Since Tamisier includes this piece in his volume of translations from the Greek Anthology, he evidently thought it came from that source, an error repeated by many after him.

[15]In Bonfons's *Fleurs des plus excellents poètes*, 3d ed. (Paris, 1601), f.82 ʳ, and signed "M.G.B.S." For the identification of these initials, see Fr. Lachèvre, *Bibliographie des recueils collectifs* 4 (Paris, 1905), 59. Bernard seems already to have read *parenti*, or else to have yielded to the impulse to fit the case more closely to Venus and Cupid—*Imitation d'Amaltheus:*

> Iulles a perdu l'œil droit, et le gauche sa mere.
> Mere et fils qui pouvoient vaincre en beauté les Dieux:
> Preste ton œil, mignon, a la belle Sidère,
> Elle sera Cyprine et toy l'Amour sans yeux.

[16]*Poésies*, Travers, ed. (Caen, 1869), 2.641. Vauquelin has *bel enfant* and *sœur*.

[17]*Œuvres* (Amsterdam, 1723), 2.938: *ex Hieronimo Amaltheo:*

> Acon a perdu son œil dextre,

epigram in Mlle de Gournay's *Egalité des hommes et des femmes* (Paris, 1622), printed "in order to fill out a page" (p. 28); the Latin ("autheur incertain") is followed by two French versions. Although *sorori* is read in the text, the translations have 'donne ton bon œil a ta mere.'[18] Similarly René Hémard, in giving an imitation in 1653, entitles it: *D'une mère et d'un fils très beaux, mais borgnes.*[19] And in the same year Nicolas Mercier, in his book on how to write epigrams, quotes the lines, reading *parenti*.[20] In his chapter on Imitation he further quotes an imitation of Amalteo by Matteo Toscano on a handsome husband married to a lame but unfaithful wife—the exchange of qualities being made, "Sic Vulcanus eris, sic erit illa Venus."[21]

If a poem becomes a classic when it reaches the schoolbooks, Amalteo's epigram entered upon this state in 1659 when it was included in the Port-Royal *Epigrammatum Delectus* (p. 332, with *parenti*). The requirements of the editors, as expressed in Pierre Nicole's Preface, were severe; for example, they condemned epigrams making sport of bodily defects, and this one must have been admitted only because it is not satirical. It even receives special

---

> Et Leoville son senestre,
> Et peut toutesfois chacun d'eux
> Effacer en beauté les dieux.
> O Acon, petit enfant, preste
> A ta sœur cest œil qui te reste:
> Ainsi vous serez par ce don,
> Elle Venus, toy Cupidon.

Pasquier quotes the Latin, reading Leovilla [*sic*], *parve puer*, and *sorori*. These at least are the readings of the 1723 *Œuvres*.

[18] The *Jardin des Muses* (Paris, 1643), contains an anonymous epigram that is in all likelihood an imitation of Amalteo. The book is at present inaccessible to me, but Lachèvre, *Bibliographie (1597-1700)* (Paris, 1909), 2.566, gives the first line of the epigram: "Jeanne et André son fils sont beaux comme le jour." It is said to be translated from the Latin of Du Bellay, but, since nothing of the kind is found among Du Bellay's Latin epigrams, this is probably one more of the many wild ascriptions of Amalteo's lines.

[19] *Les Restes de la guerre d'estampes*, Pinson, ed. (Paris, 1880), p. 126.

[20] *De Conscribendo epigrammate* (Paris, 1653), p. 33. Amalteo's epigram is cited to illustrate the type in which the argument is drawn from equals (*argumentum ductum a pari*). On theories of the epigram see the present writer's *Greek Anthology in Italy* (Ithaca, 1935), pp. 55-75.

[21] *De Conscr.*, p. 120. The author of this imitation is presumably not the Toscano mentioned earlier in this paper; his poems are included in the *Carmina* of 1576, and this one is not there; but rather another Matteo Toscano, of Rome, the author of *Anthologia epigrammatum* (Bordeaux, 1624). He is given to reworking themes of the older neo-Latin poets; but if this epigram is in his book I have passed over it.

commendation: "Epigramma a multis celebratum, nec immerito. Non enim sua elegantia, suo pretio caret." The *Epigrammatum Delectus* had a long and honorable history. Adopted in 1689 for use at Eton, it passed through many editions in the service of that school during the next hundred years. Possibly Joseph Warton's words, "that most justly celebrated of modern epigrams," are an echo of the Jansenist verdict.

Within the circle of Port-Royal, however, not every one was satisfied; Pascal dismisses the epigram as "worthless," and does so on Nicole's own principles:[22] "L'homme aime la malignité, mais ce n'est pas contre les borgnes ou les malheureux, mais contre les heureux superbes.... Il faut plaire à ceux qui ont les sentiments humains et tendres. Celle [*sc.* épigramme] des deux borgnes ne vaut rien, car elle ne les console pas et ne fait que donner une pointe à la gloire de l'auteur. Tout ce qui n'est que pour l'auteur ne vaut rien: *ambitiosa recidet ornamenta.*" No doubt there is justice in this censure. Though the point of the epigram is to praise Acon and Leonilla to the skies, there remains a certain insensitivity in making personal misfortune the source of wit. If the epigram escapes at all, it is through its artificiality: Acon and Leonilla live only in an unreal literary world.

In real life the Abbé de Montreuil borrows Amalteo's point for the verses he presented to Mme de Sévigné when she played at blindman's buff:

> De toutes les façons vous avez droit de plaire,
> Mais surtout vous savez nous charmer en ce jour:
> Voyant vos yeux bandés, on vous prend pour l'Amour;
> Les voyant découverts, on vous prend pour sa mère.[23]

---

[22]*Pensées,* Brunschvicq, ed. (Paris, 1904), 1.50. The remark occurs under the heading "Epigrammes de Martial," but Havet has shown that Pascal was following Nicole's paragraph *De epigrammatis malignis,* in which examples from Martial are cited. Certain of these, on one-eyed persons, recalled Amalteo's epigram to Pascal. Sainte-Beuve, *Port-Royal* 3.434, records a fruitless search in Martial for an epigram corresponding to Pascal's criticism.

[23]Mme de Sévigné, *Lettres,* 14 vols. (Paris: Hachette, 1862), I, 355. Anne Isabella Ritchie, *Mme de Sévigné,* Chap. 7 (Tauchnitz ed., p. 57) gives the verses accompanied by an English translation by Hallam Tennyson:

> Your right is to enthrall, -
> You charm in every way;
> But surely most of all,
> You charm us all today.

The objections raised by Pascal probably occurred to few others, and the epigram continued to find admirers in France. I list those that have come to my attention. The Latin text (with *parenti*), accompanied by a French translation, appears in the *Poésies diverses*, s.l. (1699), p. 71, of a writer otherwise unknown to me, who signs himself "L.D.S.E.Q.V." There is an imitation (implying *parenti*) by the well-known epigrammatist Antoine-Louis Le Brun.[24] Another (implying *sorori*) was made by Mme de Simiane, the granddaughter of Mme de Sévigné.[25] Voltaire quotes "ces quatre beaux vers" in the Remarks appended to his *Henriade* (1723) and involves the epigram in a historical anecdote to which we return below.[26] Baron d'Orbessan included a translation in his *Mélanges* (Paris, 1768, 3.122). Marmontel quotes the second couplet in his *Eléments de littérature*, art. "Distique."[27] The Chevalier de Boufflers, as one might have predicted, has a translation of the epigram. In his *Poésies* it is headed "De l'Anthologie."[28] Perhaps the best French version is that of the poet Claude-Joseph Dorat, published in the *Almanach des Muses* of 1766 (p. 64):

> L'œil droit manque à Dorine, et le gauche à Cidnus;
> Tous deux ont en partage une beauté celeste.
> A ta sœur, bel enfant, cède l'œil qui te reste:
> Tu vas être l'Amour, elle sera Venus.

The interest in this epigram survived the Revolution. There is a free imitation by P. Laujon, "member of the Institut," in his *Œuvres choisies* (Paris, 1811, 2.410); an anonymous French version is printed in the *Epigrammi di moderni autori* (Faenze, 1819, p. 88); and Firmin Didot, *Poésies* (Paris, 1832, p. 280), prints the Latin with a

---

> Your blindfold eyes we see,
> And deem you 'Love'—none other;
> Your blindfold eyes we free,
> And lo! you are 'Love's mother'.

[24]*Epigrammes, madrigaux et chansons* (Paris, 1714), p. 401.

[25]*Porte-feuille de Madame**** (Paris, 1715), p. 179.

[26]His text reads *Puellae* in v. 3 and (perhaps a printer's error) Leonida for Leonilla in v. 1.

[27]*Œuvres complètes* (Paris, 1818), 13.165: he reads *parve puer* and *parenti*. As first printed in the *Encyclopédie*, Marmontel's article is without this quotation.

[28]*Poésies diverses*, Uzanne, ed. (Paris, 1886), p. 175.

note on the text—preferring *blande puer* and *puellae*—and with a French translation.[29]

In Amalteo's own country the fame of his epigram begins late, and is probably an echo from France. Noticed in 1670 by Tesauro (above, n. 8), it seems first to have been translated into Italian by the Arcadian G. B. Felice Zappi:[30]

> Manca ad Acon la destra, a Leonilla
> La sinistra pupilla,
> E ognun d'essi è bastante
> Vincere i Numi col gentil sembiante.
> Vago fanciul, quell'unica tua stella
> Cedi alla madre bella:
> Così tutto l'onore
> Ella avrà di Ciprigna, e tu d'Amore.

This translation won the approval of leading critics. Muratori praises it, only remarking that for a moment the reader may take *la destra* to mean "his right hand."[31] Crescimbeni quotes it as a model in the art of translation.[32]

There are later Italian translations by Luigi Subleyras,[33] Saverio Bettinelli,[34] Pietro Ceroni,[35] Lodovico Savioli Fontana,[36] and Pietro Stancovich.[37] All the Italian versions imply *parenti* in line three.

In England again the epigram has been quite as popular as in France, though translations do not begin so early. The Latin was printed in Abraham Wright's *Delitiae Delitiarum* (Oxford, 1637,

---

[29]Didot assigns the date 1535 to the epigram, but gives no reason for so doing.

[30]*Rime* (Venice, 1725), p. 109. The earliest edition of Zappi's *Rime* is that of 1723, but this translation had already been quoted by Muratori in 1706, and may have been first printed in an academic publication that has escaped me.

[31]*Della perfetta poesia* (Modena, 1706), 2.405. Muratori supposes that the Latin epigram was "transpiantato di Grecia."

[32]*Volg. Poes.* (Venice, 1731), 1.397; the paragraph in which the epigram is quoted is not in the 1695 edition.

[33]I do not know when Subleyras's version was first printed; see the list of his publications (1759–84) in my *Greek Anthology in Italy*, p. 429. It is quoted in Bettinelli's *Opere* (Venice, 1799–1802), 21.69.

[34]*Opere*, ed. cit. 21.69: "Quel epigramma si celebre dell' Antologia."

[35]In Savioli Fontana's *Amori* (Verona, 1808), p. 87.

[36]*Ibid.* Besides his own and Ceroni's version, he prints the Latin and the versions of Subleyras and Bettinelli.

[37]*Versi* (Venice, 1818), p. 134. Stancovich has two versions.

p. 59). In *The Wits' Recreation* (1640) there appeared what seems to be the earliest English translation:[38]

> A half-blind boy, born of a half-blind mother,
> Peerless for beauty, save compar'd to th'other—
> Fair boy, give her thine eye, and she will prove
> The Queen of Beauty, thou the God of Love.

This version, with various improvements, was reprinted time and again for the next hundred years.[39] The translation by Charles Cotton is better:[40]

> Acon his right, Leonilla her left eye
> Doth want, yet each in form the gods outvie.
> Sweet boy, with thine thy sister's light improve,
> So shall she Venus be, and thou blind Love.

[38] *Musarum Delitiae . . . Wits' Recreation,* by Sir John Mennis and James Smith (repr. London, 1874), 2.59. Another of Amalteo's epigrams, on the hour-glass, had already been translated by Ben Jonson, *Underwoods,* in *Works,* Cunningham, ed., 3.285.

[39] Thus, in *Wit's Interpreter: the English Parnassus,* 3d ed. by J. C. (London, 1671), p. 28 [said to be John Cotgrove; see *DNB.*]:

> An one-eyed boy born of a half-blind mother,
> Matchless for beauty, save the one with t'other—
> Lend her thy sight, sweet boy, and she shall prove
> The Queen of Beauty, thou the God of Love.

In the seventh edition of Camden's *Remains concerning Britain* (London, 1674), among the epitaphs added at the end of the book, apparently by John Philipot or his co-editor W. D. [repr. London, 1870, p. 437], the Latin is given, much mutilated (*dextro caruit, potuit, parve puer, sorori*), and since *sorori* is read the English is patched to suit, becoming even less grammatical than before:

> Thou one-ey'd boy, whose sister of one mother,
> Matchless in beauty are, save one to th'other—
> Lend her thine eye, sweet lad, and she will prove
> The Queen of Beauty, thou the God of Love.

The original version of 1640, with only minor changes, was reprinted in *A Miscellaneous Collection of Poems, Songs, and Epigrams* (Dublin, 1721), 2.68. With greater changes it is No. 221 in *A Collection of Epigrams* (London: Walthoe, 1727) [perhaps edited by William Oldys]:

> Fair half-blind boy, born of an half-blind mother,
> Equal'd by none, but by the one the other:
> Lend her thine eye, sweet boy, and she shall prove
> The Queen of Beauty, thou the God of Love.

This version was reprinted in Hackett's *Collection of Select Epigrams* (London and Canterbury, 1757), p. 91.

[40] *Poems on Several Occasions* (London, 1689), p. 548. The translation appears, without Cotton's name, as No. 222 in *A Collection of Epigrams* (1727), where "sight" is read for "light" in verse three.

There can be little doubt that Sir Edward Sherburne's lines entitled *A Maid in Love with a Youth blind of one Eye* were suggested by Amalteo's epigram:[41]

> Though a sable cloud benight
> One of the fair twins of light,
> Yet the other brighter seems
> As 't had robb'd his brother's beams,
> Or both lights to one were run,
> Of two stars to make one sun:
> Cunning archer! who knows yet
> But thou wink'st my heart to hit—
> Close the other too, and all
> Thee the God of Love will call.

After 1689, as aforesaid, the Jansenist *Epigrammatum Delectus* made the epigram familiar to generations of English schoolboys, at Eton and doubtless elsewhere.[42] In the higher reaches, Joseph Trapp devoted to it a part of a university lecture published in 1715 when he was Professor of Poetry at Oxford.[43] Looking more closely at the epigram than most readers have done, Trapp discovers a flaw in the thought: If Acon and Leonilla are already capable of surpassing the gods in beauty, their becoming no more than gods in the end is an anticlimax. "Nevertheless," he adds, "there is in these verses the true epigrammatic spirit; particularly there is perhaps nothing more ingenious than the last line."

Amalteo's epigram is the final selection in the *Selecta Poemata Italorum* (London, 1740), edited by Alexander Pope.[44] The *Collection of Epigrams* of 1727 (repr. 1735), mentioned above (n. 40), contains three translations, two of which have been noticed, and the Latin is quoted "for its exquisite beauty." The third translation, says the editor, "for its beauty and elegance, surpasses all the others we have seen." It is anonymous:

> Young Acon wants, Lunilla wants an eye;
> And either might with gods in beauty vie.

[41]Chalmers' *English Poets* 6 (1810) 630. Sherburne's verses are compared with Amalteo by Henry Philip Dodd, *The Epigrammatists*, 2d ed. (London: Bell, 1876), p. 128.
[42]E.g., it is on p. 163 in the twelfth edition (Eton, 1752).
[43]*Praelectiones poeticae* (Oxford, 1715), 2.8.
[44]A reissue of *Anthologia, seu Selecta quaedam poemata Italorum* (London, 1684).

"That Most Justly Celebrated of Modern Epigrams"

> Those lamps, sweet youth, which shine, apart, so fair,
>   No longer with thy blooming mother share:
> Oh! let thy light adorn Lunilla's brow,
>   So shall she Venus be, blind Cupid thou.

Risking the reader's weariness, we must notice the attention paid to the epigram in the *Gentleman's Magazine* for 1745. A correspondent, signing himself "O.," submits the following translation:

> Robb'd of an eye fair Leonilla mourns;
> One eye alone sweet Acon's face adorns.
> Kind youth, to her thy single orb resign
> To make her perfect and thyself divine;
> For then (if Heav'n the happy change allow)
> She shall bright Venus be, blind Cupid thou.

A second correspondent, "T. L.," thereupon addresses the editor as follows: "Sir: The Latin epigram ... has always had many admirers; others say it has beauties, but is not without faults. To this opinion I subscribe, and have endeavored to remove them. ... :

> Lumine Acon dextro, capta est Leonilla sinistro,
>   Dis aliter formae dotibus ambo pares.
> Magne puer, pueri lumen concede puellae:
>   Sic puer hic Veneris, sic erit illa Venus.

The second line here is inspired by Trapp's observations. There now follows a second translation by "W. W.":

> Of his right eye young Acon is bereft;
> Fair Leonilla too has lost her left;
> Else heavenly beauties both; and soon might Jove
> Make her the goddess, him the god, of Love.

Finally there is a second "improved" Latin version by a nameless writer, no better than the first.[45]

Goldsmith, in *The Bee* for Saturday, October 6, 1759 (p. 8), quotes the Latin, and precedes it with an epigram "in the same

---

[45]*Gent. Mag.* (1745), pp. 101, 159, 213, 327. The author of the first translation thinks the original, which he quotes, to be "an epigram by a monk of Winchester," giving a reference to Camden's *Remains;* but I find no such statement there.

spirit," *On a Beautiful Youth struck blind with Lightning,* which he says is imitated from the Spanish:[46]

> Sure 't was by Providence design'd,
> Rather in pity than in hate,
> That he should be, like Cupid, blind,
> To save him from Narcissus' fate.

Not surprisingly, the epigram attracted Lord Chesterfield, who writes to his godson (1766) as follows:[47]

> Voici une jolie épigramme faite par le célèbre Cardinal du Perron, sur une belle dame qui avoit un enfant d'une beauté égale à la sienne, mais ils étoient tous deux borgnes—

> > Parve puer quod habes lumen concede parenti
> > Sic tu caecus Amor, sic erit illa Venus.

Thus translated into French,

> > Aimable enfant, crois-moi, fais présent à ta mère
> > De cet œil qui te reste, et te privant du jour,
> > Tu nous retraceras l'aveugle Dieu d'amour,
> > Elle sera Venus, déesse de Cithère.

> Mon intention en vous envoyant toutes ces jolies bagatelles est de nourrir vostre esprit.

Chesterfield's apparent ignorance of the first distich recalls Marmontel with whose text (*parve puer . . . parenti*) his agrees, save that he has misplaced *lumen;* but Marmontel says nothing of Du Perron, and Chesterfield may depend on the same source that he used rather than on him. The Cardinal du Perron (1556–1618) was not the author of the epigram, but one would like to know how his name came to be associated with it.[48] The French translation is

---

[46]*Poetical Works,* Dobson, ed. (Oxford, 1905), pp. 42, 192. The Spanish original has not been found. I notice a French imitation of Goldsmith's epigram in *Anthologie française* (Paris, 1816), 1.152. In the Latin epigram Goldsmith reads Leonida for Leonilla, and otherwise also his text agrees with that of Voltaire: *poterat, parve puer, puellae.*

[47]*Letters,* Dobrée, ed. (1932), 6.2740 (No. 2434).

[48]In a notice of the Earl of Carnarvon's edition of Chesterfield's *Letters,* in the *Quarterly Review* 171 (1890)298, Churton Collins says that the epigram is "certainly

probably not Chesterfield's own, if it is safe to judge by the words "Aimable enfant," which translate *blande puer* and not the text which he quotes.

Translations of Amalteo's epigram continued to appear in English. *The Poetical Farrago* (London, 1794, 1.96), presents an anonymous version that turns out, however, to be the one contributed by "O." to the *Gentleman's Magazine* in 1745, with changes in the first two lines.[49] In this form it was reprinted in *Select Epigrams* (London, 1797), whence H. P. Dodd extracted it for his well-known work, *The Epigrammatists* (London, 1870).[50] It may thus be said to have succeeded to the place of the translation from *Wits' Recreation* as the standard English version. I have not seen John Rock's *Select Translations from Amaltheus* (London, 1826). There is an anonymous translation in *Notes and Queries* for 1851.[51] John Booth, *Epigrams Ancient and Modern* (London, 1863, p. 163), includes a curious imitation entitled *On two beautiful one-eyed Sisters [sic]*:

> Give up one eye, and make your sister's two
> Venus she then would be, and Cupid you.

This presumably is translated from the German version by E. C. von Kleist: *An zwey sehr schöne, aber einäugig Geschwister:*

> Du musste, O kleiner Lykon, dein Aug' Agathen leihn,
> Blind wirst du dann Kupido, die Schwester Venus seyn.

Kleist is censured by Lessing for supposing that his single couplet, requiring, as it does, a prose title, is as fine (gleich schön) as Amalteo's self-contained original, which Lessing quotes.[52]

---

not by Du Perron, for it was published thirty years before he was born, though it has often been attributed to him, as it has also been attributed to Ménage." This is a troublesome sentence. Collins's only reference is to the *Amaltheorum Carmina;* as this was first published in 1627, he may have interchanged 6 with 5, making 1527, thirty years before Du Perron's birth. If the epigram has often been attributed to Du Perron, and has at any time been attributed to Ménage, these facts have escaped me.

49   But one bright eye young Acon's face adorns,
      For one bright eye fair Leonilla mourns, *etc.*

50Dodd, *loc. cit.* n. 41 above.

51Series 1, vol. 3, 289. The note is signed "H. A. B., Trinity College, Cambridge," and is an entirely futile answer to an enquiry made on p. 208 concerning the source of Byron's statement presently to be noticed.

52Lessing, *Zerstreute Anmerkungen über das Epigramm*, in *Gesammelte Werke*, 10 vols. (Berlin, Weimar, 1968), 7.36. Cf. Kleist, *Sämmtliche Werke*, Körte, ed. (Berlin, n.d.), p. 227.

James Davies in an article on the epigram as a literary form published in the *Quarterly Review* for 1865 quotes the Latin text with high commendation and subjoins a translation of his own. The only subsequent comment on the epigram that I can cite is that of George Saintsbury, *The Earlier Renaissance* (New York, 1901, p. 38), who refers to its fame, and quotes it as typical of its period: "Nor could, perhaps, that prettiness, with a touch of triviality, which is the note of much of this verse, be better shown."

Byron, in his controversy with William Lyle Bowles concerning Pope, quotes the epigram as evidence that physical deformity need not deprive one of charm.[53] Joseph Warton, in his *Essay on the Genius and Writings of Pope* (1756),[54] after citing the epigram as "most justly celebrated," continues: "My chief reason for quoting these delicate lines was to point out the occasion of them, which seems not to be sufficiently known. They were made on Louis de Maguiron,[55] the most beautiful man of his time, and the great favorite of Henry III of France, who lost an eye at the siege of Issoire; and on the Princess of Eboli, a great beauty, but who was deprived of the sight of one of her eyes, and who was at the same time mistress of Philip II of Spain." Byron, no doubt reading Warton at the time of his discussion with Bowles, repeats this statement.[56] Warton in turn clearly depends on Voltaire, who makes the same statement in the first of his Remarks on his *Henriade* illustrating verses that mention the "Mignons" of Henri III. He singles out Maugiron, and continues:[57] "On le comparait à la princesse d'Eboli, qui, étant borgne comme lui, était dans le même temps maîtresse de Philippe II roi d'Espagne. On dit que ce fut pour cette princesse et pour Maugiron qu'un Italien fit ces quatre beaux vers renouvelés depuis," quoting the epigram. I have found no source for Voltaire.[58]

---

[53] *Works*, Prothero, ed. 5.572–73.

[54] (London, 1772), 1.298. Warton's text has *blande puer* and *sorori*.

[55] The name is Maugiron: see below.

[56] His text of the epigram agrees with that of Warton.

[57] *La Ligue, ou Henry le Grand*, pub. surreptitiously at Geneva (1723), p. 164. In this first edition of the *Henriade*, the last sentence quoted above ends with the words "renouveléz depuis," and this apparently is the reading of all the eighteenth-century editions examined for the 1971 edition mentioned in note 63 below. In the edition of the *Henriade* by Louis Moland in *Œuvres complètes de Voltaire* (Paris: Garnier, vol. 8, 1877), p. 45, there appears a different reading: "renouvelés de l'Anthologie grecque," and this already is found in the Didot edition (1819), p. 61.

[58] The story is repeated by Forneron, *Histoire de Philippe II* (Paris, 1882–87), 3.55, but again without authority.

Indeed the last sentence here quoted raises a suspicion that the anecdote may have been fabricated by Voltaire himself. The words "renouvelés depuis" carry the assertion that the epigram known to us is a revision of an earlier one referring to the princess and Maugiron. This is not true of course; Maugiron lost his eye at the siege of Issoire in 1577, and the epigram was already in print in 1563. "On dit" is not a reassuring form of reference.

Though not above suspicion, Voltaire's account may yet rest upon a source, or at least a hint, that we have overlooked. A comparison of the one-eyed princess and the one-eyed "mignon" was possible for their contemporaries and would almost inevitably call up the famous epigram.[59] Just a year after the loss of his eye, Maugiron perished in the infamous "duel of the mignons." His death as well as the loss of his eye was deplored by the foremost poets of the day, and in their verses there is a notable tendency to advert to the figure of Venus and Cupid. Thus Ronsard says of him:[60]

> La déesse Cyprine avoit conceu des cieux
> En ce siècle dernier un enfant, dont la veue
> De flames et d'esclairs estoit si bien pourveus
> Qu'Amour son fils aisné en devint envieux.

But more interesting from our point of view is an anonymous poem quoted by L'Estoile, containing the following lines:[61]

> Cest œil perdu ne le rend point plus laid:
> Ce jeune enfant lui [Venus] aggrée et lui plaist,
> C'est tout son coeur, Maugeron, ce lui semble,
> A Cupidon de plus en plus ressemble,
> Qui n'a qu'un œil. Car s'il n'avoit point d'yeux
> Qui est celui qui lui sembleroit mieux?

---

[59]Be it noted, however, that the Princess of Eboli had lost her right eye and Maugiron his left, the wrong way round for the epigram. For the princess, who lost her eye in youth, see her portrait with a patch over the right eye in Don Gaspar Muro's *Vida de la Princesa de Eboli* (Madrid, 1877). For Maugiron, cf. Philippe Desportes, *Œuvres*, Michiels, ed. (Paris, 1858), p. 179: "de ses yeux le gauche." The loss of Maugiron's eye is noticed in several contemporary accounts, e.g., *Annales de la ville d'Issoire*, J.-B. Bouillet, ed. (Clermont-Ferrand, 1848), p. 137.

[60]*Œuvres complètes*, Paul Laumonier, ed., rev. by I. Silver and R. Lebègue (Paris, 1967), 18¹.161.

[61]Pierre de l'Estoile, *Mémoires-journaux*, Bonnefon, ed. (Paris, 1888), 1.251.

This is but a French version of a Latin poem by "C. M." in the
Tumulus Maugeronii which follows it in L'Estoile (p. 251):

> ... Quem Venus irridens: "Mavors stultissime! dixit:
> Est geminus factus, qui fuit unus, Amor.
> Est Mogeron luscus: caecus mea cura Cupido:
> Sic mihi luscus Amor, sic mihi caecus Amor."[62]

The last line here quoted might even be an echo of the last line of
Amalteo's epigram. About the same time, the Princess of Eboli was
the subject of a scandal that still captures the interest of historians:
she was said to be implicated with the famous Antonio Pérez in the
murder of Escobedo, the secretary of Don Juan of Austria.

The most recent edition of the *Henriade* offers nothing to resolve
our doubts about Voltaire's anecdote.[63] The editor has not found
an earlier comparison of Maugiron and the princess involving the
"quatre beaux vers," and in fact says flatly: "Nous ne savons pas où
Voltaire a lu le quatrain en vers latins." Amalteo's epigram which
most of Hallam's readers were supposed to have by heart apparently is not even recognized by an otherwise well informed literary
scholar in our day.

---

[62] *carus*, L'Estoile; I have altered to *caecus*.
[63] *Les Œuvres complètes de Voltaire*, vol. 2, *La Henriade*, O. R. Taylor, ed., 2d ed.
(Geneva: Les Délices, 1970), p. 632.

Analogues of Shakespeare's
Sonnets 153 and 154: Contributions
to the History of a Theme

What is perhaps most notable about Shakespeare's last two sonnets is that their theme is obviously borrowed. As is well known, the
ultimate original is an epigram by Marianus Scholasticus found in
the Greek Anthology (*AP*, 9.627). The puzzle is to know how
Shakespeare came upon it, for there is little, or rather no, likelihood that he lifted it directly out of the Anthology. Before 1603
there was no complete translation of the Anthology in print; and at
that date Shakespeare is unlikely to have opened this collection of
three thousand poems at about the middle of the volume only to
choose one of the least distinguished epigrams.[1] Literary men were
prone to know only such epigrams as had special currency either
because they had been included in one of the well-known books of
selections or because they had been put into Latin verse by one of
the humanists. It may be said at once that Marianus' epigram appears in none of the current selections.[2] Does it occur among the
more casual translations from the Anthology made by one of the

From *Modern Philology* 38 (1941) 385-401. Copyright © 1941 The University of
Chicago Press.

[1] The translation of 1603 was by Lubinus: *Florilegium . . . . interprete Eilhardo Lubino*
(Heidelberg). Ben Jonson's copy of this edition of the Anthology is preserved, and
he has underscored a number of epigrams, but not this one. (This last sentence is
based on information supplied to me by Messrs. Henry Sotheran Ltd., London, in
1931.)

[2] The best-known were the *Epigrammata Graeca* of Joannes Soter (Cologne, 1525,
1528, and Freiburg, 1544); the *Selecta epigrammata Graeca* of Janus Cornarius (Basel,
1529); Henri Estienne's *Epigrammata Graeca* (Geneva, 1570), refurbished by John
Stockwood, *Progymnasma scholasticum* (London, 1597); and Hieronymus Megiser,
Anthologia seu florilegium Graecolatinum (Frankfort, 1602). Besides these, the present
writer has examined many less-known selections, perhaps all that exist. The state-

humanists (for this seems to be the only channel left)? An attempt, now extending over some years, to control the modern influence of the Anthology, has produced for this epigram only one un-equivocal translation in the sixteenth century. Certain other epigrams were translated over a hundred times. Clearly this was not a popular one. Other material, however, rather more interesting than simple translations, has thereby come to light. We can at least, I think, now view the two Shakespearean sonnets in the perspective of a literary tradition.[3]

The Greek epigram, first printed in the *editio princeps* of the Anthology (Florence, 1494) is here given in the text of the Planudean Anthology, the only one read before the eighteenth century.[4]

Τάσδ' ὑπὸ τὰς πλατάνους ἁπαλῷ πεπεδημένος ὕπνῳ
εὗδεν Ἔρως, Νύμφαις λαμπάδα παρθέμενος.
Νύμφαι δ' ἀλλήλησι, τί μένομεν; αἴθε δὲ τούτῳ
σβέσσαμεν, εἶπον, ὁμοῦ πῦρ κραδίης μερόπων.
Λαμπὰς δ'ὡς ἔφλεζε καὶ ὕδατα, θερμὸν ἐκεῖθεν
Νύμφαι ἐρωτιάδες λουτροχοεῦσιν ὕδωρ.

Beneath these plane trees, detained by gentle slumber, Love slept, having put his torch in the care of the Nymphs; but the Nymphs said one to another: "Why wait? Would that together with this we could quench the fire in the hearts of men." But the torch set fire even to the water, and with hot water thenceforth the Love-Nymphs fill the bath.[5]

---

ment of Dowden, lately repeated (and misquoted) by Tucker Brooke, that the epigram, "had been translated into Latin 'Selecta Epigrammata, Basel, 1529,' and again several times before the close of the sixteenth century," is quite unfounded, as is also the similar lighthearted remark on the subject by Alden, *The Sonnets of Shakespeare* (Boston and New York, 1916), p. 370. The blame, however, rests in the first place on Hertzberg (*Shakespeare Jahrbuch* 30 (1894) 162), whom Dowden follows and who counted the titles of eight "Select translations" from the Anthology in Fabricius' *Bibliotheca Graeca* but never looked up any one of them to see whether this epigram was included, merely assuming that it was!

[3]Of the fourteen poems, besides the Greek epigram, here noticed, four have previously been adduced as parallels to Shakespeare: the verses of Regianus, those from Tolomei's book, the German poem on Baden, and the sonnet of Fletcher.

[4]I quote from the edition of Estienne (Geneva, 1566). There were ten editions of the Anthology between 1494 and 1600. Our epigram appears in Book IV, chap. xix (epig. 35), save that it was inadvertently omitted from the Basel edition of 1549.

[5]Lubinus' prose translation of 1603 follows:
Sub his platanis suavi domitus somno
Dormivit amor, nymphis facem apponens.

Both this epigram and the one preceding it in the Anthology (*AP* 9.626), also by Marianus, are, says a lemma, in praise of a bath named "Eros"; they explain how it became a hot spring, though originally cold. The elements of the poem which must be borne in mind are (1) the plane trees, (2) Love asleep, (3) his torch intrusted to the Nymphs, (4) their conspiracy, (5) the "reflective" phrase: "the fire in the hearts of men," (6) the heating of the waters, (7) the subsequent existence of the hot bath of "Eros."

The only Latin parallel to Shakespeare that has heretofore been quoted is the following, found in the Latin Anthology and there ascribed to one Regianus or Regianius:

> Ante bonam Venerem gelidae per litora Baiae.
> Illa natare lacus cum lampade iussit Amorem.
> Dum natat, algentes cecidit scintilla per undas;
> Hinc vapor ussit aquas: quicumque natavit, amavit.[6]

These verses are perhaps of about the same period as the Greek epigram (fifth century of our era). They may or may not have some connection with it, but they certainly do not reproduce it, and writers on Shakespeare should not carelessly call them "the Latin version" (Sarrazin, *Jahrbuch,* 31 (1895) 229; Alden, p. 371). For our purpose two points are noteworthy: the localizing at Baiae of a fancy similar to that of Marianus and the fact that these lines were hardly available for imitation until the end of the sixteenth century, when they were first published by Pierre Pithou in his well-known *Epigrammata et poemata vetera* (Paris, 1589/90).

More like the Greek epigram are the following verses of uncertain authorship:

> Baiarum dum forte capit sub mollibus umbris
>   Fessus Amor somnum murmure captus aquae,
> Ipsa facem accurrens gelida celavit in unda,
>   Ut veteres flammas vindicet, alma Venus.
> Quam primum liquor ille aeternos concipit ignes,

> Nymphae vero ad invicem: Quid volumus? simul cum hac
>   Extinguamus (dixerunt) simul ignem cordis hominum.
> Lampas vero ut combussit et aquas, calidam exinde
>   Nymphae amatoriae inter lavandum fundunt aquam.

[6]Baehrens, *Poetae Latini minores,* IV, 359. As printed by Alden (p. 370), the epigram is unintelligible. The first line means "Before [the arrival of] kind Venus Baiae, all over its shores, was cold."

Igne novo (quisnam crederet?) arsit aqua.
Flammivomis igitur fumant haec balnea lymphis,
Quod facula una omnes vincit Amoris aquas.

This epigram, which is easily accessible in Baehrens' *Poetae Latini minores* (IV, 438), ought to have been produced before this for comparison with Shakespeare and perhaps would have been except for Baehrens' note. He says that the poem is now (1882) first published by him from a Florence manuscript (Cod. Riccard. 2939) of the fifteenth century. But Baehrens was mistaken; the poem had been published among the Latin poems of Count Niccolò d'Arco (1479–1546) in the edition of 1762, seemingly from an earlier publication in 1533.[7] Though a slight uncertainty exists as to this earlier publication, it will be abundantly clear as we proceed that the epigram was known in the sixteenth century.

Meanwhile, it is of interest that Baehrens found it in a fifteenth-century manuscript. If Riccard. 2939 is of the fifteenth century, the poem can hardly be the work of D'Arco. Baehrens believed that it was ancient, because he found traces of the Latin Anthology in the same manuscript: "In quo inter plurima carmina novicia (quorum auctores ubique nominantur) casu quodam inrepsit Anthologiae excerptum." But these words plainly leave room for doubt as to the antiquity of this epigram.

It is undoubtedly a derivative of the Greek epigram, and the manner of its derivation is in harmony with neo-Latin treatment of Greek themes, though this fact is not decisive for its origin. Generally speaking, neo-Latin imitators of the Greek Anthology recognized three degrees of departure from their originals: near-translation commonly marked with the words "e Graeco"; free handling or "imitatio"; and verses merely inspired by the Greek, marked "allusio" (they also wrote replies, "responsa," to the originals). A translation "e Graeco" was hardly respectable if it employed more lines than the Greek. The present verses would pass as an "imitatio." The main theme of the original is reproduced: Love asleep, his torch stolen and plunged into the water, which there-

---

[7]*Numerorum libri iv* (Verona, 1762), p. 159, where a note says that this epigram is from the Aldine *Carminum collectio* of 1533. No such book is listed by Renouard as published by the Aldine press, but I see no reason to doubt that the editor found the verses in a sixteenth-century book. D'Arco's *Numeri* appeared posthumously at Mantua in 1546, but, unless my own notes here fail me, the present epigram is not in that volume.

upon burns and forms a hot bath. The "reflective" element of the Greek is present in "Ut veteres flammas vindicet." On the other hand, there are notable departures: the scene is at Baiae and not "beneath the plane trees," Love does not intrust his torch to his betrayer, this betrayer is not the Nymphs, but Venus, and there is an attempt at point in a new reflection at the end: "Quod facula una omnes vincit Amoris aquas" (not unlike Shakespeare: "Loves fire heates water, water cooles not love"; cf. also "tooke heat perpetuall" and "aeternos concipit ignes"). Baiae for the scene and Venus for the agent recall the Latin lines of Regianus, but I do not think that a direct connection can be established between the two epigrams. Yet an independent introduction of Baiae into the theme is perhaps more likely if the imitation is ancient and possibly contemporary with Regianus than it would be in a fifteenth-century imitation.

Baiae is again the scene in the earliest allusion to the theme that I find in the sixteenth century.[8] This is by Girolamo Angeriano, a Latin poet whose amatory verses to "Caelia" were a mine to the vernacular poets who came after him. Many of them are more or less free renderings from the Greek Anthology, but whether this is one from that source seems doubtful. His *Erotopaegnion* appeared at Florence in 1512.[9]

---

[8]One turns with some expectation to the *Hendecasyllaborum seu Baiarum libri duo* of Giovanni Pontano (1508), but he shows no certain knowledge of our theme. He has verses on the heating of the waters (*Opera omnia* [Basel, 1556], IV, 3509), but they are a play on the name of his friend Hieronymus Carbo. Another poem, however, comes, by chance, I think, somewhat nearer—"De Bathilla puella in balneis" (*ibid.*, IV, 3452):

> Baianas petiit Bathilla thermas.
> Dumque illi tener it comes Cupido,
> Atque una lavat et fovetur una,
> Dum molli simul in toro quiescit,
> Ac ludos facit improbasque rixas,
> Sopito pueroque lassuloque
> Arcum surripuit Bathilla ridens.
> Mox picta latus instruit pharetra,
> Et molles iacit huc et huc sagittas.
> Nil O nil reliquum miselli amantes,
> Nil his impenetrabile est sagittis.
> Heu cladem iuvenum senumque Baias!

[9]I have not seen this edition. The epigram is here quoted from the Naples edition of 1520, sig. C4. A second epigram (sig. B2), slightly reminiscent of our theme, begins: "Quum dormiret Amor, rapuit clam pulchra pharetram/Caelia" but continues in a totally different strain.

153

Essays on Renaissance Poetry

De Caeliae Balneo
Inclyta laudatas peteret quum Caelia Baias,
Atque salutiferis membra lavaret aquis,
Vidimus eiectis undantia balnea flammis,
Miramur, quid sit tantus et unde vapor.
Quidam inquit, simulac visa est hic Caelia nuda,
Hac cum rupe latens protinus arsit Amor.

If this is from the Greek epigram, it is "allusio" and not "imitatio";
and in any case the localization at Baiae suggests a knowledge of
"D'Arco" or Regianus. Angeriano was a Neopolitan; but, for all his
proximity to Baiae, it seems unlikely that two derivatives of a Greek
epigram—his and "D'Arco's"—should independently shift the
scene to the same place. If Angeriano had known Regianus' verses,
it would have been an easy step to substitute Caelia for Regianus'
Amor.

The next example has been somewhat doubtfully ascribed to
Mellin de Saint-Gelais. It seems to have been written about 1535
but not to have been printed until the nineteenth century.[10]

Fortune avoit à l'Amour endormy
Desrobé l'arc et carquois et flambeau,
Et le tout mis soudainement en l'eau;
Mais le garson qui ne dort qu'à demy
Ouyt le bruict, si se jecta parmy
Et tant ouvra que la plus amortie
Des ses chaleurs secheroit un amy,
Voire la mer, dont Venus est sortie.

Though again far from the Greek epigram, this is somewhat nearer
it than was Angeriano. Here the agent is no longer the Nymphs of
the Greek or Venus as in Regianus and "D'Arco" but Fortune, and
it is not the torch but Love himself who heats the waters. The last
point recalls Regianus. Unless these changes are entirely the
French author's own, as seems unlikely, we have evidently failed to
uncover at least one early treatment of the theme. It is only a guess
that this version ultimately goes back to "D'Arco," since it is somewhat easier to pass from Venus to Fortune than from the Nymphs

[10]*Œuvres complètes,* Blanchemain, ed. (Paris, 1873), III, 6. Blanchemain published
it from a manuscript of about 1535 containing Saint-Gelais's work but also the work
of other poets.

154

and since the conclusion of the *huitain* is somewhat suggestive of the last line of "D'Arco" and not at all accounted for by the Greek epigram.

Much closer to the Greek are the anonymous Italian verses already offered as an analogue to Shakespeare by M. J. Wolff and found in the *Versi et regole de la nuova poesia toscana* of Claudio Tolomei (Rome, 1539), sig. M4:

> Tradotto da M. Statio Romano
> de l'Acque di Baia
> Al lido gia di Baia, sotto un bel Platano Amore
> Dormendo stanco presso posò la face,
> Naiade Calliroe, de li gioveni amanti pietosa,
> Toltola, l'immerse nel vago freddo rio.
> Ilqual, mentre dee smorzarla, accesi et arse,
> Quinci le belle acque sempre coccenti sono.

The *Versi et regole* was the publication of Tolomei's society, if his group can be so called, for the promotion of quantitative verse in Italian, and in its time it attracted a good deal of attention. Since it is experimental, the book is made up of translations, largely from neo-Latin poets, and among the anonymous translations several are given as from this same Statio Romano who seems to be otherwise unknown.[11]

The object of the experiment being to reproduce in Italian the effects of classical verse, and not merely those of quantity, we may be sure that the translator has kept the "rule" of the Latin translators and that his Italian epigram is in six lines because the Latin of Statio was in six lines. Statio's Latin was, therefore, a translation of the Greek epigram. The substance bears this out: here we have (1) a plane tree; (2) Love asleep; (3) his torch laid by (?παρθέμενος); (4) "Naiade Calliroe" = the Nymphs; (5) a "reflective" phrase, "de li gioveni amanti pietosa"; (6) the heating of the waters; (7) the resulting hot baths—all the elements of the Greek. Yet there are changes that cannot be attributed only to the accidents attendant on double translation—there is no direct speech on the part of Callirhoë, and the localization at Baiae (with the plane tree) must be a reminis-

---

[11]Others among the pieces taken from him are also imitations of the Greek Anthology (see my *Greek Anthology in Italy* [Ithaca: Cornell University Press, 1935], p. 299). I may add that there is no question here of the author of the "Silvae" and "Thebais."

cence of one of the Baiae poems. Though "stanco" and "freddo rio" are perhaps implicit in the Greek, they are explicit here and in the verses of "D'Arco": "fessus Amor" and "gelida unda." Unless Statio's Latin version turns up, we cannot say whether he or his Italian translator is responsible for these alterations. We shall return to this version later.

Certainly no more than an "allusio" is the following epigram by Luc-François le Duchat, an associate of the Pleiade:

Naiadibus

O quae sub liquidis agitatis eburnea limphis
Brachia, Capripedum cura iocusque, Deae:
Vosne etiam puer ille subit? puer ille, sagittas
Qui tenet, et caeco vulnus ab igne facit:
Nec gelidi fontes, inimicus et ignibus humor
Vindicat a rapida mollia corda face?
Ah valeant, quibus est animo non cedere: me me
Torreat hic, undas qui quoque torret, Amor![12]

These lines read like a reflection written after reading a poem in which the substance of the Greek epigram had been set forth. Of the versions thus far examined, only that of the *Versi et regole* contains Naiads or Nymphs, but there is little likelihood that Le Duchat had this poem in mind. His source remains a missing link in our history. The reference to "gelidi fontes" and the point of the last line possibly suggest that this source belonged to the Baiae tradition (cf. "D'Arco": "gelida unda," "vindicet," and his last line) but corrected for the Naiads or Nymphs to the Greek epigram.

The only sixteenth-century translation of Marianus' epigram that I have encountered is by Fausto Sabeo, published with many other translations from the Anthology in his *Epigrammata:*[13]

In Balneum Dictum Erota. E Graeco
Sub platano viridi apposta iam lampade Nymphis,
Victus erat somno nequitiosus Amor.

---

[12]*Praeludiorum libri tres* (Paris, 1554), fol. 38ᵛ. There is a French version of Le Duchat's poem by Gilles Durant in the latter's *Imitations* (Paris, 1587; Leiden ed., 1659, p. 196).

[13](Rome, 1556), p. 791. Sabeo (c. 1478–1558), originally from Brescia, was *custos* of the Vatican Library and, he proclaims, a friend of Michelangelo (see *Anthology in Italy*, p. 212).

Inter se haec dicunt: "Nitamur lampada, Nymphae,
Suffocare, hominum quae male corda cremat."
Dumque volunt flammas extinguere, lympha calescit:
A Nymphis calidae sic oriuntur aquae.

Here are the obligatory six lines, and the translation is as near to the original as Sabeo had the skill to make it. It has crossed the mind of the present writer that Sabeo might somehow be identical with the mysterious Statio Romano of the *Versi et regole:* he has "platano" (sing.), and his "apposta lampade Nymphis" might have been turned into "presso posò la face" (cf. Shakespeare: "laid by his brand"). The "lido di Baia" would then be an importation of the Italian translator, who would also have dropped the direct speech of the Nymphs. Despite the parallels, however, there seems to be no way of passing from Sabaeus Brixianus to Statius Romanus.[14]

We return to the Baiae tradition with the German Latin poet Johann Stigel (1515–62), a friend of Melanchthon.[15] In this version, besides localization at Baiae, we have (2) Love asleep; (4) the conspiracy of the Nymphs, in direct address as in the Greek; (5) a "reflective" verse (vs. 2); but we lack (3) the intrusting of the torch to the Nymphs and notably (6) the heating of the waters and (7) the creation of the hot bath, Stigel having substituted a fancy of his own in the latter half of his poem.

> De Cupidine ad Baias Dormiente
> Dum tepidas somnum Baiarum carpit ad undas
> Qui mentes hominum versat amore Deus,
> Accedunt furtimque faces et spicula Nymphae
> Surripiunt, tacitis in sua vota dolis.
> "Vosne estis toti dominantia spicula mundo
> Quae toties questae saucia turba sumus?
> At nunc irriguum poenas date mersa sub amnem,
> Et semel ignitas doleat unda faces."
> Sic illae, gressuque petunt vada salsa citato,
> Immerguntque imis flammea tela vadis.

---

[14]Sabeo's translation may well have been made before 1539 when the *Versi et regole* was published. Another point against the identification, however, is the fact that other pieces said to be translated from Statio in the *Versi et regole* find nothing to correspond to them in Sabeo's *Epigrammata.*

[15]Janus Gruter, *Delitiae poetarum Germanorum* (Frankfort, 1612), VI, 571. Stigel's poems were collected after his death and published in 1566–69 and 1572.

Vera fides, mediis magis aestuat ignis in undis:
Immissum gelidis sulphur ut ardet aquis.
Sentit Amor fraudes, animumque citatus in iram
In medio raras colligit amne faces.
"Quis furor est nostras extinguere velle sagittas?
Illas sub cœlo nemo cavere potest."
Sic ait, et genibus lunato protinus arcu
Coniicit in miseras spicula mille Deas.
Ast illis teneris haesere sub ossibus ignes,
In quos Oceanus non satis unus eat.
Hei mihi, quid Domino frustra pugnamus Amori?
Effugere hunc ipsi non potuere Dii.

The following verses by Luigi Groto bear a certain resemblance to the epigram of Angeriano given above, and Groto elsewhere borrows from Angeriano; but in other respects they draw nearer to other versions of our theme. Thus, before the miracle the waters were "fresche" (cf. "D'Arco," "gelida"), and after it they retained their new heat and their "virtù," and so the poem ends with a point more like that of the Greek epigram than like that of Angeriano.

Quando Madonna per mia morte nacque,
Vener (cui darle il primo bagno piacque)
La portò in grembo a l'acque
(Fresche allhor, come l'altre, e senza pregio)
Che'l lido nostro hor fan caldo e egregio.
V'immerse il corpo ignudo, e 'l trasse fora.
Ma l'onde ne l'accor membra si grate,
Si belle e delicate,
D'un amoroso incendio arsero allhora,
E quel soave ardor serbono anchora.
E di tanta virtù piene restaro
Dapoi che'l nudo e bel corpo lavaro.[16]

Two rather faint echoes of the theme in Ronsard may here be recorded. The first occurs in his "Stances de la fontaine d'Hélène" (1578):

Ie voulois de ma peine esteindre la memoire:
Mais Amour qui avoit en la fontaine beu,

---

[16]Luigi Groto, *Rime* (Venice, 1587), p. 21. The *Rime* first appeared in 1577.

> Y laissa son brandon, si bien qu'au lieu de boire
> De l'eau pour l'estancher, ie n'ay beu que de feu.[17]

The second is found in a sonnet following the "Stances":

> Amour du rouge sang des Geans tout souillé,
> Essuyant en ceste eau son beau corps despouillé,
> Y laissa pour iamais ses feux et sa teinture.

We promised some way back to present evidence of the influence, within the sixteenth century, of "D'Arco's" version of the theme. Certainly, the lines now to be quoted seem to betray that influence, but are they from the sixteenth century? I have seen them twice printed, once in the *Anthologia epigrammatum* of Matteo Toscano (Bordeaux, 1620, p. 145), and again in the *Carmina illustrium poetarum Italorum*, edited by G. Bottari (Florence, 1719–26, IV, 182). Toscano's volume is, I have supposed, made up of his own compositions.[18] But Bottari gives the epigram as the work of Matthaeus Faetanus of Naples, a writer I fail to trace beyond Bottari's collection.[19] If the verses were unknown before 1620, they are, of course, unavailable for comparison with Shakespeare; but, with the reader's patience, good reason will appear for supposing them to have been known before 1599. They follow:

> De Amore ad Baias Dormiente
> Dum Baiis dormiret Amor prope littus in umbra,
> Murmure detentus lene fluentis aquae,
> Conspexere illum Nymphae multo igne coruscum,
> Et raptas lymphis supposuere faces.
> Quis gelidam credat subito exarsisse liquorem
> Atque inde aeternos emicuisse focos?
> Nec mirum, his flammis, toties quibus arserat aether,
> Vos quoque perpetuum si caluistis aquae.

The resemblance to the version of "D'Arco" is striking: the same number of lines, localization at Baiae, similarity of construction in

---

[17]*Œuvres*, Marty-Laveaux, ed. (Paris, 1887–91), I, 332.

[18]Toscano, originally of Rome, died in 1624 at Condom in France (see *Anthology in Italy*, p. 257).

[19]Quadrio (*Storia*, II, 364) mentions a Giovanni Matteo Faitano as one of thirty-nine contributors to Offredi's *Rime di diversi autori eccellentissimi libro ix* (Cremona, 1560), but I have at present no means of connecting this writer with Bottari's Faetanus.

the *dum*-clause (vs. 1) and in *Quis.... credat* (vs. 5), and further
coincidence of vocabulary: "umbra," "murmure detentus (captus),"
"aeternos focos (ignes)," "gelidam liquorem." There are three important differences: the present epigram returns to the Nymphs of
the Greek where "D'Arco" introduces Venus; this epigram lacks a
"reflective" phrase corresponding to "ut veteres flammas vindicet,"
and the final reflection is unlike that of "D'Arco." One is forced to
conclude that the writer mainly imitates "D'Arco" but also knew the
Greek epigram and naturally sought to evince his originality by a
new ending.[20]

Sonnet 27 of Giles Fletcher's *Licia* (1593) was long ago brought
into connection with Shakespeare by Sir Sidney Lee:

> The chrystal streames, wherein my love did swimme,
> Melted in tears, as partners of my woe:
> Her shine was such, as did the fountaine dimme,
> The pearllike fountaine whiter than the snow;
> Then lyke perfume, resolved with a heate,
> The fountaine smoak'd, as if it thought to burne:
> A Woonder strange, to see the colde so great,
> And yet the fountaine into smoake to turne.
> I searcht the cause, and found it to be this:
> She toucht the water, and it burnt with love.
> Now by her means it purchast hath that blisse,
> Which all diseases quickly can remove.
>   Then if by you, these streames thus blessed be
>   (Sweet) graunt me love, and be not woorse to me.

This sonnet, as Janet Scott has observed, is an imitation of
Angeriano's epigram quoted above.[21] It was a tenet of sixteenth-
century poetics that the sonnet corresponds in modern literature to
the epigram of the ancients,[22] and certainly sixteenth-century son-
neteers turned willingly to the epigram, Greek and neo-Latin, for
materials. Since, however, epigrams are as a rule shorter than sonnets, the efforts of these poets to stretch such material over the

---

[20]This reworking of themes from older neo-Latin poets is found more than once
in Toscano's *Anthologia*.

[21]Janet G. Scott, *Les Sonnets Elizabéthains* (Paris, 1929), p. 313. Twenty-three of
Fletcher's sonnets are from Angeriano. Is Fletcher's imaginary "Licia," then,
perhaps a quasi-anagram of Angeriano's lady "Caelia"?

[22]See the evidence quoted in *Anthology in Italy* (pp. 56–57), to which much more
could be added.

frame of the sonnet are often interesting and merit study from anyone who wants to know their minds and their methods. We cannot afford space to analyze Fletcher's procedure in detail: the first quatrain is his own, as is also the final "reflection." Attention is due to the lines:

> Now by her meanes it purchast hath that blisse,
> Which all diseases quickly can remove.

The notion that the bath became not only hot but medicinal is perhaps implicit in all versions of the theme, but Fletcher's is the first to make it explicit. Very likely the suggestion came to him from Angeriano's "salutiferis aquis"; compare "tanta virtù" in Groto's poem, which may also be a derivative of Angeriano.

Fletcher's sonnet, after Angeriano, is somewhat off the main stream, to which we now return with a sonnet by Jean Grisel, seemingly the only sonnet before Shakespeare to be built strictly on this motive. It was published in Grisel's *Premières œuvres poétiques.*[23]

> Amour, lassé de courir par le monde,
> S'alla poser dessus le bord d'un bain,
> Où plus l'endroit estoit d'ombrage plein;
> Puis s'endormit au murmure de l'onde.
> Là mainte Nimphe arrivant vagabonde,
> Voyant ce dieu ne mouvoir pied ny main,
> Mit dedans l'eau le feu dont l'inhumain
> Rend sa nature en malice fœconde.
> Au lieu d'esteindre on vit que le flambeau
> Du bain jazard eschauffa toute l'eau,
> Tant que depuis chaude elle est demeurée.
> Qui s'en estonne? il a bien sceu chauffer
> Par tant de fois l'Océan et l'Enfer
> Et le lambris de la voute etherée.

The reader cannot have failed to see that Grisel is here reproducing the Latin epigram of Toscano or Faetanus, for the concluding "reflection" can hardly have had any other source:

> Nec mirum, his flammis, toties quibus arserat aether,
> Vos quoque perpetuum si caluistis aquae.

---

[23](Rouen, 1599), p. 79. Grisel was a native of Rouen, but virtually nothing more is known of him (cf. Goujet, *Bibl. Fr.*, XIII, 451).

Here, too, are the Nymphs, "ombrage" echoes "umbra," "murmure de l'onde" is "murmure aquae," "depuis chaude elle est demeurée" translates "aeternos focos," and "Qui s'en estonne" represents "Nec mirum." Save that Baiae is not mentioned, very little is altered. Only the addition of the "reflective" sentiment "le feu dont l'inhumain / Rend sa nature en malice fœconde" is perhaps notable, since this element is absent from the Latin version; but probably it is here no more than padding. Baiae belongs to the atmosphere of classical Latin and is naturally omitted in a vernacular poem.

Since Grisel imitates the epigram of Toscano or Faetanus, that epigram was available before 1599, and hence the epigram on which it, in turn, was based—"D'Arco's" version—must have been available in the sixteenth century.

The German poem in eight eight-line stanzas brought forward by Taussig in 1904 (*Jahrbuch,* 40, 232) need not detain us, since it was not published until 1624;[24] but a summary may be interesting as showing one more early variation of the theme. The poem "explains" how the medicinal baths of Baden near Vienna became warm: Venus and Cupid come to a spring, and fall asleep, Cupid having laid beside him his torch, arrow, and weapons. A maiden of the place saw them, said, "Ah, that is the god that burns my heart, I will play a trick on him," and plunged the torch deep in the spring. The waters took fire from the unquenchable torch. Amor awoke in alarm, looked for his brand, and found it in the spring. Drawing it forth he said: "Henceforth whoever bathes here shall feel my fire." And ever since, Baden has had the virtue and power of healing old and young.

I see no way of determining how the writer of this poem came by the subject. He has evidently altered the circumstances to suit his purpose. Certainly, he is not dependent on Stigel, who omits the very point here emphasized, namely, the creation of the warm bath; that, like Stigel, he makes Love draw the brand from the spring is probably an accidental resemblance. We might guess that his source, if not the Greek epigram itself, was closer to it than the Baiae poems, since these all omit point (3)—the intrusting of the torch to the Nymphs, here represented, as in the Italian version, by Love's laying his weapons aside: "Ihr Sohn legt neben sich sein

[24]It has been ascribed to Christoph von Schallenberg (1561–97).

162

Fakel, Pfeil und Waffen." The insistence in this poem on the cura-tive power of the bath probably has no other origin than the fact that the waters of Baden are actually medicinal.

Such is the history, as far as I am able to trace it, of the theme before it came to Shakespeare. Evidently there are missing links. From the material at hand, then, the most likely account seems to be the following. The verses of Regianus are probably independent of the Greek epigram. Those of "D'Arco" are an imitation of the Greek and were perhaps composed about the same time as Regi-anus' epigram and in the same atmosphere. That they were known in Italy in the fifteenth century is certain from their appearance in a manuscript of that period in the company of humanist poems. The Greek Anthology was first printed in 1494. The earliest modern exercise on the theme is that of Angeriano (1512), possibly suggested by the Greek epigram but more likely by one of the Latin epigrams to which, in any case, it probably owes its localization at Baiae. From Angeriano's poem that of Groto may be derived, while that of Fletcher certainly is. The verses of "D'Arco" were printed in 1533, and from them are descended the remaining Baiae poems—those of Faetanus or Toscano, Grisel, and Stigel; but these are corrected to the Greek epigram by the restoration of the Nymphs, whose place had been taken by Venus in Regianus and "D'Arco," and by Caelia in Angeriano. Saint-Gelais's "Fortune" suggests that his original belonged to the uncorrected Baiae tradition, whereas Le Duchat's "Naiades" suggests the corrected version, though neither his nor Ronsard's allusion to the theme can be satisfactorily accounted for. Meanwhile, a fairly close translation, now lost, of the Greek epigram occasioned the Italian version published in the *Versi et regole* (1539), though even here the influence of the Baiae poems, presumably "D'Arco," is felt in the addition of Baiae to the plane tree for the *mise-en-scène*. The only direct translation that we have from the Greek epigram, before Lubinus' prose version of the Anthology, is that of Sabeo published in 1556. The German poem on Baden cannot be accounted for but seems close to the Greek epigram. Thus we have two traditions—the one that of the Baiae poems springing, perhaps, from "D'Arco's" epigram (itself an im-itation of the Greek), the other directly from the Greek epigram. There is interplay between the two traditions, but on the whole the tradition of the Baiae poems is the stronger.

Shakespeare, Sonnet 153
Cupid laid by his brand and fell a sleepe,
A maide of *Dyans* this advantage found,
And his love-kindling fire did quickly steepe
In a could vallie-fountaine of that ground:
Which borrowd from this holie fire of love,
A datelesse lively heat still to indure,
And grew a seething bath which yet men prove,
Against strang malladies a soveraigne cure:
But at my mistres eie loves brand new fired,
The boy for triall needes would touch my brest,
I sick withall the helpe of bath desired,
And thether hied a sad distemperd guest.
   But found no cure, the bath for my help lies,
   Where *Cupid* got new fire, my mistres eyes.

Sonnet 154
The little Love-God lying once a sleepe,
Laid by his side his heart inflaming brand,
Whilst many Nymphes that vou'd chast life to keep,
Came tripping by, but in her maiden hand,
The fayrest votary tooke up that fire,
Which many Legions of true hearts had warm'd,
And so the Generall of hot desire,
Was sleeping by a Virgin hand disarm'd.
This brand she quenched in a coole Well by,
Which from loves fire tooke heat perpetuall,
Growing a bath and healthfull remedy,
For men diseased, but I my Mistrisse thrall,
   Came there for cure and this by that I prove,
   Loves fire heates water, water cooles not love.

We have remarked that there is a field for interesting observation in the study of the composition of sixteenth-century sonnets made from epigrams, and we may add in passing that such observation would be fruitful if begun with the French Pléiade, who employed such sources frankly and were conscious artists. Broadly speaking, there can be but two methods of stretching an epigram upon the frame of the sonnet. The one method makes an entire sonnet out of an epigram by stretching and diluting (compare Grisel above), while the other (frequent with Ronsard) agglutinates the epigram and other matter borrowed elsewhere or original.

In these two sonnets Shakespeare, whether consciously or not, has given examples of both methods. In Sonnet 153 the borrowed theme is set down compactly in the first six lines and a half, and is "agglutinated" to the poet's original conceits that follow. In Sonnet 154 the borrowed theme runs into line eleven but has to be diluted. The dilution is cleverly made a cement by carrying a motive of its own, virginity: "that vou'd chast life to keep," "but in her maiden hand," "and so . . . . by a Virgin hand disarm'd." Sonnet 153, however, is the more original in the sense that more of it is wholly given up to the poet's added inventions. In Sonnet 154 he is more interested in the epigram, in getting it into sonnet form. He had to invent for it a pointed ending, and this perhaps suggested to him the fancies to which he gave scope in Sonnet 153 by the alternate method of composition.

Granted the uncertainty of this last point, let us, nevertheless, look more closely at Sonnet 154. Of the elements belonging to the theme we here lack (1) localization, whether plane trees, shade, or Baiae; but we have (2) Love asleep, (3) his torch laid by, (4) the Nymphs, (5) a "reflective" phrase: "that fire / Which many legions of true hearts had warm'd," and, of course, (6) the heating of the waters and (7) the resulting hot bath. This analysis obliges us to eliminate as possible sources of Shakespeare all the Baiae poems that we have found, since all these pass over (3), the torch laid by or handed to the Nymphs. This, although the insistence on the eternal heat of the bath in both sonnets at first sight seems to reflect those poems: "tooke heat perpetuall" and "D'Arco," "aeternos concipit ignes" and although one pauses on Grisel's "Là mainte Nimphe arrivant vagabonde" recalling "Whilst many Nymphes. . . . / Came tripping by." As for this last parallel, indeed, lines 3–4 of Sonnet 154 seem to be mainly padding, like lines 7–8. If they are, it is noteworthy that the borrowed element of this sonnet, as well as that of 153, is contained in just over six lines—the six lines that Shakespeare would have found in a Latin translation of the Greek epigram or in the Greek epigram itself.

To return for a moment to the matter of priority. A very literal reader of Sonnet 154 might notice that the first two lines are deficient in sense; they make the love-god in his sleep perform the act of laying aside his brand:

> The little Love-God lying once a sleepe,
> Laid by his side his heart inflaming brand.

Noticing this difficulty, Shakespeare in his second attempt wrote very plainly:

> Cupid laid by his brand and fell a sleepe.

Is he so likely to have gone in the opposite direction? But the main object in Sonnet 153 is compression. Here we have two lines compressed into one. Next "a maide of Dyans" says compactly all that in 154 is spread over two lines and a half (and "a maide of Dyans" is further from the original "Nymphs" retained in 154). The padding is left out. Still more notable, the "reflective" phrase, something like which he certainly found in his original, is wholly sacrificed in 153. This point is, perhaps, decisive for the priority of 154. Finally, he compressed so well in lines 1–5 of 153 that he had to dilute again in line 6, and "heat perpetuall" of 154 becomes "A datelesse lively heat still to indure." We may be sure that the eternity of the heat was not so emphasized in his original.

Though Shakespeare is closer to the Greek epigram than he is to the Baiae poems, his management of the theme suggests that he did not draw immediately on the epigram. That he omits localization is perhaps without significance; but other points are worth notice. Love's brand is laid by his side, not laid by, or handed to, the Nymphs. There is no conspiracy of the Nymphs in direct address. The act—"This brand she quenched in a coole Well by"—is not represented in the Greek. There is as little likelihood, therefore, that the translations by Sabeo or Lubinus were known to Shakespeare.

We recur to the beginning of Sonnet 154:

> The little Love-God lying once a sleepe,
> Laid by his side his heart inflaming brand.

This slight absurdity occurs in the Italian version of the *Versi et regole,* and in no other version that we have found:

> Amore
> Dormendo stanco, presso posò la face.

That version, furthermore, is fairly close to the original, in six lines but without the dialogue of the Nymphs. Where the Greek has "placing it by [in the care of] the Nymphs" (Sabeo: "apposta iam lampade Nymphis"), the Italian and the English say, "Laid it by his side," "presso posò" (cf., however, also the German poem on Baden). "The fayrest votary" (singular) might represent "Naiade Calliroe." "Took up that fire" looks like "toltola"; and the act is described in the Italian as by Shakespeare: "l'immerse nel vago freddo rio," where also "freddo rio" and "coòle Well" represent a point not made in the Greek. There is less correspondence between the "reflective" phrases of the two versions; but "heat perpetuall" could be sufficiently accounted for by "sempre coccenti." There might even be a small involuntary—and hence all the more significant—memory of "già" in Shakespeare's "once" in his first line.

On the other hand, I seem to find fatal objections to regarding this Italian version as Shakespeare's immediate source. First, the Nymphs of the Greek epigram reappear in Shakespeare, and it would be too much to suppose that he had restored them accidentally out of "Naiade Calliroe." Second, the reflective phrase, "That many legions of true hearts had warm'd," is somewhat closer to πῦρ κραδίης μερόπων than to "de li gioveni amanti pietosa," which, besides, occurs too early in the poem. Third, while the bath is certainly implied in the Italian, it is not actually mentioned as in the Greek and in Shakespeare. Again, Shakespeare in both sonnets regards the torch as really quenched—a point that the Greek leaves somewhat uncertain, while in the Italian the torch is not quenched. Of these objections the most important is the first concerning the Nymphs.

As we have noted, by whatever channel the Greek epigram came to Shakespeare, he has reproduced it in both sonnets faithfully to the end in the creation of the warm bath. At that point, however, he adds the thought, not in the Greek, that the bath is curative for disease, and this becomes the point of both sonnets. If our modest collection of analogues has any weight, it suggests that this thought probably was not in the sources from which Shakespeare drew the epigram. None of our examples at all close to the Greek shows this trait, which tends rather to support the suggestion of Sidney Lee that this motive may show the influence of Fletcher's sonnet on a similar theme.

Thus Shakespeare's immediate source still eludes us, though we know somewhat better than before what we should expect to find.

In the state to which the question is brought by the present paper, it is noteworthy that the mistaken translation of Νύμφαις λαμπάδα παρθέμενος ("laid by his side"; "presso posò la face"; "legt neben sich sein Fakel") occurs only in the three versions for which we are unable to suggest a direct source. More light on Statio Romano might prove interesting.

Spenser's "Adamantine Chains":
A Cosmological Metaphor

In the following pages, an attempt to account for a phrase in Spenser's *Hymne in Honour of Love* will be the occasion for touching upon certain nuances in the handling by the Renaissance poets of the perennial theme of cosmic organization. Since the *topos*—the creation of the world, often as here by Love—is perennial, and the steps in the process are fixed, commentators have had no difficulty in illustrating this part of Spenser's poem from the countless statements of the theme that he might have known.[1] No one, I suppose, expects to find a unique source for Spenser. A Renaissance poet in a mood of high seriousness would feel bound to know a topic of this kind so thoroughly that he could handle it with originality while keeping within the confines of philosophical tradition. Spenser's phrasing is intended to guarantee his competence—an allusion to precosmic light, Love's "infused fire," man's "deducted spright," the technical concept of "mixture" (the elements "mixe themselves," v. 91). He takes care to be scientifically correct, and commentators have justifiably turned to philosophical or near-philosophical literature to illuminate his thought. But as one reads their findings and considers the precision of Spenser's language, the phrase "adamantine chains" for the Platonic bond of the ele-

Reprinted from Luitpold Wallach, ed., *The Classical Tradition.* Copyright © 1966 by Cornell University.

[1]Suggested parallels are collected in the "Variorum" Spenser edited by E. Greenlaw, C. G. Osgood, and F. M. Padelford, *Minor Poems* 1 (Baltimore, 1943), 662–81. Especially to the point is Rosamund Tuve's article, "A Medieval Commonplace in Spenser's Cosmology," *Studies in Philology* 30 (1933) 133–47; cf. her "Spenser and the *Zodiake of Life*," *Journal of English and Germanic Philology* 34 (1935) 1–19. More recently, Robert Ellrodt's book *Neoplatonism in the Poetry of Spenser* (Geneva, 1960) sheds new light on the antecedents of Spenser's thought, but offers nothing on the specific subject of this paper.

ments calls attention to itself as something not found in that literature and as untraditional at a point where the tradition is strong and consistent. I judge that the commentators regard it as only a poet's whim. Certainly the point seems small, but perhaps *hae nugae seria ducent.*

Love, born of Venus, taking wings of his own heat (kindled originally from heaven's life-giving fire), moves through dark chaos with light lent by his mother from her own goodly ray—

> Then through the world his way he gan to take,
> The world that was not till he did it make;
> Whose sundrie parts he from them selves did sever,
> The which before had lyen confused ever.
>
> The earth, the ayre, the water, and the fyre
> Then gan to raunge them selves in huge array.
> And with contrary forces to conspyre
> Each against other, by all meanes they may,
> Threatning their owne confusion and decay:
> Ayre hated earth, and water hated fyre,
> Till Love relented their rebellious yre.
>
> He then them tooke, and tempering goodly well
> Their contrary dislikes with loved meanes,
> Did place them all in order, and compell
> To keepe them selves within their sundrie raines,
> Together linkt with Adamantine chaines;
> Yet so as that in every living wight
> They mixe themselves and shew their kindly might. [74-91]

While most poetical cosmogonies follow Ovid (*Met.* 1.5 ff.) in identifying the original chaos with the war of the elements and taking "separation" and "uniting" as one step, Spenser keeps in touch with Plato's *Timaeus* (31C-32C, 53A-B) in imagining a moment after "separation" and before "uniting" when, he says, the elements threaten each other and are not yet in their right places. In language that allows for the *Timaeus,* yet is indicative of the contrasting and combining "qualities" (earth dry and cold, water cold and moist, etc.), the elements are characterized by "contrary dislikes" and "loved meanes," and it is by the latter that they are united. Thus the adamantine chains merely repeat the idea of "loved meanes" in a more palpable metaphor. This follows Plato, who explains the union of the elements as a proportion with extremes and means and calls it metaphorically a "bond." Adamant is a substance of a high metaphorical potential; the specific meanings the word may have are easily subordinated, and its obvious etymology—*adamas,* "the unconquerable," "the durable"—invites metaphorical application. Plato himself employs adamant in cosmic construction in the "adamantine spindle" of Necessity in the *Republic* (618c). Furthermore, the expression "adamantine chains" itself is used proverbially in Greek and perhaps still more in Latin.[2] Dionysius I thought his tyranny was secured ἀδαμαντίνοις δεσμοῖς (Plutarch, *Dion.* 7 and 10); Psyche is bound by Cupid *adamantinis nexibus* (Mart. Capella 1.7); St. Augustine uses the phrase to designate a strong argument;[3] in Manilius (1.923) it refers to the end of the Roman civil wars: "Adamanteis discordia vincta catenis"; and perhaps most commonly, the Latin poets in describing the underworld bind with adamantine chains the monster Cerberus (Ovid, *Met.* 7.412; Seneca, *Herc. fur.* 808) and various sinners: Coeus in Valerius Flaccus 3.224–5; the Giants in Statius, *Theb.* 4.534; Pluto prepares such chains for sinners in Lucan 6.801. All this is true, and suggests the possibility of Spenser's image, but the fact seems to be that in all the vast cosmogonical literature (so far as I have explored it), no one but Spenser (and a few poets to be mentioned later) applies this expression to the bond of the elements. Traditional *topoi* tend to carry their metaphors with them and to resist others. Besides, "adamant," though it exists in literature almost entirely as a synonym for durability, was felt to have a material reference, often "steel," and the association with iron appears in a common cliché, ἀδάμας καὶ σίδηρος, though this expression is itself always, I believe, metaphorical. But everyone knew that the cohesive principle of the world was a function and immaterial, whether Plato's mathematics or the coincident qualities of the elements or the action of the Stoic Spirit (specifically Physis) or of the Christian Trinity (specifically of the Logos-Son and the Holy Spirit) or of some other demiurge: Amor, Pax, Concordia, Clementia, Amicitia (for when Plato says that the

---

[2]See Stephanus' Greek *Thesaurus* and the *Thesaurus Linguae Latinae* under *adamas* and its derivatives.

[3]"Rationes, quae illam propositionem adamantinis, ut dicitur, catenis innexae consequuntur" (*De duab. anim.* 23; *PL* 42.110); cf. Plato δέδεται, καὶ εἰ ἀγροικότερόν τι εἰπεῖν ἔστιν, σιδηροῖς καὶ ἀδαμαντίνοις λόγοις (*Gorgias* 508E).

Essays on Renaissance Poetry

bond gave the world friendship, φιλίαν, this concept soon rose from the predicate—or was resurrected, if φιλία alludes to Empedocles' Philia or Philotes—to become the active subject of the statement). Whatever the agent, the range of metaphor for the bond (and the agent of course is the bond) remained remarkably discreet.[4] It may reside only in the verb of binding—συνδεῖν, ligare, nectere, or the like—or in such a verb with an instrumental noun, "quasi quodam vinculo" (Cicero, *De nat. deor.* 2.45.115), or a noun suitably qualified, as δαιμονίῳ δεσμῷ (Timaeus Locrus 99B), "concordi pace ligavit" (Ovid, *Met.* 1.25), ἀρρήκτῳ τινὶ φιλίας δεσμῷ (St. Basil, *Hom.* 2 *in Hexaem.*, PG 29, 33A). One may distinguish between the primary bond of the elements and the derived bond of the "mixed" world: "Sitque haec discordia concors, / quae nexus habilis et opus generabile fingit" (Manilius 1.142-43); "aeterno complectens omnia nexu, / O rerum mixtique salus, Concordia, mundi / et sacer orbis Amor" (Lucan 4.189-97). Roman writers favor *pax* and *foedus*: "Alterno religatus foedere mundus" (Manilius 3.55); "Pugnantia semina foedus perpetuum tenent" (Boethius, *Cons.* 2, metr. 8, where also *frena*). Less nobly, Prudentius' elements are slaves: "Dum servant elementa suum famulantia cursum" (*Contra Sym.* 2.803). Those of Martianus Capella, in a figure whose background need not be traced here, are married: "[Hymenaeus] semina... arcanis stringens pugnantia vinclis...: namque elementa ligas vicibus mundumque maritas" (*De nupt.* 1.1). Farther afield, in Dionysius the Areopagite divine Peace holds all things together with something like bars or bolts, ὥσπερ τισὶ κλείθροις τῶν διῃρημένων συμπτυκτικοῖς (*De div. nom.* 11.1). But later writers generally repeat with modest variations the expressions of the ancients. The twelfth-century cosmogonists delight in accumulating such figures; for example, Alanus ab Insulis: "[Natura] fidei nexu civilia bella refrenans / et fratrum rixas, elementis oscula pacis / indidit, et numeri nodo meliore ligavit" (*Anti-claudianus* 1.194-96 Bossuat). Dante's universe is a book "legato con amore in un volume" (*Par.* 33.86). For Ficino, Love is the "nodus perpetuus et copula mundi" (*Comm. in Symp.* 3.3). In

[4]The examples mentioned here are limited so far as possible to explicit references to the elements, but the metaphor was soon extended to the cohesive principle in all being—by Posidonius according to Jaeger (*Nemesios von Emesa* [Berlin, 1914], pp. 101 ff.), already in the *Epinomis* according to J. A. Festugière (*La révélation d'Hermès Trismégiste 2, Le dieu cosmique* [Paris, 1949], 216-17).

Pontano's *Urania*, "aequa compage ligavi [sc. Juppiter] / Nexibus alternis et amico singula vinclo" (*Opera*, 1513, f. 18ᵛ). Du Bartas reverts to marriage: "le nœud du sacré mariage / Qui joint les elemens" (*Sem.* 1, *Jour* 2, 245–46). Rabelais sees the elements bound together by Debt (*Tiers livre*, ch. 3).

All this language keeps to function and contemplates no actual material, which would in fact be "earth." Yet there is little objection to "adamant" on that account, if the word is taken as a synonym for "durable" (= ἄρρηκτος). And in fact there is a metallic or quasi-metallic metaphor that has been supposed to have been in Spenser's mind. In annotating this passage, the late Charles G. Osgood assumed as a matter of course that the adamantine chains are the *aurea catena Homeri* (Iliad 8.18–26), and Emil Wolff in an interesting book on this metaphor in English literature, states without argument: "Die 'adamantine chaines' sind hier an die Stelle der goldenen Kette getreten."[5] The assumption is that the *aurea catena Homeri* was the traditional metaphor for the bond of the elements and that Spenser so regarded it. For the tradition there has been adduced the *Roman de la Rose*: "La bele chaeine dorée, / Qui les quatre elemens enlace" (16,786–87 Langlois), and for Spenser's acceptance of it, *FQ* 4.1.30:

> For all this world's fair workmanship she [Atê] tride
> Unto his last confusion to bring,
> And that great golden chain quite to divide,
> With which it blessed Concord hath together tide.

Nevertheless, the assumption will not, I think, bear scrutiny as an explanation of the chains of the *Hymne in Honour of Love*. The *aurea catena* has indeed a tradition as representing the union of the elements, but a rather obscure one, far from being the main tradition of this metaphor, and it does not seem to have affected the Platonic creation sequence with which Spenser is here working. Pierre Lévêque, in a careful study of the *aurea catena* metaphor,[6] is able to cite for this meaning only the same three witnesses that Karl

---

[5] Osgood, "Variorum" Spenser, *Minor Poems* 1.513–14; Wolff, *Die goldene Kette: die Aurea catena Homeri in der englischen Literatur von Chaucer bis Wordsworth* (Hamburg, 1947), p. 19.

[6] *Aurea Catena Homeri, une étude sur l'allégorie grecque* (Annales Littéraires de l'Université de Besançon 27; [Paris, 1959] 23–28. Lévêque's aim is to be as exhaustive as possible.

Reinhardt had cited in his doctoral dissertation[7]—Eustathius on the Iliad and two anonymous scholiasts on Homer and Hesiod—all apparently of the twelfth century; but the notion seems to be part of a more widely attested allegory, not of Iliad 8.18–26, where Zeus speaks of the golden chain (σειρά) let down from heaven, but of Iliad 15.18–21, where he reminds Hera how he suspended her from heaven, attaching anvils to her feet and binding her hands with an "unbreakable golden bond" (δεσμὸν . . . χρύσεον ἄρρηκτον). An allegory invented or adopted by the Stoics saw in this scene the binding of the elements, and this golden δεσμός was sometimes assimilated to the golden σειρά of Iliad 8.[8] This interpretation was of course known to the Renaissance, and might be found, for example, in the useful *Mythologia* of Natale Conti (2.4, Juno). But this was and is a learned curiosity, well out of the main stream of the *aurea catena* metaphor. In the main tradition, the golden chain represents the Stoic εἱμαρμένη or universal chain of causes, or the Neoplatonic chain of being.[9] It extends down from the highest being to the lowest, "lessening down / From infinite perfection to the brink / Of dreary nothing" (Thomson, *Seasons*, "Summer" 334–36), and so keeps in touch with Homer's original picture of a σειρά extending downward rather than a δεσμός that ties together.[10] Proclus indeed, who is an authority on this matter, since his world is everywhere in chains of one kind or another, seems to refer the golden chain to the Platonic transcendent triad, making it prior to the lower bond taken "in three senses," bond of Mind, of Soul, and of Nature (elements).[11] Proclus' considerable

[7] *De Graecorum theologia capita duo* (Berlin, 1910).

[8] Lévêque, *op. cit.*, pp. 27–28; F. Buffière, *Les mythes d'Homère et la pensée grecque* (Paris, 1956), pp. 115–17; J. Pépin, *Mythe et allégorie* (Paris, 1958), pp. 161–62.

[9] Most of the examples in Wolff's *Die goldene Kette* illustrate this meaning, and it is this chain that is the subject of A. O. Lovejoy's well-known book, *The Great Chain of Being* (Cambridge, Mass., 1936).

[10] The authority of Macrobius (*In Som. Scip.* 1.14, 15) may be largely credited with fixing this meaning in the tradition; Thomson seems almost to be translating Macrobius' description: "Invenietur . . . a summo deo usque ad ultimam rerum faecem una mutuis se vinculis religans et nusquam interrupta connexio; et haec est Homeri catena aurea."

[11] *In Tim.*, Diehl, ed., 146E and 173F. In 146E, he describes the δεσμός (Mind, Soul, Elements) as διὰ πάντων τεταμένος καὶ ὑπὸ τῆς χρυσῆς σειρᾶς συνεχόμενος. In 173F: "Strong [κρατερός] is the bond [δεσμός] from Mind and Soul, as Orpheus also says, but greater and the cause of greater goods is the unification of the golden chain [χρυσῆς σειρᾶς]." He repeatedly cites the lines of "Orpheus" (frg. 166 Kern): αὐτὰρ ἐπὴν δεσμὸν κρατερὸν περὶ πάντα τανύσσῃς, / σειρὴν χρυσείην ἐξ αἰθέρος ἀρτήσαντα.

authority is against identifying the specific bond of the elements with the golden chain. And again, why should anyone who was supposedly thinking of a golden chain write "adamantine chains" instead? Yet even that is possible. Three years after the appearance of Spenser's *Hymnes,* one might read in Sir John Davies' poem on the immortality of the soul, *Nosce Teipsum* (1599), the following vigorous lines:

> Could Eve's weake hand, extended to the tree,
> In sunder rend that adamantine chaine,
> Whose golden linkes effects and causes bee,
> And which to God's owne chaire doth fixt remaine?[12]

This is a classic description of the golden chain of Homer—effects and causes, fixed to the throne of God, and manifestly golden, since what is a chain apart from its Links? It is called "adamantine" no doubt in the sense of "solid, unbreakable," the word being abstracted from its material reference yet retaining enough of it to effect, with "golden," a pleasant irritation of paradox. But this has nothing to do with Spenser's *Hymne,* even if Davies borrowed the words from it. This chain is not the bond of the elements and does not occur in a cosmological setting; it is God's universal plan, especially as regards the soul.[13] Spenser, when writing his hymn, was thinking only of the bond of the elements and thinking only in the tradition of the cosmological theme, where he would encounter principally the cautious range of metaphor that we have surveyed and seldom a golden, never, I believe, an adamantine chain— except in the small group of poets to which we now turn.

The only place, so far as I can discover, in which Spenser would find this application of the proverbial adamantine chains is in the French poets of the Pléiade group, with whose work he is well known to have been familiar. The exact expression seems to belong to Jean-Antoine de Baïf, but Ronsard prepares the way and perhaps explains how Baïf came to adopt it. In Ronsard's earliest cosmogony (he has several), the pindaric *Ode de la Paix* (1550), Peace violently (perhaps Orphically) rummages the womb of the All to bring forth its "obscur fardeau," which she proceeds to "dismember" in four quarters and put together with adamantine *nails,*

[12] *The Complete Poems,* A. Grosart, ed. (London, 1876), 1.53–54.
[13] Cf. Lévêque, *op. cit.,* ch. 2.

"lia de clous d'aimant."[14] The Empedoclean γόμφοι suit the tone and give the poet the happy opportunity of insinuating into his pindaric ode a phrase of Pindar (κρατεροῖς ἀδάμαντος δῆσεν ἅλοις).[15] He was well aware that he was substituting nails for the usual "bond."[16] When Ronsard uses the expression "adamantine bonds," it is in a different cosmic context. In his *Hymne des Astres* (1555), the stars are kept in place by a "lien aimantin" in a passage based on Marullus' *Hymnus Stellis* where Marullus has "solida catena."[17] But Marullus, the chief inspirer of Ronsard's philosophical hymns, may have given the start for the usage we are interested in. In his *Hymnus Aeternitati* 25, in reference indeed to time and not immediately to the elements, he writes: "Perpetuoque adamante ligas fugientia saecla," perhaps thinking of Plato's adamantine spindle, but verbally close to Ovid in a different context: "adamas licet adliget illud" (*Tristia* 4.8.45). Ronsard duly reproduces this expression in his *Hymne d'Eternité* (1556), 80–81:

> Tu nourris l'univers en éternelle paix,
> D'un lien aimantin les siècles tu attaches.[18]

Ronsard will return to our consideration shortly in another phase of the subject.[19]

Elsewhere I shall show in more detail that J.-A. de Baïf's long *Hymne de la Paix* is largely a paraphrase, or even a translation, of

[14]*Œuvres complètes*, Paul Laumonier, ed. (Paris, 1914–), 3.6.

[15]*Pyth.* 4.71; noted by Laumonier. Cf. also Horace, *Carm.* 3. 24.5: "Figit adamantinos . . . Necessitas clavos."

[16]If we assume, as seems likely, that Ronsard had in mind the ἀόρατοι γόμφοι of *Timaeus* 43A, with which the ephemeral frame of the human body is constructed, we may infer that his universe is less durable than Plato's. For the various views expressed by him on such matters, see Isidore Silver, "Ronsard's Reflections on Cosmogony and Nature," *PMLA* 79 (1964) 219–33.

[17]*Œuvres, ed. cit.*, 8.153.

[18]*Michaelis Marulli Carmina*, A. Perosa, ed. (Zürich: Thesaurus Mundi, 1951), p. 114; Ronsard, *ed. cit.*, 8.251.

[19]Spenser's idea of writing philosophical hymns may well have been inspired by Ronsard, and Ronsard certainly took the idea from Marullus, who had supplied Latin literature with this form which it lacked. Marullus's hymns, I believe, are intended to be "Orphic," since the Orphic Hymns were highly venerated in his milieu. Their content is Neoplatonic and Stoic, but he works in as many expressions as he can from the Orphic fragments. In this he resembles Proclus, who in expounding Neoplatonic doctrine likes to believe that it is sanctioned by Orpheus, for him ὁ θεολόγος. About half of Marullus' deities are organizers of chaos; and the ordering of chaos was the chief theme associated with the name of Orpheus.

parts of the fourth book of the *Zodiacus vitae* of Palingenius (Manzolli).[20] After some prefatory verses, the hymn proper begins with a paraphrase of the following lines of the original:[21]

> Praeterea caelum, tellus, aerque, fretumque
> Atque ignis, demum totius machina mundi
> Hoc stat et hoc durat tot iam per saecula nexu.[22]
> Nam nisi tantus amor *firma compage* teneret
> Omnia, pugnarent vinclis elementa solutis:
> Non caelum terris lucem radiosque calentes
> Nec generandarum praeberet semina rerum,[23]
> Aera finitimum consumeret improbus ignis [etc.].

In reproducing this passage, Baïf makes the alterations that I note by italics:

> Le ciel, la terre, l'air, et la mer, et le feu,
> Et tout le monde entier, d'un amiable neu
> S'entretienent conjoints. Cette belle machine
> Sans la bonne amitié tomberoit en ruine,
> Car s'ils n'estoyent liez de *liaisons d'émant,*
> On verroit rebeller tout mutin élement
> Et guerroyer l'un l'autre: et soudain *toutes choses*
> *Dans l'ancien chaos retomberoient encloses.*
> Le ciel refuseroit aux terres son ardeur,
> Et de ses chauds rayons la vitale tiedeur
> Ne departiroit plus les benines semences,
> Dont toutes choses ont leurs premieres naissances.
> Le feu sec bruleroit l'air son moite voisin [etc.].

It is the French poet, not his source, who brings in the adamantine chains. Perhaps significant also is his expansion on the contingent return of chaos.

Curiously enough, Baïf's intrusion of this phrase into this context can be closely paralleled from another French poet of the same

---

[20]Baïf, *Euvres en rime*, Marty-Laveaux, ed. (Paris, 1883), 2.223. The *Hymne* appeared in Baïf's collective *Euvres* of 1572–73.

[21]Palingenius, *Zodiacus vitae* 4 (Cancer) 457–64. Palingenius believes in five elements.

[22]*Hoc nexu*, i.e., by the bond of God's love just mentioned.

[23]Cf. Macrobius, *Sat.* 1.8.8: "Cumque semina rerum omnium post caelum gignendarum de caelo fluerent."

group. In 1575, Ronsard published a small pamphlet entitled *Les estoilles à Monsieur de Pibrac,* containing six poems, the title piece being a "Hymne des Estoilles," paraphrasing, once more, Marullus' *Hymnus Stellis.* In the same year, his younger friend and former secretary, Amadis Jamyn, published his own *Œuvres poétiques,* including a "Hymne des Estoilles," also paraphrasing Marullus.[24] Marullus alludes to the bond as follows:

> At ipsa coelo lucida sydera
> Affixa cursus deproperant suos,
>   Secura privati laboris,
>   Dum stet opus *solida catena*
>
> Naturae et aeterni imperium Iovis.

Ronsard's version of this is:

> Ainsi vous plaist, Estoilles.
>
> Et toutefois loing des misères
> Qu'aux mortels vous versez icy,
> Vous mocquez de nostre soucy,
> Tournant voz courses ordinaires,
> Et n'avez peur de rien,
> Tant que *le fort lien*
> De la saincte Nature
> Tient ce monde arresté
> Et que la magesté
> Du grand Jupiter dure.

Jamyn writes:

> Mais les lampes au Ciel fichées
> Hastent leur branle coutumier,
> Et ne se meslent empeschées
> D'un affaire particulier,

---

[24]Ronsard, *et. cit.,* 17.37; Jamyn, *Œuv. poét.* (Paris, 1575),f. 51^r; Marullus, *ed. cit.,* p. 122. Ronsard's poem seems to have been written early in 1574 in allusion to a celestial phenomenon of the time. What relation Jamyn's poem may have to Ronsard's is uncertain; the only comment I have seen is that of Marcel Raymond, *Bibliographie critique de Ronsard en France (1550–1585)* (Paris, 1927) p. 91: "J. suit Marulle plutôt que Ronsard." Yet influence of a sort may exist in what seems like a determined effort on Jamyn's part to avoid the phrasing and form of Ronsard's paraphrase of the same original.

Spenser's "Adamantine Chains"

> Pourveu que l'œuvre de nature
> Et l'Empire de Jupiter
> En sa constante beauté dure,
> Et puisse les ans dépiter,
> *Lié d'une aimantine chaisne.*

Very possibly Jamyn may have taken the phrase from Baïf, whose *Euvres* had recently appeared. There the exact words he uses are found, not in the *Hymne de la Paix,* but in a more notable composition, *Les Muses,* which deserves our attention for its own sake.[25] This poem embodies a hymn to Love, designated as a sacred hymn ("hymne sainct") and sung by Orpheus. It has not, I believe, been analyzed before. The hymn is embedded in the story of the Argonauts; Jason goes to fetch Orpheus and finds him singing and playing his harp before his cavern, and the magical effect of his music on nymphs, wild beasts, and trees is described in detail. Orpheus' hymn to Love, which then follows, is a complete composition in itself, and we may suppose that Baïf, who believed in the ancient "effects" of music and presumably in the importance of Orpheus as the exemplar of the *prisca theologia,* has taken unusual pains with it.[26] It must be an "Orphic" hymn. It is carefully constructed in hymn form (invocation, the god's *benefacta,* final prayer).[27] As an Orphic hymn it is inevitably a hymn to Love the Creator:

> O premier né (disoit il) je te chante,
> Amour aislé, dont la force alechante
> D'un nœud fertil toutes choses conjoint,
> Et d'éguillon semencier les époint.

Love, now addressed as a shining star ("Astre luisant"), is celebrated for arranging chaos, described as war among the elemental qualities, from which he himself springs:

> De gaillarde alegresse
> Saillant dehors de ceste mace épesse,

---

[25]*Euvres, ed. cit.,* 2.71–91.

[26]For Baïf's profound interest in the "effects" of music, see Frances A. Yates, *The French Academies of the Sixteenth Century* (London, 1947) *passim;* see also D. P. Walker, "Orpheus the Theologian and Renaissance Platonists," *Journ. of the Warburg and Courtauld Inst.* 16 (1953) 100–120, and "The *Prisca Theologia* in France," *ibid.,* 17 (1954) 204–59.

[27]Aphthonius, *Progymnasmata* 8, on encomia; but encomia (for men) and hymns (for gods) have the same form.

179

Tu debrouillas ce desordre, ô bon Dieu,
A chacque chose assignant propre lieu.[28]

He fixes the vault of heaven (presumably a fifth element) and
below it ranges fire, air, water, and earth,

de rebelles accords,
Entr' alliant les membres de ces corps.

He creates sun and moon in the region of fire and adds the celestial
poles to delimit time. And so, Orpheus continues:

Depuis, ô Dieu, *de chaine adamantine*
Ayant lié ceste belle machine

—and having formed the earth (lakes, hills, etc.) and created the
animals (the special creation of man is passed over, as is usual in
these cosmogonies; Love is only Physis), Love proceeds with his
function of vitalizing and preserving:

Depuis porté dessus tes aisles gayes
Par tout le monde hault et bas tu t'égayes, ...
Tous animaux et nous hommes chetifs,
Ici tu poinds, de ta flamme douc' aigre
Grillant les cœurs.

His role as preserver is emphasized:

Tout te craint, Dieu; à ta douce puissance
O premier-veu, tout rend obéissance.
Si tout le monde en toy ne s'asseuroit,
Par le discord il se démembreroit.
Mais par tes dons, Semencier, tout s'asseure.

The hymn ends with a formal and summarizing invocation:

Je te saluë, ô Dieu, qui sur ton aisle
Premier vuidas la masse universelle
Du vieil chaos, faisant évanouir

[28]The sense in which Love is born of Chaos is explained, e.g., by Ficino, *Com. in
Symp.* 1.3 (Plato, *Symp.* 178B).

Spenser's "Adamantine Chains"

La vieille nuit, le jour épanouir.
Je te saluë, Amour, de qui la grace
Des choses tient en son estre la race,
Par qui tout vit, par qui tout ce qui est
Pour vivre meurt, et pour mourir renaist.

Divided by anaphora into two quatrains, this prayer might be read as invoking the Father or the creative Son ("Let there be light") in "ô Dieu," and in "Amour" the vitalizing and preserving Holy Spirit (identified since Abelard as *Caritas*). Just possibly that may be the intention; "par qui tout vit" sounds like an allusion to "in ipso enim vivimus et movemur et sumus" (Acts 17:28), and if Aratus, quoted here by Paul, anticipated Christian truth, why should not Orpheus, prime exponent of the *prisca theologia,* hint at creation by the Trinity and know about divine grace that keeps the "race of things" in being?[29]

The hymn begins with what also might be taken as an Orphic ambiguity in the address to the creator as "premier né," clearly Protogonos (i.e., Phanes or Eros) of the Orphic fragments, but possibly also suggestive of Christ the "first born" (Matt. 1:25; Heb. 1:6), to whom in Christian cosmogony the physical creation is "appropriated."[30] "Premier veu" and "astre luisant" presumably also refer to Phanes. In the setting and in the theme of creation, Baïf has the Orphic *Argonautica* in view, but whereas the *Argonautica* describes the magical effects of Orpheus' singing after his hymn as its result, Baïf discreetly describes them before Orpheus sings, and his hymn is elaborated with only a general similarity to the hymn in the Greek poem.[31] He has laid several other sources under con-

---

[29]It is difficult to know how far one may go in finding implications in such a passage. What is said above may be thought to go too far; but the typology of Orpheus and Christ is deep-rooted in the tradition; see E. R. Curtius, *European Literature and the Latin Middle Ages,* Eng. tr. (New York, 1953), p. 244. See Walker, "Orpheus the Theologian," p. 109, for Orpheus' supposed foreknowledge of Christian doctrines: monotheism, the Trinity, and creation according to Genesis (but the last less often attributed to him than the first two). Guy Lefèvre de la Boderie (1570) interprets Orph. frg. 168 Kern to mean that Orpheus, in speaking of Eros as the son of Wisdom, refers to the Son and the Holy Spirit (Walker, "The *Prisca Theologia,*" p. 227).
[30]See H. Pinard, "Création," in *Dict. de Théol. Cath.* 3.2.2034-2201.
[31]Orphic *Argonautica* 377-443 Abel. Orpheus sings of "the dark night of old chaos, how it changed its nature and heaven came into being; of the genesis of the earth and the depths of the sea; of Eros the eldest, the self-sufficient, the all-wise, how he begat all and separated one thing from another"; also of Kronos and Zeus,

tribution. From Ovid comes part of his description of chaos and part of his account of the formation of the earth.[32] And as expected, he makes considerable use of Marullus' *Hymnus Amori*.[33] From it he takes the epithet "Astre luisant" ("splendidus sydus"); for the *concordia discors* he echoes Marullus' striking phrase "pace rebelli" in "rebelles accords" (Marullus of course does not have the "chaine adamantine," merely writing "mutuis nectis ... catenis"); but what Baïf chiefly owes to Marullus is most of the twenty lines he devotes to Love as the propagator of life.[34] Yet his emphasis on this function at the beginning and at the end of the hymn—"la force alechante / D'un nœud fertil ... d'éguillon semencier les époint ... par tes dons, Semencier, tout s'asseure"—goes beyond Marullus and suggests an independent apprehension of Love as the σπερματικὸς λόγος.[35]

Describing the magical effects before Orpheus sings, Baïf does

---

the birth and strife of the gods, and of the generation of men. The corresponding hymn in the *Argonautica* of Apollonius of Rhodes (1.496–511) is less suggestive (e.g., no mention of Eros), and the setting (a banquet) is different. Baïf's setting (visit of Jason to Orpheus' cavern) resembles the setting of the Orph. *Arg.* (visit of the heroes including Orpheus to the cavern of Chiron), and I think this source gave Baïf the general form of this episode. But he has filled it out from other sources; for example, the magical effects of Orpheus' singing include effects on the sea-gods ("A son chanter les Nymphes ... hors leur moite repaire / Poussoyent leur chef," etc.) taken from Catullus 64.17–18; the effect on the birds—i.e. the swallow, "Qui s'oubliant et de plus loing voler / Et de son nid, pend surprise dans l'air"—is not, as one might expect, from Orph. *Arg.* 439, ταρσοῖς κεκμηῶσιν, ἑῆς δ'ἐλάθοντο καλιῆς, but from Silius Italicus 11.467–468 (Ruperti), "Immemor et dulcis nidi, positoque volatu, / Non mota volucris captiva pependit in aethra."

[32]E.g., soft and hard are "qualities"; Ovid, *Met.* 1.18–20, "Quia corpore in uno / ... pugnabunt ... mollia cum duris": "Quand en un corps ... la chose molle avec la chose dure ... avoit debat"; *Met.* 1.38, "Addidit et fontes et stagna immensa lacusque": "Ayant fait que les eaux dorment en lacs."

[33]Marullus, *ed. cit.*, 110.

[34]E.g.,

> "Puissant Amour, maugré leurs moites ondes,
> Du vieil Forcyn les filles dans leurs creux
> Tu vas brusler de tes pétillans feux."

> "mediisque in undis
> Improbus Phorci nimia puellas
> Lampade aduris."

[35]I know of no source for *nœud fertil* and *Semencier;* the latter word is rare as a noun in this sense or perhaps unique in this passage. The idea of course is unexceptionable; cf. Ficino's statement of the subject of the *Timaeus:* "Sit ergo huius libri subiectum ipsa universa natura, id est, seminaria quaedam et unifica Virtus toti infusa mundo" (*In Tim. Plat.* c. 1).

not pretend that his hymn will move trees. But after the song, he mentions its effect on Jason:

> Cet hymne sainct le poète Eagride
> Avoit fini, quand Jason Esonide
> Il apperceut, qui n'avoit le pouvoir,
> Tout épris d'aise encor de se mouvoir:
> Si doucement ceste douce merveille
> Avoit ravi son âme par l'oreille.

It can hardly be doubted that Baïf here reproduces the effect on the listening heroes of Orpheus' hymn of creation in the *Argonautica* of Apollonius of Rhodes (1.512-15): "He ended, and stayed his lyre and divine voice; but though he had ceased they still bent forward with eagerness all hushed to quiet, with ears intent on the enchanting strain (ὀρθοῖσιν ἐπ' οὔασιν ἠρεμέοντες κηληθμῷ), such a charm of song (θέλκτρον ἀοιδῆς) had he left behind in their hearts."[36] But perhaps it is more interesting that the founder of the Académie de Poésie et de Musique represents Apollonius with what may be called the standard formula for musical "ecstasy," the ultimate effect of solemn music: "Avoit ravi son âme par l'oreille." This phrase, perhaps invented by the Pléiade, seems to have crossed the Channel with their influence.[37]

This accomplished hymn to Love would have deserved the attention of Spenser, if we could assume that he knew it. The assumption is not unlikely, but the most I would assert is that the use of "adamantine chains" in this context ensures that the *Hymne in Honour of Love* has a French background. The content of Baïf's hymn coincides with only a part of Spenser's; the disposition of material is different (e.g., Spenser omits the molding of the earth); and the

---

[36]R. C. Seaton's translation (Loeb Library).

[37]See Gretchen L. Finney, "Ecstasy and Music in Seventeenth-Century England" in *Journ. Hist. Ideas* 8 (1947), 153-86, esp. 175-81, where references for the following are given: Du Bellay: "harmonie . . . tirant l'âme par les oreilles"; Ronsard: "Avecque ta voix nompareille, / Leur tires l'âme par l'oreille, / D'un vertueux enchantment," and in another poem: "ta voix . . . pour attirer une âme par l'oreille"; Du Bartas (compare Baïf): "sons, / Qui par le charme doux de leur douce merveille, / Emblent aux escoutans les âmes par l'oreille"; William Strode: "thus pleasingly to teare, / The soul forth of the body by the eare"; T. Crashaw: "soul snatch out at his ears / By a strong ecstasy"; T. Stanley: "The music of this heavenly sphere, / Would steal each soul out at the eare"; and similarly Spenser: "Every deed and word that he did say, / Was like enchantment that through both the eyes / And both the eares did steale the hart away" (FQ 6.2.3). I give these instances at length, since the fortune of this phrase may parallel that of the adamantine chains.

handling of the hymn form is not quite the same (e.g., Spenser makes more of the topic "honorable birth" from Venus, and his final invocation is in the manner of the Homeric hymns, embodying a promise to sing again on another occasion).[38] There is no Orphism in Spenser's hymn. What can perhaps be compared is the insistence in both hymns on Love's essential fire that sustains the generations: "brusler de tes pétillans feux," "de ta flamme douc'aigre grillant les cœurs"; "are increast through secret sparks of his infused fyre," "to quench the flame which they [animals] in burning fynde"; it goes "par tout le monde hault et bas," "both most and least," and is a πῦρ τεχνικόν that transcends the common elemental fire. With due caution, since similar themes demand similar language, some verbal similarities may also be noted:

> So ever since they [elements] *firmely have remained,*
> *And duly well observed his beheast;*
> Through which now all these things that are contained
> Within this goodly cope, both most and least,
> *Their being have,* and dayly are increast
> Through secret sparks of his infused fyre
> Which in the barraine cold he doth inspyre.
> *Thereby they all do live, and moved are*
> To multiply the likenesse of their kynd.

[38]The formal aspect of Spenser's hymn is seldom noticed by the commentators, who mostly search philosophical treatises for the thought and neglect the Renaissance hymns to Love, except indeed Benivieni's *Canzone d'Amore,* which is in canzone form. I find no mention in the "Variorum" Spenser of Philippe Desportes' hymn to Love (*Chant d'Amour* in *Œuvres,* A. Michiels, ed. [Paris, 1858], pp. 50-53) which is in hymn form and in a stanza similar to Spenser's. It begins like Spenser's hymn with the poet's own experience:

> "Puis que je suis épris d'une beauté divine,
> Puis qu'un amour céleste est roy de ma poitrine...."

> "Love, that long since hast to thy mighty powre
> Perforce subdude my poore captived hart...."

And the final invocation, like Spenser's, imitates the Homeric form of a promise; both poets offer to sing again in a higher style:

> "O Dieu puissant et bon, seul sujet de ma lyre,...
> Donne-moy pour loyer qu'un jour je puisse faire
> Un œuvre à ta louange éloigné du vulgaire,
> Et qui ne suive point le trac accoustumé."

> "Then would I sing of thine immortall praise
> An heavenly Hymne, such as the Angels sing,
> And thy triumphant name then would I raise
> Bove all the gods, thee onely honoring."

Mais par tes dons, Semencier, *tout s'asseure,*
Se perpetuë, *en son estre demeure,*
Et d'une paix immuable conjoint,
Suit volontiers ta force qui l'époint. . . .
Je te saluë, Amour, de qui la grace
Des choses *tient en son estre* la race,
Par qui tout vit, par qui tout ce qui est
Pour vivre meurt, et pour mourir renaist.

If "thereby they all do live" echoes "par qui tout vit," Spenser caught the allusion to Acts and made it overt in "and moved are." As for the adamantine chains (singular in Baïf), both poets add this metaphor after they have mentioned the real nature of the bond— "rebelles accords" in Baïf, "loved meanes" in Spenser, but Spenser, who compresses the topic "placing of the elements," brings in the chains at once, completing the idea of "loved meanes," before passing to "mixture," while Baïf, who expands on "placing," introduces the metaphor after this expansion in a resumptive phrase as he too passes to "mixture." The position of the metaphor is thus essentially the same in both poems, and in both the effect is to assure us that the world is firmly made and safe, which is the effect that Plato himself gains with the metaphor of the bond.

Some reason, more than a passing phrase of Marullus, may be suggested to explain why these Renaissance poets thought this metaphor appropriate. There is not much exaggeration in saying that the intrusion of a new metaphor on an old topic may have some significance in a time when every usage of antiquity was observed and venerated. The acceptance of this reassuring phrase may, I think, be a very small and subtle indication of the special Renaissance feeling of uneasiness about the world. For Ronsard, the feeling has been well brought out by A.-M. Schmidt, who finds it characteristic of Ronsard's universe that "son harmonieuse ordonnance n'est jamais définitivement acquise, mais toujours conquise par les vertus providentielles de Dieu"; Ronsard is conscious of "la tendance de l'univers à toujours glisser vers l'anarchie."[39] There is no need to bring up again the speech of Ulysses on "degree" in Shakespeare's *Troilus and Cressida* (1.3.75ff.); but this speech, like the passages quoted below from Ronsard, makes it

[39]Albert-Marie Schmidt, *La poésie scientifique en France au seizième siècle* (Paris, 1938), pp. 86–87.

clear that the threatened discord of the universe was a far from unconscious symbol of the political and social discord that menaced the sixteenth century at every hand and was in fact unleashed in France in the wars of religion. Ronsard indeed, perhaps from his own invention, goes so far as to personify the *Discordia* of the elements. In classical Latin, *Discordia* seems always to personify human strife.[40] In Ronsard, this figure by an intentional fusion is at once the cosmological strife that threatens the foundations of the world and human strife often seen as a divine scourge. In a passage of his *Hymne d'Eternité* where he is following Marullus fairly closely, he suddenly deserts his model to introduce a development of his own. Addressing Eternity (God), he avows that the deity is attended by Puissance (a "virtue" of God)—

> pour donner la mort
> A quiconque vouldroit favoriser Discord,
> Discord ton ennemy, qui ses forces assemble
> Pour faire mutiner les Elementz ensemble
> A la perte du Monde, et de ton doulx repos,
> Et vouldroit, s'il pouvoit, rengendrer le cahos.
> Mais tout incontinent que cet ennemy brasse
> Trahison contre toy, la Vertu le menasse,
> Et l'envoye là bas aux abysmes d'Enfer,
> Garroté pieds et mains de cent liens de fer.[41]

These iron bonds are not very different from adamantine (steel) bonds, though they recall the hundred brazen bonds with which Virgil binds Furor (*Aen.* 1.295–96) and the unspecified chain with which Satan is bound in the Book of Revelation (20:1–3). In Ronsard's *Exhortation pour la Paix* (1558), Peace drives Discord out of Chaos:

> La Paix querella
> Au Chaos le discord, et le chassa delà
> Pour accorder ce Tout.[42]

---

[40]See *ThLL* and P-W., s.v. There may of course be mediaeval or Renaissance instances that I have overlooked; the usage seems not, however, to be known to the twelfth-century cosmogonists, inventive though they are in this realm. I have in mind here only the word; there are of course other avatars of the Empedoclean Neikos. Indeed Ronsard's concept of the barely arrested dissolution of the universe strongly recalls Plato's *Politicus* myth (272E–273D), in which also the cosmic perils have ethical overtones.

[41]*Œuvres complètes, ed. cit.*, 8.249.

[42]*Ed. cit.*, 9.25.

In *La Paix, au Roy* (1559), Discord is again clearly both cosmic and social, chained in hell by La Paix the creator but destined to be unleashed (*deschaîné*) when God wills to punish mankind by war.[43] Peace, assisting Nature and God, pacifies the original chaos and arranges the world:

> Après avoir par ordre arrangé la machine
> Et lié ce grand Corps d'une amitié divine,
> Elle fist atacher à cent cheines de fer
> Le malheureux Discord aux abysmes d'Enfer.

As in Baïf and Spenser, the elements are united by "une amitié divine" (cf. "rebelles accords" and "loved meanes"), and this is followed by "chaînes de fer" (cf. adamantine chains). Here, however, the satanic Discord is abstracted from the process, and the chains (really repeating "lié d'amitié") are appropriated to him. Renaissance feeling has dissociated these ideas and enlarged the concept of discord. Such a monster is properly bound in material chains.

The ancient equivalent of Ronsard's satanic Discord, at least in the Roman poets, is no doubt Chaos itself, often referred to as being in the underworld or as being the underworld itself and its denizens. In a view known to Manilius (1.125–27), Chaos is dispatched thither, it seems, in the form of its own darkness:

> Seu permixta Chaos rerum primordia quondam
> discrevit partu, mundumque enixa nitentem
> fugit in infernas caligo pulsa tenebras.

There it menaces the created world; so Valerius Flaccus 1.831–32:

> Ingenti iacet ore Chaos, quod pondere fessam
> materiem lapsumque queat consumere mundum;

and Lucan 6.695–96:

> Eumenides Stygiumque nefas Poenaeque nocentum
> et Chaos innumeros avidum confundere mundos.

[43]*Ed. cit.*, 9.108. Cf. Rev. 20:3, where the chained Satan after a thousand years "must be loosed a little season." In the *Ode de la Paix* (1550), creative Peace sits by the throne of God together with "l'horrible Dieu de Violence" (*ed. cit.*, 3.7), but this deity seems only to be War. Possibly related to Ronsard's usage is Ovid, *Fasti* 1.103–24, where Janus as Chaos reduced to order sends forth Pax while *rigidae serae* hold Bella in check; but Ovid does not distinctly link up these ideas.

In plainer language, the elements are ever straining to break their bond; in Lucan's storm scene (5.634–36):

> Extimuit Natura Chaos; rupisse videntur
> concordes elementa moras, rursusque redire
> Nox manes mixtura deis—

a passage that commentators on Spenser might well note as a parallel to *FQ* 7.6.14.[44] There, after Mutability had brought on darkness by tampering with the moon, "all the heavenly crew"

> Were much afraid and wondred at that sight,
> Fearing least Chaos broken had his chaine,
> And brought againe on them eternall night.

If Spenser follows Lucan here, he has assimilated Chaos to the chained elements.

The breaking of the bond clearly would confound heaven and hell and would thereby release the enemies of Zeus who are bound in Hades for their rebellion against him; so Claudian, *De rapt. Pros.* 1.42–45:

> Paene reluctatis iterum pugnantia rebus
> rupissent elementa fidem penitusque revulso
> carcere laxatis pubes Titania vinclis
> vidisset caeleste iubar.

We are not entitled, I believe, to see in this connection between Chaos (or the rebel elements) and the imprisoned enemies of Zeus much more than an association of ideas on the part of the poets.[45] But the association alone, given Ronsard's concept of a chaotic or

---

[44]It is not mentioned in the "Variorum" Spenser.

[45]Ancient allegory of the enemies of Zeus apparently did not take this direction even when it might seem to suggest it: the quarrels of the gods symbolic of the war of the elements (ascribed to Theagenes, Diels-Kranz, *Vorsokr.* 1.52); the Titans symbolic of the elements, e.g. Koios, with Aeolic κ for π, signifies ποιότης, "quality" (Zeno, frg. 100, *SVF* 1.28 von Arnim); the gods who assisted Hera (chaotic matter) when she was suspended by Zeus are "demons having to do with matter" and cast by Zeus into the lower world, i.e. our world (Celsus ap. Origen, *c. Celsum* 6.42; Celsus charges that the Christians borrowed such ideas for their Satan); see J. Pépin, *op. cit.*, pp. 98, 128, 451. The personification or even worship of the elements themselves evidently also takes another direction; see H. Diels, *Elementum* (Leipzig, 1899), pp. 44–49.

satanic Discord bound in chains, might suggest to a humanist poet, scrupulous of ancient usage, the propriety of transferring to the rebel elements the adamantine chains so conspicuously applied by the Roman poets to the denizens of Hades. Valerius Flaccus relates how the Titan Coeus

> vincla Iovis fractoque trahens adamante catenas
> Saturnum Tityumque vocat spemque aetheris amens
> concipit,

while Statius pictures among the monsters of Erebus

> Centauros solidoque intorta adamante Gigantum
> vincula.

Even the binding of Cerberus in Ovid might seem relevant: "Tirynthius heros . . . restantem . . . nexis adamante catenis Cerberon abstraxit." Spenser, we may mention, translates this passage for the binding of the Blatant Beast (*FQ* 6.12.35, 38): "Like as whylome that strong Tirynthian swaine / Brought forth with him the dreadful dog of hell / Against his will fast bound in yron chaine." Ovid's *adamante* is rendered as "iron" to harmonize with Spenser's context.[46] It is the wicked enchantress Acrasia who is bound with adamantine chains (*FQ* 2.12.82.6): "But her in chaines of adamant he tyde." And Milton (*PL* 1.47-48) true to this usage sends Satan

> To bottomless perdition, there to dwell
> In Adamantine Chains and penal Fire.[47]

We have gone the long way round to suggest that the adamantine chains give to the creation passage a shade more assurance than

[46]The Blatant Beast, himself bound with an iron chain, is led about like an ordinary dog, and adamant, the stuff of metaphor, would be incongruous in a realistic scene. Spenser's source in Ovid was identified by H. G. Lotspeich ("Variorum" Spenser *ad loc.*).

[47]Osgood (n. 5 above) offers as verbal parallels to Spenser's phrase this passage of *Paradise Lost* and the binding of Prometheus in Aeschylus, *Prometheus Vinctus* 6. What the term "adamantine chains" most readily brings to mind is the punishment of rebels against the divine order. The personified "Discord with a thousand various mouths" who is among the attendants of Chaos and Night in Milton's hell (*PL* 2.967) is clearly the ethical *Discordia* of Virgil, *Aen.* 6.280, but perhaps a cosmic allusion is not excluded.

Plato's "fairest" bond, and that such assurance was needed. The present world, "indissoluble," according to Plato, "by any other than the one who joined it together" (*Tim.* 32c), and made by him "as eternal as might be" (37D), was known unequivocally by most Stoics and Christians to be doomed to destruction. Plato's point has a different color when restated by the Protestant poet Du Bartas:

> Or les sacrez anneaux de la chaine, qui lie
> Les membres de ce Tout, sont tels que quand il veut,
> Celuy qui les a joints seul desjoindre les peut.[48]

Destruction "when He wishes" is in God's plan from the beginning. In our Platonic hymns to creative Love, the point must be left with the optimistic turn that Plato gives it, but the threat nevertheless commonly forces itself in as a contingency and is elaborated. The *machina mundi*, says Palingenius in the passage quoted above, endures by reason of the bond of God's love, *hoc nexu*, for if Love did not, *nam nisi*, hold the elements *firma compage*, fire would consume air, and so forth. The syntactical form invites a second mention of the bond, and a second mention suggests a *variatio*, here *firma compage* and in Baïf's paraphrase *liaisons d'émant*. A *variatio* is likely to be a bolder metaphor. Palingenius perhaps reflects the every-popular *metrum* of Boethius on this *topos*, itself a hymn to creative Love, in which the common *foedus* and *ligat* of the statement are varied with *frena* in the conditional clause (*Cons.* 2, metr. 8):

> Quod pugnantia semina
> Foedus perpetuum tenent, . . .
> Hanc rerum seriem ligat
> . . . Amor.
> Hic *si* frena remiserit,
> Quidquid nunc amat invicem
> Bellum continuo geret.

(The formula is duly retained in Chaucer's imitation in *Troilus and Criseyde* 3.1753–64: "That elements that been so discordable / Holden a bond perpetuely duringe . . . al this doth Love; . . . and if

---

[48]*Semaine* I, *Jour* 2, 302–304.

that Love ought lete his brydel go, . . . lost were all").[49] Baïf does
not forget to include the conditional sentence in his hymn to Love
("Si tout le monde en toy ne s'asseuroit, / Par le discord il se démembreroit"), and earlier in the poem it may have influenced him
to repeat "rebelles accords" in the strong metaphor "chaine
adamantine." From Spenser's hymn the condition has, so to speak,
disappeared, but the cosmic threat is strongly felt in the elements'
"rebellious yre," in the need of Love to "compell" the elements to
keep their places, and in their being linked with adamantine chains.
In another Spenserian passage (*FQ* 4.10.35), however, the formu-
lation appears in full—mention of the bond, conditional sentence,
bolder metaphor--and this fact may be taken as confirming what
has been suspected, that this passage depends on Palingenius:

> By her [Concord] the heaven is in his course contained,
> And all the world in state unmoved stands,
> As their Almightie maker first ordained,
> And bound them with *inviolable bands;*
> *Else would* the waters overflow the lands,
> And fire devoure the ayre, and hell them quight,
> But that she holds them with her *blessed hands.*[50]

---

[49]In Alanus ab Insulis, *Anticlaudianus* 2.242-45 (R. Bossuat, ed.), Concordia, herself being concord, need only utter the conditional sentence:
"*Ni* stabili nexu, concordi foedere, pace
perpetua vicibusque meis elementa ligassem,
intestinus adhuc strepitus primordia rerum
dissona concuteret germanaque bella moverent."
Instead of *si, dum* is also available; cf. Prudentius (above): "Dum servant elementa
. . . cursum," and Marullus (above): "Dum stet opus . . . Naturae." The *topos* again
has analogies with Plato's *Politicus* myth (n. 40, above), and Boethius' "Hic si frena
remiserit" is not far from Plato's metaphor of the pilot of the universe "letting the
helm go," οἷον πηδαλίων οἴακος ἀφέμενος (272E). This metaphor reappears in the
Orphic hymn (58, 8) to Eros, where Love is the pilot: πάντων οἴηκα κρατύνεις.
[50]Rosamund Tuve, in her first article (n. 1, above), p. 143, offers the lines from
Palingenius in Barnabe Googe's translation as a "parallel . . . interesting in connection with this passage on Concord and other Spenserian passages"; in her second
article she goes no further on this point. Apart from the frame of the sentence, the
words "fire (would) devoure the ayre" seem to render "aera . . . consumeret . . . ignis" directly rather than to be deduced from Googe's "the fiery flame / This
Ayre . . . would consume"; but in any case "would devoure" is clearly Palingenius'
"consumeret." Further, "the heaven" is very likely his "caelum"; and in the preceed-
ing stanza Concord is called "Mother of blessed Peace and Friendship trew," a
concept that quite possibly reflects Palingenius, who proceeds next to the praise of
Peace (4.474, "gignit Amor pacem") and of Friendship (4.502).

191

Timothy Kendall's *Trifles*
and Nicolas Bourbon's *Nugae*

Professor Lathrop's recent study of the relations of Turbervile and Kendall to Cornarius' *Epigrammata Graeca* once more demonstrates that, if we would understand the ways of many an English versifier in the sixteenth century, we should turn to the neo-Latin poets.[1] This is not only true for English verse, but also for French, Spanish, and to some degree for Italian.

Lathrop rightly defends Kendall, and on the right grounds, against the charge of plagiarism in the *Flowers of Epigrams* where he lays no claim to originality; yet it must be allowed that, by our standards, Kendall errs in not distinguishing his own work as translator from that of others whose English versions he adopts.

Kendall's book, as it was published in 1577, is divided into two parts, each having a title-page of its own. The first part is *Flowers of Epigrammes out of sundrie the moste singular authours selected;* the second, *Trifles* by Timothe Kendal *devised and written (for the moste part) at sundrie tymes in his yong and tender age.* From these titles it would seem that he looked for the reputation of originality from the

From *Modern Language Notes* 44 (1929) 19–22. Copyright © 1929 The Johns Hopkins University Press.

[1]H. B. Lathrop, "Janus Cornarius's *Selecta Epigrammata Graeca* and the Early English Epigrammatists," *MLN*, X43 (1928) 223–29. Lathrop still misses one poem of Turbervile's that comes from the Anthology (unless it be referred to on p. 225, where, under "Turbervile, p. 205," the quotation is wanting—I regret that I cannot refer to the edition of Turbervile used by Lathrop); this is *The Epicure's Counsell* (Chalmers, *English Poets*, 2.615), an elaboration of *AP*, 7.325, well known from the Latin of Cicero, *Tusc.* 5.101; on p. 616 (Chalmers), Turbervile has a second poem in reply to this.

A few *lapsus calami* should be corrected in Lathrop's article: on p. 227, whatever the intermediary Latin epigram, *The Cittyes* 7 is ultimately from *AP* 9.366 (not 127); on p. 228, *Timocritus a warrior* should be referred to *AP* 7.160 (not 250), *The frounyng fates* to *AP* 7.308 (not 9.308), *It makes no matter* to *AP* 10.3 (not 7.288), and *Shunne thou the seas* to *AP* 7.650 (not 668).

Trifles, though not from the *Flowers.* Accordingly, Bullen[2] and Whipple[3] speak of the *Trifles* as if they were original in our ordinary sense of the word. The closing lines of the poem introductory to the *Trifles* mark the author's modest feeling of greater responsibility for them than for the *Flowers* preceding:[4]

> Now, reader, lend thy listnyng eare,
>   and, after syngyng Larke,
> Content thy selfe to chattyng Crowe
>   some homely notes to marke.

In the opening lines of this poem, Kendall names two poets who have preceded him in the writing of 'trifles':

> Borbon in France beares bell awaie
>   for writyng trifles there;
> In Englande Parkhurst praysed is
>   for writyng trifles here.

Parkhurst had supplied Kendall with one large section of his *Flowers;* but Bourbon, though one of the better-known and more prolific of the neo-Latin epigrammatists, finds no place there.[5] He finds a place, though his presence is not acknowledged, in the *Trifles,* the title of which is obviously transferred from his *Nugae.*[6]

---

[2]*DNB.*

[3]T. K. Whipple, *Martial and the English Epigram from Sir Thomas Wyatt to Ben Jonson* (Berkeley, Calif., 1925), p. 322.

[4]Likewise in the list of "aucthors out of whom these Flowers are selected" (p. 2 of the Spenser Society's reprint) it is implied that what follows Fo. 113 (p. 243) belongs originally to Kendall exactly as what follows Fo.38 belongs originally to Poliziano.

[5]He is mentioned for his fame together with his friend Salmon Macrin, and with Muret, in Kendall's epistle "To the Reader" (reprint, p. 8).

[6]*Nicolai Borbonii Vandoperani Nugae* (Paris, 1533); *Nugarum libri octo* (Basel, 1540). Parkhurst's epigrams had for title, *Ludicra sive epigrammata juvenilia* (London, 1573). The elder Nicolas Bourbon (1503–50) needs a better biography than the notices in the *Biographie Universelle* and the *Nouvelle Biographie Générale,* both of which are taken from Niceron. Much of Bourbon's verse is autobiographical; yet these notices of his life make nothing of the imprisonment he complains of in a series of poems, or of what seems to follow it, his residence in England at the Court of Henry VIII. I have seen no clearer account of Bourbon's career than the brief note by Edmund Lodge, accompanying Holbein's portrait of Bourbon in the *Facsimiles of Original Drawings by Hans Holbein in the Collection of His Majesty for the Portraits of Illustrious Persons of the Court of Henry VIII,* published by John Chamberlaine (London, 1884). He addresses Anne Boleyn in a poem on his release from prison (*Nug.* [1540] p. 418); other verses are to the Duke of Richmond, Sir William Butts, Cranmer, Latimer, and Cromwell. The biographers mention J. C. Scaliger's adverse criticism of Bourbon, but fail to account for Bourbon's apparently subsequent epigram in praise of Scaliger (*Nug.* [1540], p. 465, not in the edition of 1533).

The extent to which, in the *Trifles,* Kendall levies upon Bourbon is expressed in the following table:[7]

Kendall	Bourbon
p. 252: As water cleare.	p. 55: Sordida stagnina est.
No stabbyng glave.	p. 149: Quaeris quid timeam.
p. 254: By riches none.	p. 74: Pulchra (Dei donum).
a) p. 255: The churlishe chuffe.	p. 224: Mularum vitam vivit.
The ayre, the yearth.	p. 32: Aer, terra, fretum.
p. 257: This silver coine.	p. 328: Aes, ferrum, argentum.
p. 258: Tyme bringeth lurking.	p. 442: Profert in lucem.
The cursed play.	p. 173: Filia avaritiae.
p. 260. Who dyes in Christ.	p. 235 (cf. p. 330): Qui moritur Christo.
This age hunts.	p. 124: Haec aetas venatur.
The bowe that bended.	p. 264: Amittit vires qui.
b) p. 261: Loves rigorous rage.	p. 96: Compescit rabiem.
p. 268: The fem, the floud.	p. 100: Foemina, flamma, fretum.
c) His first wife.	p. 368: Vixdum in marmore.
p. 269: To combersome a clog.	p. 369: Res uxor nimis est.
A husband of his wife.	Commoda tum demum.
p. 277: My Titus, if.	p. 310: Tu si vales, Pucri.
p. 281: Learned thou wast.	p. 292: Scribere quur. [?]
My front well framd.	p. 350 (or again at end of the volume): Corporis effigiem.
d) p. 284: Mark miser yesterday.	p. 27: Marcus avarus heri.
p. 296: Take in good parte.	p. 22: Sic studium. [?]
p. 302: Post cineres virtus.	Quoted from *Nug.,* p. 74; second line of the epigram translated by Kendall on p. 254.

The epigrams above marked a, b, c, d, ultimately come from the Greek Anthology: (a) *AP* 11.399; (b) 9.497; (c) 9.133; (d) 11.169.[8]

Though it was the convention to ascribe such verse as Kendall's to the writer's "yong and tender age," and though even in this statement Kendall could be echoing Bourbon (*Nug.,* p. 21 *et*

---

[7]Pages of Kendall according to the Spenser Society's reprint (1874); pages of Bourbon according to the *Nugae* of 1540.

[8]Bourbon owes some 85 epigrams to the Anthology, Kendall, through several media, about 90. The epigram marked (c) he elsewhere (p. 137) takes from another intermediary, Cornarius.

passim), the courteous reader will take him at his word. It is not necessary to think that Erasmus and "good old Mantuan" were the only neo-Latin authors employed in English schools; and it is possible that Kendall there became acquainted with Bourbon's *Nugae*. The sources of the remaining "trifles" surely are likewise to be sought in popular neo-Latin writers; perhaps some of them in Parkhurst's *Ludicra,* a book at present inaccessible to me and, I suppose, to most others. We may hope that the persons who give us reprints of books like Kendall's *Flowers* and Weever's *Epigrammes* will in time present us with reissues of influential books such as Walter Haddon's *Poemata* and Bishop Parkhurst's *Ludicra,* or even with a readable edition of John Owen's *Epigrammata.*

With some real knowledge of the professedly original part of Kendall's book, we can more fairly judge him, understand his own view of what he was doing in the whole. He plainly regards the *Flowers of Epigrams* merely as an anthology of translations; perhaps he supplies some, but in general he takes them where he finds them. The *Trifles,* on the other hand, are his own; perhaps he has translated a certain part of them from the Latin poets old or new, but in doing so he reserves the right to adapt the original freely to purposes of his own. A case in point is his treatment of Bourbon's *Quaeris quid timeam,* a rueful love-poem, almost a Latin sonnet in form:

> Quaeris quid timeam, Beate frater?
> Non hastas ego, non acuta tela;
> Non vim, non rabidi pericla belli,
> Non ignes, odium, minas, ruinas,
> Non ventos, mare, fulmen, astra, monstra,
> Non pestes, furias, famem, tyrannos,
> Non per caeca vagas sepulcra formas,
> Non spectra horrida noxiosve manes,
> Non quidquid (breviter) solet timeri
> Vulgo, quodque putant, nocere posse:
> Formidabilius malum puella est
> His, et tristius, imminentiusque:
> Cui me perdere si libet licebit.

> No stabbyng glave, nor stycking knife,
> Nor darte dread I, that reveth life
> No fencers skill, no thrusting pricks,
> No thundering threates of despirat Dicks,

No chyllyng cold, no scaldyng heate,
No gnashing chaps of monsters greate,
No plague, no deadly vile desease,
No broilyng blaze, no swallowyng seas,
No ganglyng greefe, no cares that crushe,
Of these I recke not of a Rushe.
An ill there is which doeth remaine,
That troubles more and putts to paine:
A fawnyng frende moste mischief is,
Whiche seekes to kill yet semes to kisse.

Michel Guy de Tours: Some Sources and Literary Methods

Blanchemain, in his edition of Guy de Tours, notices two or three instances in which the poet has lifted lines bodily from Ronsard, and remarks that Guy is evidently at no pains to conceal these borrowings.[1] Other examples of this practice could be added to those observed by Blanchemain,[2] and in fact so far is Guy from concealing his character of *ronsardisant fidèle* that he founds upon it his chief claim to the attention of posterity (" Au jardin de deffunct Monsieur de Ronsard"):

> O beau jardin, s'il te demeure encor
> Quelque tresor d'un si rare tresor,
> Enrichis-en ma muse peu vantée,
> A celle fin que nos plus tards nepveux
> Puissent sçavoir que j'estois un de ceux
> Qui de Ronsard ont leur gloire empruntée.[3]

From *Modern Language Notes* 58 (1943) 431–41. Copyright © 1943 The Johns Hopkins University Press.

[1] *Premières Œuvres et Souspirs amoureux de Guy de Tours* and *Le Paradis d'Amour*, 2 vols. ("Trésor des vieux poètes français") (Paris, 1878), 2.105. Guy published his poems in 1598, and in 1611 a prose-novel, *Les Amours de Paris et de la nymphe Œnone*. Notices by François Colletet (quoted by Blanchemain), Goujet, and La Monnoye contain no information that cannot be deduced from his books. He was born at Tours, probably about 1562, the son of a prosperous lawyer, Michel Guy (d. 1595), *procureur au siège présidial de Tours,* and himself entered the legal profession. After his father's death he seems to have settled in Paris. He gives a portrait of himself in an *envoi* to his poems (*ed. cit.* 2.98). There is an article, not accessible to me, by L. Langlois in *Bull. de la Soc. archéol. de Tours* (1903–04), concerning one Anne Méon as the Anne of Guy's sonnets.

[2] E.g., "Belle, ne garde point à Pluton ta beauté" (*ed. cit.* 1.64) = Ronsard, "Ne garde point à Pluton ta beauté" (*Œuv.*, Marty-Laveaux, ed. [Paris, 1881], 1.63).

[3] *Ed. cit.* 2.65. Guy has two other sonnets on Ronsard (*ed. cit.* 1.29 and 2.87), the first addressed to the "roi des poètes françois," as he calls him, as still living, the second an epitaph. A native of Tours, he may have met or at least seen Ronsard

No doubt the very fact that writers, like Guy were unable to quit the "jardin de deffunct Monsieur de Ronsard" is a reason why their Muse is "peu vantée," but Guy's manner of decorating his poems with flowers from that source is so frank as to amount to a kind of originality. Besides whole verses he has culled a good many phrases and epithets. In the lines just quoted, for example, the phrase "nos plus tards nepveux" is, as I recall, a Ronsardian expression. Like Ronsard he fell in love at the age of twenty, 'Sur mes vingt ans,'[4] with a girl of fifteen, "belle fleur de quinze ans," like Cassandre.[5] I have not attempted to collect such parallels, but we shall meet with others as we proceed. More interesting is the founding of entire sonnets upon Ronsard, a practice of which at least two instances occur, one the introductory sonnet to Guy's *Mignardises,* the other the final sonnet of his *Souspirs.* Unless other cases have escaped my notice, as is quite possible, Guy may have thought it somehow appropriate to make more or less open allusions to his master at these points. The first example follows:[6]

Ronsard
Dessus l'autel d'Amour planté sur vostre table
Me fistes un serment, je vous le fis aussi,
Que d'un cœur mutuel à s'aimer endurcy
Nostre amitié promise iroit inviolable.
Je vous juray ma foy, vous feistes le semblable,
Mais vostre cruauté, qui des Dieux n'a soucy,
Me promettoit de bouche et me trompoit ainsi:
Cependant vostre esprit demeuroit immuable.
O jurement fardé sous l'espece d'un Bien!
O perjurable autel! ta Deité n'est rien.
O parole d'amour non jamais asseurée!
J'ay pratiqué par vous le proverbe des vieux:
Jamais des amoureux la parole jurée
N'entra (pour les punir) aux oreilles des Dieux.

Guy de Tours
Dessus l'autel d'Amour je veux ce mois icy

---

there. Since Marcel Raymond's *L'Influence de Ronsard sur la poèsie française* (Paris, 1927) concludes with the year 1585, Guy does not come within its scope; he is mentioned casually (2.218, 349) as a continuator of the "Catullan" style.
[4]*Ed. cit.* 1.28; Ronsard, *ed. cit.* 1.55 ("Sur mes vingt ans").
[5]Guy 1.64; Ronsard 1.11 ("un beauté de quinze ans").
[6]Ronsard, *Sonnets pour Hélène,* in *ed. cit.* 1.286; Guy 2.29.

Michel Guy de Tours

Ce beau mois consacré à l'alme Cytherée,
Vous jurer saintement, ô ma belle Nérée,
Que serez desormais mon amoureux soucy.
Mais je veux qu'en après vous me juriez aussi
Que seulement de moy serez enamourée;
Ainsi nostre amitié l'un à l'autre jurée
Luira tousjours en nous d'un feu bien esclairci.
O d'Amour et du Ris, Venus douce nourrice,
Soit que tu sois en Cypre, en Paphe, ou en Eryce,
Entens ces juremens et ces mystiques vœux!
Et fais que ton enfant à jamais soit contraire
A qui d'elle ou de moy sera si temeraire
De premier les enfreindre et d'en rompre les nœuds.

With his opening phrase Guy has, quite intentionally, given the signal that his sonnet is to be compared with Ronsard's. The connection once seen, his more hopeful treatment of the theme gains a certain piquancy from comparison with the melancholy ending of his model, and such must have been his intention; for no doubt he imagined that his readers would always be verbally familiar with the "king of French poets." Guy's sonnet has further interest as illustrating the imperceptible diffusion of classical themes, since, as I shall show elsewhere, its original, Ronsard's sonnet, is little more than an "inspired translation" of a Greek epigram by Callimachus.

The final sonnet of the *Souspirs* is founded on the penultimate sonnet of the *Sonnets pour Hélène,* but the manner of derivation differs from that in the case just cited.[7]

Ronsard
Je faisois ces Sonnets en l'antre Piéride,
Quand on vit les François sous les armes suer,
Quand on vit tout le peuple en fureur se ruer,
Quand Bellone sanglante alloit devant pour guide:
Quand en lieu de la Loy le vice, l'homicide . . .
Estoyent tiltres d'honneur. . . .
Pour tromper les soucis d'un temps si vicieux
J'escrivois en ces vers ma complainte inutile. . . .

Guy de Tours
Triste je souspiroy cette plainte amoureuse,

---

[7] Guy 1.97; Ronsard 1.292.

Assis dans le giron de la belle Eraton,
Quand l'horrible Megere et sa sœur Alecton
Rendoient de toutes parts la France malheureuse,
Quand les François mutins, d'une dague outrageuse
S'entrecoupoient le fil que leur tramoit Clothon, ...
Quand nos princes Bourbons et les princes Lorrains
Avoient pour s'esgorger le coutelas aux mains. ...
Pour n'ouyr leurs débats ny le bruit des canons
Ny voir les estandars de tant de gonfanons,
J'escrivois en ces vers mon amoureuse plainte.

In this instance Guy does not alter the sentiment of Ronsard, but makes it his artistic aim to vary the expression—"dans le giron de la belle Eraton" for "en l'antre Piéride," "l'horrible Megere et sa sœur Alecton" for "Bellone sanglante"—usually with amplification. It is an exercise of the schools, where the sixteenth-century pupil was taught to vary a given Latin sentence in as many ways as possible *styli exercendi gratia*. Both poets unquestionably felt genuine concern for their country in the Civil Wars, but then they doubtless had other strong feelings which they never expressed in their verses. It seemed proper to express this one in this way at the end of a book, because they had literary precedents; for Ronsard must have been prompted here by the well-known ending of Virgil's *Georgics*. Yet the French poets, one observes, in their situation, unlike Virgil felt no need of excusing their *studia ignobilis oti;* quite the contrary.

The sixteenth-century poets, forever pillaging the same treasuries of themes, were well broken to the ruses of style, and it was from invention in treatment more than from invention in subject that they looked to celebrate their triumphs. Hence it is instructive to follow a theme as it passes through different hands, as we have good opportunity to do in our next example of Guy's borrowing. We go therefore the long way round. A poet of the Anthology, Meleager of Gadara, is the author of some verses which may be translated as follows:[8]

O flower-nurtured bee, why do you brush Heliodora's skin, deserting the flowers of spring? Do you mean to show that she has that which is both sweet and false, the sting of love ever bitter to the heart? Yes, I think so—that is it. My friend go back where you came from: your message is no news to me.

[8]*AP* 5.163. I follow here the text of the Planudean Anthology as read in the sixteenth century.

Meleager's poem is not certainly, but very probably, the original of the *basium* of Joannes Secundus that we read next. Secundus invites the bees to leave the spring flowers and come to his lady's lips, but warns them of her "sting." This degree of transformation in an ancient theme is about what one learns to expect from the rhetorically-trained Latin poets of the Renaissance.[9]

Mellilegae volucres, quid adhuc thyma cana rosaque
   Et rorem vernae nectareum violae
Lingitis aut florem late spirantis anethi?
   Omnes ad dominae labra venite meae.
Illa rosas spirant omnes thymaque omnia sola
   Et succum vernae nectareum violae.
Inde procul dulces aurae funduntur anethi,
   Narcissi veris illa madent lacrimis
Oebaliique madent invenis fragrante cruore,
   Qualis uterque liquor, cum cecidisset, erat,
Nectareque aetherio medicatus, et aëre puro,
   Impleret fetu versicolore solum.
Sed me iure meo libantem mellea labra
   Ingratae socium ne prohibete favis.
Non etiam totas avidae distendite cellas,
   Arescant dominae ne semel ora meae
Basiaque impressans siccis sitientia labris,
   Garrulus indicii triste feram pretium.
Heu non et stimulis compungite molle labellum:
   Ex oculis stimulos vibrat et illa pares.
Credite, non ullum patietur vulnus inultum:
   Leniter innocuae mella legatis apes.

The poem is neatly arranged. After stating his theme in the first four lines, Secundus slows the motion and gives body to the piece by "accumulation" in the floral passage of eight lines, and then finally exhibits his wit in three fancies addressed to the bees: (1) Do not exclude me from her lips, (2) Do not extract all the sweetness therefrom, and (3) Do not sting her, for she has stings equal to your own.

This was exactly the thing for the Pléiade. Ronsard turned it into an ode in 1550, Baïf into a long "Anacreontic" published in 1555,

---

[9] *Basia*, Ellinger, ed. (Berlin, 1899), p. 15. I have put vv. 5–12 in italics for reasons that will be apparent below.

and Belleau into two sonnets in his *Bergerie* of 1565.[10] Ronsard expresses the whole substance of Secundus' poem except that he omits point (1); his intention is fulfilled when he has transformed the Latin elegy into a graceful *chanson*, and has shown what he can do by way of invention in the floral passage, for, while crowding the points at the end, he has rehandled and augmented this passage, giving to it two out of his four stanzas. One sees that therein lies the main artistic interest of his poem. Baïf's treatment is characteristic of him: in some sixty lines he follows Secundus straight through, taking the floral passage more lightly (4 lines), but amplifying heavily on the three final points. Belleau's treatment is more interesting, since his opposite problem—compression of the material into sonnet-form—was more difficult:[11]

> Mouches qui massonez les voustes encirées
> De vos palais dorez, et qui dès le matin
> Volex de mont en mont pour effleurer le thym,
> Et suçotter des fleures les odeurs savourées:
> Dressez vos ailerons sur les lèvres sucrées
> De ma belle maistresse, et baisant son tetin
> Sur sa bouche pillez le plus riche butin
> Que vous chargeastes onc sur vos ailes dorées.
> Là trouverez un air embasmé de senteurs,
> Un lac comblé de miel, une moisson d'odeurs:
> Mais gardez-vous aussi des embusches cruelles.
> Car de sa bouche il sort un brasier allumé,
> Et de souspirs ardans un escadron armé,
> Et pour ce gardez-vous de n'y brusler vos ailes.

Slight as it is, this sonnet shows originality and thought. The floral passage is omitted, mainly no doubt as an unnecessary ornament, but possibly also because Belleau recalled that Ronsard had retained it as the chief "effect" of his ode. Again, of Secundus' three final points, Belleau chooses only the last, that which gives warning of the lady's dangerous power, but he expresses it under the new figure of a brand and fiery sighs, not as in Secundus and Meleager by a "sting." Thereby the point: bee . . . sting . . . counter-sting, is lost, no doubt intentionally, because it would seem too clever and

---

[10]Ronsard, *éd. crit.* by Laumonier, 2.55; Baïf, Marty-Laveaux, ed. 1.260; Belleau, Gouverneur, ed. 2.280, 289.

[11]In Belleau's second sonnet, *Mais las! où volez-vous*, the theme is handled in a similar manner, but with a variation of language.

would "steal" the whole sonnet, ruining the tone. In any case, a new point is welcome and shows the writer's wit.[12]

What remained for Guy to do in rehandling this theme? We have seen him transposing sonnets of Ronsard; on this occasion he revises Belleau, as is clear, for example, from his final point, where "brandon" is from Belleau's "brasier":[13]

> Fille du ciel, O menagere Avette,
> Ne lasse plus tes vollans avirons
> Pour effleurer à petits becs larrons
> Les belles fleurs qui naissent sur Hymette.
> Sans te peiner d'une aussi longue traite,
> Sur ceste bouche ou bien aux environs,
> Tu peux suçcer un milier de fleurons,
> Mainte Hyacinthe et mainte Paquerette.
> Icy la fleur qui naquit d'Adonis
> Croist à foison, ici sont épanis
> Les lyz, les tyms et le Girofle encore;
> Mais garde toy, dérobant leur douceur
> Pour t'enrichir, qu' un brandon ravisseur
> Ainsi qu' à moy le cœur ne te devore.

He has lightened the sonnet by reducing Belleau's twelve-syllable lines to the more common ten-syllable measure; but his main inten-

[12]Similarly J. C. Scalinger, who paraphrases Secundus' poem in the form of an Anacreontic (*Poemata* [Heidelberg, 1600], p. 457), also scants the floral passage, but makes the final point with *venena*. One may doubt whether this touches the true *decorum* of the theme better than "sting" or "brand"! Scaliger's *Anacreontica* appeared in 1574. An English version also comes to hand. At least I think it has not been noted that the verses of a madrigal by John Wilbye (publ. 1609), described by E. H. Fellowes as one of the most widely-known of all English madrigals, is a, probably direct, reduction of Secundus' poem (Fellowes, *English Madrigal School* 7 [1920] 87, and compare *English Madrigal Composers* [Oxford, 1921], p. 212):
> Sweet honey-sucking Bees, why do you still
> Surfeit on Roses, Pinks, and Violets,
> As if the choicest Nectar lay in them
> Wherewith you store your curious cabinets?
> Ah make your flight to Melisuaviae's lips;
> There may you revel in Ambrosian cheer,
> Where smiling Roses and sweet Lilies sit
> Keeping their spring-tide graces all the year.
>
> Yet, sweet, take heed, all sweets are hard to get;
> Sting not her soft lips, Oh beware of that!
> For if one flaming dart come from her eye
> Was never dart so sharp, ah then you die!

[13]Guy, *ed. cit.* 1.33: the sixth sonnet, "La Bouche," in a series entitled "Pourtrait de son Ente." The phrase, "à petits becs larrons," is taken from Belleau's second sonnet.

tion is clear: he thought that Belleau had erred in omitting the floral passage, and hence he restores it, neatly enough, in his version.[14] There is no reason, however, to suppose that Guy knew the original *basium* of Secundus. Rather, we have here another instance of his loyalty to Ronsard, from whose ode he very likely imagined Belleau's sonnet to have been made; for that Guy had Ronsard in mind is evident, since, true to his habit, he has lifted the address, "Fille du ciel," directly from Ronsard's first line.[15]

From all this we get some idea of Guy's artistic personality. He is no bewildered imitator; whether he appropriates a phrase or a line from another, or reworks an entire sonnet, he proceeds deliberately, with some purpose; but his purposes, it seems, amount to little. We should be unjust, however, in this last instance to measure the superiority of Belleau by comparing the small differential between the two French sonnets with the large differential between Belleau and Secundus. We ought to know what Guy could do in making a sonnet from a comparable Latin poem. Such knowledge fortunately is at hand. Like so many sixteenth-century poets Guy has drawn a handful of his poems from the *Erotopaegnion* of Girolamo Angeriano. I summarize these borrowings:[16]

Guy de Tours	Angeriano
Mon Anne et Cupidon (1.61)	Caelia fatur, Amor (a4)
Le premier qui peignit (1.69)	In tabula primus (e4)
Mon Anne voyant (1.70)	Forte videns natum (e3)
Mon Anne trouvant (1.71)	Quum dormiret Amor (b2)
Pourquoy te myres-tu (1.74)	Quid speculum spectas (e4)
Lorsqu' un petit papillon (1.84)	Papilio fulgens (c4)
Mon Anne un jour (1.85)	Pectine formosos (c4)
Bien-heureuse tu chante (1.87)	Tu felix cantas (c4)
A cause que ta beauté (1.88)	Ecce tumet forma (d1)
Lorsqu' une fievre (1.93)	Quum mea ferventi (e2)

[14]Yet the *brandon* certainly arises somewhat abruptly out of Guy's bouquet of flowers—another reason, perhaps a principal one, why Belleau had been obliged to suppress the floral passage.

[15]Few sixteenth-century "floral passages" fail to include the flowers mythologically sprung from men. Secundus gives us Narcissus and Hyacinthus (vv. 8–9), and Ronsard, Hyacinthus and Ajax, replacing Narcissus by Ajax because of his bracket, "fleurettes ensanglantées." Secundus had similarly bracketed Narcissus and Hyacinthus, but by an undesirable pun that Ronsard was unwilling to reproduce: "Qualis uterque liquor, cum cecidisset, erat." Guy in an effort to vary the language of Ronsard takes virtually the only metamorphosed mortal left under "fleurettes ensanglantées," namely Adonis.

[16]References are to Guy, *ed. cit.*, and to Angeriano, *Erotopaegnion* (Naples, 1520).

Michel Guy de Tours

These ten poems from the Latin of Angeriano are all found in the third book of Guy's *Souspirs*. Only the first and the last are sonnets, the remainder taking the form of Anacreontic odes or *chansons*, except *Le premier qui peignit*, which is a poem in six quatrains, and *Pourquoy te myres-tu*, which is a single quatrain. Hence in most instances he has chosen a metrical form that imposes no restraint, but permits him to follow his originals with little modification. The first of the two sonnets, again, is made from an epigram that happens to contain just enough material to fill the sonnet-form. But in making the second sonnet he was faced with a problem of reduction comparable with that faced by Belleau in dealing with Secundus.

De Caelia Convalescente

Quum mea ferventi langueret febre puella,
  Purpureo et starent candida membra toro,
Induit invisum Mors lurida protinus ensem,
  Et petit infestis aurea tecta rogis.
Irruit, at postquam vidit sine labe papillas,
  Et quales praefert flava Minerva oculos,
Obriguit retroque dedit vestigia, et inquit:
  Non haec lethaeam digna subire ratem.
Sic fata infernas pudibunda recessit ad umbras,
  Ausaque sic nigro verba tonare Jovi:
Quaecumque aetherio sub regno regna morantur
  Sunt nostra, una precor Caelia morte vacet.
Annuit hoc Pluto, facta est dea, et illico cedunt
  Nubila, et intonsus dat quoque Phoebus opem.
Sperandum est, postquam Mors importuna pepercit,
  Facta dea ut nostras audiat illa preces.

Lorsqu' une fievre forte agitoit ma Maistresse,
La Mort vint à son lict, recrespant de sa main
Le bois soupplement fort de son dard inhumain,
Afin de la tuer au fort de son angoisse.
Mais si tost qu'elle vist la fleur de sa jeunesse
Et le mont jumelet de son trop chaste sein,
Elle ne voulut pas achever son dessein,
Et sans luy faire mal, incontinent la laisse.
Et disoit s'en allant: Une telle beauté
Ne doit jamais sentir ma fiere cruauté,
Ny morte devaller au manoir Plutonique.
Les enfers ne sont pas dignes de tel honneur;

Apres cent ans d'icy, sans mort et sans douleur,
Le ciel s'enrichira de sa face angelique.

In setting up the situation Guy (vv. 1–8) follows the original closely
(vv. 1–7), but thereafter sacrifices the action (withdrawal of Death
to Hades, her plea to Pluto, transformation of Caelia into an immortal goddess), and makes the rest of his sonnet merely a laudatory speech by Death, of which vv. 9–12 are no more than varied
statements of v. 8 in Angeriano. The final point is thereby lost;
Guy's "After living a hundred years, without death she will become
an angel in heaven," seems much inferior to Angeriano's "It is to be
hoped that now, having become a goddess, she will hear our
prayers." Yet there is something to be said for Guy. Angeriano's
poem, though rather long, is properly an epigram, and hence justifies a somewhat complex narrative by a striking point at the end.
Though the sixteenth-century sonnet had been sufficiently crossed
by the classical and neo-Latin epigram to make it seek something
like the epigrammatic final point, it retained its true lyric nature so
far as to keep these points subdued. Belleau seems to respond to
this feeling in his transformation of Secundus' final points. The
sonnet had to remain "passionate," and too smart a conclusion
would tend to throw it from the emotional climate of love-poetry
completely into the intellectual climate of wit. Perhaps therefore
Guy does well enough to sacrifice the point of his original, and,
naturally, the complex narrative that leads to it and is in any case
too complex for a sonnet; but it is hard to escape the impression
that he has impoverished his borrowed theme far more than Belleau, in Guy's estimation, impoverished his by omitting the floral
ornament.[17]

[17]The poems here noticed are, of course, only a small portion of Guy's production. I have observed only two other borrowings: an elegy entitled *Songe* (1.52) from
Ovid, *Amores* 1.5, quite literally translated save that it is cast as a dream and sixteen
rather empty verses are added at the end; and secondly an epigram, *A Pacollet* (2.77),
reproducing Buchanan's well-known *In Zoilum* (*Poemata* [Leiden: Elzevir, 1628],
p. 329).

The Classics In
Sixteenth-Century France

I

The Renaissance represents the historical moment when European thought was ready to come to terms with the whole of its ancient heritage, and not merely with some part of it. Yet the process of coming to terms was not simple nor immediately complete, and it helps to define the character of the period to observe those points at which the electric fluid flowed freely and those at which it encountered a non-conductor, through failure either of understanding or of sympathy. For this purpose the penetration of humanism into the realm of vernacular literature, as addressed to a popular and not merely a learned public, may be particularly telling; and not least in France, where the successive literary movements of the sixteenth century are linked together and at the same time distinguished from each other precisely by an increasing involvement in the classical revival. This general trend reaches maturity only in the formation of the "classical" style, and the full assimilation of the drama, in the seventeenth century.

The school of the Rhétoriqueurs, carried over from the fifteenth century, is famous for its verbal ingenuity, not to say jugglery, yet is not without reflections of humanism, which shine with increasing light in one of its later representatives, really a "transitional" figure, Jean Lemaire de Belges (d. after 1514).[1] The mannerism of the

---

From *The Classical Weekly* (January 30, 1950) 131–38. Reprinted by permission of *The Classical World*.

[1] The standard work on the Rhétoriqueurs is Henry Guy's *L'Ecole des rhétoriqueurs* (Paris, 1910), being the first volume of his *Histoire de la poésie française au xvie siècle*. Important among them are Jean Molinet, Jean Meschinot (*Lunettes des princes*), Octovien de Saint-Gelais, Jean Marot, Jean Lemaire (*Illustrations de la Gaule*), and Guillaume Cretin. They eschewed what is simple and natural, and exercised their

Rhétoriqueurs begins definitely to give way to style in Clément Marot and his generation about 1530, and the change is involved with humanism. It may even be asked whether mannerism in European literature has not been fostered by the free application of rhetorical and aesthetic theory, while style has been gained, or regained, and guarded by imitation. Marot writes Epistles, Eclogues, Elegies, and Epigrams after the model of the Latin and the neo-Latin poets, and even takes up some Greek themes; his style at its best is direct, crisp, racy, and pointed. Yet in almost equal measure, with his allegories, abstractions, and acrostics, he is still a rhétoriqueur. His *Adolescence Clémentine* was published in 1532, the same year that saw the appearance of Rabelais' *Pantagruel,* in which the new humanistic education is set above the old education in no uncertain terms. Rabelais' work is already a palmary example of the mingling of "popular" and classical materials which is characteristic of the rest of the century; and it is significant of his own and his readers' development that the classical element greatly increases in his later books. Probably the most decisive part of it comes from Lucian. Lucian is also the model for the free-thinking *Cymbalum Mundi* (1537) of Bonaventure des Périers. Platonism, on the other hand, is a decisive influence on the queen of Navarre, but a Platonism hardly direct from Plato, though Des Périers had trans-

---

invention chiefly on patterns of verse, rhyme, and alliteration; whence modern criticism, which is fundamentally classical, has found it difficult to view them with sympathy, and tends to see in them the decadence of mediaeval school-rhetoric. Yet their bias is endemic in European literature, with its rhetorical schooling, and had appeared in the troubadours before them as it was to appear in the Précieux and Euphuists after them. The following, very mild, example of their manner is taken from Molinet's *Complainte de Grece,* written about a decade after the fall of Constantinople: for that reason, but hardly for any other, the *Complainte* might be compared with Shelley's *Hellas,* written in another manner at the other end of these events.

O saincte Eglise, angelique conserve,
Mon corps preserve et prie pour tes serfs;
Vieng reboutter l'ereticque leupserve [= lynx]
Qui me tient serve et veult que je le serve
Et que m'aserve a ses dragons desers;
Afui des airs, volle par les desers,
Et si me sers, donnant a mes serfs vie
Qu'ils n'aient mort, s'ils ne l'ont deservie.

Admirers of the poetry of the late Charles Williams will probably like this. Modern practitioners of mediaeval verse-forms, however, proceed on the principle of imitation, whereas the Rhétoriqueurs themselves consciously followed an "art"; they published a number of elaborate *Arts de rhétorique* setting forth their devices.

lated the *Lysis* for her. Much the same is true of the Platonism of Antoine Héroet, whose verse-paraphrase *L'Androgyne* (1542) is made directly from the Latin Plato of Ficino, but whose *Parfaite Amye* only reflects Italian literary ideas of "Platonic love."

The fifteen-forties mark a critical moment in French literature, perhaps not yet sufficiently understood; but we are safe in saying that this period is characterized by a growing appreciation of the classics and of the Italians. The suppression of heretical and skeptical ideas—with one or the other of which the writers of the thirties tended to sympathize—probably had little importance, unless it was to foster a turning away from the northern humanism of Erasmus to the literary ideas of the South. The fatal defect of the Rhétoriqueurs, which had not been their fulness of rhyme but their emptiness of ideas, had been little amended by the school of Marot, and was now painfully evident in the triviality of Mellin de Saint-Gelais and others. With the example of the classics and the Italians before them, men craved something better; and modern literary history, from its topsy-turvey viewpoint, sees the decade filled with "precursors" of the Pléiade.

Still less was the progress of classical scholarship affected by the burning at the stake of Etienne Dolet (1546), against whom the principal charge of blasphemy rested on his having added the words "rien du tout" to his translation of σὺ γὰρ οὐκ ἔσει in the Platonic *Axiochus*, 369 c: '*quand tu seras decedé... tu ne seras plus rien du tout.*' It was precisely in this period that France took the leadership of Europe in this department, if indeed she had not already done so in the person of Guillaume Budé. Though humanist studies had been pursued in various colleges of the University since the fifteenth century, it was the foundation in 1530 of the Royal Readerships (Collège de France), largely through Budé's efforts, that gave them the final lift upwards; and most of the great scholars who came forward in the forties were pupils of the first Royal Readers, Toussain and Danès. In order to indicate the brilliance of the period, one has only to mention Adrien Turnèbe, Jean Dorat, Pierre Ramus, Denys Lambin, Marc-Antoine Muret, and, somewhat younger, Henri Estienne. To Budé's interest in lexicography, antiquities, and law, they added a special emphasis on textual criticism, and, unlike Budé, put forth their best efforts upon the poets, and especially the Greek poets.

The outlook of this generation of scholars, their emphasis on the poets of Greece and Rome, made possible a fruitful relationship between them and the rising generation of French poets, whose publications begin in 1549–50. Of these poets, Ronsard and Jean-Antoine de Baïf and, briefly, Joachim du Bellay were pupils of Jean Dorat, while Etienne de Jodelle and Remy Belleau attended the college of Boncourt, where they had as masters George Buchanan and Muret. The interest of the scholars in the ancient poets gave them an interest in forming and encouraging the poets of the present, and these poets in turn, having seized upon the ancient idea of the *vates* and the *doctus poeta*, remained close to the world of scholarship throughout their lives. In the high sense of their calling, imbibed from humanism, they pass well beyond Marot and Saint-Gelais and set French poetry upon a new plane.

The manifesto of the new school, Du Bellay's *Deffence et Illustration de la Langue françoyse*, appeared in 1549. Its alleged unfairness to the earlier schools is only superficial; the main contention, that they were lacking in ideas and in density of style, is perfectly right. Du Bellay sees this as poverty of language, and the theme of the first part of the *Deffence* is that with cultivation—specifically the naturalization of more Greek and Latin words—French is capable of becoming a vehicle of the highest thought. Words represent ideas. The second part is directly addressed to the future poet, who is to "illustrate" the language and literature by imitating the ancients in the several literary types, by boldly coining new words especially from the Greek, by thoughtful attention to the music of his verse, and by preparing himself through devoted study. The practical method recommended throughout it *"l'immitation des Grecz et Romains,"* though formal rhetoric is not ignored. And animating the whole is the spirit of patriotism; France is to have a language and literature on a level with the ancients. These are the tones of Italian humanism, rather different from the Erasmian and northern humanism of the earlier French school.

The great interest of the *Deffence* is that the young poets stood ready to carry out its program. Let us see briefly where they succeeded and where they overshot the mark and failed. Certainly it was going too far when J.-A. de Baïf attempted to introduce a quantitative versification into French; but nowhere did the Pléiade succeed better than in their gift of music to French poetry. In this, too, imitation played a major role (not demonstrable here), and perhaps chiefly the imitation of Virgil, whose very mood together with his music deeply penetrated Du Bellay and Ronsard. Again they sometimes went too far in the attempt to bring Greek words into French, though they are more discreet than their later critics admitted. Even towards the end of his life Ronsard still could sigh:

Ah! que je suis marry que la Muse françoise
Ne peult dire ces mots comme faict la Gregeoise,
Ocymore, dyspotme, oligochronien:
Certes je les dirois du sang Valesien.

He contrives, we see, to use them (impossible though it is), and that in a funerary poem for members of the royal family! But it is important that he recognizes a limit. Rabelais, who revels in similar words, has them in place in his comic style.

Where the Pléiade most obviously failed was in their ambition to naturalize the greater types of ancient poetry. Ronsard's Pindaric odes are notorious, though possibly modern criticism does them less than justice. His epic poem, *La Franciade,* which he was unable to finish, is still more obviously a failure, and the failure is the more striking because the Pléiade, with the Renaissance generally, saw in the "long poem," as Du Bellay calls it, the highest type of poetry. The tragedies of Jodelle, despite his friends' enthusiastic reception of *Cleopatre* (1552), miss the essence of drama.[2] Nevertheless, here a seed was sown that would grow and flower within a hundred years in the French classical drama. And in general these efforts were perhaps not so much failures as premature attempts; for even the epic poem was, if not a French, at least a European possibility. As the first to introduce the greater forms into French poetry, these poets deserve respect for their gallant enterprise; but their true poetic sensibility was not of the same order as their ambition, and was chilled in the effort to "fill up" the forms. Even the formal eclogue defeated them, though it lives on the themes of love and of nature to which they were sensitive; all wrote eclogues, but none of their eclogues comes to life. At best there is Remy Belleau's *Bergerie,* in which, significantly, the bucolic themes are poured into the modern hybrid mold of Sannazaro's *Arcadia.*

[2]Be it noted that Aristotle's *Poetics* was just dawning above the horizon even for the Italian critics whom Du Bellay followed; in the *Deffence* it is mentioned once in passing.

Indeed it is when thus detached from the original form that their imitations often produce the best effect. The classics were of pervasive value to them in supplying themes, figures, "passages," and phrases, inset everywhere in their poems and more or less transmuted according to the skill of the individual poet. To such borrowings their work, like that of Tasso and Milton, owes much of its richness and texture. The Renaissance emphasis on imitation, realized through the rhetorical resources of *"copia"* and *"dilation,"* here receives its justification, as does also the full reception of antiquity, which enabled these poets to cast their nets widely for materials—in Aratus, Lycophron, and Stobaeus as readily as in Virgil or Horace. Yet it was not an indiscriminate pillaging; in themes as well as in vocabulary there were things that the French Muse *"ne peult dire,"* and he who would precisely evaluate the classicism of the Pléiade should note the limits of their seemingly casual borrowings.

The limitation lies chiefly in the bases of their poetic sensibility, which remained "popular" and, if you like, "mediaeval" (i.e. largely within the realm of courtly love). Nearly as basic and familiar was the Latin tradition; while the pure Greek tradition was too remote to be directly assimilated, though near enough to exert an attraction. Poetical sincerity was attainable when the second or even the third of these levels could be integrated with the first; for while the Pléiade could not, in their time, write seriously, and hence sincerely, at the merely popular level, neither could they write sincerely if they entirely took leave of it. (Tasso, for example, saw this situation very clearly.) In much of their early work they were fortunate in following the neo-Latin poets—Marullus, Navagero, Angeriano, J. Secundus—who had already modulated many an ancient theme, Greek and Latin, into a tonality between ancient and modern feeling. They could use the personal poetry of Ausonius, Horace, and Catullus, and could safely advance as far as the Alexandrian and late Greek writers. Thus the Greek Anthology was a fortunate discovery for them, and equally so the *Anacreontea,* discovered and published by the young Henri Estienne just at the right moment (1554). Even the Alexandrian epigram best met their mood when "pre-digested" by a neo-Latin poet. Thus the votive epigrams of the Anthology had been imitated with Latin (and Venetian) personality by Andrea Navagero in his *Lusus pastorales;* these modern transcriptions appealed to Du Bellay, who carried them over into French in his *Divers Jeux Rustiques,* among which the *Vœu d'un Vanneur de blé aux vents* is recognized as one of the finest lyrics of the Renaissance. This vibrant lyric poem could not have been elicited from the chiseled restraint of the Greek original (*Anth. Pal.* vi. 53) without passing through the unconscious, modern tonality of Navagero's Latin.

Within their home grounds of the personal lyric, therefore, the Pléiade still would be nothing without the imitation of the ancients—when the models were fortunately chosen. And in this sphere we may even speak of a successful formal influence. Their best poems are among their sonnets and *chansons,* but sonnets crossed by the concept of the Alexandrian epigram and *chansons* crossed by the concept of the Horatian and Anacreontic ode. That is the Renaissance style. Ronsard, who fails with Pindar, succeeds with Horace:

> O Fontaine Bellerie
>   Belle fountaine cherie
>   De nos Nymphes quand ton eau
>   Les cache au creux de ta source
>   Fuyantes le Satyreau,
>   Qui les pourchasse à la course
> Jusqu'au bord de ton ruisseau:
> Tu es la Nymphe eternelle
>   De ma terre paternelle:
>   Pource en ce pré verdelet
>   Voy ton Poëte qui t'orne
>   D'un petit chevreau de lait,
>   A qui l'une et l'autre corne
>   Sortent de front nouvelet.
> L'Esté je dors ou repose
>   Sus ton herbe, où je compose
>   Caché sous tes saules vers,
>   Je ne sçay quoy, qui ta gloire
>   Envoira par l'univers,
>   Commandant à la Memoire
>   Que tu vives par mes vers.
> L'ardeur de la Canicule
>   Ton verd rivage ne brule,
>   Tellement qu'en toutes pars
>   Ton ombre est espaisse et dru
>   Aux pasteurs venans des parcs,

Aux bœufs las de la charruë,
Et au bestial espars.
Io! tu seras sans cesse
Des fontaines la princesse,
Moy celebrant le conduit
Du rocher percé, qui darde
Avec un enroué bruit
L'eau de ta source jazarde
Qui trepillante se suit.

The fluid phrasing within successive stanzas, almost imitative of the flow of the fountain Bellerie, is not a Horatian effect, but very accomplished and pleasing; the engagement of the poet's own personality in the scene is far more prominent than with Horace; and there are other alterations; yet there is an essential sympathy between Ronsard and his model, and one may even hesitate whether to call these famous lines an imitation or an inspired translation of their famous original.

II

Verse-translations from the classical poets had been made by certain of the Rhétoriqueurs; and Marot, Saint-Gelais, Héroet, and others had made the practice more general in the thirties and forties. Very possibly this activity of the earlier poets inspires the animus of Du Bellay, who in facing the problem of the "illustration" of the language, sharply repudiates the idea that translation is sufficient. He gives two chapters to it. Translations are bound to be lacking in native vigor, and the higher the qualities of the original the less possible translation becomes; whence the poets cannot be translated at all. This is true enough; yet something has slipped through the meshes of the argument, for the modern languages owe much to translation, and even while Du Bellay wrote, Amyot was preparing his Plutarch. As a matter of fact, all the Pléiade, including Du Bellay himself, offer verse-translations, though these are usually short or fragmentary.

Translation of the classics into French was no novelty of the Renaissance. Already the thirteenth century had in French a *Rhétorique de Cicéron* (*De inventione* plus *Ad Herennium*); parts of Seneca and Suetonius; Vegetius; Paulus Diaconus; and three versions of Boethius' *Consolatio*. Five more translations of the *Con-*

solatio were made in the fourteenth century. Pierre Bersuire (d. 1362), the friend of Petrarch, now translated what was known of Livy, and Nicolas Oresme (d. 1382) translated from Latin the *Politics, Ethics, Economics,* and *De caelo* of Aristotle, bringing into French such words as *démocratie, sophiste, poète,* and *métaphore.* At this time or shortly afterwards French translations were made of Aristotle's *Problemata* and *Physiognomica;* of Terence, of Cicero's *De amicitia, De senectute,* and *De officiis,* of Sallust, parts of Ovid, Seneca's *De remediis* and *Epistolae,* Lucan, Valerius Maximus, Suetonius, Josephus, Augustine's *De civitate dei,* Cassian, Orosius; of Ptolemy's *Tetrabiblos* and of Justinian's *Institutes,* Books x-xii. Many of these translations were diffused by the printing-press in the last decades of the fifteenth century, and some of them, Oresme's for example, were still printed in the sixteenth. Transitional is the version of Caesar's *Commentaries* by the humanist Robert Gaguin, printed in 1495.

This is a very fair showing, even if the list betrays the special interests of the Middle Ages. Doubtless the taste of the sixteenth century was more catholic, yet so far as Latin authors are concerned the emphasis is not very different. The rhétoriqueur Octovien de Saint-Gelais translated, or travestied, the *Aeneid* (1509); while a more acceptable translation of the *Metamorphoses* was produced by François Habert (1557). Horace, whom the Middle Ages had left in Latin, now began his long struggle with the translators, which has never ceased (*Art poétique* by Peletier, 1545; *Satires* by Habert, 1549; *Odes* by Mondet, 1579; etc.). Of Cicero's works, *De officiis* remained the favorite of the moralizing Renaissance, being thrice translated in the course of the century. Seneca's moral essays are well represented, but the tragedies less well, only *Agamemnon* being translated (twice) before 1590. Most of the familiar Latin classics were translated or retranslated, but one notes a certain shyness as to the "new" Latin authors recovered by the humanists. Of the "new" Cicero, the *Familiares* were put into French by Etienne Dolet (1541) and completed with the other epistles by François de Belleforest (1566); many of the orations were translated; but not the *Brutus.* Tacitus, a "new" author, was translated by Etienne de La Planche (1555, 1582); but Plautus appears only in J.-A. de Baïf's version of the *Miles* (1572),[3] Catullus only in casual

[3]On the other hand, there was more than one complete translation of Terence.

versions by the poets; while Lucretius, Tibullus and Propertius, Quintilian, Silius Italicus, the younger Pliny, and most of the minor "new" authors were ignored by the translators. The impact of the Renaissance is more evident in the translation of Greek authors, virtually all of whom were "new." With the recovery of Greek, the natural impulse of the Latin West was to resume the work of Boethius and late antiquity, and of William of Moerbeke, and turn these Greek authors into Latin. Typical is the great Latin-translation project of Pope Nicholas V in the fifteenth century. Since what the Renaissance mostly craved was the Wisdom of the ancients, this and other like projects mainly contemplated the prose authors. Besides, the poets were more difficult to render adequately. Of Homer, after the complete prose-translation made by Pilatus (c. 1360) for Boccaccio and Petrarch, the fifteenth century provided a prose-translation begun by Valla and finished by Francesco Aretino (c. 1460), and this was replaced in the sixteenth century by the closer *ad verbum* of Andreas Divus (1537). At length a Latin verse *Iliad* was completed by Eoban Hess (1540) and an *Odyssey* by Simon Lemnius (1549). Of the drama, there was virtually nothing until Erasmus and Buchanan translated some few plays of Euripides in the sixteenth century. The vernacular translators inevitably follow the lead and emphasis of the humanists, and indeed commonly are only translating their translations.

In French, the first important translator is Claude de Seyssel, Archbishop of Turin, who devoted himself to the historians, translating Thucydides (1527), the *Anabasis* (1529), Diodorus (1530), Eusebius (1532), and Appian (1544). His express object was to supply his countrymen with the political wisdom of the Greeks, and this worthy aim was not lost from sight by his successors. He knew no Greek; but where Latin versions were wanting—as for Diodorus and the *Anabasis*—he was indebted to the almost incredi-

---

An anonymous *Therence en françoys* (c. 1501, and reprinted in 1539) contains a prose and a verse translation—the prose, it seems, a fifteenth-century version by Guillaume Rippe, the verse probably by Gilles Cybille. A second translation in verse, the work of Jean Bourlier (1566), was reprinted at least four times, and revised in 1583 by M.-A. de Muret. The translators, in the spirit of the age, advertise Terence as a moralist; and doubtless all agreed with Montaigne that, compared with Plautus, Terence "*sent bien mieux son gentilhomme*" (*Essais* 2.10). Professor Marie Delcourt, however, has shown that the literary influence of Plautus was greater than the scarcity of translations might suggest.

ble generosity of his friend, the prince of Greek exiles, Janus Lascaris, who made Latin versions for his sole use. The wisdom of the Greek poets is doubtless less available than that of the prose-writers; the want of good humanist versions made them less accessible to would-be translators; and the manifesto of the Pléiade warned the poets of 1549 not to make the attempt. The fortunes of Homer are instructive. No one could tolerate the prose *Iliad* of Jehan Samxon (1530), which wanders away into a kind of mediaeval *roman de Troye*. Serious translation was undertaken by Hugues Salel, a poet of the school of Marot, whose verse-translation of *Iliad* 1-2 appeared in 1542, of 1-10 in 1545, and of 11-12 with part of 13 posthumously in 1554. Nothing further was done while the Pléiade were at the height of their vogue; and here Du Bellay's influence seems evident. Twenty years later, however, Amadis Jamyn, the protégé of Ronsard, published his version of Books 12-16; and finally a complete *Iliad* (Books 1-11 by Salel and 12-24 by Jamyn) appeared in 1577. Of the *Odyssey*, Books 1-2 were translated by Jacques Peletier in 1547 and Books 1-3 by Jamyn in 1582, but a complete translation was only produced by Salomon Certon in 1603. The drama fared even less well. Only four translations were published: Sophocles' *Electra* by Lazare de Baïf (1537), Euripides' *Hecuba* in an anonymous version (1544) probably by Guillaume Bochetel with the help of Amyot, *Iphigenia in Aulis* by Thomas Sebillet (1549), and after the significant interval Sophocles' *Antigone* by J.-A. de Baïf (1572). On the other hand, excessive attention was given to minor works and trifles. Short flights were more in the order of the day. Brevity combined with cleverness or a love-theme or both drew attention to Musaeus' *Hero and Leander,* translated from the Latin by Clément Marot; to Moschus' *Amor fugitivus,* also translated by Marot and by at least five others in the course of the century; to the *Battle of the Frogs and Mice,* which found four translators; to the *Anacreontea;* and to the Greek Anthology. Brevity combined with moral wisdom was equally attractive. The Anthology offered not only amatory and ingenious comic and "epideictic" epigrams, but well-turned moral observations which found many translators; Hesiod's *Works and Days* appeared in four French translations, as did also Naumachius' advice on marriage and the Golden Verses of "Pythagoras"; ps.-Phocylides in three. Though not so brief, Nicander was translated by Jacques Grévin (1567), Aratus, not quite entire, by Remy Belleau (1568, 1578), and Oppian by Florent Chrestien (1575). Du Bellay had made an exception for poems of useful content. Be it noted also that the major Greek poets had little to offer in the contemporary poetical vein of courtly love.

Translations from the Greek prose-authors appeared on every hand. I estimate within the century approximately 300 such translations, some of them attaining several editions. Probably no other European language can show so many. Here we may note a few peculiarities of emphasis. Lucian, for example, is distinctly an author dear to the earlier part of the century, in the atmosphere of "thoughtful laughter" associated with Erasmus. In 1529 Geoffroy Tory published *Trente Dialogues,* and the rhétoriqueur Simon Bougouyn *Des vraies Narrations avec l'oraison contre la Calomnie.* Three other versions of the *Calumny,* the Renaissance favorite, appeared before 1560; but on the whole Lucian does not retain the favor he enjoyed in the time of Rabelais and Des Périers.[4] Romantic love, so little emphasized by the major Greek poets, was quickly scented out in the Greek Romances. All the Romances then known were in French before the century ended. Amyot's first published work was his translation of Heliodorus (1547), and to this day his *Daphnis and Chloe* of Longus (1559) rivals his Plutarch in popularity. Once more the later Greek temperament was found by the Renaissance more sympathetic than the classical.

What the translators thought the public would accept from the philosophers is of some interest. In Plato they begin with the shorter dialogues, and rather on the periphery: *Crito* (Vallambert, 1542; Du Val, 1547); *Axiochus* and *Hipparchus* (Dolet, 1544); *Lysis* (Des Périers, 1544); *Ion* (Richard Le Blanc, 1546); *Apology* (François Hotman, 1549). After 1550 there began to appear the superior translations of Loys Le Roy: *Timaeus* (1551); *Phaedo,* with *Republic* x and passages from *Phaedrus* and *Gorgias* (1553); *Symposium*

[4]There was, however, a complete *Œuvres de Lucian* by Filbert Bretin in 1582. The indefatigable J.-A. de Baïf offered nine *Devis des Dieux pris de Lucian* turned into verse. In this trick he had been preceded by Clément Marot, who similarly versified one of the *Dialogues of the Dead;* and after Baïf one dialogue each was so turned by Etienne Forcadel and Jean Le Masle. Lucian's dialogues in Latin verse are found in the works of more than one humanist. Similarly Jacques de la Tapie gave Plutarch's *Marriage Precepts* in verse (1559) and Pierre Trédéhan the *Theages* of Plato (1564). Antoine Héroet's *Androgyne de Platon* (1542) obviously belongs to this tradition of verse-paraphrase, which has a long history (see E. R. Curtius, *Europäische Literatur und Lateinisches Mittelalter* [Bern, 1948], pp. 155 f.).

(1559); part of Book III of the *Laws* (1562); and finally a complete *Republic* (1600). An earlier *Symposium* by Mathurin Heret (1556), *Euthyphro* by Jean Martin (1579), and a new *Lysis* by Blaise de Vigenère (1579) complete the list, unless we add the verse *Theages* of Trédéhan and Héroet's *Androgyne*. Popular interest in Aristotle remained where the fourteenth century had left it. There were new translations of the *Ethics* by Le Plessis (1553) and of the *Politics* by Le Roy (1568), while the *Economics, De mundo, Physiognomica*, and *Problems* were translated more than once. That is all, unless we add the *Secreta secretorum*, continually reprinted in the fourteenth-century version of Tignonville. By way of contrast, the *Manual* of Epictetus was translated three times—by Antoine du Moulin (1544), by André Rivaudeau (1567), and by Guillaume du Vair (1591). Marcus Aurelius was put into French by Pardoux du Prat (1570). Esoteric wisdom was in great popular demand; there were translations of Horapollo and Artemidorus, and two translations of the Hermetic writings. Of more serious interest again, a strong emphasis rests on the Greek ecclesiastical writers, of whom many translations appeared. We may mention the long series published by the younger Fédéric Morel between 1583 and 1615.

The technical wisdom of antiquity also had its share of attention. Indeed, after Seyssel's historians, the next important effort of translation was that laid out on the medical writers just before and after 1540 by certain persons—Pierre Tolet, Jean Canappe, and others—associated with the circle of Etienne Dolet. The mathematicians were the special concern of Etienne Forcadel in the last quarter of the century. Even the tacticians Aelianus and Onosander found themselves speaking French.

But the main emphasis was always on moral and political wisdom. If among the Greek orators Isocrates sometimes seems to be the favorite of the Renaissance, that is largely because just three of his writings were translated again and again—*Nicocles, ad Nicoclem*, and *Demonicus*. These pieces answered to the contemporary concern with the education of a prince; and one or another of them seems regularly to have been set for royal personages who were learning Greek. There exists a manuscript translation of *ad Nicoclem*, probably by Marguerite of Navarre; Queen Elizabeth of England and James I seem also to have translated from them. The similar admonitions of Agapetus, twice translated into French in the sixteenth century, were set for the young Louis XIII, and his translation was published (1612). A typical book of our period is the *Manuel Royal* of Jean Brèche (1541, 1544), consisting of extracts from Isocrates together with Plutarch's advice *To an Uneducated Prince;* and this was characteristically improved on after 1550 by Loys Le Roy in *Trois livres d'Isocrate,* with extracts from other Greek writers on kingship (1551, 1568).

No wonder, then, that the historians fared better with the French translators than any other group of ancient authors, since for the humanist centuries history was "philosophy teaching by examples." Seyssel's translations continued to be printed, and no one undertook to replace his Thucydides, Eusebius, or *Anabasis.* Of the other Greek historians, Herodotus was translated by Pierre Saliat (1556); Diodorus by Macault (1535), completed by Amyot (1554); Polybius by Meigret (1542); Josephus entire or in part six times by different translators; Dio by Des Rosiers (1542); Herodian by Jean Colin (1541) and again by Jacques De Vintimille (1554); Appian by Des Avenelles (1558) and by Tagault (1559); Arrian by Witart (1599); Procopius and Agathias by Fumée (1587); and Zonaras by Jean de Miremont (1563) and again by Jean Millet (1583). Absent are Dionysius of Halicarnassus and Xenophon's *Hellenica,* though Jacques de Vintimille is reported to have translated the latter. Vintimille (a Greek by birth) translated the *Cyropaedia* (1545); the *Memorabilia* was translated by Jean Doublet (1582); but perhaps the main interest in Xenophon was in the *Economics,* translated by Geoffroy Tory (1531), by F. de Ferris (1562), and by Etienne de la Boétie (1571).

On the foregoing evidence one could almost postulate that the author destined completely to meet the temper of the age was Plutarch, who combined in the most congenial way the moral and the political emphasis. On the whole, the *Moralia* seems to have caught the attention of translators earlier than the *Lives.* Between 1521 and 1572 (the date of Amyot's *Moralia*), I count thirty-one translations of various essays, many of them printed more than once. The record goes to the *Marriage Precepts,* of which no fewer than seven different versions, including Amyot's, appeared. Of the *Lives,* only one considerable translation preceded Amyot's (published in 1559), that of eight lives by the diplomat George de Selve (1543).

Amyot's Plutarch is no ordinary translation. If one is sometimes inclined to think that it has played a part in French history comparable to that of the Authorized Version of the Bible in English history—the men of the French Revolution quoting Plutarch as the men of the Puritan Revolution quoted Scripture—let it be noted that Amyot approached his task in something of the spirit of one translating a sacred text. A scholar of serious attainments, he laid a solid foundation, gathering a large "apparatus" on his author, and consulting manuscripts in France and Italy, so as to constitute a reliable text. He might thus have produced a superior edition of Plutarch in Greek; but his aim was the more difficult one of recreating this perfected Plutarch as a Frenchman speaking French without an accent. On this subject he expended the utmost artistic energy. His search for expressions that should be both immediately significant to the French reader and true to the forms of ancient life has been followed by René Sturel and other scholars through the successive editions of the *Lives;* for Amyot was continually amending. The result was not only to put into the hands of Frenchmen a lively and reliable version of an author whom they were born to embrace as their own, but also quite definitely to "illustrate" the French language and give it new resources. Amyot's Plutarch is the most important monument of French prose between Calvin's *Institutes* (French version, 1541) and Montaigne's *Essais* (1580). Indeed it is no paradox to say that Amyot had already written a considerable part of Montaigne's *Essais,* of which page after page is found to be either a simple transcription or a paraphrase of Amyot's Plutarch.

III

Montaigne, the most important writer of the last part of the century, is thus not only the heir of the whole classical revival, but in particular demonstrates the value and use of the remarkable activity in translation that precedes him; for Amyot, though the chief, is by no means the only translator he uses—Saliat's Herodotus, for example, is another of his favorite sources. With Montaigne's sources is bound up the evolution of the *Essais,* and therewith the creation of this modern form of literature.[5] When he retired to his estate of Montaigne in 1570 to become a gentlemanly

[5]See Pierre Villey, *Les Sources et l'Evolution des Essais de Montaigne* (Paris, 1908), on which what follows is mainly based.

author, his idea seems to have been no more than to compile from his reading one of those collections of *Lesefrüchte* that were then popular, and that reflected in the vernacular the scholar's *Miscellanea* or *Variae Lectiones*. The earlier *Essais* are of this type; but they already possess an "attitude," which is that of Seneca's moral imperative, and thus far reflect a traditional, and almost mediaeval, classicism, since Seneca had always been one of the *auctores*. A change comes, according to Pierre Villey, with the full revelation of Plutarch's *Moralia* in Amyot's translation of 1572. Plutarch liberated him from Seneca, and while always a moralist, he escaped through Plutarch from Senecan dogmatism into a simple observation of the ways of men. Since, however, these ways are seriously contradictory, Montaigne became a relativist and was ready to be deeply influenced by yet a third ancient book, which he came upon at this time (c. 1576), namely Sextus Empiricus' *Outlines of Pyrrhonism*, probably in the Latin version of Henri Estienne (1562). He became a skeptic. (He had a medal struck with the motto ΕΠΕΧΩ; moreover, ten of the famous inscriptions in his study are from Sextus.) Retreating somewhat from this view, he finally realized that what he was really searching for was himself—"Michael, who concerns us nearer than man." The discovery of the value and reality of one's private existence was evidently one made over and over again in the Renaissance, whether in spite of or because of the attention paid to the ancient moralists. It is not that in a great rain of classics Seneca, Plutarch, and Sextus fell by accident on the head of Montaigne; he found them out because they answered to his instincts—instincts molded by the circumstances of his life. His essays continue to mingle instances from his own experience with instances drawn from antiquity, with which he evidently felt at one; but to the great Renaissance question, Can reason apprehend a moral law, he returns a negative answer, after gazing into the well of ancient wisdom from which his age always expected the answer.

It remained to see if more positive results would come from the attention to ancient political experience; and already Bodin was reviving from antiquity the concept of natural law, while Montaigne's friend La Boétie was distilling from Plutarch the ideal of political liberty. In the sixteenth century all serious thought was engaged with the ancients, and, whether for or against them, found its problems in them.

To none of the Renaissance writers do the early writers of Greece have much to say as spirit to spirit. Montaigne's authors are preferably those of the Empire, and, despite the influence of Plutarch and Sextus, his culture is mainly Latin. Latin, as every one knows, was his "native" language, taught him (*à la* Quintilian) before French, and which his masters at the Collège de Guienne only succeeded in corrupting. As these masters included Buchanan and Muret, we receive the statement, as intended, with astonishment. Luckily he could always steal away to read Ovid, who gave him at eight years of age his first feeling for literature. He made only a beginning at Greek, and forgot most of it. The innumerable verse-quotations in the *Essais* are chiefly from the Latin poets, among whom, with Virgil, Horace, and Ovid, Lucretius is conspicuous. In this Latin bias his "common sense" takes its departure from the sixteenth century and looks forward to the seventeenth. Then, Malherbe, for example, who routed the last followers of Ronsard and set French poetry once more on a new career, "had no use for Greek literature," and among the Latins "*celui qu'il estimoit le plus étoit Stace . . . et après, Sénèque le tragique, Horace, Juvenal, Ovide, Martial*" (Racan). This is already the true accent of the seventeenth century. Ronsard and his fellow enthusiasts for Greek were viewed as representing a false step in French literature (they returned to esteem only with Sainte-Beuve in the nineteenth century), and their Hellenisms were expelled from the poetic vocabulary. There must be nothing not immediately intelligible to the "*honnête homme*," who (though the expression is of later currency) was of the "*génie latin*."

Yet the substantial gains of the sixteenth century could not be lost. Seventeenth century "classicism" stood on the shoulders of the classical revival, and could eventually, in a moment of social stability, pass beyond the intimate chamber music of the Pléiade to fill the larger forms of the drama in verse and the funeral oration in prose—it could be at once sincere and oratorical; but this would not have been possible without the experiments of the sixteenth century. The moral question persisted, in which now the classics competed with a new devotional sentiment. And more and more, with the revival of "natural law," the political experience of antiquity seemed significant. Plutarch's reputation was maintained and enhanced. In the eighteenth century, Montesquieu would gladly save him from the stigma of being a Greek author, confiding to his notebook: "*Ils* [the Greek writers] *avoient moins d'esprit que les auteurs*

romains—Plutarque presque le seul—aussi avoit-il profité des Latins."
Every one knows what Plutarch meant to Rousseau, to the young
Napoleon, to Mme. Roland and the heroes of the Revolution, who
found in him, and in Tacitus, their own ideal of liberty. He fell a
victim of the guillotine with Robespierre and St. Just—so at least
Macaulay hopefully intimates, who writes his epitaph in acid.[6]

The classics did not create the Renaissance, but the Renaissance
found in them, in its own time, the larger world and the liberation
of spirit that it craved—in the aesthetic, and still more in the moral
and political, sense. From the fifteenth century to the Revolution,
the ancient poets, moralists, and historians were not merely a lesson
for children, but—like the Bible, largely through translations—
influenced and combined with the deepest expressions of European sensibility. They were profoundly meaningful because they
clarified and interpreted his own situation for modern man.
Hence, for one thing, all those classical quotations. Has experience
since the French and the Industrial Revolutions so far transcended
the experience of antiquity that this is no longer the case? Society
speaking through the parents of American school children seems
to return an affirmative answer, bidding the young not to study
Latin and Greek but cooking and chemistry. Society speaking
through the poets—Mr. O'Neill, for example, or Messrs. Eliot, Au-
den, Jeffers, and Toynbee—seems to return a different answer.
Whose voices are more likely to represent the real sensibility of our
time? As in the Renaissance, so now, no doubt there are parts of
ancient literature that chime with our own sensibility more than
others, we can hardly say why. For Ronsard it was the Alexandrian
and Roman personal lyric; for Montaigne and generations of
Frenchmen (and not only Frenchmen) it was Plutarch; for the
modern age perhaps it is Greek drama, Plato, and Thucydides?

[The foregoing article is in part based on the annotated survey of
scholarly work concerned with the translations from the Greek, together with a list of the translations themselves, contributed by me
to *A Critical Bibliography of French Literature*, D. C. Cabeen, ed. vol.
II, *The Sixteenth Century*, Alexander H. Scheetz, ed. (Syracuse, N.Y.:
Syracuse University Press, 1956), pp. 263–70 (Bibliography) and
pp. 305–309 (Translations).]

[6]Macaulay's attack on Plutarch occurs in his essay "History" (*Critical and Historical
Essays by Lord Macaulay, in Three Volumes* [Boston and New York: Houghton Mifflin
Co., 1900], I, 251–58, 263 f.).

Classical Poetry in
Renaissance Poems on Peace

One way of understanding the sensibility of the Renaissance is to study the commonplaces that are repeated with most complacency in regard to some matter of universal concern. Years ago the late Theodore Spencer applied this method with success to the subject of Death.[1] If not quite so universal as that, our more cheerful subject of Peace is certainly one on which the Renaissance had plenty to say and in which it was deeply concerned. War reigned throughout the period, and accordingly there was a high output of writings about peace. The divine invention of the printing-press continually opposed the diabolical invention of artillery. The poets played their part, and the latest poet of the age might well have echoed the first: "I'vo gridando pace pace pace." But the wars periodically died away into peace before starting up again—so many wars, so many peace settlements; and it was for these moments of rejoicing that, on the whole, the typical peace poems were written. Alas! one who had written many such poems might well be allowed a cry of despair in his sixtieth year (Ronsard, 1584):

> J'ay veu guerres, debats, tantost trèves et pais.
> Tantost accord promis, redéfais et refais,
> Puis défais et refais; j'ay veu que sous la lune
> Tout n'estoit que hazard et pendoit de Fortune.

In the study from which this paper is extracted, I have analyzed a large number of poems on the topic of peace, taking into account the ideas of the time, the historical moment, the sources, and so forth. Only a few poems will be mentioned here, and only a few instances of the influence of the ancient poets upon them. I may

---

[1] Theodore Spencer, *Death and Elizabethan Tragedy: A Study of Convention and Opinion in the Elizabethan Drama* (Cambridge, Mass.: Harvard University Press, 1936).

remark, however, that the stream of peace poetry was more abundant in France than elsewhere—perhaps for good reason. It begins already at the end of the fourteenth century with Eustache Deschamps, and continues through the fifteenth; Alain Chartier, Pierre de Nesson, Jean Regnier, and others wrote notable peace poems, and we may admit that no Renaissance poem possesses the haunting beauty of Charles d'Orléans' *ballade;* "Priez pour paix, doulce Vierge Marie . . ." The Rhétoriqueurs continued the tradition (Jean Molinet, *Le Testament de la Guerre;* Jean Marot, *Le Voyage de Venise*), and Clément Marot, Sagon, and others followed suit. The first verses of serious intent written by Antoine de Baïf were his poem *Sur la Paix avec les Anglois* for the peace settlement of 1549–50 in connection with which the Constable Montmorency had secured Boulogne for France. The same peace brought out Ronsard's *Ode de la Paix,* which deserves a high place in his total *œuvre,* and a high place among the peace poems of the century.

I shall not dwell long on this Pindaric ode, though it contains many echoes of the classical poets; its chief topics transcend what the classical poets have to give. These topics are Cosmic Peace and Hope of the French Monarchy. Yet cosmic peace deserves to be mentioned as one of the major topics of Renaissance peace poetry though it is not strongly represented in the ancient poetical tradition. That the world is a truce among four mutually hostile elements was an idea that had many ramifications, and especially appealed to late mediaeval writers. Cusanus and Ficino had made it go far. Ronsard's poem describes the formation of the world by the creator La Paix; passes to the divinely-permitted invasion of Discord, and traces the divinely-intentioned history of the French Monarchy from Francion to the restoration of peace by Henri II, ending with the hope of his further conquests and those (to include the Indies) of his son. A minor treaty with the English hardly justifies all that. It has not perhaps been noticed that this poem was written at the height of the activity of that great and strange apostle of world peace, Guillaume Postel. Postel had absorbed the mystical mediaeval tradition about peace, upon which he had superimposed the Cabala; but his chief hope at this time was in the French monarchy, and he prophesied a final era of peace to be ushered in by its conquests. For proof he traced the French nation back to Japheth and Gomer, but contrived to include the story of Francion. He had recently determined cabalistically that this very year, 1550, would begin the new era.[2] But that suggestion is apart. Ronsard's poem is not cabalistic, but seems clearly to depend on Ficino for its esoteric matter. That realization even leads us to a wisp of Greek poetry. La Paix, who has no traditional personality, acts the part of the cosmic Aphrodite ("Car partout où voloit la belle / Les Amours volloient avecq'elle," 66-67), and that fact allows the poet to address her in such enigmatic lines as these (311-18):

> L'effort de ta divinité
> Commande à la necessité
> Ploiant' sous ton obéissance:
> Les bestes sentent ta puissance
> Aléchés de ton dous amer:
> De l'air la vagabonde troupe
> T'obéist, et celle qui couppe
> Le plus creus ventre de la mer.

How does Peace rule necessity? and what has that fact to do with beasts, birds, and fishes? Ronsard's reader would need to have in hand Ficino's Commentary on the *Symposium* (5.11) to know that Love "rules before Necessity," because Love's power "begins in God, that of Necessity in created things," a point that Ficino supports by citing the *Orphic Hymn to Aphrodite:*

> καὶ κρατέεις τρισσῶν μοιρῶν, γεννᾶς δε τὰ πάντα
> ὅσσα τ'εν οὐρανῷ ἐστι καὶ ἐν γαίῃ πολυκάρπῳ
> ἐν πόντου τὲ βυθῷ.

"Thou rulest the three Fates, and givest birth to all things that are in heaven and in the fruitful earth and in the depth of the sea"—"le plus creus ventre de la mer." By such devious routes do the ancient poets sometimes come to the modern, especially to Ronsard who magpie-like is ever ready to snatch a glittering fragment for his nest.[3]

---

[2]The year 1550 is determined in *Candelabri typici . . . interpretatio,* (Venice, 1548), p. 49. Among the publications of Postel that I have seen, the appeal to the history of Francion occurs only in *L'Histoire mémorable des expéditions* (Paris, 1552). On Postel see now William J. Bouwsma, *Concordia Mundi: The Career and Thought of Guillaume Postel (1510–1581)* (Cambridge, Mass.: Harvard University Press, 1957).

[3]Ronsard often compounds his sources. Here he seems to have crossed the verses of the *Hymn to Aphrodite* with a recollection of the similar expressions of Lucretius (1.1-15): "aléchés de ton dous amer" perhaps equals "perculsae corda tua vi." Cf. his *La Paix, au Roy* 178-83.

The greatest outburst of peace poetry, perhaps of all time, came in 1559 with the peace of Cateau-Cambrésis, which was indeed an important event in European history. May I be permitted to recall this occasion very briefly, since the poems about to be mentioned are involved in it. In the war between Henri II of France and Philip of Spain, Philip's very able general Emmanuel-Philibert of Savoy had completely destroyed the French army under the Constable Anne de Montmorency at Saint-Quentin in August, 1557. Montmorency, Saint-André, the Marshal of France, and other notables were taken prisoner. But a new French army under the Duke of Guise redressed the balance (Guise took Calais in January, 1558); and toward the end of August, 1558, the two hostile armies, with the kings present, faced each other near Amiens, expecting to fight a decisive battle. Instead of battle, peace supervened. The chief commissioners for Henri II were the Cardinal of Lorraine, Montmorency, and Saint-André; for Philip, the astute Granvelle (Bishop of Arras), the Duke of Alba, and William of Orange. After nearly six months of negotiations, the treaty, which was a general European settlement, was signed at Cateau-Cambrésis at the beginning of April, 1559, and though disappointing to many Frenchmen, was celebrated with unprecedented fervor when peace was proclaimed on the 7th. Among its terms, Philip of Spain (who had lost Mary Tudor in November) was to marry Henri's daughter Elizabeth, and the Duke of Savoy Henri's sister Marguerite. It was during the fêtes preceding these marriages at the end of June that Henri suffered the accident from which a few days later he died.

Ronsard had followed each step of these events with a new poem, from his *Exhortation pour la Paix* of late September, 1558, to poems for the marriage of Marguerite and Savoy. But he was only the leader of a full chorus of songsters both in French and in Latin who raised their voices even before April 8. We make no attempt to enumerate them here. Jacques Grévin in his *Chant de Joie de la Paix*, the privilège of which is dated precisely April 8, already feels himself anticipated by the Pléiade, if it is to them that his word "brigade" refers:

> Et suivant la troupe heureuse,
> La brigade industrieuse,
> Favorite d'Apolon,
> Qui ja gaillarde s'appreste
> A descrire la conqueste

De la PAIX sur Mars felon:
Et qui a ja la nouvelle
De la celeste pucelle,
Par la douceur de ses vers
Annoncée à l'univers,
Je viens d'une humble caresse
Saluer ceste déesse.

What had the ancient poets to contribute to the celebrations of Cateau? Something, no doubt, since the moment was one in which the incidence of classical influence in French poetry was high. In what follows we glance first at the Greek poets, and then at the Latin.

Apart from Aristophanes' peace plays, which were little known in the Renaissance, surviving Greek poetry offered only incidental passages on the topic of peace; yet some of these passages are important. From Hesiod (*Theogony* 901-903) comes the very idea of Eirene as one of the Horae, linked with her sisters Dike and Eunomia, as well as the implication (*Erga* 119, 145-46) that peace was the condition of the Golden Generation. Often the Greek poets are content to elaborate the concept of "peace and plenty"—πλοῦτος καὶ εἰρήνη—already expressed in the odyssey (24.486). Most famous of Greek poems on peace was a paean of Bacchylides, of which Stobaeus has preserved a fragment: "Peace is the mother of great blessings for mankind—of wealth and the flowers of sweet-tongued song: that on spangled altars the thighs of cattle and of long-haired sheep flame for the gods with yellow fire; ... in ironbound shields the busy spiders set their looms, and rust subdues the pointed spear and two-edged sword. . . ." The figure of the spider weaving in the weapons of war lived on in the Greek tradition (Sophocles, Euripides, Theocritus), while the Roman poets prefer the figure of the rusted armor (Horace, Tibullus, Ovid). But the Renaissance revived the Greek spider—for example, Ronsard, *Exhortation* 185.6:

Au croq vos morryons pour jamais soyent liez
Autour desquelz l'araigne en filant de ses piedz
Y ourdisse ses retz.

Further instances of this figure are too numerous to mention. The fragment of Bacchylides and eight others from various Greek poets make up the chapter περὶ Εἰρήνς of Stobaeus' *Florilegium*. What a tempting "source" for a Renaissance poet! The entire chapter, already a peace poem in itself, was transcribed in a Horatian metre by the neo-Latin poet Girolamo Vida to make a notable hymn *To Peace*. The same idea came to the English humanist John Leland, who in his *Laudatio Pacis* also runs these fragments into one poem. There may be other Renaissance echoes of this attractive chapter of Stobaeus.

The French poets of peace avail themselves but rarely of these Greek sources. Hitherto undetected is a fragment of the *Cypria* that Ronsard, after his manner, has picked up to account for the origin of war in his *Exhortation pour la Paix* (87–102): Zeus began the Trojan war to relieve Earth of the burden of excess population. The fragment is preserved in a *scholium* on *Iliad* 1.5: if Ronsard chanced to use the Homer published by Hervagius at Basel in 1535, the *scholium* appears on the first page.[4] But it is Guillaume des Autels, a poet badly neglected by modern scholarship, who distinguishes himself among the poets of Cateau-Cambrésis by turning to the Greeks for his "inventions." He is also unique in celebrating the treaty from both sides. Presumably in April, when the treaty was signed, he published with Wechel in Paris a *Remonstrance au peuple francoys* (to accept the peace), followed by an *Eloge de la Paix à Pierre Ronsard*, an *Eloge de la Trefve à Joachim du Bellay*, and an *Eloge de la Guerre à Estienne Jodelle*. He then departed for Brussels, hoping to win the favor of Philip II, whose subject he had become when Article 18 of the treaty gave his native Charolais to the Spaniard. And in July he published with Plantin in Antwerp a long poem on the peace, *La Paix venue du ciel*, dedicated to the Bishop of Arras. A résumé of this poem follows:

Once the god of Wealth poured his bounty upon France and Flanders; but afterwards, owing to the wickedness of men, Justice fled to her father Jupiter and induced him to punish them. But God will yet listen to prayer if a just remnant is found. Now Até creates contention, and Peace also departs. The horrors of war ensue, and would have been protracted had not a just remnant, the

---

[4]From the *scholium* Ronsard takes the notion that both the Theban and the Trojan wars had this origin, and he seems to echo the scholiast's prose expression: βαρυμένην ὑπ' ἀνθρώπων πολυπληθίας in "trop chargée / d'hommes qui te foulloyent"; from the *Cypria* itself, compare: "Après elle alluma la querelle Troyenne" and ῥιπίσσας (alluma) πολέμου μεγάλην ἔριν (querelle) Ἰλιακοῖο.

kings Henri and Philip, been imbued with faith, and the limping prayers gone up to entreat Jove's mercy. Conciliated by the Prayers, and by Saint Madeleine and Saint Clothilde, Jupiter bids Peace return to earth, taking with her Astraea, the Graces, Concord, Amalthea, and two Hymenaei. But Peace cannot get down to Earth without help. Mercury therefore is instructed to attach to her ivory car the ends of six golden chains, and to place the other ends in the hands of six mortals—the Cardinal of Lorraine, Montmorency, Saint-André, the Bishop of Arras, the Prince of Orange, and the Duke of Alba. Mercury travels far and wide handing a chain to each of these deputies. They pull: "Les deputez soigneus à leur œuvre entrepris / Suent tous en tirant ce beau char de haut pris." So Peace returns to earth. And who are these two? They are the Hymenaei, who will unite Spain with France and France with Savoy. Let peoples and kings cherish Peace and her sisters; as long as Bonne Loy and Justice are present, La Paix also will remain.

The poem did Des Autels no good. He was back in Paris by the end of the summer.

The outline no doubt already reveals the classical sources that Des Autels has rather ingeniously woven together in a poem of Rhétoriqueur design. Nor has he failed to keep in touch with Christian belief—Peace comes through the Grace of God. Here I draw attention to only one or two of the classical features. At the beginning of the poem, the god of Wealth is introduced with traits that blend Aristophanes' *Plutus* with Aristophanes' own source, Hesiod:

> Ce Dieu que l'on dit estre et aveugle et boyteus,
> Qui suyt les effrontez et qui fuyt les honteus,
> Qui règne sur la terre et dessus le dos large
> De la mer, que de naufs estrangères il charge,
> Ce Dieu fils de Ceres, qui en donnant le bien,
> N'avise point à ceus qui le méritent bien,
> Versoit l'or et l'argent par tout à grandes sommes.

The blind god of Wealth, who follows the shameless and avoids the modest, is of course from Aristophanes' *Plutus* (28–31, 86–91, etc.), while the rest of the description follows Hesiod, *Theogony* 969–74: "Demeter and the fair goddess bore Plutus, ... a good deity who goes over the land and the broad back of the sea, everywhere; and any chance person into whose hands he may fall he makes wealthy and bestows great riches upon him." Every now and then Des Autels renders his sources line for line. The Horae are: "Bonne Loy et Justice et la Paix florissante" [as in Hesiod (*Theog.* 902)]: Εὐνομίην τε Δίκην τε καὶ Εἰρήνην τεθαλυίαν and the Homeric Prayers from *Iliad* 9.502–503:

> Filles de Jupiter, les Prières boyteuses, . . .
> Leur habit est tout blanc, plus net que précieus,
> Leur visage est ridé, et louches sont leurs yeus.

> καὶ γάρ τε Λιταί εἰσι κοῦραι μεγάλοιο
> κωλαί τε ῥυσαί τε παραβλῶπες τ' ὀφθαλμώ.

When Peace departs from mankind, all the gods go with her. For this development Des Autels takes leave of his Greek sources and paraphrases the last lines of Catullus 64. When Justice entreats Jupiter to punish mankind, the scene is of course from *Works and Days* 256–62: "The maiden Justice . . . sits down beside Zeus Cronion and tells him of men's unrighteousness, until the people pay for the folly of their princes who, with evil mind, turn justice aside in crooked utterance":

> L'arc de vengeance il bande alors sur les provinces
> Pour leurs propres pechez ou pour ceus de leurs princes,
> Qui ont mal conseillez detourné de l'endroit
> Que monstroit la raison, la practique du droict.

All leads up to the final "invention" borrowed, surely, from Aristophanes' *Peace*. Here, it will be recalled, Trygaeus, flying to heaven in search of Peace, learns from Hermes that War now reigns, and has cast Peace into a pit, heaping stones over her to keep her down. Trygaeus summons the men of Greece to bring spades, crowbars, and ropes, and to "pull out Peace, the darling of mankind." In a vigorous scene, he exhorts Boeotians, Spartans, Megarians, and Athenians to pull their hardest; and at last, chiefly by the efforts of the farmers (who are the Chorus), Peace is drawn forth, accompanied by her attendants Harvest and Games. They descend to earth with Trygaeus, and the play ends with the marriage of Trygaeus and Harvest (i.e., Abundance) amid cries of "Hymen

Hymenaeus." Des Autels has taken only the general idea, which suits his purpose admirably. He has retained none of the boisterous spirit or homely imagery of the Greek. Aristophanes' simple ropes have become golden chains—perhaps a reminiscence of Homer (*Iliad* 8.19–20). The attendants of Peace—Astraea, the Graces, Concord—are chosen from another tradition, but the Hymenaei— so aptly made present for the royal marriages—may well have been suggested by Aristophanes.

In this poem the resources of Greek poetry have for once been rather fully exploited by a Renaissance poet celebrating peace. And here, without much doubt, is an instance of the rare influence of Aristophanes' *Peace,* which seems not to have been collected by those who have followed the fortune of Aristophanes in French literature. It does not exhaust Des Autels' Greek "inventions"; a future editor of his poems will note that the *Eloge de la Paix à Pierre de Ronsard* is built upon the Hesiodic Shield of Heracles, another rather uncommon source for Renaissance poets.

If the direct influence of the Greek poets interests us by reason of its rarity, the influence of the Roman poets claims attention by its abundance and importance. Indeed thought about peace, in the West, had always looked back to the experience of the Roman Empire, and now in the day of the national state, it was not only Postel who hoped for peace in a renewal of the *pax Romana* by the French monarchy or some other power. The Roman poets had been the voice and conscience of the Roman world-mission; and that poets like Ronsard desired to be the Virgils of the new day is nowhere clearer than in their peace poetry. If this proved to be a compound of idealism, solicitation of Court favor, and propaganda, the poets were not on wholly different ground from Virgil and Horace, not to say Calpurnius and Claudian.

Roman ideas about peace owed much to Hellenic and Hellenistic thought, but had a warmth and force of their own. Already the Venus who overpowers Mars in Lucretius' Prologue is an Aphrodite-Eirene of Greek speculation, but presented with Roman emotion and richness. Greek too is the constant alliance of the notions of peace and agricultural prosperity, yet made thoroughly Italian in the *Bucolics* and *Georgics* of Virgil and in the only Latin poem we have directly in praise of peace, Tibullus 1.10. It is through Virgil, seconded by Calpurnius, that the Renaissance came to associate peace poetry with the pastoral eclogue. One of the great themes is that of the Golden Age and its possible return. It is bound up with the hopes and the propaganda of the Empire, mysteriously in Virgil's fourth *Eclogue,* explicitly in Calpurnius' prophecy that the reign of Nero would be an *aurea aetas* (reduced in the event to an *aureum quinquennium*). With the hopes of the Golden Age went also the concept of the Peace Hero who would secure its return and win thereby a special immortality. With this figure, sprung from a Hellenistic background in the mystique of kingship, is associated the divinity of the Roman Emperor. Augustus as Peace Hero is hailed by Horace in terms suitable for Pax herself in an ode (Carm. 4.5) that the Renaissance did not fail to echo, while the occasion it celebrates, Augustus' return from Spain, was commemorated by the Senate in the great Ara Pacis Augustae. If for once great poets were in harmony with government, it was because the Roman Empire was justified by a lofty ideal, Concord and Peace, and was conscious of it. The imagination of the poets extends to the symbolic Roman coinage, which is itself a kind of poetry and lingers in our visible idea of Peace. Even here the symbols have mostly a Greek background: Pax with cornucopia or caduceus; with olive spray in hair or hand; with wheat ears; as Concordia, symbolized by clasped hands; as Justitia—a figure with the scepter of Justice and the olive branch of Peace; with the wings and laurel wreath of Victoria; Roman-all-too-Roman as *Mars pacifer* or setting foot on the necks of the conquered; while even as the Empire declined, coins and medallions hopefully announce the return of an *aurea aetas.*[5]

The Romans had thus carried Greek ideas about peace into their own climate of sensibility, and had made them at home in the West. In the Renaissance, the neo-Latin poets—Mantuanus among the first—had virtually organized these themes into a *laudatio pacis,* which can be recognized, though with many variations, in subsequent peace poetry. It made almost obligatory a series of topics associated with the Roman Peace by the ancient poets: for example, public rejoicing; domestic repose; Peace with Fides and other Companions; the Golden Age; the restoration of agriculture; the

---

[5]See Hans Christ, *Die röm. Weltherrschaft in der antiken Dichtung* (Tübinger Beiträge) (Stuttgart-Berlin, 1938); for the coins, Carl Koch in Pauly-Wissova-Kroll, RE xviii, 4 s.v. "Pax"; a selection of coins referring to the Golden Age is reproduced by Michael Grant, *Roman History from the Coins,* (Cambridge, Eng., 1958), pl. 25.

seas open for commerce; the laws again in force—items that Malherbe in praising peace would run off so roundly:

> Elle met les pompes aux filles,
> Donne aux champs les moissons fertilles,
> Et de la majesté des lois
> Appuyant les pouvoirs suprêmes,
> Fait demeurer les diadèmes
> Ferme sur la teste des Rois.

In filling up these ready topics the Renaissance poets sometimes recall the original phrases of the ancient poets, but perhaps more often seek a *variatio* of their own.

It may be of interest to ask to what degree these poets strove in their turn to adapt the Graeco-Roman motifs to present circumstances. The occasion—say, the peace of Cateau—surely made its demands on an "occasional" poem. For one thing the terms of this treaty did not encourage thoughts of a world-conquest by the French monarchy. Instead, Ronsard now (in the poem *La Paix, au Roy*) urges upon his sovereign the topic "domestic repose":

> Il vaudroit beaucoup mieux . . .
>   gouverner vostre Royal ménage, . . .
> Qu'acquérir par danger des lauriers triomphans:
> Il vaudroit beaucoup mieux joyeusement vivre,
> Ou bâtir vostre Louvre, ou lire dans un livre.

Neither was the treaty of Cateau-Cambrésis going to usher in the Golden Age. In fact it ushered in the wars of religion. But the topic is mandatory in a peace poem, so it is either introduced at an early point as the good time eclipsed by war, or otherwise handled with discretion. Jacques Béreau has this discretion in his eclogue *De la Paix:*[6]

> Quelques traces bien tost du Saturnien Age
> Doibvent recommencer sous le règne puissant
> D'Henry. . . .
> Encores de leur gré produyront les campagnes
> Le froment nourricier, encore des montagnes

[6]Jacques Béreau, jurisconsult and poet. His *Eclogues et autres œuvres poétiques* were published at Poitiers in 1565.

Heureux fleuves de laict et de vin couleront,
Et les chesnes encor le roux miel sueront.

It sounds like the Golden Age, but, cattle and vineyards being on the hills, all is quite good sense. Even in this minor example language redolent of the high mood of ancient poetry attempts to raise the present occasion to that level, and at the same time sets up a tension between the associations of the language and the basic meaning. That is perhaps a peculiar Renaissance effect, neither ancient nor modern. Thus the Roman Peace Hero merited apotheosis; but every good Christian may hope for heaven. Ippolito Capilupi foresees this for Henri II and Philip of Spain, in Horatian phrases:

Hac iter vobis erit ad beatas
Aetheris sedes superumque menses,
Et choro accepti ferietis altum
Vertice Olympum.

But if we expect to find this discretion—this *allegoria* of a Roman poetical language—in every poem, we may be disappointed. The power of classical style may triumph over all other considerations. An extreme example is the *Damon* of the Venetian poet Navagero. Never was the Virgilian tone more successfully caught than in this bucolic poem, which celebrates the peace following the expulsion of the French from Milan in 1512. The peace hero is Pope Julius II. We may perhaps read "deus" as "saint" when Navagero declares: "Tu nostra ante Deos in vota vocaberis omnes," but can we extend this interpretation to the altars and rites of heroicization that Damon will inaugurate for Julius?

Ipse ego bina tibi solemni altaria ritu,
Et geminos sacra e quercu lauroque virenti
Vicino lucos Nauceli in litore ponam.
Hic ripa passim in molli viridante sub umbra,
Vere novo dum floret ager, dum germinat arbos,
Dum vario resonant volucrum nemora avia cantu,
Annua constituam festis convivia ludis.

Every word and every concept is Virgilian. The twin altars for one hero are from the heroization of Daphnis in Virgil's fifth *Eclogue;*

236

they are placed in a sacred grove in accordance with the heroization of Hercules in *Aeneid* 8.271; the homely setting beside the provincial stream is from the heroization of Octavian in the third *Georgic,* where Virgil contemplates raising a temple in his honor beside the Mincius. Personal allusion is reduced to the name Naucelus—the Noncello at Pordenone, where Navagero was staying temporarily. But it is hard to place the altars anywhere but in the wonderland of Virgilian pastoral.

It has not escaped attention that Navagero's *Damon* delighted the French poets. Remy Belleau in his *Chant de la Paix* of 1559 adopts, among other details, the two altars by the riverside, and having to celebrate two peace heroes of Cateau-Cambrésis, conveniently assigns one altar to the Cardinal of Lorraine and the other to Montmorency:[7]

> Et quant à moy, sous les ombres mollets
> De ces coudriers, près cette eau qui jargonne
> Dessus le sable, il faut que je façonne
> De gazons verds deux petits autelets. . . .

He explains for whom they are intended, and continues:

> L'autel premier d'un verdroyant lierre
> Tout à l'entour aura les fronts couverts,
> L'autre sera entaillé d'une pierre,
> Où tous les ans je chanteray ces vers:
> "Dessous leurs pieds et la manne et le miel
> Naisse tousjours," [etc.]

For a French shepherd, the tone is lowered from the Virgilian grandeur of Navagero; the altars are "petits autelets" and are made of turf—*arae gramineae* being correct for country gods (cf. Horace, *Carm.* 1.19.13). Later they are somewhat grander, the one having its sides covered with ivy, the other encased in stone—details faintly suggesting tombs.

From Belleau no doubt the motif passed to Jacques Béreau, who, however, requires only one altar, since he celebrates Montmorency

---

[7]Remy Belleau's use of *Damon* is pointed out by Eckhardt in his *Remy Belleau* (Budapest, 1917), p. 127.

alone. Moreover, ignoring Navagero, he has gone back directly to Virgil:

> Noble Montmorency, en ferme souvenance
> Du bien par toy receu, qui nous as de souffrance
> Heureusement mis hors, en un val écarté,
> Joignant mon petit Loy de longs vergnes planté
> De saules et de houx, de peupliers et d'érables,
> Un brave pavillon de feuillées aimables
> Treillesé et couvert proprement te feray,
> Et dedans un autel de gazons dresseray
> Dessus lequel sera ta figure élevée
> De blanc marbre, tenant en une main l'épée,
> En l'autre un olivier; et puis aux deux costez
> De cest autel seront deux ronds pilliers entez
> Où graver je feray pour durable mémoyre
> De tes rares vertus et de tes faicts l'histoyre.

For bucolic simplicity, Béreau has altered Virgil's marble temple into a rustic arbor. He now has both Navagero's altar (borrowed from Belleau) and Virgil's temple, which has no altar, and he places the one inside the other. But Virgil's temple contained Caesar's statue, and adopting this for Montmorency, Béreau rather oddly sets it upon the altar. The result—a white marble statue of the Constable, sword in one hand and olive branch in the other (the Roman Pax-Justitia), standing upon an altar—may suggest that the Virgilian picture is merging into a Renaissance funerary monument, an impression that grows as the poet places two pillars at the sides of the altar, and inscribes upon them *pour durable mémoyre* the virtues and deeds of his hero. Actually the ancient hero cult had partly the character of the cult of the gods and partly that of burial or funeral rites, as is the case in the death and heroization of Daphnis in Virgil's fifth *Eclogue*. But Montmorency was still alive.

Ronsard in his turn goes to Navagero and Virgil, in this case for the apotheosis of Henri II (*Bergerie* of 1565).[8] Forests, plains, and streams

> murmurent en tout lieu
> Que le bon Henri est maintenant un Dieu.

[8]Ronsard's dependence on Navagero is noted by Paul Kuhn in *RHL*, 1914, pp. 311 ff.

And the shepherd Angelot continues:

> Sois propice à nos vœux: je te feray d'ivoire
> Et de marbre un beau temple au rivage de Loyre,
> Où au retour de l'an, aux jours longs et nouveaux,
> Je feray des combatz entre les pastouraux.

And:

> Nous ferons en ton nom des autels tous les ans,
> De grands gazons de terre.

Apparently we have not much right to expect in Renaissance pastoral a high degree of discretion in regard to the realities. The basic thought: "I honor Montmorency" or "I venerate the memory of Henri II" is transposed into a fairyland setting, and details have meaning in the context of the poem and not elsewhere. One can only criticize putting the costly marble and ivory temple of the *Georgics* within the means of the simple shepherds of the *Eclogues*. Yet it is disappointing that poems for an occasion show so little responsibility. The Renaissance knew Virgil's *Eclogues* as masquerades, accepting, for instance, an ancient opinion that the dead Daphnis of *Eclogue* 5 is Julius Caesar. We might expect these poets to do as much as they thought Virgil had done to close the gap between poetry and reality. But before we dismiss the heroization of the pastorale as mere fantasy, let us look at a real Renaissance monument.

The visitor to the Louvre who pauses among the Renaissance sculptures, Salle de Jean Goujon, after admiring Goujon's *Diane à l'Anet* and the equally familiar *Three Graces* of Germain Pilon, may well spare a moment's attention for a monument beyond, of the following description. From a central pedestal rises a twisted "salomonic" column of white marble with rose-colored marble encrustations, before which on a marble pedestal stands a "Virtue" in bronze, while two similar "Virtues" stand on their pedestals at the sides. The column originally upheld an urn in which reposed the heart of the deceased. This is the *monument funéraire du cœur* of the Constable, Anne de Montmorency, erected in 1573 by his widow, Madeleine of Savoy, in the Paris church of the Célestins. It came to join the *monument du cœur* of Henri II (to which belonged

239

The *monument funéraire du cœur* of the Constable
Anne de Montmorency. Courtesy of the Musée du
Louvre, Paris.

the *Three Graces*) since the king on his deathbed had requested that his heart and that of the old Constable should repose together. Montmorency's monument was designed by Jean Bullant, and the bronze figures at least were executed by Barthelemy Prieur.[9]

The "Virtues" especially claim our attention. These draped figures represent Peace, Abundance, and Justice, a Roman triad, each with her attributes and with appropriate emblems on the pedestal beneath her feet. Peace, on the viewer's left, bending slightly forward, holds a torch downwards as though in the act of burning a plumed helmet and certain weapons at her feet—the destruction of weapons being a regular peace theme. Abundance, in the center, extends a bunch of grapes and a spray of vegetation in her right hand and holds up a large cornucopia in her left. Justice (said to have the features of Montmorency) holds up a tall sword in her right hand and extends a wheat-ear in her left—again a Pax-Justitia as in Béreau. The emblems on the pedestals have been misplaced in the Louvre reconstruction.[10] Originally, beneath the figure of Peace, an elaborate design (now placed below Justice) showed, in the center, an armillary sphere, from the sides of which hung festoons of oak and other leaves, fruit, and rosettes; under the sphere were clasped hands; under the hands, wheat sheaves; and above the sphere a heart. Perhaps we may read: cosmic peace (the sphere) and earthly peace (the clasped hands, a Roman emblem) with its abundance (the sheaves), and the hero's civic virtue (oak leaves).[11] Below Abundance another complicated design (now below Peace)

[9]The reconstruction of the monument in the Louvre is faulty in important respects. The bronze figures and their pedestals are unpleasingly huddled together, whereas originally they were spaced out forming an ample composition agreeable to the eye, and the column, rising close behind the central figure, was thus in better proportion to the whole. For the displaced panels see below. See the careful study by Cripps-Day, "Le monument funéraire de Montmorency connêtable de France" in *Gazette des beaux-arts* (1928), pp. 62–74. I am greatly obliged to my friend Professor Isidore Silver for information about the present state of the monument.

[10]The following description of the emblems is taken from the article by Cripps-Day, together with the very clear illustration in the following book: J. A. Piganiol de la Force, *Description de Paris et ses environs* (Paris: Théodore Legras, 1742), vol. 4, pp. 58–62, which also contains copies of the inscriptions. I am greatly obliged to my friend Professor Henry Guerlac for bringing this book to my attention.

[11]The heart placed above the sphere might be taken to signify Montmorency's repose in heaven beyond this world, but it may only be intended to indicate the nature of the monument. To similar effect, just above, the word *cœur* is repeated sixteen times in the inscription, a French sonnet to the hero's noble heart, which was placed below the feet of Peace.

displayed cornucopias, the balance of Justice, a caduceus (signifying peace and commerce), and two olive branches; in side panels, a gauntleted hand raised a drawn sword tipped with a laurel wreath, and a scabbard stood decorated with fleurs de lys, also with wreath above, sword and scabbard being emblems of the Constable of France.[12] Below the figure of Justice there was only the coat of arms of Montmorency (now missing). Inscriptions below the figures proclaimed the glory of Montmorency and the nobility of his heart. The twisted column, lifting aloft the heart of the hero, dominates the whole composition.[13] Rich and strange, it lends to the monument an air of the marvelous, which is among the aims of superior art.

This composition in marble and bronze deserves to be joined with the poems that celebrate Montmorency as the peace-bringer of Cateau-Cambrésis.

[This paper was written to be read at the Association Guillaume Budé, Congrès de Lyon, 1959, and in my absence was presented by my friend Professor Isidore Silver, who also very kindly prepared the résumé published in the *Actes du Congrès* (Paris, 1960).]

[12]The sword and scabbard are now affixed to the wall behind the monument.
[13]Prototypes of the twisted column are found in St. Peter's in Rome and are traditionally said to be derived from the Temple of Solomon.

The "Lost" *Cohortatio Pacificatoria* of Jacques Peletier du Mans

Ten years ago, Professor V.-L. Saulnier presented in this journal a hitherto unpublished work of Jacques Peletier, his Funeral Oration for Henry VIII.[1] It is the aim of the present paper to restore to students of Peletier his Oration on Peace, published in his lifetime, but regarded by modern scholars as lost.

The conviction that it is lost has rested on the, usually good, authority of André Boulanger in his edition of Peletier's *L'Art poétique* (1930). Thus Paul Laumonier, referring to Boulanger, surmised that Ronsard's *Exhortation pour la paix* of 1558 may have been inspired by the "*Exhortation à la paix*" of Peletier, and regretted that "cette œuvre est malheureusement perdue."[2] Tchemerzine, in his *Bibliographie des éditions originales et rares,* reserves a niche for this work, with only the words, "Exhortation 1558 in-8," to mark the place.[3] Such reticence seems excessive, however, since the knowledge of such a title depends on La Croix du Maine, who gives details:[4] "L'Exhortation de la Paix entre Charles V, Empereur des Romains, & Henry II du nom, Roi de France, imprimée à Paris chez André Vechel, l'an 1558, tant en Latin qu'en François." Still referring to Boulanger, Henri Chamard in 1939 devoted a short paragraph in his *Histoire de la Pléiade* (II, 299) to this "lost" work of Peletier:

> Nous n'avons pas conservé l'œuvre latine que rédigea J. Peletier avant de quitter Lyon, à la fin de 1557: *Exhortatio pacificatoria ad christianos*

From the *Bibliothèque d'Humanisme et Renaissance* 22 (1960) 302–19. Reprinted by permission of the Librairie Droz.

[1]*BHR*, 11 (1949) 7–27.
[2]Ronsard, *Œuvres complètes,* ed. crit. by Paul Laumonier, IX (Paris: Droz, 1937) 26, n. 2.
[3]Vol. IX (1933) 153.
[4]*Bibliothèque françoise,* Rigoley de Juvigny, ed., I, 427.

principes Carolum V et Henricum II. Nous savons seulement par La Croix du Maine qu'il la fit paraître à Paris, chez André Wechel, en 1558, avec une version française, également perdue. On peut supposer sans invraisemblance que Peletier y traduisait déjà des sentiments analogues à ceux de Ronsard [in his *Exhortation pour la paix*]. Et ces sentiments étaient unanimes, si l'on en juge par l'explosion de joie qui partout accueillit le mémorable traité de Cateau-Cambrésis (3 avril 1559).

One may already ask how it is "likely" that in 1558 Peletier would have addressed sentiments of the sort to Charles V, who had abdicated in 1555, and was now dying in the convent of Yuste. In 1558, surely, such sentiments would be attached to Philip II.

Let us see how Boulanger came to hold the view that this work is lost. Primarily it was because, though he had before him Peletier's own testimony about the oration, he persisted in reading it through what he understood La Croix du Maine to be saying. As we shall see, La Croix du Maine is correct enough after his fashion, but capable of providing a false scent. Boulanger writes of Peletier in 1558 as follows:[5]

> Dès son retour [from Lyons to Paris], il fit imprimer chez Wechel, à la paix, adressée à Henri II et à Charles Quint, qu'il avait terminée avant son départ de Lyon, tandis que Ronsard, peut-être pris d'émulation, publiait un poème de sujet identique.

Apart from the conjecture about Ronsard, this adds to La Croix du Maine the statement that Peletier had finished his work before he left Lyons (i.e., in 1557). The reason for this addition is given in a footnote:

> Il en est question dans la lettre latine à Jean Peletier citée *supra* [a letter from Peletier to his brother, printed in Jacques Peletier's *In Euclidis Elementa . . . demonstrationum libri sex,* Lyons, J. de Tournes and G. Gazeau, 1557]: "Certe Oratio nostra Pacificatoria nos rerum non ignaros esse testatur"; et dans l'*Orat. Pictav.*, p. 290 [*Oratio Pictavii habita,* Poitiers, Buchet, 1579; ed. by Laumonier, *Rev. de la Renaiss.* 5 (1904). 290]: "Latine scripsimus Cohortationem pacificatoriam ad Principes Christianos." Cet ouvrage, cité par La Croix du Maine, est perdu.

[5] *L'Art poétique de Jacques Peletier du Mans* (Paris: Les Belles Lettres, 1930), p. 26 and n. 69.

Boulanger accepts from La Croix du Maine the date 1558, but is obliged to suppose that the work was completed (i.e., in manuscript) before Peletier's departure from Lyons, since Peletier mentions it in a letter printed in 1557. It would be more natural to assume that it was *published* before 1557. Finally, discarding the titles given by Peletier himself, or unable to choose between them, Boulanger made up a Latin title partly from Peletier's words and partly from La Croix du Maine:[6] "1558. *Exhortatio pacificatoria ad christianos principes Carolum V et Henricum II.* Paris (perdu ainsi que la trad. française parue la même année)." And yet in another connection he refers to a passage in Peletier's *De Constitutione Horoscopi commentarium* (1563) in which the author a third time names his work: "Exinde [after his funeral oration for Henry VIII, 1547] cohortationem pacificatoriam scripsi ad Principes Christianos, quo tempore inter Carolum quintum Caesarem et Erricum secundum bella fiebant." The clause, "quo tempore," etc., most certainly does not refer to 1557 or 1558.[7] A more excusable assumption from La Croix du Maine's notice is that the *Cohortatio Pacificatoria* was published under the author's name.

As a matter of fact, it appeared anonymously at Lyons in 1555. I take the following notice from the beginning of the second volume of Alfred Cartier's *Bibliographie des éditions des De Tournes,* Paris, 1937 (No 288, p. 381):

> Ad Principes ‖ Christianos ‖ Cohortatio ‖ Pacificatoria ‖
> *Et nunc, Reges, intelligite: erudimini ‖ qui iudicatis*
> *terram.* ‖ Psal. II. Lugduni ‖ apud Ioan. Tornaesium ‖ M.D.L.V.
> ‖ Cum privilegio Regis. In-4 de 29 p. Rom.
> Le privilège est daté "Fonsbellaquei, IIII, Non. Maias, M.D.L.V."
> Bibl. Nat.—Le Mans.—Brit. Mus.

That a copy exists at Le Mans is interesting.[8] The title corresponds with Peletier's own reports, and is quite individual, not paralleled, I believe, in the extensive peace literature of the time.

---

[6] *Op. cit.,* p. 2 ("Bibliographie").

[7] Boulanger refers to this passage, *op. cit.,* p. 14, n. 26. It is quoted by Saulnier, *op. cit.,* p. 8. I have not myself seen the *De Const. horos.* However, the dating clause, "Quo tempore," etc., is also in the passage cited from the *Orat. Pictav.,* following the words Boulanger quotes.

[8] I have not investigated this copy. My references are to that in the British Museum (596. e. 2 [2.], microfilm).

De Tournes, Peletier's friend and "imprimeur ordinaire,"[9] published in this same year his *Art poétique,* his *L'Amour des Amours,* and his *Dialogue de l'ortographe* (2d ed.). It is noteworthy that the *privilège* of the *Cohortatio,* that of Peletier's *Art poétique,* and that of his *In Euclidis Elementa* (printed by De Tournes in 1557) all are dated "Fontainebleau, May 4, 1555."[10] The reference in a letter of 1557 to a work published in 1555 becomes easy and natural. That Charles V is among those addressed, as reported by La Croix du Maine, is inevitable.

But we need not dwell on these points, since the identity of the book is put beyond doubt by information available to us concerning the French translation. This information is of considerable extent, and only escaped the notice of Boulanger because he failed to look up Du Verdier as well as La Croix du Maine! Among the anonymous works listed at the end of the letter "E" in Du Verdier we find:[11]

Exhortation aux Princes Chrétiens pour le fait de la Paix, notamment à l'Empereur Charles V, & au Roi très-Chrétien Henri II, imprimée à Paris, in-40. par André Wechel, 1558.

Sentences contenues en cette Exhortation

Tu veux maintenant, ô César, renouveler & renforcer ta fortune, la mettant à pair contre celle d'un Roi, duquel la grandeur florissante se va haussant de plus en plus; & d'autant que plus t'y opposes, plus elle se fortifie & se tient droite. [Etc.]

Du Verdier continues to quote for a page and a half; but this first sentence is quite enough to show that the French *Exhortation* of 1558 was an exact translation of the Latin *Cohortatio* of 1555, where we read (p. 6):

Tu nunc tuam fortunam instaurare ac redintegrare eniteris, eamque ex adverso Regis fortunae collocas, cuius florida ac vegeta virtus se in sublime magis ac magis attollit: quae quanto fortius obsistis, tanto contentius obnititur & firmatur. [Etc.]

[9]Boulanger, *op. cit.,* p. 23.
[10]No other books printed by De Tournes, so far as one may judge from Cartier's *Bibliographie,* received a *privilège* at this time and place. The *Dialogue de l'ortographe* and *L'Amour des Amours* are without *privilège.*
[11]*Bibliothèque françoise,* I, Rigoley de Juvigny, ed., 561.

Du Verdier gives us ample material for comparison.[12] Indeed the book had considerable interest for him, since he prints a still longer extract in his article on Guillaume Postel, where he reproduces the whole tirade against Postel (see below) contained in the *Cohortatio* and hence in the French *Exhortation*.[13] Here again the *Exhortation* is for him the work of "un Auteur incertain," and apparently he does not associate it with Peletier, with whom he was acquainted in Peletier's later years.[14]

To sum up, La Croix du Maine somehow knew that the anonymous French *Exhortation* of 1558 was Peletier's work, and that this work also existed in Latin.[15] Du Verdier's quotations from the French book prove that the *Cohortatio* is the Latin version, as we already had reason to believe from Peletier's own statements and from the circumstances of its publication. Peletier, so far as I know, says nothing of a French translation, but it would perhaps be an excess of skepticism to doubt that it was from his own hand.[16] Finally, the French *Exhortation,* apart from Du Verdier's extensive transcriptions, remains lost or at least unrecognized.[17]

But it is more important that we have the original *Cohortatio Pacificatoria*. It is clearly the work of a superior writer. Compared with much of the peace-propaganda of the time, it is remarkable for avoiding on the whole the traditional and well-worn *topoi,* and concentrating on the real situation, though we must at once add

[12]In this place he has extracted sentences from various parts of the book, disregarding the original order.
[13]Du Verdier, *Bibl. fr.* II, 115-17.
[14]Here Du Verdier inadvertently gives the wrong date 1557. Abel Lefranc, in writing about Postel (*Histoire du Collège de France* [1893], pp. 192-94), makes much of this "anonymous pamphlet," expressing himself almost as though he had it before him; but in fact he depends on Du Verdier II, 115, giving the wrong date 1557, and overlooking the better notice in I, 561. W. J. Bouwsma also overlooks it in his *Concordia Mundi: The Career and Thought of Guillaume Postel* (Cambridge, Mass., 1957), p. 24, where he refers to this pamphlet. In any case, it makes a difference to know that the attack dates from the spring of 1555, and not from 1557, when Postel lay in prison, and also a difference to know that the anonymous assailant was Peletier.
[15]In compiling a *Bibliothèque françoise* La Croix du Maine had no responsibility to Latin titles. When he adds "tant en Latin qu'en Francois," he presumably does not mean "printed in Latin and French by Wechel" but "a work existing in Latin and French."
[16]Nothing indicates that it was printed in Peletier's peculiar orthography.
[17]It may well turn up, now that we know what to look for, namely an anonymous *Exhortation aux Princes Chrestiens* (A. Wechel, 1558). I have made no special effort to find it.

that the humanist author sees this situation wholly in a moral view, and not at all from the practical standpoint of the chancelleries. The oration is of course imaginary. Peletier pretends that he is addressing the assembled princes of Europe, but after the proem "fixes his eye" (*intueor*, he says) on Charles V and Henri II, and to them in turn addresses his argument. This argument proceeds from the point of view of the good of the "Christian Republic" and the iniquity of sacrificing it to private ambition. The oration, though long (nearly 10,000 words) is well formed after the rules of deliberative oratory. It is admirably written in a style of Ciceronian amplitude and rhythm, with a rich and correct diction, and is lighted throughout by the *sententiae* that Du Verdier was pleased to collect from the French version. At mid-point it rouses its, perhaps now restless, audience by a startling digression on Guillaume Postel, and toward the end sounds the solemn note there deemed desirable by striking out into the region of prophecy. A brief peroration "repeats the proposition and recapitulates the chief arguments."[18]

It is unnecessary here to reproduce *in extenso* a fairly long text which is available both in the Bibliothèque Nationale and in the British Museum. The greatly abbreviated paraphrase that follows is intended to give some idea of the content of the discourse, and in occasional quotations, the sound of Peletier's voice; it is intentionally disproportionate in emphasizing the latter parts of the oration. Finally, we shall append some remarks on the content, including a guess as to why it was published without the author's name, and some comments on its possible influence.

To Christian Princes, an Exhortation to Peace

When about to speak on the subject of Peace, Christian Princes, I decided to rest my whole argument (undertaken in the name of all Christians) upon Christ, Prince of all the world and Author of peace. [*De Pace verba facturus, Principes Christiani, omnem dicendi rationem, quae omnium Christianorum nomine a me instituta est, ad summum illum totius orbis Principem Christum Pacisque authorem, referendam esse decrevi.*] Otherwise, in these turbulent times it seemed unlikely that you would hear me, or that your armies rushing into conflict could stand and listen to a talk about peace. And I reflected that if I, a "new man" and scarcely known even in my own country should appear as adviser

[18]Melanchthon, *Elementa Rhetorices.*

before such exalted "heroes" as you, I would only incur the charge of ambition or rashness. . . . But suddenly some impulse—why do I say "some"? nay, roused by the clear voice of Christ himself, I have been emboldened to enter your presence. Yet I do not claim a special grace. I do what any Christian should do. That shining light that spreads through the air and illumines the eyes of every good man kindled my mind to speak to you for peace and to enlighten you. I have no eloquence, I can only speak from my heart. Christ will furnish the *auctoritas,* the gravity of the subject will be its own *ornatus.*

Whither shall I turn, Christian Princes? to whom direct my speech? You are all above me, and your presence distracts my mind. On you, however, Caesar Charles, on you, King Henry, I fix my eyes—on you both, who are preëminent in this assembly of heroes and have in your keeping the safety and peace of the whole Christian Republic. . . .

All that I ask of you, Caesar, is that you judge your own case, and see that peace is for your personal interest. From your many wars you have gained honors and triumphs such that no king ought to hope for greater. Do not yourself despise a fortune that others deem splendid. Yet you are straining to renew it, pitting it against the fortune of a king whose lively "virtue" ever rises higher and higher. You must know that virtue contending often with virtue becomes its equal. You cannot defeat the King of the French, but you have a chance of victory: bind him in the bonds of peace, conquering at the same time the King and yourself the Emperor.

You recall how rich France is. Long since, she surpassed all Christendom in piety, justice, and military glory; today she surpasses herself. [*Nam quum ab antiqua Regnorum memoria caeteras Christianae ditionis gentes religione, iustitia, bellicisque laudibus superaverit: haec certe hodie seipsam superat. Quae species totius Regni? quae Principum maiestas? quae Senatorum dignitas? quae nobilium praestantia? quae militum virtus? quae pulchritudo urbis? quae humanitas civium? quae celebritas civitatum? quae forma regionum? qui agri? quae fruges? At haec omnia Regem circumstant; haec omnia Regi parent & praesto sunt.*] What are you waiting for, Caesar? For the French people to become disloyal? It is against their nature. For them to revolt? They know better. For the nobles to desert the King? They are too well treated. For pecuniary trouble to beset him? That will sooner happen to you. . . .

By experience over the years you have become wise and practiced; but the same passage of time has taught the observant to see through your policy. . . . Princes are but men; their desires may be infinite, but only a jot of what they hope for rewards their efforts. But honor grows from honor; complete from another's, Caesar, what you think you lack. Become the King's friend; you will impart to him a touch of your glory, and he and all he has will be on your side.

Your lofty intellect, O Caesar, forbids me to advise you to seek now

249

a time in which to con over your past deeds, and to enjoy the repose you have earned and the glory that has advanced with your years. It should be clear to you, as it is to others, that your present labors serve your glory at the risk of your life. . . . Here perchance you will give me Crassus' answer to the Parthian legation. When they pressed him to negotiate, alleging the hardships of war, his age, and the benefits of peace, he replied: "We shall soon have an occasion for talking of peace in Seleucia" [Plutarch, *Crassus* 18]. But I know that you have no such thoughts, and my "legation" has none but its stated purpose of pleading the cause of the Christian Republic. I speak from no private interest, receiving no promises nor pay. But your dissensions, O Emperor and O King, come just to this: that whatever either of you has gained from the other in war is less to the advantage of the victor than to the detriment of the Republic.

And now in turning to you, Most Christian King, I see a greater task before me, in that in one and the same cause your position is quite dissimilar. The same arguments that recall Caesar from war appear to lead you on to war and away from peace. His age and past glory restrain him, while the prime of life prompts you to meet the future and expect its fruition. . . . I confess that your fortunes are in the ascendant and that fair opportunities await you on every hand. Perhaps you do right to seize the occasion of attaining the highest power. You have brave soldiers, an obedient people, loyal nobles. But (forgive me) you lack the supreme title of felicity. Do you not see that all these gifts of fortune, or rather of God, are incomplete and unsure without the aid of peace? . . . War is costly in the lives of the best and ablest men. As carried on today, it wipes out cities before you can get them in your power. The retort of Cineas to Pyrrhus is applicable to you. [If the end of world conquest is tranquillity, why not enjoy tranquillity now without the trouble? Plutarch, *Pyrrhus* 14]. He made the king recognize that tranquillity is the end of action. This pagan utterance may be taken as a kind of prophecy, of which the true meaning becomes clear in Christian times. Christians are brothers; for a Christian king to lead his brother in triumph is a reversion to pagan forms. Now of course I do not urge sloth upon the king; I urge his true business, Religion and Justice. War is not the only source of royal grandeur. Uphold, Henry, a title [Most Christian] more glorious to you than the victories you pursue.

If you aim to give a display of kingly virtue, how will that be done by enlarging your realm at the expense of the Empire? As I just said to you, Caesar, that the king's virtue, so well fortified, is hard to quell, so, O King, the Emperor's glory, deep-rooted and gained by the highest virtue, is hard indeed to overthrow. You are equally matched. Therefore make peace. I think that God has made you equal for that very purpose.

The "Lost" *Cohortatio Pacificatoria*

I hear you reply, O King, that you do not reject peace, but that you will not remit any part of your rights. Nor do I ask it. But you have already provided so well for the future that you will lose nothing by accepting peace. For a time at least, lay aside your plans for war, and think only of the miseries your people suffer. [*Atque interim reliquam miserorum multitudinem ab interitu, exitio, miserabilique luctu eripueris. Omnium aetatum, omnis sexus greges per tuam Galliam palantes, fame valetudine, erroribus confecti: Patres effoeta senectute, patria, domo, liberis carentes, nullum iam mortis genus vita miserius putant. Matres inter brachia infantulos vagientes e media flamma atque hostium cruentis gladiis ereptos efferunt: & belli inclementiam fugientes, nullum consistendi locum reperiunt in quo temporis calamitatem vitare possint. Tibi vero, Caesar, qui vultus, qui sensus in hoc luctu populari? . . . an forte tuus non gemit populus?*]

You both aim to conquer the world, a thing impossible among so many sovereign powers. Since the fall of Rome, each has defended his own liberty. In time, an inferior power may be conquered, an equal power hardly ever. There has been a long history of conquering and being conquered, and armies ever recruited anew. In your time, it is no longer yours to command as you will, but your peoples' to obey as they will. Your realms are large and prosperous; you merely injure them both in your struggle. If you must seek supreme power, remember that he has it who has learned to enjoy his own in peace. With the insatiable mind of an Alexander, who sighed for more worlds to conquer, you will live in perpetual poverty.

You both wish to restore the Church; but that will not be done by destroying it through war. Internal dissensions are ruining it. Not only do old heresies spawn again, but new ones raise their heads. While you are occupied in war, false prophets rise to subvert your realms and even to assail the power of Christ. Has there not appeared in your time a man so bold as to pretend to divinity? who has thought to abrogate the law of Christ and promulgate a new one? Postel is the man I mean, the most criminal and audacious that earth ever bore. [*Quid? nonne his vestris temporibus homo prodiit, qui in divinitatem irrepere aggressus sit? qui legem Christi antiquare ac novam promulgare cogitaverit? Postellum illum dico, omnium hominum quos unquam terra tulit sceleratissimum atque audacissimum: tranquillitatis Christianae, quasi non satis perturbata sit, flagitiosissimum perturbatorem.*] Modeling himself on Mohammed, who at first adopted Christianity for the purpose of deceiving the pious, he tried a similar strategem, and affected fasting and godly sermons. . . . He even lured educated men to hear him by his title to learning and philosophy. For he is learned, and has devoted an active though unfortunate effort to studies, as his various works show. An able mathematician, he was professor of this subject some years ago with a salary from the crown. I mention this so that persons of intelligence may see that the man is not mad but astute and

Essays on Renaissance Poetry

vicious. Perceiving that nowadays noblewomen have power, he set himself to catch their favor, and published a book entitled: *De l'admirable victoire des femmes,* with the foolish theme that women would one day come to dominate men, and that he had been sent to earth to redeem the female sex as the male sex had been redeemed by Christ (whether that is more impious or ridiculous it would be hard to say). Twisting philosophical doctrines to adorn this nonsense, he was held by sane men to be insane, and so escaped punishment, but gained the credence of the ignorant, who are the greater number. He proclaimed that the end of the world was at hand, offering it to us within two years, and then adding two years more, as though he possessed the secrets of eternity. Meanwhile the impostor, either thinking his fraud firmly founded or tired of dissimulation, unequivocally declared his intention of attacking royal power, professing at the end of his book to be the avenger of tyrants and the defender of liberty. That you may know that he intended his impiety to be complete, while he was in France he pretended with I know not what devious fancies that his mother was one Jeanne, who the histories say drove the English from France. But seeing that his designs were exposed and that his frauds made no headway in these enlightened times, he is said to have fled to Austria. Unable to remain there, he betook himself, Venetian Fathers, to your land, and today lives in your city of Padua, where again he has published a book, written in Italian, more remarkable for nonsense than the rest. For he has imagined that another virgin, whom he now calls Venetian, is his mother, presenting himself (I quote) as "the first-born son of the restitution." . . . When I think of all that, I am not only indignant, but shudder all over. And now what does he do but declare that he has "twice tasted of death" (his words again), and that he will live a third time. In fact he has his own forerunner, who has taken the name of John, the servant and emissary of his crimes. I would not bring this matter up with you, Christian Princes, nor deem this human monster worth notice, if it were not clear how his shamelessness imperils the Christian religion, your peoples, and your thrones. Meanwhile you bestow your attention elsewhere. Watch out lest from the commotions of your time the waves mount higher, which you may some day wish to calm too late. . . .

Undeniably there is a vicissitude in human affairs. Peace may bring slackness and overconfidence. Contraries subsist on contraries. But good heavens! in your time the balance between war and peace has been upset for ever. As one of your wars grows out of another, how can there ever be peace? . . . You hold your power from God for the sake of the people. Your peoples are one in the blood of Christ, yet you attack and slay them. Christ came in a time of universal peace to show that he loved men of peace. He came in a time of universal monarchy; but inasmuch as the like has never existed since, clearly by his coming he approved a division of rule, reserving absolute sovereignty for Divine Wisdom alone. Should Christ speak to you, he would denounce your wars. Well, he does speak. Behold his anger at seeing your discords "worse than civil" [Lucan 1.1]. His voice, his light seek to reach you. Are your senses so stopped by darkness that they cannot be quickened by that shining light?

Suppose God purposes to establish universal peace in your time, and you are found opposing Him. See lest He cast you down. It is He who bestows empires and kingdoms. He works through the acts of men, but often in such a way that the outcome is marvelous in our eyes. For if we observe and connect the events of the recent past, and project the future, all these modern innovations, the intellectual ferment [*concitiones ingeniorum*], the stirrings of peoples and nations, seem to promise a new face for the World [*novam quandam Mundi faciem*]. For some years you have enjoyed plenty; if you waste it in war, you will be unable to meet the possible disasters of the future—a depression, perhaps, or pestilence. Now in fact the heavens present such a figure of the times as to surpass in wonder not only living memory but the whole of recorded history. And here, Christian princes, permit me while speaking to you to put in something for the benefit of the philosophers. I shall not be straying from the matter in hand.

The permutations of the apsides—the one, that of Venus and the Sun, entering about two hundred years ago the sign of the solstice, where the Moon and the second power of Jupiter hold sway, the other, of Mercury, which a hundred years ago entered the dominion of Mars—have brought into the world an enormous abundance of good things, likewise a variety of literature, of arts, and of inventions, the most ample in history. It might seem that human wits had reached their natural limit. There remains only the congress of Saturn and Jupiter in the watery trigon before the Great Conjunction in the head of the Zodiac, for mortals always the most significant of all. Many recent events have anticipated this, more and greater will usher it in. That conjunction—that it is which amends the times, alters customs and laws, stirs minds to grasp at innovation, transfers realms, and in short reforms and renews the whole appearance of the world. [*Permutationes Apsidum, altera solis & Veneris ducentis abhinc, plus minus, annis, Solstitii Signum ingressa, in quo Lunae imperium & secunda Iovis potestas: altera Mercurii, quae ante centum annos in Martis dominium intravit, opum ac delitiarum profusissimam copiam Mundo induxerunt: itemque literarum artium, inventorumque varietatem post homines natos amplissimam intulerunt: ut videantur hominum ingenia suae, quantum fert natura, facul-*

tatis summum gradum attigisse. Superest unus Saturni & Iovis congressus in Trigono Aqueo ante Maximam illam & mortalibus semper notatissimam Coniunctionem in capite Signiferi: quam tot eventus paulo ante elapsi praeverterunt, plures ac maiores praeibunt. Illa, illa est quae tempora corrigit, mores ac leges mutat, ingenia excitat ad res novas capessendas, regna transfert, totam denique orbis effigiem reformat & instaurat.] Disturbance precedes it, stability accompanies it, a decline and infancy, as it were, follows it. [He links the Great Conjunction with the times of Sulla, Caesar, Augustus, Christ, and Charlemagne.] But that of our time (which, however, few of us will see), good heavens! what great and wonderful effects it will bring! But I need not enter into predictions, especially of things that the experienced already foresee from the course of events.

The purpose of these remarks is not to frighten anyone, but that you, Christian Princes, may not seem to have been without a premonitor, and if anything strange and unexpected happens in your time, though it may surprise men generally, you may retain your presence of mind, and remember your rank and almost divine virtue.

I do not mean that human history depends on the stars in the sense that all is not controlled by God. The arrangement is such that external causes intervene, God using the celestial bodies as signs, or men as instruments, so that mortals may have an "indicator" [*obiectam materiam*] of their human lot, and perceiving God's will through intermediary things, refer all to His glory. Nor am I among those who predict the end of the world in our time, cloaking their own dreams in the decrees of the stars. Why, by the way, do they think it should be inferred from the revolution of the small circle round the equinoctial points rather than from the circuit of the apsides? But such foreknowledge is not given to men. God has granted us a small and shadowy knowledge, reserving to Himself for ever the knowledge of secret things.... We must reject divination in those things of which no example or species has existed from the beginning of the world. Since the end of the world will be a unique occurrence, and all judgment by the stars depends on the comparison of a long succession of phenomena, how shall we define the end of the world by any position of the heavens? Only God can mark the end of a circle.

To return to our subject, it is your duty to consider what outcome you should expect from the great disturbances of the time, and to put your trust in God and not in your own power.

In contending for your private advantage, you disturb the whole Christian Republic, and your gains last but a moment, for death comes soon. But if two such great princes were to join in making peace, all difficulties would vanish. Great matters require the efforts of great men. If you proceed with no private interest, with only the good of the Republic at heart, the outcome will be happy. And you will win the more gratitude and glory the more unlikely it seems that so continuous a war can be terminated without bloodshed.

To end as we began, O Christian Princes: decide that above all things you should make peace. The will of Christ, the safety of your peoples, the position you hold demands it. Peace was Christ's chief message and his legacy to his own. He has been expelled from your realms; call Him back with Peace. . . . Consider that God is judge. The cry of the people comes to His ear. The suppliant Church implores your help. Do not let it be said that so long a war was caused solely by the private greed of princes. Seize the opportunity of unexampled glory. . . . For a peace made for the safety of all Christians, you will be praised to the skies by all the world. And each of you will win the highest award from the supreme Prince. May God Himself, Best, Greatest, King of kings, Lord of hosts, Judge of controversies, Author of victories, so guide your counsels with His boundless goodness and wisdom that the Christian people may be brought from this long and wretched tossing of the storm into the port of tranquillity, and at last, with Christ leading, enjoy life eternal in the kingdom of Heaven. Amen. *Nisi conversi fueritis gladium suum vibravit, arcum suum tetendit, et paravit illum.* Psal. VII.

The astrological section of this speech—a development unparalleled, so far as I know, in a work of this kind—betrays the personal bias of Peletier, who was an accomplished astrologer, having learned the art in his youth in his father's circle.[19] He gives here a very full statement of his point of view. Astrological prescience, though only *probabilis* and *umbratilis,* is a precious indication to us of the will of God and a guaranty that the world is not ruled by chance. It is based on a comparison of the successive configurations of the heavens and of the events in human history that have run parallel to them. It is interesting that Peletier lays special emphasis here on the flowering of the human intellect in successive periods, and thus gives due place to the founding of universities in the Middle Ages, which are also the age of faith.[20] Since prediction is based on a study of the past configurations of the heavens, it is impossible to predict the end of the world, for this will be an un-

---

[19]Albert-Marie Schmidt, *La Poésie scientifique en France au seizième siècle* (Paris, 1938), p. 9, and p. 7, n. 3.

[20]*Cohort.,* p. 25. In the time of Caesar, "maxima illa ingeniorum lumina dominatrix Roma produxit"; the age of Charlemagne saw the "ditionis Christianae incrementum Academiarumque institutionem," and "Iustitiam . . . ac religionem aetas illa sanctissime coluit."

precedented event. The significance of repetition, we may recall, had been demonstrated for Peletier a few years before at the beginning of the reign of Henri II, though in this case the repetition was chiefly that of the calendar:[21]

> Ce n'est doncq' point par un sort hazardeux,
> Que de Henry tu [France] as eu iouissance,
> Le veuil celeste a esté l'entredeux
> Qui à Fortune a osté la puissance:
> Le iour fatal auquel il print naissance
> De Iuppiter son nom heureux tenant,
> Qu'estoit Phebus en son Mouton regnant,
> Au nombre d'ans de vingt huit parfait,
> Un mesme nom, ordre & mois reprenant,
> Regner Henri, France renaistre a fait.

Henri II, born March 31, 1519, succeeded Francis I March 31, 1547. But even more remarkable than the coincidence of dates is the fact that in these two years March 31 fell on the same day of the week, Thursday, the *dies Jovis,* for Jupiter is the patron of rulers. Henri's age also is significant, twenty-eight being "the second perfect number."[22] And—"Phebus en son Mouton regnant"—it was the spring of the year:

> O bel accord des occultes raisons
> A celles là, qu'evidence nous donne!

Here clearly one could rely on the "eventuum similitudo et comparatio,"[23] assured that "le veuil celeste . . . à Fortune a osté la puissance."[24]

Regarded as the work of an anonymous writer, the attack on Postel seemed to Abel Lefranc significant and interesting.[25] Clearly it is still more interesting when we realize that the writer is Jacques Peletier, who must now be reckoned among the enemies of Postel. That Postel, the veritable apostle of peace, should be made the

---

[21] *Congratulation sur le nouveau règne* (1547) in *Les Œuvres poétiques,* Marcel Françon, ed. (Rochecorbon: Gay, 1958), p. 269; see the editor's note, p. 76.

[22] Marcel Françon, *loc. cit.*

[23] *Cohort.,* p. 26.

[24] More fully: The will of God has intervened (*entredeux* = *empêchement*) to wrest the power from Fortune, and to order the concurrence of times and events in such a way as to give a sign to men of the importance of Henri II.

[25] Above, n. 14.

chief object of attack in an oration on peace, seems ungrateful as well as paradoxical. The passage is clearly marked off by the author as a digression, and as such its rhetorical aim is partly to be as entertaining as possible. But it was hardly realistic to drag before the princes of Europe as a chief threat to religion and monarchy one who had just been pronounced insane by the Inquisition. To be sure, the unreality allows Peletier to touch on the religious question (an important reason for peace between Charles V and Henri II), without involving himself in matters that might be exacerbating; the important Diet of Augsburg had just opened on February 5.[26] Postel was fair game, and I do not know whether we should search for any personal reason for Peletier's hostility, beyond the likelihood that he was really indignant at Postel's mistreatment of both religion and astrology. Even so, the attack is remarkably envenomed. Though his account of Postel's doctrines is intentionally a travesty, it is mostly a possible one; and his information about Postel is up to date. It is noticeable that the mathematician Peletier remembers only that Postel had been Royal Reader in Mathematics, omitting the oriental languages.[27] He knows that, as he writes, Postel is in Padua and has published a book in Italian. His description makes clear that this is *Le prime nove del altro mondo,* which must therefore have been published before May 4.[28] He also knows that Postel had been pronounced insane by the Venetian Inquisition, a judgment rendered shortly before February 24.[29]

[26]Meanwhile Henri II maintained some sort of alliance with the German Protestants. He was also still allied with the Sultan, and hence Peletier takes care to avoid the common topic of all Renaissance peace manifestos, that the Christian princes should make peace among themselves and combine against the Turk.

[27]Postel was Royal Reader in Mathematics and Oriental Languages from 1538 to 1542. Is it conceivable that in writing this sentence Peletier thought of himself as a candidate for the chair in Mathematics? There was an appointment in Mathematics in 1555, but presumably after the death of Oronce Finé in October.

[28]Postel published two books in Italian in 1555, *Le prime nove . . .* at Venice (?), and *Il libro della divina ordinatione* at Padua (Bouwsma, p. 303). Peletier knows only one work; his description might almost have been inferred from the title alone: *Le prime nove del altro mondo, cioè l'admirabile historia et non meno necessaria et utile da esser letta et intesa da ogni uno, che stupenda, intitulata La Vergine Venetiana.* But he clearly has read the book; compare the description in Bouwsma, *op cit.,* p. 158–60. Peletier's earlier statement that Postel had once taken Joan of Arc to be his "mother" seems improbable (Bouwsma, p. 24; cf. Lefranc, *op. cit.,* p. 193).

[29]Bouwsma, p. 22. Postel had gone from Vienna to Venice and Padua at the beginning of 1555. He was adjudged insane by the inquisitors in February, but either because they, like Peletier, did not really think him insane, or, what is likely, because of Postel's persistence, they finally condemned him in the autumn of the same year, and he was thrown into prison.

Peletier thought highly of his *Cohortatio,* and especially valued it as witness to his political insight—*nos rerum non ignaros esse testatur.* A man of many gifts, he had undoubtedly thought of employment by the Court in some public capacity, and his appointment in 1547 to deliver the funeral oration of Henry VIII had seemed to be a step on the way. But he had been disappointed. His feelings at the time the *Cohortatio* was published are expressed in the prefatory remarks to his *Art poétique*:[30]

> Disant ceci, je me raporte une souvenance de l'amour que j'ai toujours porté au public: tel que quand j'ai vu ma fortune dedire mes intancions quant aus affaires de manimant, l'un des moyens que j'ai tousjours estimé qui rand les hommes non seulement prudans, mais doctes et savans: Je me suis avisé d'impetrer mon meilleur tans pour me retirer sus mes Livres: pour accommoder mon etude à l'utilité des studieus: en epiant ce pendant, comme d'une solitude, quelle part doit tourner cette Nue, mais plus tôt cette Tempête et emocion universelle de la terre.

Whether these words were written before or after the writing of the *Cohortatio* perhaps does not matter; the oration gives substance to the statement that he kept his eye on the agitated state of public affairs.[31]

Composed at least ten months before the Truce of Vaucelles (February 5, 1556), the *Cohortatio* takes its place in the propaganda for peace leading up to that agreement. Rumors of the decline in the health of Charles V had been spread abroad for some time—in January, 1555, the report was that he had been thought dead—so that Peletier's advice to him to retire was safe enough (he abdicated

---

[30]Boulanger, ed., p. 60.

[31]In annotating this passage, Boulanger is brought to say: "C'est vers la même époque [!] que Peletier, très préoccupé de la guerre entre Henri II et Charles-Quint [!], composa une *Exhortation à la Paix* qui parut en 1558." He parallels the phrase "Tempête et emocion universelle de la terre" with phrases from the *Euclidis Elementa* and the Epistle to Jean Peletier; to which we can now add the reiteration of this concept throughout the *Cohort.,* e.g., p. 24: "magnae illae commutationes rerum . . . commotiones populorum et civitatum." Here may be noted the recurrence in the *Cohort.* of a thought already expressed in the funeral oration for Henry VIII. In the *Cohort.,* Charles V is advised not to contend in his old age against the flourishing "virtue" and fortune of Henri II. In the funeral oration (*BHR* II, 13), Henry VIII is commended for having made peace with Francis I: "Car certainement vouloir entretenir guerre en aage desjà si advancé, et encores contre ung roy insupérable des hommes et de fortune, c'est faire une playe incurable à sa prospèrité, et à sa vertu." This is in fact the nucleus of the argument in the *Cohort.*

in October). The oration, intended for a French public, keeps the French king mostly in view. The "arguments" addressed to the emperor are in fact flattery of Henri II, and a chief point made to Henri is that his "virtue" and fortune are now the equal of Charles's, and hence that it is time for peace. Ready for publication on May 4, the pamphlet, whether intentionally or not, was in good time for the Conference of Marcq (or Gravelines) which opened on May 25, under the auspices of Mary Tudor, for the purpose of finding a basis of peace between Charles and Henri. This conference had been inspired by Montmorency, who aimed at peace in opposition, as usual, to the Guises; and Montmorency had reason to fear that the king was inclined to follow the ambitious policy of the latter.[32] Peletier's oration might pass as propaganda for the party of Montmorency. Taking a definite stand when affairs were extremely fluid, and the tide might turn against him (for the king was hardly in peaceful mood), the author prudently remained anonymous and in a position to repudiate or claim his work as occasion prompted. And in fact the Conference of Marcq failed, chiefly because, as Charles wrote to his brother Ferdinand on June 8, the French merely reiterated all the "vielles querelles." Throughout the remainder of the year, Peletier may have been well content to leave his oration unacknowledged.[33] But the Truce of Vaucelles early in 1556 would seem to justify all that he had said, and in 1557 he could point with pride to his "oratio pacificatoria" as proving his competence in public affairs.[34]

So long as it was supposed that Peletier's *Cohortatio* or *Exhortation* was written in 1558 (or 1557) and reflected the feeling then current, it was easy to guess that it may have expressed sentiments analogous to those of Ronsard's *Exhortation pour la Paix* and may have "inspired" that poem. Now that we know that it belongs to the spring of 1555 and reflects the feeling that preceded Vaucelles

---

[32]Henry Lemonnier in Lavisse, *Histoire de France* V, II, 159.
[33]For the feeling in November, see the letter of Pibrac to the French ambassador in Rome, quoted by Chamard, ed. of Du Bellay, *Œuvres poétiques* VI, 3, n. 1: "Habet hic annus incredibilem expectationem pacis. . . . Nullum vero tempus commodius est, ut de pace agatur, quam quando res bello bene geruntur, quod non accepisse tunc, sed pacem dedisse videamur, in quo maxima laus est. Fit tamen, nescio quo modo, ut suae felicitati statuere Principes nesciant modum, nec cohibere offerentem se fortunam, ... Quae Henrici felicitas [of equality or better in the war] ne non satis valeat ad concordiam metuo." Had Pibrac read Peletier's *Cohortatio?*
[34]Peletier's letter to his brother is dated "V Id. Aprilis Lugduni," presumably 1557.

rather than that preceding Cateau-Cambrésis, the likelihood of a direct relationship to Ronsard's poem diminishes, even if we assume that Ronsard knew the anonymous oration and knew who wrote it. That is not, of course, an improbable assumption, and the possibility of some relationship remains. Nothing could be founded on the coincidence of titles, since Ronsard's *Exhortation pour la Paix* is a sort of palinode to his *Exhortation au camp du Roy pour bien combattre* published a few weeks earlier. But something might be made of the coincidence of form, Ronsard's *Exhortation pour la Paix* being a well-made deliberative oration or declamation in verse, a type of composition that he had never attempted before.[35] Again, the enclosing thought of Ronsard's poem, stated in the exordium and repeated in the peroration, is the same as that of Peletier, namely that Christians should not make war on brother Christians—

> Non, ne combatez pas, vivez en amitié,
> Chretiens, changez vostre ire avecque la pitié,
> Changez à la douceur les rancunes ameres,
> Et ne trampez vos dars dans le sang de vos frères,
> Que Christ le fils de Dieu, abandonnant les cieux,
> En terre a rachetez de son sang precieux.   [vv. 1–6]

Conceivably this general attitude might have been suggested by Peletier, though no topic is commoner in Renaissance peace propaganda than this one, which, for example, informs the pacifist writings of Erasmus, to name no others. Ronsard addresses Christians in general and Christian soldiers in particular, not the Christian princes; and his argument unrolls in a series of topics far removed from those of Peletier.

Yet the sentiments of Peletier's oration were not altogether unsuited to the situation that ended in the treaty of Cateau-Cambrésis. Peletier was urging Henri II in 1555 to make peace though peace might not seem to be to his advantage, and that is pretty much what, in a different sense, Henri did in 1559. It is likely that the French translation was brought out in 1558 at a moment when it was deemed appropriate; and, until we learn better, it would seem most appropriate to the latter part of the year

---

[35] I have dealt with Ronsard's use of such forms in "Rhetorical Doctrine and Some Poems of Ronsard." See below, p. 291.

when the peace conference was in session.[36] It may thus be later than Ronsard's *Exhortation,* which probably was published at the beginning of October, also by Wechel. However that may be, it is not in Ronsard's *Exhortation,* but in his poem *La Paix, au Roy,* published when peace was proclaimed in the following April, that we find a passage to compare with Peletier. This poem is also a declamation in form, it is addressed to a Christian prince, and is "deliberative," since the aim is to persuade Henri to be satisfied (as many Frenchmen were not) with the settlement now made. The argument therefore again turns on the advantages of peace. In vv. 203-24 we read:

> Sire, je vous supply de croire qu'il vaut mieux
> Se contenter du sien, que d'estre ambitieux
> De sur le bien d'autruy: malheureux qui desire
> Ainsi comme à trois detz hazarder son empire
> Soubz le jeu de Fortune, & duquel on ne sçait
> Si l'incertaine fin doibt respondre au souhait.
> Que desirez vous plus? vostre France est si grande:
> «L'homme qui n'est content, & qui tousjours demande
> «Quand il seroit un Dieu est mal-heureux, d'autant
> «Que tousjours il desire & n'est jamais contant.
> Bien? imaginez vous des Flamens la victoire,
> Quel honneur auriez vous d'une si pauvre gloire,
> D'avoir un Roy, Chrestien comme vous, enchainé
> Et par vostre Paris en triomphe mené?
> Il vaudroit mieux chasser le Turc hors de la Grece,
> Qui miserable vit soubz le joug de detresse,
> Que prendre un Roy Chrestien, ou de meurtrir de coups
> Un peuple en Jesuschrist baptisé comme vous.
> Il vaudroit beaucoup mieux, vous qui venez sur l'age
> Ja grison, gouverner vostre Royal menage,
> Vostre femme pudique, & voz nobles Enfans
> Qu'acquerir par danger des lauriers triomphans.

These arguments, so different from most of the topics of this poem, may remind us of several "sentences" in Peletier's oration.

---

[36]The public mood of the earlier months of the year, after the victories of Calais and Thionville, or of the summer, when Ronsard's *Exhortation au camp* was in order, would seem to offer no very favorable atmosphere for a call to peace. Yet this is conjectural; the discovery of a copy of the book might put the matter in a different light.

Two can be cited from the French *Exhortation* in Du Verdier's excerpts:[37]

> Les Princes, quoiqu'ils soient excellens, ... si sont-ils hommes pourtant, & ont à reconnoître ce qu'ils ont d'humain en eux, par cela mêmement qu'ils peuvent assez étendre leurs désirs, voire jusqu'à l'infini, mais à peine la moindre satisfaction de leur attente ensuit-elle leurs efforts.... Celuy a tout, qui se connoît assez avoir; mais à celuy qui tousjours désire, autant fait faute ce qu'il a, comme ce qu'il n'a point, & faut par nécessité qu'il demeure en perpétuelle indigence.

Again, "What victory is so deplorable as that gained by a Christian king over a king of his own kind? what other glory before Christ has the triumph of the one over the other except that the victor has defeated his brother king, despoiled his brother king, led his brother king in triumph?"[38] And the advice to Henri to turn from the danger of war to a life of domestic *otium,* now that old age is approaching, seems like an application to him of the argument Peletier had more appropriately addressed to Charles V.[39] A few days earlier, in the *Chant de liesse,* Ronsard had congratulated him on being "en la fleur de tes ans," but Henri's fortieth birthday had intervened on March 31.[40]

Let us return to the year 1555. The community of sentiment once thought likely to exist between Peletier's oration and Ronsard's *Exhortation* really exists, so far as the historical moment is concerned, between the *Cohortatio* and Du Bellay's poem on the Truce of Vaucelles, *Discours au Roy sur la Trefve de l'an M.D.LV.* (1556 n.s.).[41] Indeed between two French writers, the one advocating a peace in advance and the other welcoming its consummation, a similarity of outlook might be expected, without an assumption

[37]Du Verdier, I, 562; *Cohort.,* pp. 8, 16–17.

[38]*Cohort.,* p. 12: Quae tam luctuosa victoria, quam ea quam Rex Christianus a Rege sui ordinis reportat? quid aliud habet laudationis coram Christo quod alter de altero triumphaverit, nisi quod victor Regem fratrem debellaverit? Regem fratrem spoliaverit? Regem fratrem in triumpho duxerit? quid hoc est aliud quam Christianismum ad gentium ritus revocare?

[39]*Cohort.,* p. 9 (above, p. 250). Peletier applies to Henri II the advice of Cineas to seek tranquility now (*Cohort.,* p. 12, above, *ibid.*), but unlike Ronsard recommends to him a leisure devoted to public service.

[40]*Chant de liesse* 107–109, in *Œuv. compl.,* ed. crit., IX, 137–38.

[41]*Œuv. poét.,* Chamard, ed. VI, 3.

that one had influenced the other.[42] The following parallels, however, may be worth noting. Thus Peletier had argued that to make peace was to Charles's interest, and that though it might not seem to be to Henri's interest, it would redound to his credit to make peace when he was able to pursue war successfully.[43] Du Bellay makes this difference sharper. Charles has received the truce—

> La Trefve bien heureuse & profitable à tous,
> Mais plus utile à luy, & plus louable à vous:
> Plus utile, d'autant qu'en seureté plus grande
> Il jouist du repos, que son aage demande:
> Et plus louable à vous, d'autant que le bon heur,
> Sire, vous asseuroit de r'emporter l'honneur,
> Et vous avez trop plus, tenant ja la victoire,
> Prisé le bien public que vostre propre gloire.   [71–78]

Taking pity on his subjects, Henri has accepted the truce after "conquering himself"—a topic that Peletier had recommended to Charles.[44]

> Car vous n'avez plus tost apperceu l'Empereur
> Incliner à la Paix, que soudain la fureur
> S'est esteincte dans vous au plus fort de l'affaire:
> Et content d'avoir peu domter vostre adversaire,
> Avez domté vous mesme: & pour le commun bien
> Vous estes souvenu d'estre Roy Treschrestien:
> Non un Jules Cesar, un Pyrrhe, un Alexandre,
> Qui ne prenoient plaisir qu'à sang humain espandre.   [143–50]

Similarly Peletier had very emphatically reminded Henri of the responsibilities of his title "Très-Chrétien."[45] In deploring that a Christian king should think of leading another Christian king in

---

[42]Note, however, that Du Bellay's sonnets on the Truce of Vaucelles, *Regrets* 123–26 (*Œuv. poét.*, ed. cit., II, 151–53), mostly present a different view, reflecting the dismay of the papal Court. The doubts they express about the treaty seem in some measure to be shared by the poet, and not to be merely "reportage" as Chamard says they are (*Du Bellay* [1900], p. 326; *Hist de la Pléiade*, II, 289).

[43]*Cohort., passim*, and esp. pp. 5–6, 14–15 (above pp. 249–50).

[44]*Cohort., p.* 6 (above, p. 249).

[45]*Cohort.*, p. 13: Nomen illud insigne a maioribus tuis tibi relictum vide quid moneat: maximus ille Christianitatis titulus vide quid te requirat. Sustine, Henrice, sustine nomen profecto longe gloriosius, quam quod ab iis quas persequeris victoriis proficiscitur.

triumph, Peletier asks: "Quid hoc est aliud quam Christianismum *ad gentium ritus* revocare?"[46] So Du Bellay in imagining a triumph for the king:

> Mais apres voz charroys!
> Je ne ferois marcher les Princes & les Roys,
> Les bras liez au dos à la mode Romaine,
> Triomphe des Gentils. [213-16]

But more suggestive perhaps than these parallels is the fact that, like Peletier, Du Bellay constantly reverts to the topic of Henri's "virtue" and "fortune" (in vv. 35-38, 55-58, 79-82, 102-20, 123-24, 207, and in the closing lines of the poem 247-50)—for example:

> Ainsi quand l'Empereur, Sire, feit ses efforts
> Pour prendre des François les villes & les forts, ...
> Vous luy feistes sentir des la premiere attainte,
> Combien vostre grandeur commande sur la crainte,
> Et combien la vertu peult au cueur d'un grand Roy
> Quand il a, comme vous, la Fortune pour soy. [27-36]

> Celuy vrayment, celuy est doublement vainqueur,
> Vainqueur de son hayneux & de son propre cueur,
> Qui peult durant le cours de sa bonne fortune
> Suyvre de la vertu la trace non commune. [79-82]

[46]*Cohort.*, p. 12 (above, n. 38).

Erasmus and France:
The Propaganda for Peace

The reputation of Erasmus in the period after his death has been the object of considerable interest in recent years following the impression made by Marcel Bataillon's *Erasme et l'Espagne* (Paris, 1937) and, more recently, by Andreas Flitner's essay *Erasmus im Urteil seiner Nachwelt* (Tübingen, 1952).[1] The vicissitudes of an influence felt to be important, yet at the same time widely suspect, are something of a critical index to European moral sentiment. It is clear also that the reception of this influence has differed with the climate of opinion from country to country as well as from time to time, and it would seem desirable to fill up the outline, so admirably sketched by Flitner, at points where our present information is relatively thin. One such point is to be found in France in the latter part of the sixteenth century. To this broad subject, however, the following pages aim to make only a limited, though material, contribution by calling attention to some adaptations and translations of the *Dulce bellum inexpertis* and the *Querela Pacis* that have hitherto been overlooked. These items may be considered as supplementing in particular the 'Notes sur quelques traductions d'Erasme en français' which form the appendix to Dr. Margaret Mann Phillips' *Erasme et les débuts de la réforme française* (Paris, 1934). Dr. Phillips' list includes, as a matter of fact, no translations of the *Bellum* or the *Querela*.

Let it be said at once that none of the books here considered is a straightforward and professed translation of the whole of either of

From *Studies in the Renaissance*, 8 (1961) 103–27. Copyright © 1961 by The Renaissance Society of America.
[1]See also G. J. de Voogd, *Erasmus en Grotius* (Leiden, 1947); A. Renaudet, "L'héritage d'Erasme," *Rivista di Letterature moderne* 1 (1950) 1–30; Pierre Mesnard, "La Tradition érasmienne," *BHR* 15 (1953) 359–66.

the works in question. No. 4, *Les Louanges et recommandations de la paix*, is nothing but a translation from the *Bellum*, but it renders only selected passages. No. 5, Sevin's *Complainte de la paix*, our most important discovery, presents the whole of the *Querela*, but in the form of an adaptation rather than a translation. In nos. 2 and 3, Claude Colet's *Oraison de Mars* and Guillaume Aubert's *Oraison de la paix*, considerable portions of the *Bellum* are translated, while other passages of the *Bellum* or of the *Querela* are assimilated without literal translation. No. 1, Clichtove's *De Bello et pace opusculum*, takes topic after topic from Erasmus, but the developments are mostly Clichtove's own. I have included Clichtove's attractive little book not only because it depends on Erasmus, but also because I believe that, though it had only one edition, it had some influence in transmitting these Erasmian topics to writers of the more popularly-directed pleas for peace, in particular to writers of poems and literary orations. Such writings, especially poems on peace, are numerous in sixteenth-century France, and in scanning them one finds oneself with a certain frequency in the presence of Erasmian topics and images.[2] This more general influence will form part of another study; we are concerned here only with some actual translations which show in their own way how Erasmus continued to play a part in the discussion of peace during the quarter century after his death.[3]

What strikes us first perhaps is that this role is anonymous and surreptitious.[4] Whereas more recent writers sometimes place peace under the patronage, so to speak, of Erasmus' name, Erasmus' name was precisely the stumbling block in the sixteenth century. In the five books here discussed as taken wholly or in part from him,

[2] Among orations permeated with Erasmian influence, I note Richard Pace, *Oratio in pace nuperrima composita* (London: Pynson, and Paris: Gourmont, 1518), with a French version, *Oraison en la louenge de la paix*, published by Gourmont at the same time; and [Jacques Peletier,] *Cohortatio pacificatoria* Lyons: De Tournes, 1555) (see above, p. 243). Among poems, in varying degrees influenced by Erasmus, François Sagon, *Chant de la Paix* (Paris, 1538, 1544, etc.); Pierre Habert, *Traicté du bien et utilité de la paix* (Paris, 1568, 1570); Antoine du Verdier, *Antitheses de la paix et de la guerre* (Lyons, 1568), dependent on Clichtove rather than on Erasmus; anon., *Advertissemens aux trois Estatz sur l'entretenement de la paix* (Paris: Tabert, 1576).

[3] I have not followed the fortunes of the *Bellum* or the *Querela* outside of the propaganda for peace, but may note that the section "Misères des soldats et gens de guerre" in P. Boaistuau's *Le Théâtre du monde* (1558) is in part translated from the *Bellum*.

[4] Cf. Dr. Phillips' article, "Erasmus and Propaganda, a study of the translations of Erasmus in English and French," MLR 37 (1942) 1-17, where, however, p. 5, the point is made only with reference to the earlier translations of Louis de Berquin.

his name does not once appear. In fact, the reader is deliberately put upon a false scent. The *Louanges* are said to be "extraictes de l'Ecriture saincte"; Sevin's *Complainte de la paix* is "recueillie de plusieurs auteurs" (which is false); Aubert professes to be the interpreter of "les plus renommés auteurs des langues étrangeres." Not even Colet can be absolved. We do not expect him to mention Erasmus in a poem; but he fills his margins with references to authorities, among which his chief authority Erasmus is conspicuously absent. Nor does Clichtove mention Erasmus, whose friend he had been. Clichtove wrote with his eye upon the Sorbonne, with whose strictures, however, he was in any case in agreement. The later books, falling between 1544 and 1570, belong to the moral atmosphere of the Council of Trent and the indices, but are yet within a twilight zone compared with the obscurity that followed the latter date. I have found no translations from the *Bellum* or the *Querela* after 1570.

It would be interesting to know by whom and within what limits the name of Erasmus was invoked after say 1559. The only one of his works to be continuously reissued in France was the harmless but useful *Apophthegmata,* and it alone appeared in translation under the author's name several times between 1543 and 1557 (but not again until 1574).[5] Montaigne mentions Erasmus only once: those who have performed some impressive public act are imagined by us in accordance with it, demons as of wild shape, Tamerlane as a monster, Erasmus as uttering nothing but adages and apophthegms.[6] Such was Montaigne's picture, or the picture he knew his readers would respond to—the author of apophthegms. Larger claims have been made for Montaigne's dependence on Erasmus, but these remain to be proved, as do other claims for Erasmus' influence in this period.[7] The time was yet far off when Guy Patin would make a cult of "le divin Erasme," "l'in-

[5]M. M. Phillips, *Erasme et les débuts,* pp. 204-208. Exceptional is a professed translation (*ibid.,* p. 203) of the suspect *De Esu carnium* (Lyons, no name of printer, 1561) by one Robert Prevost (a Protestant?), who was also the translator of Sleidan.

[6]*Essais* 3. 2: "Qui m'eut faict voir Erasme autrefois, il eust esté malaisé que ie n'eusse pris pour adages et apophthegmes tout ce qu'il eust dict à son valet et à son hostesse."

[7]Pierre Villey, *Les Sources et l'évolution des Essais de Montaigne,* 1. 126, records a possible echo of the *Querela Pacis.* Renaudet, *art. cit.,* accepts Montaigne as Erasmian in spirit; says that after the St. Bartholomew massacre opponents of the government were readers of Erasmus, instancing Fr. Hotman and the authors of the *Vindiciae contra tyrannos;* and asserts that the "politiques" were Erasmians, but offers no evidence. I note that Erasmus is occasionally mentioned by Bodin.

comparable Erasme." Still, in the nature of the case, the influence of Erasmus was doubtless greater than the tangible evidence shows. The manipulations of his text with which we are concerned suggest indeed that the common reader was not likely to recognize their source; but Aubert and Sevin at least must surely have expected the more learned reader to see what they were up to.

The ecclesiastical authorities evidently thought Erasmus' influence still formidable. His works were condemned *in toto* by the index of Paul IV in 1559, and this is the date of the last unexpurgated edition of the *Adagia* (in which the *Bellum* is Adage 3001) to be published in France. The index of 1564 limited the ban to certain works only and called for the expurgation of the *Adagia*. Accordingly the next French edition, that of Chesneau, 1570, gave the *Bellum* in abbreviated form, though not slashed so completely as in the notorious edition of Paolo Manuzio (Florence, 1575), made with papal authorization.[8] There had been no editions of the separate *Bellum* or of the *Querela* in France since 1530. However, the editions of both works available to our translators before 1570 were complete and unexpurgated; it was only after that date that the call for retrenchment took effect, not only in the editions of the *Adagia* by Chesneau and Manuzio, but in the expurgatorial indices of 1584 and after. Even in these last, the *Bellum* suffered more than the *Querela*, which, though purged of considerable passages, nevertheless retained its identity; it had never been specifically named in the prohibitive indices. The secret character of our translations perhaps is due less to official stigma than to the general feeling that Erasmus was a dangerous author. The burning of Louis de Berquin could hardly have been forgotten. Among his translations from Erasmus condemned by the Sorbonne in 1525/1526 was that of the *Querela Pacis*.[9] There was indeed a special fear of translations as such; a Latin text circulating among scholars might do less harm than a translation that would fall into the hands of the multitude, unprepared to read with the qualifications that men of learning might be expected to take for granted.

[8] On Erasmus in the indices, see especially F. H. Reusch, *Der Index der verbotenen Bücher* (Bonn, 1883), I, 347–55; Preserved Smith, *Erasmus* (New York, 1923), pp. 421–22; Andreas Flitner, *op. cit.,* pp. 38–46.

[9] Allen, *Opus Epist.* VI, 65, seems to say that the *Querela Pacis* itself was condemned on June 1, 1525; it was, however, an anonymous translation, presumably Berquin's (Du Plessis d'Argentré, *Collectio judiciorum* [Paris, 1728], II, 42; M. M. Phillips, *Erasme et les débuts,* p. 118).

But the translations we have to present were safe enough. The portions of the *Bellum* put into French by our writers are harmless. If this adage seemed specially objectionable because of its attack on the friars, its assertion that Aristotle is incompatible with Christian doctrine, its doubts about the moral grounds for war against the Turk, its reprobation of the clergy for preaching war, and perhaps its attack on the memory of Julius II, none of these passages appears in the translations. Colet employs the earlier parts of the *Bellum* in which war is found to be contrary both to nature and to Christian doctrine, and Aubert does much the same, though adding in less direct translation the charge that wars originate in the vices of kings. The anonymous *Louanges* selects passages dealing with the contrast between war and the professions of a Christian, together with a passage on the hardships of a soldier's life and the prohibitive cost of war. Sevin, however, in his adaptation of the *Querela Pacis* to the circumstances of the Wars of Religion, retains the passages (later to be condemned) in which ecclesiastics are severely handled by Erasmus, though he tends to soften their impact.[10]

Josse Clichtove

De Bello et pace opusculum, Christianos principes ad sedandos bellorum tumultus & pacem componendam exhortans. Paris, Simon Colinaeus, 1523 (August 3); 8°, 50 ff. + 1 f. Index.

Erasmus mentions Clichtove with some frequency in his letters, and usually has a good word to say of him, even after he became convinced, about 1525, that Clichtove had aligned himself with the Sorbonne: "Clithoveus quidam, homo mihi quondam amicus, nec prorsus alienus a Musis; sed hunc in suum pertraxerunt consortium" (*Epist.* 1805 Allen, dated 1527).[11] If he read the treatise *De Bello et pace* when it appeared in 1523, he may well have regarded it

---

[10] For the *Bellum*, page-and-line references ("Latomus") are to *Erasme, Dulce bellum inexpertis*, texte édité et traduit par Yvonne Remy et René Dunil-Marquebreucq (Berchem-Brussels, 1953, Collection Latomus VIII); for the *Querela Pacis*, references (LB) are to the *Opera omnia* (Leiden, 1703–1706), IV.

[11] Josse Clichtove (1472–1543) is known as an early opponent of Luther (*Antilutherus*, Paris, 1524), and as the editor of many works of Lefèvre d'Etaples, whose pupil he had been. A Fleming, he studied in Paris from c. 1488, taking the divinity degree in 1506. Tutor to the young Bishop of Tournai in Paris, 1513–1517, he received a benefice in Tournai in 1519, and about 1525 a canonry at Chartres which he held for the rest of his life. The best account of Clichtove is still that of J. A. Clerval, *De Judoci Clichtovei... vita et operibus* (Paris: Picard, 1894); on his relations

at first with some favor as the work of a friend, so much of it echoes his own writings on peace (though without acknowledgment), even going beyond him in protest against the warmongering of clergymen.[12] About half the chapters of the *opusculum* begin with topics suggested by the *Bellum* or the *Querela Pacis*. Yet the work is Clichtove's own; he knows the traditional thought about peace independently of Erasmus, and he fills out his topics with a wealth of instances from biblical and classical history and from the poets, among whom Mantuan is a favorite. Moreover, he departs from Erasmus on such essential matters as the virtue of fighting the Turk and the justification of war for the recovery of territory. He seems to have aimed at avoiding the apparent exaggerations of the *Bellum* and the *Querela*, as if hoping to serve the cause of peace the better by remaining within the bounds of the possible.

In his preface, Clichtove explains why a plea for peace is needed, and declares that he writes as a Christian, not as a German, Englishman, or Spaniard.[13] Defining peace (ch. 1), he divides it in the mediaeval fashion, after Augustine, between *pax mundi* and *pax Domini*.[14] Peace is the condition of the natural world from stars to stones (2).[15] Peace reigns in heaven, war is from hell (3).[16] Christ in all his words and acts taught only peace (4).[17] The blessings of peace are enumerated (5); war, in contrast, is worse than plague and famine and the cause of both (6).[18] Christian princes should

---

with Erasmus, see P. S. Allen, *Opus Epist. Des. Erasmi* IX, 160 n., and E. V. Telle, *Erasme de Rotterdam et le septième sacrement* (Geneva: Droz, 1954), esp. pp. 329–345. There is a facsimile reprint of the *De Bello et pace opusculum*, the Marqués de Olivart, ed. (Madrid, 1914) (not seen by me).

[12]However, Clichtove has nothing like Erasmus' attack on the mendicant monks in *Bellum* 86, 1006–85. He may not have known this passage unless he possessed a copy of the latest edition of the *Adagia* (January 1523), where it appeared for the first time; but very likely he knew it and deplored it, since his attitude towards the regular clergy was altogether opposed to that of Erasmus (see E. V. Telle, *op. cit.*, *passim*).

[13]In the preface, echoes of the title and first sentence of the *Querela:* "extorris illa [Pax] finibus nostris miseram luget suam sortem, quia ubique gentium profligata sit," etc. (cf. *Querela Pacis, undique gentium eiectae profligataeque*); quotation from Silius Italicus, as in *Querela* 629E.

[14]Erasmus does not make this traditional distinction.

[15]The greater part of ch. 2 follows *Querela* 626B–627A in detail.

[16]Erasmus does not so contrast, but mentions peace in heaven (e.g., *Bellum* 56, 580) and reiterates that war is from hell (*Bellum* 26, 154; 52, 517, etc.).

[17]Inspired by *Bellum* 54, 547 ff. and *Querela* 629D.

[18]Traditional *laudatio pacis* and *vituperatio belli*, not from Erasmus, though some

not make war on each other (7);[19] worse than civil, such wars are fratricidal (8);[20] the pagans fought more humanely than we do (9).[21] It is shameful to display the cross on military banners (10);[22] and clergymen ought not to incite princes to war (11);[23] they should encourage them to fight the enemies of the faith (12).[24] Here and in the next chapters (13-16), Clichtove departs rather widely from Erasmus; acceptable reasons for a *justum bellum;* the testimony of Augustine on this point; war sometimes justifiable between Christians and even for the recovery of territory.[25] War is a punishment sent from God for our sins; He must be appeased (17-18).[26] When differences arise, princes should at once send envoys and negotiate without cupidity, making nonaggression pacts (19).[27] Let them remember that they are brothers in the spirit, recall the miseries of their subjects, fear the wrath of God, and, if they must fight, let it be against the enemies of the orthodox faith (20).[28]

---

details inevitably agree with the same *topoi* in *Bellum* 44, 409-420 and *Querela* 639B.

[19]Passages of N.T. enjoining peace; vindictive passages of O.T. explained as allegorical or superseded. This is Erasmian; cf. *Bellum* 68, 748-790, *Querela* 630A-F. Remarks on the hostility among nations (f. 16ᵛ: "Iam Gallum esse apud Britannos capitale est," etc.) are from *Querela* 638D (cf. *Inst. princ. Christ.* 610). The conclusion that war may be condoned as a last resort, here frankly accepted, is barely admitted by Erasmus in *Querela* 637F.

[20]This topic, and much of the expression, from *Bellum* 52, 519-529.

[21]From *Bellum* 64, 689-691, 736-747; cf. *Querela* 633C.

[22]From *Bellum* 42, 365-70, and *Querela* 635B-C and 740F (the naming of special cannon for the apostles).

[23]From *Querela* 634C-635B (the equivalent *Bellum* 40, 351-64 was added by Erasmus in 1526; see below).

[24]Unqualified advocacy of a Turkish war is not Erasmian, though it is well known that Erasmus' attitude shifted (cf. Allen, *Opus Epistolarum* VIII, Epist. 2279 and 2285 introd.). Clichtove ascribes opposition to a Turkish war to Luther (who also changed his mind on the matter), but may be striking at Erasmus through him as Erasmus came to think he did in the *Antilutherus.* In editions of the *Bellum* before 1523 there is only the brilliant passage (84, 969-96) against fighting the Turk; passages added in January 1523 include a concession (92, 1075-85) to the common view, and this is already in *Querela* 638B.

[25]On the *justum bellum* see below. Clichtove here condones war for the recovery of territory with reluctance, emphasizing the cost in blood and wealth (he echoes *Bellum* 48, 481-504 or *Querela* 640A), but permits it as a last resort—otherwise a prince might gradually lose all his territory.

[26]A traditional topic significantly omitted by Erasmus.

[27]Compare *Bellum* 84, 958-68, *Querela* 636B, and *Inst. princ. Christ.*, last sec. But Clichtove's ideas on arbitration are more concrete than those of Erasmus.

[28]In this recapitulation several sentences echo *Bellum* 52, 519-36.

Essays on Renaissance Poetry

We cannot pass over the possibility that Clichtove's work may in turn háve influenced Erasmus' *Bellum,* though what we say on this point is a suggestion and by no means a certainty. Erasmus revised the *Bellum* for the edition of the *Adagia* published by Froben in February 1526.[29] Apart from scattered sentences, there are three substantial additions: 40, 350–364, against clergymen who preach war; 64, 692–736, on the superior humanity in war of the ancient pagans compared with the brigandage of the sixteenth-century soldiery; and 70, 791–820, an extension of Erasmus' reprobation of those who twist Scripture to justify war. The first of these passages is presumably not influenced by Clichtove, since the equivalent is in the *Querela,* which Clichtove himself echoes.[30] But Clichtove's influence on the other two passages is conceivable. The first of them is inserted in a train of thought which before 1526 stated that the ancients waged war more humanely than we, and civilized the peoples they conquered. This thought is repeated in the *Querela* (633c) with the explicit contrast that *modern princes fight for trivial causes.* Clichtove (ch. 9) states that the reading of ancient history shows that the pagans fought with more moderation; he gives many examples, and ends (f. 21) by observing that *now soldiers fight lawlessly like brigands:* they leave their honest callings to rush into war and to live by rapine. Erasmus' insertion in the 1526 *Bellum* is similar: if you read the history of the pagans, you will find generals who avoided war and sought reconciliation (examples different from Clichtove's), but now those are called soldiers who rush into battle in hope of gain: *Christian warfare is brigandage.*[31]

Between the lines of the second passage one might read a reply

[29]Latomus, Introd., p. 10.
[30]*Querela* 634F: "Evangelici praecones ... e suggesto sacro classicum canebant." Clichtove, f. 26r: "Qui vero suggestum conscendunt, ... classicum canunt bellicum." *Bellum* 351: "Alius e sacro suggesto promittit omnium admissorum condonationem, qui sub eius principis signis pugnarint."
[31]Clichtove, f. 19v: "Caeterum si antiquorum annales ... cuiquam evolvere vacat, invenientur profecto ethnici ... multo maiore moderatione ... gessisse bella quam hac tempestate gerant inter se ... Christiani.... (f. 21v): Nunc autem detonante bello, qui prius artis alicuius exercitio ac usu victum sibi honeste quaeritabant, artis opus relinquunt, ad bellum catervatim properant, ut, illius praetextu, rapto vivant, ditentur spoliis," etc. Erasmus, *Bellum* 1526: "Si revolves ethnicorum historias, quam multos reperies duces qui miris artibus bellum declinarint.... Nunc inter Christianos vir fortis habetur si quis eius gentis quicum bellum est hominem forte obvium in nemore, non armatum sed pecuniis onustum, ... occiderit.... Et milites vocantur qui spe lucelli ultro provolant ad pugnam.... Itaque, si veteris militiae disciplinam contempleris, Christianorum militia latrocinium fere est, non militia."

to one of Clichtove's main points. Clichtove had devoted three chapters to the doctrine of the *justum bellum,* attempting (in ch. 15) to define the narrow limits within which a ruler might justly go to war for the recovery of territory. Before 1526, Erasmus had barely mentioned this doctrine in his *Bellum* (60, 637), and it is not referred to as a doctrine in the *Querela,*[32] but he had dealt briefly with it in the *Institutio principis Christiani* (LB, IV, 609)—princes easily persuade themselves that any war they wish to wage is "just"—and this charge is brought into the *Bellum* in 1526 in an added sentence (60, 638–640) and again in the long insertion in question (70, 791–820). The insertion chiefly extends the thought that precedes it, namely the iniquity of those who interpret Scripture so as to justify war. He quotes them as saying that the words "Nolite esse solliciti de crastino; benefacite iis qui oderunt vos" were valid only during the Lord's lifetime, and as saying: "Porro sicubi similia docet Paulus aut Petrus, *consilii sunt, non praecepti.*" Now Clichtove, after quoting Luke 6:30 ("Of him that taketh away thy goods, ask them not again") and I Cor. 6:7 ("Why do ye not rather take wrong? why do ye not rather suffer yourselves to be defrauded?"), admits that one might reasonably take these verses as *consilia* and not as *praecepta.*[33] By this kind of interpretation, Erasmus says, kings are encouraged in their vices.[34] He adds: "Haereseos suspectus est qui vehementer dehortatur a bello, et qui talibus commentis diluunt vigorem evangelicae doctrinae... orthodoxi sunt et pietatis Christianae doctores: doctor vere Christianus nunquam bellum probat; fortassis alicubi permittit, sed invitus ac dolens." In writing the first clause,[35] he could hardly fail to be thinking of the action of the

---

[32]Erasmus appears to avoid the term *justum bellum,* even when he alludes to the notion that rulers find reasons for war (e.g., *Querela* 636B–C; 639F) or himself allows war for defense against "barbarians" or for internal tranquillity (*Querela* 637F).

[33]*De Bello,* f. 36ʳ: "Caeterum his haud ineptam responsionem adhibebit quispiam, quae ex evangelio et Paulo nunc deprompta sunt, non esse praeceptoria dicta sed consilium tantum exprimentia, quod amplecti aut praetermittere cuique liberum sit."

[34]Clichtove also allows (f. 34ᵛ) that Christ's telling Peter to put up his sword (John 18:11) should not be used as an argument against a "defensio moderata" of one's own person. In the *Bellum,* just before the new insertion, Erasmus disposes of this text, and denounces as impious and ignorant the interpretation of Luke 22:36 ("he that hath no sword let him sell his garment and buy one") as justifying a "moderata defensio" (*Bellum* 70, 787–90).

[35]Stepped up from *Querela* 635A; "Immo iam eo prope rediit res, ut stultum et impium sit adversus bellum hiscere."

Sorbonne against Berquin, and against himself through Berquin, then going on. He may have been aware that it was to Clichtove that the examination of Berquin's translations had been entrusted.[36] The second clause recalls the kind of concession to the defenders of war that Clichtove was willing to make, and "orthodox doctor" (and censor) is of course what he was. Erasmus' feeling against him was, understandably, rising at this time.[37] Yet surely Clichtove's rightful place is in the last clause with Erasmus himself; a way out is left for him in accordance with the conciliatory attitude usually assumed by Erasmus toward the canon of Chartres.

Claude Colet

L'Oraison de Mars aux dames de la Court, ensemble la Responce des Dames à Mars, par Claude Colet Champanoys. Plus l'Epistre de L'Amoureux de vertu aux Dames de France fugitives pour les guerres. A Paris, chez Chrestien Wechel, 1544. Avec privilège. 4°, 64 pp. [B.N. Rés. p.Ye. 390].

Second edition, augmented by Colet's *Epigrammes*, etc., Paris, Wechel, 1548; 8°, 144 pp. [B.N. Rés. x. 2537].

A conspicuous part of the propaganda for peace in the sixteenth century in France is in the form of poems, either "remonstrances" in the absence of peace or "réjouissances" on the occasions of its fleeting return. Such poems were commonly published as separate pamphlets, as in the present case of Colet's *Oraison de Mars*, published to celebrate the Peace of Crépy. The influence of Erasmus,

[36]E. V. Telle, *op. cit.*, p. 332. Berquin's translations were seized on March 7, 1525 and were considered by the faculty on May 20 (the *Querela Pacis* separately on June 1). Erasmus was kept informed of the proceedings both by Noel Beda and by Berquin. The latter was arrested in January 1526, and his translations were finally condemned on March 12. Though unique copies of the other translations survive in the library of the University of Geneva, no copy of the French *Querela Pacis* is known to exist, if indeed the book was printed [see bracketed addition at end of this essay]. Erasmus relates an anecdote of its good effect on a French bishop to whom Berquin had given it: from an enemy of Erasmus he was turned into a friend (*Opus Epist.* VIII, 213).

[37]In a letter of December 24, 1525 to Nicholas Everard (*Epist.* 1653), finally convinced that Clichtove had covertly attacked him in the *Antilutherus*, he calls all Clichtove's writings "begutarrii libri" ("bigoted"), and includes Clichtove among the "nebulones" whom Luther had armed against him. Clichtove openly criticized Erasmus in his *Propugnaculum Ecclesiae* of May 1526, and was answered in an *Appendix de scriptis Clithovei* published in August (LB IX, 811); Allen, *Opus Epist.* IX, 160 n.; Telle, *op. cit.*, p. 334.

as we have said, is traceable in many of these poems; what brings Colet's work before us here is the peculiarity that considerable portions of the second of the two poems it consists of, the *Responce des Dames à Mars,* are simply verse-paraphrases from the *Bellum* and the *Querela.*[38]

The first poem indeed, the *Oraison de Mars,* may be taken as an example of the "influence" of Erasmus. The god of war pleads his own case in a rather straightforward manner, without the irony of, for example, Jean Molinet's ever-popular *Testament de la Guerre.* War or dissidence, he asserts, is a universal principle; nation differs from nation, the arts contend one with another, even individual men are divided within themselves, the planets have different orbits, the elements are mutually hostile, spirit and flesh are at variance. These are Erasmian topics in reverse.[39] Mars continues on his own: the greatest honors are reserved for military heroes; it is not war, but God, who advances or retards the day of a man's death; not death therefore, but only the glory attending it, is attributable to war. The *Oraison* is not meant to be very convincing, and is only a prelude to the much longer *Responce.*

After some introductory lines, the first argument of the *Responce des Dames* begins as follows (pp. 27–30):

> Premierement, contemplant la nature
> Du corps humain, de toute creature,
> On trouvera que Dieu divinement
> L'homme créa avec entendement,
> Prest à pourvoyr au salut de chacun,
> Non pas pour nuyre ou mal faire à quelqu'un.
> Cela est cler par la grand' difference
> Des animaulx, qui sont en leur naissance
> D'armes munis, les Lions furieux,

[38]Claude Colet was a native of Rumilly in Champagne, and served in Paris as maître d'hôtel to the Marquise de Nesle. His poem, which had been in preparation for some time, is dedicated in a prose epistle to Charles de Hautecourt, seigneur de Richeville, as to a personal friend. Besides this work, he published several translations, including the ninth book of *Amadis de Gaule* (1553).

[39]Nation differs from nation (cf. *Querela* 638D); the arts contend (*ibid* 628D); individuals are at variance within (*ibid.* 629D); heavenly bodies, elements, body and soul are harmonies of opposites (*ibid.* 626B–C). Mars represents himself as born of Justice, but says that when Justice fled from earth he was left behind to be nursed by Folly. The notion of having him pronounce his own eulogy may have been suggested by the *Moriae encomium* rather than the *Querela Pacis.*

Tigres legers, Regnarts industrieux,
Ours despiteux, decepvans Crocodilles,
Loups affamés, Elephans mal habilles. . . .
L'homme n'est pas de sa nature ainsi:
Car le grand Dieu, comme il est trescongnu,
Des animaulx l'homme seul créa nud,
Et qui de soy ne peult faire un seul pas,
Et ne congnoist ny peult prendre repas. . . .
    Par ce propos, ô Mars, tu peuls entendre,
Que Dieu créa l'homme imbecille et tendre
A ce semblance et divine figure,
Pour faire bien à toute créature:
Ce qu'ont congnu les bestes brustes mesmes,
Qui se voyans estre en perils extrêmes,
Et ne pouvans plus trouver subterfuge,
Ont accouru à l'homme pour refuge.

This passage (sixty-four lines without the omissions) will be recognized as a verse-paraphrase of the "portrait of man" which forms the first striking development of the *Bellum:*

> Primum igitur, si quis habitum modo figuramque corporis humani consideret, an non protinus intellecturus est naturam, vel potius Deum, animal hoc non bello, sed amicitiae, non exitio, sed saluti, non iniuriae, sed beneficentiae genuisse? Nam ceterorum animantium unumquodque suis instruxit armis: taurorum impetus armavit cornibus, leonum rabiem unguibus . . . elephantos, . . . crocodilum. . . . Solum hominem nudum produxit. . . . Nec fari novit, nec ingredi, nec cibum capere. . . . Proinde Deus in hoc mundo velut simulacrum quoddam sui constituit hominem, ut ceu terrenum quoddam numen saluti prospiceret omnium. Sentiunt hoc ipsa etiam bruta, cum videamus non mitia solum, verum etiam pardos et leones . . . in magnis periculis ad hominis opem confugere.[40]

The second argument of the *Responce des Dames à Mars* is to the effect that the whole doctrine of Christ favors peace and is opposed to war (pp. 30–33):

Et s'il nous fault prendre la loy divine,
Nous trouverons que toute la doctrine

---

[40]Ed. Latomus, 20, 52–24, 115. At one point Colet slightly alters the original order; he omits 94–98 on the liberal arts, and gives 99–108 before 89–94 (Colet, p. 29).

> De Jesu Christ n'exhorte qu'à pitié,
> A charité, à paix et amitié. . . .
>   Salomon Roy de tout le peuple Hebrieu,
> Representant la figure de Dieu,
> Non sans raison feit construire le temple, . . .
> Car Salomon en langage Hebraïc
> Nous signifie un homme pacific. . . .
>   Voy un petit comment sainct Pol met peine
> A collauder ceste Paix tant humaine, . . .
> Sainct Jehan, sainct Pierre, et ceulx qui ont escript
> Tant sainctement des faictz de Iesu Christ,
> Ne proposoyent en praedication
> Que charité, paix et dilection.

Colet has here gathered passages from a later page of the *Bellum:* 'Universam illius doctrinam excute: nihil usquam reperies quod non spiret pacem, quod non sonet amicitiam. . . . Quid undique sonant omnes Pauli litterae, nisi pacem . . . ? Quid Ioannes loquitur . . .? Quid aliud Petrus?'[41] and: "Christi typum habebat Salomon, quod Hebraeis pacificum sonat: ab hoc sibi templum exstrui voluit."[42] But with these passages he mingles others derived from the *Querela Pacis*,[43] and it is with the *Querela* that he continues (pp. 33–34):

>   Escoute un peu ce que dit Isaye. . . .
> Il nous promet un Roy doulx et clement,
> Non un tyrant, non un triumphateur,
> Non un Satrape. . . .
> Mesmes alors que sa mort approchoit,
> Pour son dernier mandement ou edict,
> En enseignant ses Apostres, leur dit,
> Entr' aymez vous.

Compare *Querela* 629D: "Egregius ille vates Esaias cum coelesti afflatus spiritu Christum illum rerum omnium conciliatorem venturum annuntiaret, num Satrapam pollicetur? . . . num triumphatorem? Nequaquam. Quid igitur? Principem pacis. . . . [630E]

[41] 54, 547–66.
[42] 52, 537–39.
[43] E.g., p. 31: "David aussi parlant du redempteur/ . . . Disoit son siege estre mis en la tente/ . . . de la Paix" seems to be from *Querela* 629E rather than from *Bellum* 54, 545.

Vide quanta sollicitudine commendet moriturus: Diligatis, inquit, invicem."

Colet now enters upon a long description of the benefits of peace (pp. 35–38) and the horrors of war (pp. 39–43), and elaborates on the hardships of a soldier's life (pp. 44–47). These standard topics are of course treated by Erasmus in the *Bellum,* and most of Colet's details come from this source, though not taken in Erasmus' order.[44] The next development, a contrast between the Ten Commandments and the demands of Mars (pp. 48–53), is Erasmian in manner but not in content.[45] The poem ends with a wish to ban Mars from France, and a long appeal to rulers to consider the misery of their peoples and make perpetual peace (pp. 54–57).

To summarize roughly the dependence of Colet's *Responce* on Erasmus: the first four pages of the argument are a verse-translation from the *Bellum;* the next five pages render passages of the *Bellum* and the *Querela,* but not consecutively; the next thirteen pages contain numerous details from Erasmus; the last ten pages do not depend textually on Erasmus though written in his spirit. There is thus a gradual divergence from the text of Erasmus. Colet may have set out to paraphrase the entire *Bellum,* only to find such a procedure too confining, and he may have finished the poem hurriedly to meet the date of the Peace of Crépy.[46] At all events, about two-thirds of this poem of 815 lines is in varying degrees dependent on Erasmus.

Note. Erasmus' contrast between the animals born fully equipped for fighting and man born naked is one of the great commonplaces of ancient literature (Erasmus chiefly follows the preface to book 7 of Pliny's *Natural History*); but nowhere is it employed as Erasmus employs it, to point the moral that man is therefore intended to be peaceful.[47] Since this is Erasmus' peculiar contribution to the *topos,* the few places in other writers where it appears in this form are

[44]*Bellum,* ed. Latomus, pp. 24, 44–50, 66. For example, Colet, p. 39: "Par toy [War] lon voit maintes villes construictes / Depuis mil ans, en un moment destruictes." Cf. *Bellum,* 46, 423: "Tot saeculis exstructae florentissimae civitates una procella subvertuntur."

[45]In *Querela* 635D–E, Erasmus similarly goes through the Lord's Prayer, contrasting the demands of war with each phrase. The vices enumerated in Colet's contrast recall *Querela* 639C–D.

[46]In the dedicatory epistle (dated Paris, September 16, 1544), he recalls that Hautecourt had seen the unfinished *Responce* some time before, but says that he had felt incapable of finishing it until prompted by recent events.

[47]On the contrary, the conventional answer is that man is the best fighter of all,

necessarily due to his influence. After Colet, it is used in peace poems by J.-A. de Baïf in his poem *Sur la Paix avec les Anglois* (1550), by Ronsard in his *Exhortation pour la Paix* (1558), and by Pierre de Brach in an *Ode de la Paix* (1576). Baïf may have taken the topic from Colet, but his version is too colorless to make his source certain; Ronsard may have remembered Baïf's poem, but he seems to have consulted Erasmus directly; De Brach clearly echoes both Ronsard and Erasmus.[48]

Guillaume Aubert

Oraison de la Paix, et les moyens de l'entretenir: et qu'il n'y a aucune raison suffisante pour faire prendre les armes aux Princes Chrestiens, les uns contre les autres. Aux tresmagnanimes & trespuissants Henry, & Philippes Roys de France, & d'Espaigne, Par G. Aubert de Poictiers, Advocat en la court de Parlement de Paris. A Paris, par Benoist Prevost.... Avec privilège, 1559. 8⁰, 22 ff. Privilège dated 10 May 1559. [B.N. Lb³¹.93.]

Guillaume Aubert (c. 1534–c. 1601) is known to literary history as an associate of the Pléiade and as the editor of the first collective

---

since he possesses reason and can forge and use all weapons. Colet gives Mars this argument in the *Oraison* (pp. 15-16):

> N'a pas donné dame Nature aux bestes
> Ongles et dents et cornes en leur testes? . . .
> Et si lon dict qu'il est assez congnu,
> Qu'elle voùlut créer l'homme tout nud,
> Pour demonstrer qu'il est plus ordonné
> A chercher paix, que pour la guerre né,
> Je vous respond qu'icy divinement
> L'homme en esprit garni de jugement . . .
> N'a eu bezoign d'estre armé par Nature,
> Car il pourra de luy mesme choisir,
> Et se forger les armes à plaisir.

[48]Ronsard (*Œuv.*, éd. crit., IX, 21) seems to translate part of a sentence of Erasmus: "Ah malheureux humains, ne scauriez vous congnoistre / Que la nature, helas, ne nous a point fait naistre / Pour quereller ainsi"; Erasmus: "An non protinus intellecturus est naturam . . . animal hoc non bello . . . genuisse." De Brach (*Poèmes* [1576], f. 105ʳ) echoes Ronsard, e.g., in "Mais nous, miserables hommes, . . . / Vestus d'une tendre peau, / Par où la vie est blessée, / Estant seulement percée / De la pointe d'un couteau"; cf. Ronsard, *loc. cit.*: "Mais vous, humains, à qui, d'un seul petit couteau / Ou d'une esguille fresle, on perseroit la peau." But De Brach goes on to include points from Erasmus that are not in Ronsard; e.g., "Nous qui portons au visage / Portraicte la sainte image / D'un Dieu qui n'aime que paix"; Erasmus, *Bellum* 22, 109: "Deus in hoc mundo velut simulacrum quoddam sui constituit hominem."

edition of the poems of Du Bellay (1569). He contributed to the *Tumulus* of Jean Brinon (1554), and, with Ronsard, Baïf, and Nicot, is one of the speakers in the philosophical *Dialogues* (1557) of Guy de Bruès, where with Baïf he takes the skeptical point of view. While pursuing a legal career in Paris, he also aspired to employment at court, and is said to have been presented to Henri II precisely in the winter or spring of 1559 when his *Oraison* appeared. The occasion of the speech, which may have been delivered orally, was the treaty of Cateau-Cambrésis signed at the end of March. In publishing it, Aubert joined his friends (Ronsard, *La Paix, au Roy;* Belleau, *Chant pastoral de la Paix;* etc.) in swelling the unprecedented torrent of literary acclaim that greeted this settlement. If Aubert hoped that his oration would further his chances of preferment, these hopes were no doubt cut short by the death of the king in July; it was not until 1588 that he received a royal appointment.[49]

In the *Oraison de la Paix,* the author's stated purpose is to inquire how the peace concluded at Cateau-Cambrésis may be made permanent. He does indeed make some proposals to this end, but for the most part the speech deals with the iniquity of war, and large parts of it are either translated from the *Bellum* of Erasmus or otherwise dependent on it. We may note the details of this dependence in following an outline of the *Oraison:* (1) introduction stating the occasion and the purpose of the speech; (2) proof that war is contrary to nature and to the will of God; (3) the causes of war in the ambition of kings, their greed, craving for glory, and wish to recover lands they have lost; (4) two laws that would put an end to war; (5) conclusion.

1. After presenting his qualifications, as a lawyer, to deal with international affairs, and congratulating the kings on the recent settlement, Aubert introduces his argument with a confession that his matter is borrowed: "Et pensez que . . . ce n'est point moy qui parle à vous, mais bien sont-ce les plus renommés auteurs des langues estrangeres, qui se servent seulement de moy comme d'un truchement pour vous faire entendre ce dont ils ont assez de fois

---

[49]On Aubert see G. Fagniez in the *Mémoires de la société de l'histoire de Paris* xxxvi (1909) 47–56; for his rather numerous publications, divided between literature and law, see also Niceron, *Mém.* xxxv, 264. Cf. Bruès, *Dialogues,* Panos Paul Morphos, ed. (Baltimore, 1953).

adverti plusieurs autres princes et grands monarques de la terre"
(f. 7ᵛ).

2. The first four pages (ff. 8ʳ-9ᵛ) of the proof that war is contrary to nature are translated from Erasmus' *Bellum:* "Pour donc
commencer, ie vous supplie, Roys magnanimes, contempler à par
vous comme la nature a faict naistre l'homme en ce monde, et si elle
l'a produit pour faire la guerre à son pareil. Luy a elle baillé des
cornes furieuses comme aux taureaux? (f. 8ʳ) . . . Oultre toutes ces
choses, la bonne et sage nature a donné à l'homme le ris pour tes-
moigner sa ioye, et les larmes pour montrer la misericorde" (f. 8ᵛ).
[*Bellum* 20, 52: "Primum igitur, si quis habitum . . . corporis
humani consideret, an non protinus intellecturus est naturam . . .
animal hoc non bello sed amicitiae . . . genuisse? . . . Taurorum
impetus armavit cornibus." *Bellum* 22, 81: 'Uni risum attribuit,
alacritatis indicium. Uni lacrymas, clementiae et misericordiae
symbolum."] Aubert here omits Erasmus' further elaboration of
this point (*Bellum* 22, 85 fifi 24, 115); paraphrases the description of war (*Bellum* 24, 116-130); and reproduces in full the
speech of outraged Nature: "Que eust elle dit, la bonne mere nature voyant ce triste spectacle devant ses yeux? Eust elle pas usé à
tresbon droict de telles ou semblables parolles? 'Quels monstres,
quels fantausmes . . .?' (f. 9ʳ) . . . Certainement la sage et prudente
Architecte des choses, Nature, eust lors usé de telles ou sembables
menaces' (f. 9ᵛ). [*Bellum* 30, 210: "An non merito huiusmodi verbis
sit exsecratura facinus impium? Quod novum spectaculum ego
video?" *Bellum* 32, 235: "Haec atque id genus alia premulta diceret,
opinor, architectrix illa rerum Natura."][50]

Aubert concludes this part of his oration with a lively passage (ff.
10ᵛ-11ᵛ) in which he imagines a converted savage from La France
Antarctique (Brazil) being sent to France by the navigator
Villegaignon and arriving at Amiens when the armies were facing
each other there just before the conference of Cateau. Would not
such a visitor from another world be astonished at the conduct of
supposed Christians? "Sont-ce là les Chrestiens desquels
Villegaignon m'avoit parlé avecques tant de louanges dans les sol-

---

[50]Aubert continues (f. 10ʳ-10ᵛ) to demonstrate the peace of nature with the
example of the elements and the stars. This commonplace is not found in Erasmus'
Bellum, but is in the *Querela Pacis* 626ʙ-ᴄ, which Aubert probably follows (cf.
Clichtove, ch. 2).

itudes de mon pais?"[51] This Brazilian and his reactions are evidently a genial substitute for Erasmus' stranger from another world—from the lunar world of "Empedocles" or one of the innumerable worlds of Democritus: "an non ubivis potius iudicabit habitare Christianos quam in hisce regionibus . . .?" (*Bellum* 56, 584—58, 611).

3. Aubert's discovery of the causes of war in the vices of rulers is also obviously inspired by the *Bellum,* and many passages are direct translations, but since he does not here follow Erasmus' order, it would be tedious and serve no purpose to pick out the Erasmian sentences. One example may suffice (f. 13^r): "car les plus aspres malheurs de la guerre tombent ordinairement sur ceux qui les ont moins merités, comme sur les laboureurs, sur leurs femmes, sur leurs enfants. . . . Mais le proffit qui en peut advenir, c'est à dire la proye, les rapines, et les larcins, tombent en la gueule de ceux qui sont les plus prompts à piller, et mieux exercités à volleries et brigandages, faisants quelques-fois durer la guerre tout à leur escient, par ce qu'ils n'esperent trouver meilleur rencontre, sinon alors qu'ils voyent la Republique embrouillé de seditions, courir fortune, et en danger de faire un malheureux naufrage." [*Bellum* 76, 861–869: ". . . hic maxima pars malorum in eos redundat qui minime digni sunt malo, nempe ad agricolas, ad senes, ad matronas. . . . Ceterum, si ex re omnium pessima quicquam omnino commodi potest colligi, id totum ad sceleratissimos aliquot latrones derivatur, . . . et quibuscum nunquam melius agitur quam in summo reipublicae naufragio."]

4, 5. The two "laws" proposed by Aubert (f. 20^r) for ending war are: (1) that any two monarchs who have a grievance against each other should submit their case to a board of their own choosing, to consist of other princes, great noblemen, and men of learning; and (2) if either rejects the findings of the board and mobilizes his army, he is to be outlawed and driven from his throne by an alliance of all other Christian princes. These two laws are not Erasmian, though Erasmus does advocate arbitration in *Bellum* 84, 959. But when Aubert goes on (f. 20^v) to encourage the kings to fight just one war, the war against their own vices, he is again translating from the *Bellum* (68, 763 ff.). His conclusion, that the kings should

---

[51] Aubert clearly had been reading André Thevet's famous book, *Les Singularitez de la France antarctique,* which had recently appeared (1557), and which was highly esteemed by Ronsard and his friends.

join in a crusade against the Turks is again unerasmian, though Erasmus does not altogether forbid it.[52]

"Les Louanges et Recommandations de la Paix"

Les Louanges & Recommandations de la Paix, extraictes de l'escriture saincte. Plus est monstré que cest chose fort deshonneste, que les Chrestiens ayent guerre ensemble. Avec une Suasion à faire la Paix, au regard du grand trauail qu'il faut souffrir à mener la guerre, & des grans fraiz qu'il y faut faire. A Lyon, par Iean Saugrain, 1563. 8°, 8 ff. n.num., sig. A–B[4]. [B.N.Lb[33].96.]

A second edition is listed by Baudrier, *Bibliographie lyonnaise* III, 256, as published by Benoît Rigaud, Lyons, 1568. [Copies at Aix and Besançon.]

This anonymous pamphlet is made up of four sections, all translated from the *Dulce bellum inexpertis*. The first section (sig. Aii–Aiii[v]), with the heading *Les Louanges . . . extraictes de l'escriture saincte*, is from *Bellum* 52, 532 to 54, 572, where Erasmus shows that war is contrary to the teaching of Christ; the translator justifies his title by placing the biblical references in the margin. The second section, *Que cest chose fort deshonneste . . .* (sig. Aiii[v]–Aiv) is from *Bellum* 52, 515–535: Christians being more than brothers, war between them is worse than fratricidal. The third section (sig. Aiv–Bii), *Suasion à faire la paix*, etc., is from *Bellum* 48, 481—50, 514, on the hardships of a soldier's life and on the cost of war. The fourth section (sig. Bii–Biv), not mentioned on the title page, has the caption: *Que plusieurs Chrestiens au fait de guerre sont pires qu'infidelles & payens*, and this fairly describes the contents of *Bellum* 64, 712—68, 760, which is here translated. In all, these selections present little more than a ninth part of the *Bellum* (140 lines out of 1228).

The first sentences of the booklet follow, together with the original Latin (*Bellum* 52, 532-539):

Jesus Christ salue les siens avec le bienheureux salut de paix: laquelle il leur a donnée et laissée, comme un don trespecial. En ses sacrées

---

[52]A Latin translation of Aubert's *Oraison* was published in the next year by a young Finnish student in Paris, Martinus Helsingus: *Oratio de pace deque eam rationibus retinendi . . . gallicè conscripta & habita a G. Auberto . . . in Latinum vero idioma nuper a Martino Helsingo tralata* (Paris: F. Morel, 1560) [B.N.Lb[31].94]. It is dedicated to John, duke of Finland. The translator was apparently unaware that much of what

prieres là, qu'il a faictes à Dieu son pere, il le requiert fort entre autres choses, que les siens (c'est à dire les Chrestiens) soyent un avec luy, ainsi qu'il est un avec son pere. Desia en cecy tu entens une chose encor' plus grande que Paix, qu'amitié, ne que concorde. Salomon qui signifie en Hebrieu pacifique, estoit la figure de Iesus Christ: par iceluy Roy Dieu a voulu que son temple fust edifié.

Felici pacis omine [Christus] salutat suos; discipulis praeter pacem nihil donat, praeter pacem nihil relinquit. In sacris illis precibus illud praecipue Patrem orat ut, quemadmodum ipse idem erat cum eo, ita et sui, hoc est Christiani, idem essent secum. Iam plus audis quam pacem, plus quam amicitiam, plus quam concordiam. Christi typum habebat Salomon, quod Hebraeis pacificum sonat; ab hoc sibi templum exstrui voluit.

Charles Sevin

Complainte de la Paix dechassee et bannie pour le Iourd'huy hors du Royaume de France, auquel elle souloit faire seur repos & gracieuse demourance, recueillie de plusieurs aucteurs. Par M. Charles Seuin, Chanoine d'Agen. Adressee à Iuges equitables & non suspectz. A Paris, chez Claude Frémy, 1570. Avec privilège. 8°, 52 ff. [B.N.Lb³³.421.]

Charles Sevin, a native of Orléans and canon of the cathedral church of St. Etienne at Agen, was an intimate friend of Julius Caesar Scaliger, also of Agen, eight of whose published letters are addressed to him. Sevin edited the first collection of Scaliger's letters in 1555. Other literary friends were Salmon Macrin, Charles Fontaine, and Jean Dampierre. Sevin died in 1575, perhaps about the age of sixty-five or seventy, since Scaliger addresses a letter to him as early as 1529. His two published works—the *Complainte*, with which we are concerned, and *Sermons, ou Exhortations au peuple chrétien et catholique*, 1569 (2d ed., 1575)—belong therefore to his old age, and both were evidently inspired by his concern over the civil wars.[53]

---

he was translating from the French already existed in Latin in Erasmus' original—e.g., f. 16ʳ: "siquidem usu saepissime venit, ut maiora belli incommoda in eos cadant, qui minus ea promeruerunt," etc. (cf. the original, above).

[53]La Croix du Maine, *Bibl. fr.*, Rigoley de Juvigny, ed. I, 117; Du Verdier, *Bibl. fr.* I, 309; Jules Andrieu, *Histoire de l'Agenais* (Paris-Agen, 1893), I, 230, n. 1, with a reference to the following publication which I have not seen: *Un Cantique inédit de Charles de Sevin d'Orléans*, Tamizey de Larroque, ed. (Auch, 1878).

Sevin's *Complainte de la Paix* is an adaptation of Erasmus' *Querela Pacis*, but an adaptation that follows the original so faithfully from beginning to end that one is tempted to call it the first French translation we have, since that of Berquin was suppressed, or rather the only extant French translation before that of Mme Bagdat in 1924. Sevin, to be sure, pretends that the book is wholly his own. The name of Erasmus nowhere appears; in the title, the words "recueillie de plusieurs aucteurs" are a mild deception, or a deceptive confession; and at the end (f. 49^v) the text is signed: "Prononcée ce 22 Juin 1569. C.S."

The object of the adaptation is to make the *Querela Pacis* pertinent to the civil wars of France in 1569—an object not difficult to attain since the *Querela* is so general in character as to be applicable to any of the wars of the sixteenth century. Throughout, Sevin alters "mortales" and the like expressions to "François"; he makes the *Querela* a trifle more dramatic by inserting the address "Messieurs" or "Messieurs les juges" more often than the original calls upon "Christian princes"; he inserts some sentences bearing directly on the religious wars, and occasionally enlarges on Erasmus' thought when it seems especially pertinent; on the other hand, he omits or adapts some sentences in which Erasmus deals severely with the religious orders (though most of what is said against the clergy is retained) and also passages referring to persons of Erasmus' time such as Julius II and Henry VIII. Yet by and large the *Querela* was relevant as it stood, and for pages at a stretch Sevin is content merely to translate. Between omissions and enlargements, the *Complainte* fills about the number of pages that one would expect in a French translation of the *Querela*.[54]

Sevin's method is fairly represented by the opening sentences of the book. In the *Querela*, Peace begins her harangue as follows:

Si me, licet immerentem, suo tamen commodo sic aversarentur, eicerent, profligarentque mortales, meam modo iniuriam et illorum iniquitatem deplorarem: nunc cum me profligata protinus fontem omnis humanae felicitatis ipsi a semet arceant, omniumque calamitatum pelagus sibi accersant, magis illorum mihi deflenda est infelicitas quam mea iniuria.

[54]The *Complainte* runs to roughly 22,000 words, Mme Bagdat's translation of the *Querela* to roughly 20,000.

Sevin alters "mortales" to "la France," and makes some insertions, here indicated by italics:

Si *la France* me reiectoit & bannissoit pour quelque sien prouffit & utilité (combien que seroit à tort & sans l'avoir merité) ie ne ferois autre chose pour le present, que deplorer le tort & l'iniure qu'elle me feroit, pour demonstrer sa follie & combien elle est mal advisée. *Mais ayant puys n'agueres delaissé & abandonné tous autres Royaumes & pays, pour venir me recreer & soulager avec elle quelque temps & prendre quelque soulas & repos:* Moy (dis-ie) qui suis la source & fontaine de tout bien, de tout plaisir & felicité humaine, voyant qu'elle me dechasse *par tous endroicts de ce Royaume, & de sa compagnie avec armes & violence:* Considerant aussi que en me dechassant, elle se provoque un abisme de miseres & calamitez: I'ay à present plus grande occasion de deplorer son malheur & son infortune que mon iniure.

Yet though ready to expand or paraphrase wherever he deems it desirable, Sevin for page after page, as we have said, has only to translate the text before him. An example is the following passage on mutual aid as a law of nature:[55]

Eoque tum corporum, tum animorum dotes ita [Natura] partita est, ut nemo sit omnium tam instructus, quin infimorum etiam officio nonnunquam adiuvetur; nec eadem attribuit omnibus nec paria, ut haec inaequalitas mutuis amicitiis aequaretur. Aliis in regionibus alia proveniunt, quo vel usus ipse mutua doceret commercia. Ceteris animantibus sua tribuit arma praesidiaque, quibus sese tuerentur; unum hominem produxit inermem atque imbecillum, nec prorsus aliter tutum, quam foedere mutuaque necessitudine.

Car nul seul ne fut iamais si doué de noblesse d'esprit, ou de corps, qu'il n'ait eu besoin d'estre soulagé et aydé de son inferieur. Pource que iamais nature n'a donné à un seul, tout: ne mesmes graces semblables. Afin que ceste inequalité devint et fust faicte presque semblable, par support mutuel et communication frequente de mutuel service. Exemple. Une region, un pais, est copieux et abondant de ce qui defaut en un autre. Afin que l'usage mesme monstrast aux hommes commutation et eschangement de marchandise, pour soulager l'un l'autre. Nature a donné armes aux bestes pour se deffendre, et conservation de leur vie. Mais elle a produit l'homme seul tout nud, sans armes et sans deffense, et mesmes tout imbecille: Afin qu'il se sentist et congnust ne pouvoir estre autrement asseuré que par alliance et amytié mutuelle.

[55] *Querela* 627D; *Complainte*, f. 7^r.

Where Sevin feels called upon to modify the text of Erasmus, his governing principle is the adaptation of the sentiments to present circumstances. Sometimes he interpolates a short sentence in an appropriate context. Thus where Erasmus speaks of the strength that comes from union and concord, Sevin adds: "Les Rheistres ne fussent iamais venus manger nostre pain, ne boire noz vins, s'ilz nous eussent veu d'accord et vivre en paix."[56] Allusion to the German mercenaries suits Erasmus' point and brings it up to date. In other cases he is obliged to resort to a degree of ingenuity. An instance is his treatment of a notable passage in which Erasmus launches into the praise of France as the most prosperous, best governed, and most Christian nation in Europe: the other Christian powers should rejoice in her good fortune, but instead they give way to envy and greed and conspire to ruin her:

> Si Christiani corporis unius membra sunt, cur non gratulatur quisque alienae felicitati? . . . Etenim, si verum fateri volumnus, quid aliud commovit, et hodie commovet, tam multos ad armis lacessendum Franciae regnum, nisi quod est unum omnium florentissimum? Nullum latius patet, nusquam Senatus augustior, nusquam Academia celebrior, nusquam concordia maior. . . . O rem monstrosam! parum consultum putant Reip. Christianae, nisi pulcherrimam ac felicissimam ditionis Christianae partem subverterint.[57]

Sevin, whose wish is not to praise but to shame the France of his day, turns the passage to his purpose on the key of *autrefois:*

> Si les François sont tous d'un Royaume, d'une mesme nation, d'un commun langage, que ne soulagent ils mutuellement le Royaume de France, sans ainsi le mutiler, destruire, et mettre en proye? Ce Royaume n'a il esté autrefois le plus pacifique, . . . le plus riche et opulent de toute la Chrestienté? Trouvera lon aux Royaumes, Parlements plus sains? . . . Se trouvera il aux autres Royaumes, Universitez . . . plus fameuses? . . . Ce sont les François mesmes qui ont infecté la Religion et la ieunesse.[58]

The *Querela* is the more easily adaptable to Sevin's purpose since Erasmus treats the wars among European nations as civil wars within the Christian republic. That religion therefore plays a large

---

[56]*Querela* 641A; *Complainte*, f. 46ʳ.
[57]*Querela* 633E–F.
[58]*Complainte*, f. 25ᵛ.

part in the argument is also to Sevin's purpose, but this aspect of the *Querela* might be expected to require careful handling by the canon of Agen. Certainly he softens many of Erasmus' more provocative expressions, but on the whole he retains most of the impact of Erasmus' criticism of ecclesiastics. Whether we interrogate him on the passages censured by the Sorbonne in Berquin's translation, or on those expunged after Sevin's time by the Index Expurgatorius, it is clear that these passages embarrassed him only to a limited extent. He translates all but one of the passages censured in Berquin.[59] The one he omits is phrased in Erasmus' most startling manner, and is open to a dubious interpretation that Erasmus himself endeavors to forestall; it is not needed for the argument.[60] In another passage, that in which peace fails to find herself at home in the religious orders or even in a single monastery, Sevin extracts the sting from the whole, and leaves out an offensive sentence. Presumably he did not think that the religious houses of his day were as bad as that; yet he keeps enough of the indictment to make the point.[61] The whole passage on the monasteries is expunged in

[59]The ten passages censured in Berquin's translation will be found in Du Plessis d'Argentré, *Collectio judiciorum*, II, 45. One or two of them were rendered offensive only by Berquin's interpolations. Sevin translates (f. 12ʳ) from *Querela* 628F, "que lon nomme communément evesques" (*communément* = *vulgo* expunged also in the later indices); and (f. 12ᵛ) from *Querela* 629A, "Saint Pol défend et se courrouce amèrement de ce que un Chrestien plaide et aye procès contre un autre Chrestien," which in Berquin's version the Sorbonne declared Saint Paul never said (Erasmus had in mind I Cor. 6:7–8).

[60]*Complainte*, f. 22ᵛ. The passage is *Querela* 632B: "Tot hodie sacramentis infundi coelestem spiritum affirmant Theologi. Si verum praedicant, ubi peculiaris spiritus illius effectus, cor unum et anima una? Sin fabulae sunt, cur tantum honoris hisce rebus defertur? Atque haec sane dixerim, quo magis Christianos suorum morum pudeat, non quo sacramentis aliquid detraham." Berquin's translation, which is exact, drew the following emphatic comment from his censors: "Haec propositio diabolico spiritu in divinorum Sacramentorum contemptum excogitata, in Spiritum Sanctum, qui per Sacramenta datur, blasphemia est et schismatica." The trouble lies in apparently requiring a state of grace, or the indwelling of the Holy Spirit, to be exhibited in moral conduct if the (supernatural) efficacy of the sacraments is to be believed in. Erasmus explains that he only means that Christians *ought* to show this effect. He is on safer ground in a bold expression of similar intent in *Bellum* 98, 1185: "Si fabula est Christus, cur non explodimus ingenue? . . . Sin is vere est *et via, et veritas, et vita*, cur omnes nostrae rationes ab hoc exemplari tantopere dissident?" Here there is no question of the supernatural effect of ritual. The indices, however, found no fault in the former passage.

[61]*Complainte*, f. 12ᵛ, from *Querela* 629B: "Tot factiones sunt, quot sunt sodalitia: Dominicales dissident cum Minoritis . . . Quin idem sodalitium factionibus scinditur. . . . Optabam vel in uno quopiam monasteriolo latitare. . . . Invita dicam . . . nullum adhuc reperi, quod non intestinis odiis ac jurgiis esset infectum." In

the later expurgatorial indices.[62] Other important passages that these indices were to condemn seem not to have troubled Sevin on religious grounds. Thus two substantial omissions were called for by the later indices in Erasmus' long arraignment of the clergy who preach war.[63] Sevin gives both passages pretty faithfully.[64] In the first, two sentences interpolated by him seem intended to reinforce rather than to adulterate the argument.[65] In the second, he omits an obscure historical reference to cardinals created by war, and, less excusably, Erasmus' picture of cross fighting cross on the ban-

---

Sevin, Peace cannot dwell long in the monasteries "à cause d'une infinité de bar-bouilleries et factions," but the trouble is that the orders (not named) scorn the life of others, like the Pharisee scorning the Publican, "et pour dire tout en un mot, chascun se plaist en son habit, en sa profession, *et si magnifie son patron, qui est bonne et saincte chose*" (not in Erasmus); and finally "ie abandonnay promptement *tous telz* cloistres et monasteres" (softening *in uno* and *nullum*). Peace next looks for harmony between married couples, hoping that "inter hos citius contingat locus, quam inter eos qui tot titulis, tot insignibus, tot ceremoniis absolutam charitatem profitentur." This comparison is omitted by Sevin. If correctly reported, Berquin had made a special point of placing marriage above the cloister: "Je n'ai point encore trouvé un seul monastère, qui ne soit infecté de debats et haines intestines. Paix trouveroit plutôt lieu en mariage qu'avec ceux qui par tant de titres, par tant de signes, par tant de cérémonies si vantent d'avoir parfaite charité."

[62]References are to the Spanish and Roman indices as reported in Erasmus' *Opera* LB, x, 1818. Here all is expunged after *forsitan agnoscat aliquis* to *Pudor sit recensere* in *Querela* 629A–C. Erasmus is made to say the opposite of what he really says. He says: "St. Paul thinks it intolerable that Christian should litigate with Christian; but now . . . bishop contends with bishop; but perhaps one might pardon them because they have joined the company of the worldly ever since they began to have the same possessions as they." By omitting "because" etc., the index makes him say only: "But perhaps one might pardon them"! Note that, unlike the Sorbonne, the index found no fault in the citation of St. Paul, but, like the Sorbonne, objected to the reference to the temporal possessions of the clergy. Sevin (f. 12ʳ) is if anything more emphatic than Erasmus in condemning ecclesiastics who contend at law "pour raison de quelque benefice"; he retains the citation from St. Paul; but he renders the last part of the sentence ambiguously: "N'est ce chose indigne à la dignité sacerdotale? Mais (me direz vous) cela est desia tout commun et usité. Il ne s'en faut plus soucier. Or bien donq qu'ilz iouissent hardiment de leurs droits, qui leurs sont desia acquis: comme par longue prescription." ("Verum his quoque forsitan ignoscat aliquis quod longo iam usu propemodum in profanorum consortium abierunt, posteaquam eadem cum illis coeperunt possidere.")

[63]*Querela* 624C–E ("Immo ne . . . ad perniciem") 635B–E ("Iam ipsa castra . . . fratri machinaris").

[64]*Complainte*, f. 28ʳ–29ᵛ.

[65]"La plus part des ministres [Protestant clergy], qui bouttent et inflamment le feu, ce sont moynes reniez, apostatz des quatre ordres mendiennes. Une partie des soldatz mesmes ce sont prestres et gens d'Eglise devenuz bandoliers à toute perdi-tion et licence desbordée." This last is suggested by Erasmus, and the first sentence is probably intended to redress the balance.

ners of opposing armies. These omissions amount to a very few lines; he omits more, as it happens, from the intervening passage which the indices do not condemn, namely a development relating to the wars between France and England and to Pope Julius II. Evidently he thought the English wars and Pope Julius no longer relevant.

Erasmus himself had complained of the interpolations made by Berquin in the latter's translations of his books. Had he seen the interpolations and the omissions made by Sevin, he might not have been altogether pleased; yet after all he might have been content to know that his *Querela* could still be used as a plea for peace in the civil wars of France.

[This article was written in the belief that Louis de Berquin's translation of the *Querela Pacis* was lost. A few years later, however, the existence of a copy in the Houghton Library of Harvard University was announced by the librarian James E. Walsh (*Harvard Library Bulletin* 17, 1 [October 1969]), with notice also of a copy in Brussels; and the translation is now available in the edition of E. V. Telle, *La Complainte de la Paix* (Geneva: Droz, 1978). Berquin's version was probably unknown to Charles Sevin, whose translation differs from it.

For more recent notice of the appearance of other works of Erasmus in France in the sixteenth century, besides the *Dulce Bellum* and the *Querela Pacis,* see Margaret Mann Phillips, "Erasmus in France in the Later Sixteenth Century," *The Journal of the Warburg and Courtauld Institutes,* 34 (1971) 246–61.]

Rhetorical Doctrine and
Some Poems of Ronsard

The ease with which the young Du Bellay could proclaim that "le poète et l'orateur sont comme les deux piliers qui soutiennent l'édifice de chacune Langue"[1] at least betrays the assurance with which the new school of writers, whom he represents, set out to turn French literature into a "humanism in the vernacular" following the similar movement in Italy; for humanism, looking back to Rome, had placed *orationes* and *poemata* (and *epistulae*) in the center of literary instruction and production. Whether the French orators of Du Bellay's time "sustained" the language to any important extent may be doubted, but, while it might be interesting to study the reality against his ideal, we shall leave that for another occasion and seek instead to detain Professor Wichelns, whose own humanism is far from being departmentalized, with a few remarks on some poems in which Du Bellay's colleague Ronsard apparently aims to be at once both *poète* and *orateur*. The subject may even claim a certain novelty, since the presence or absence of rhetorical patterns (we shall have as little as possible to do with style) in Ronsard's poems seems not to have engaged the attention of the critics.[2]

There may be good reason for that. For one thing, Ronsard himself saw his activity as a poet in sharpest contrast to that of the orator in the matter of form. As a poet he gave his allegiance to the doctrine of poetic inspiration, the *furor poeticus* that Renaissance Platonism had brought into new prominence. His art, he insists, is

Reprinted from Donald C. Bryant, ed., *The Rhetorical Idiom: Essays in Rhetoric, Oratory, Language and Drama Presented to Herbert August Wichelns.* Copyright © 1958 by Cornell University.

[1] *La Deffence et illustration de la langue françoyse* 2. 1.
[2] See Paul Laumonier, *Ronsard poète lyrique* (Paris, 1909); Henry Franchet, *Le Poète et son œuvre d'après Ronsard* (Paris, 1923); Robert J. Clements, *Critical Theory and Practice of the Pléiade* (Cambridge, Mass., 1942).

altogether unpremeditated, and the spirit bloweth where it listeth. He says as much again and again; for example, in 1563, in reply to a Calvinist opponent who had ridiculed the "confusion" of his latest poems, he accepts as praise a criticism intended to be injurious:[3]

> Tu te moques aussi dequoy ma poësie
> Ne suit l'art miserable, ains va par fantaisie,
> Et dequoy ma fureur sans ordre se suivant,
> Esparpille ses vers comme fueilles au vent. . . .
> Hà si tu eusses eu les yeux aussi ouvers
> A derober mon art, qu'à derober mes vers,
> Tu dirois que ma Muse est pleine d'artifice,
> Et ma brusque vertu ne te seroit un vice.
> En l'art de Poësie, un art il ne faut pas
> Tel qu'ont les Predicans, qui suivent pas à pas
> Leur sermon sceu par cueur, ou tel qu'il faut en prose,
> Où toujours l'Orateur suit le fil d'une chose.

His poetic "fury" may seem to scatter verses like leaves in the wind, yet there is present an artifice beyond the art of the preacher (especially of the Calvinist preacher, *prédicant*) and of the orator who follows "le fil d'une chose."

Yet the contrast was more obvious and vital for the humanist poet than it may be in a time when poets and orators have moved farther apart. The struggle of Ronsard's early career, from which he emerged as "the prince of French poets," had not been purely literary, to secure the acceptance of a new poetical style, but a matter of ambition also, to make his way at court, and to be recognized as the official *poète du roi*, a title which he had deserved, not by courtly versicles à la Saint-Gelais (though he could write them if need be), but by his elaborate odes addressed to the king and other great persons and touching upon public events. Ronsard had assimilated the ancient view that poets and kings are equally divine and divinely inspired and belong together, and that the role of the

---

[3] *Responce aux injures* in *Œuvres*, éd. crit. by Paul Laumonier (Paris, 1914-), XI, 159-60 (vv. 847-72). Ronsard's verses contain a personal barb, since the critic, Bernard de Montmeia, was a Protestant clergyman, and a personal retort, since he had addressed Ronsard as "jadis poète, et maintenant prebstre." See the relevant passage from his poetical pamphlet quoted by Professor Isidore Silver in "Ronsard's Homeric Imagery" (*Modern Language Quarterly* 16 [1955] 350); e.g., "tes derniers escrits, . . . / Où n'y a nul propos d'ordre s'entre-suivant, / Mais tout y est confus."

royal poet is not merely to praise but also to advise and admonish.[4] He thus occupies ground that the orator might well dispute. The difference, as he says, is in the manner; and it might be illustrated by comparing the delphic obscurity and "brusque vertu" of his *Ode de la Paix* of 1550 with the arrangement of his *Exhortation pour la Paix* of 1558, which we examine below. He avoids the processes of rhetoric by adherence to the rhetorical doctrine of Imitation—by assuming, so far as he knows how, the lyric personality of Horace or Pindar. To be sure, as an excellent critic of his Pindaric odes has remarked, they are often unpindaric precisely in exhibiting an *esprit de suite*.[5] A prose argument ("le fil d'une chose") can be extracted from them by putting aside, with little difficulty, the "veil of fiction." But such matters are relative; this deeply embedded influence of rhetoric upon lyric poetry—if such it be—would long resist the solvent of poetic fury. It is rather a remark of the poet's own that throws us back upon rhetoric. In the Preface to his *Odes* of 1550, he regards these poems, properly enough, as encomia, but uses such language as to suggest that he thinks of encomia in the terms of school rhetoric:[6]

> Outre que ma boutique n'est chargée d'autres drogues que de louanges et d'honneurs, c'est le vrai but d'un poète Liriq de celebrer jusques à l'extremité celui qu'il entreprend de louer. Et s'il ne connoist en lui chose qui soit dinne de grande recommandation, il doit entrer dans sa race, et là chercher quelqu'un de ses aieus, jadis braves et vaillans, ou l'honnorer par le titre de son païs, ou de quelque heureuse fortune survenue soit à lui, soit aus siens, ou par autres vagabondes digressions, industrieusement brouillant ores ceci, ores cela, et par l'un louant l'autre, tellement que tous deus se sentent d'une méme louange.

[4]See Alice Sperduti (Mrs. Robert E. Wilson), "The Divine Nature of Poetry in Antiquity," *Trans. Amer. Philol. Assoc.* 81 (1950) 209-40, and Franchet, ch. 3, "La Gloire." In practice, Ronsard's advice and admonitions do not greatly differ from flattery, since he kept them within the bounds of what he knew would be acceptable; cf. Isidore Silver, *The Pindaric Odes of Ronsard* (Paris, 1937), ch. 4, "Relations with Princes."

[5]Silver, *Pindaric Odes*, p. 21.

[6]*Œuvres*, éd. crit. by Laumonier, I, 48. Ronsard does not, I think, anywhere use the word *encomion*; but his strophic odes in imitation of Pindar, since they are seldom *epinicia* or victory odes, may usually be classed with the general laudatory ode or *encomion* written by Pindar and his contemporaries, though no example (unless *Nemean* 11) survives; so Silver, *Pindaric Odes*, p. 20. It is not, of course, this ancient lyrical *encomion* that the writers on rhetoric have directly in view, but the epideictic prose oration.

This naïve and cynical confession, which must have made the recipients of Ronsard's odes look twice at the poems in their honor, smells strongly of the rhetoric books and is indeed founded on the topics recommended for encomia—family and ancestors, country, and the goods of fortune (note also the technical term *digressions*). In the language of rhetorical instruction, Ronsard is saying that if in the person praised excellences of Mind and Body are insufficient, one must dwell on External Circumstances.[7] Yet no such statement seems to be found in the handbooks, nor is it likely to be there.[8] It may reflect experience; since no doubt the problem was real enough for a Renaissance court poet committed to the laudation of persons who might be more conspicuous for rank than for their own achievements. But the context suggests that, though lapsing into rhetorical terminology, Ronsard's thought remains in the sphere of Imitation and that he may have believed that these shifts represented the practice of his model, Pindar.[9]

As we cast about in Ronsard's extensive literary production for examples of rhetorical form or evidence of a knowledge of rhetori-

[7]Topics of praise are regularly said to be found in "external circumstances and in qualities of body and mind or character"; e.g., *Ad Herennium* III, vi, 10: "Laus igitur potest esse rerum externarum, corporis, animi" (and see Caplan's note, Loeb tr., p. 174); cf. among others Cicero, *De Inventione* II, lix, 174; Quintilian III, vii, 12. Ancestors, country, and the gifts of fortune fall under External Circumstances. The *Progymnasmata*, taking a biographical order, advise beginning with Birth (τὸ γένος), divided into Nation, Country, Ancestors, Parents; and proceeding to Education (ἀνατροφή), and so to Deeds (πράξεις) distributed under Mind, Body, and Fortune (so Aphthonius 8, and cf. Hermogenes 7, Theon 8, and Menander in Spengel-Hammer, *Rhetores graeci* III, 369 ff.). Ronsard brings in Fortune more in the manner of Cicero and the Auctor ad Herennium.

[8]What we find is: If he is of illustrious descent, show that he is worthy of his ancestors, if of humble origin, that he has risen by his own merits (*Ad. Her.* III, vii, 13; the latter possibility is elaborated by Theon 8 *sub fin.*). Obviously Ronsard's formula comes closer to the recipe for censure: If he is of illustrious descent, show that he has been a disgrace to his forebears!

[9]The passage continues: "Telles inventions encores te ferai-je veoir dans mes autres livres, où tu pourras . . . contempler de plus près les saintes conceptions de Pindar, et ses admirables inconstances" (cf. "vagabondes digressions"). That he has Pindar in mind throughout appears to be the assumption of other readers of the Preface; Franchet, p. 127, Silver, *Pindaric Odes*, p. 77. Oddly enough, it is the contrary practice that impressed at least one sixteenth-century critic of Pindar: If the victor's ancestry is faulty, the poet thinks it right to make allusion to such faults when praising him; "si quos maiorum criminibus innocentia probitateque mederi videt, praesentem virtutem sic defendit, ut tamen aculeos domesticae infamiae non eximat. . . . Si alicuius maiores novit iustitiam cum audacia mutavisse, sic untranque non tacet, ut simul vitiorum horrorem cum virtutum facibus inserat" (Ulrich Zwingli, Pref. to Ceporinus' *Pindar* [Basle, 1526], p. 4).

cal doctrine (apart from style), we generally meet with an ambiguity like the one just noticed. Imitation applied to a literary tradition deeply involved in rhetoric may produce rhetorical forms without much consciousness of theory. If on occasion Ronsard thought of his encomiastic odes in terms prescribed for epideictic, did he recognize that in turning from these directly to the writing of Hymns he was still working within the same *genus*? He might have learned from the handbooks that the hymn differs from the encomium only in that hymns are addressed to gods and encomia to men.[10] And in fact, though he is capable of using the word "hymn" very loosely,[11] he gives this title only to poems in which some aspect of divinity is ascribed to the subject. But he stretches this concept pretty far. The *Hymne du treschrestien Roy de France Henry II,* for example, probably qualifies because it turns on the commonplace that the king is on earth what "Jupiter" is in heaven. Doubtless in Ronsard's hymns imitation plays the leading role; in form, they follow the "epic" type of the Homeric Hymns, Callimachus, and perhaps Proclus; and for matter and scope, the *Hymni Naturales* of the neo-Latin poet Marullus. Following Marullus, in a mood descended from the Stoics, the poet sees divinity everywhere—hence the *Hymne du Ciel,* the *Hymne des Astres,* the *Hymne de la Mort,* the *Hymne de l'Or.* Possibly, therefore, we must conclude that it is by coincidence or caprice that he has "hymns" on subjects that the rhetorical handbooks actually propose for encomia: *L'Hymne de la Philosophie; de la Justice; du Printemps; de l'Esté; de l'Autonne; de l'Hyver.*[12] Yet these are not subjects employed by the hymn writers

[10]Aphthonius 8; Theon 8; Hermogenes 7; but the distinction, already familiar to Plato (*Rep.* 607A: ὕμνους θεοῖς καὶ ἐγκώμια τοῖς ἀγαθοῖς), is found everywhere; see H. W. Smyth, *Greek Melic Poets* (London, 1906), pp. lxxvi ff. Menander (Spengel-Hammer, III, 331 ff.) discusses various types of hymns under "epideictic." The traditional relationship presumably justifies Melanchthon in so classing certain Psalms: "Sunt Psalmi quidam generis demonstrativi, qui describunt Christum, hi possunt haberi pro brevibus panegyricis" (*Elementa Rhetorices* in *Opera,* Bretschneider, ed., XIII, col. 449).

[11]In the Preface of 1550 already cited (éd. crit., I, 46), he speaks of Pindar's "hinnes écris à la louange des vainqueurs Olympiens." But the nontechnical usage of antiquity was equally broad; see Smyth, *Melic Poets,* p. xxviii, n. 2.

[12]Cf. Aphthonius 8: "Subjects of encomia are persons and things, seasons and places; ... things, such as Justice and Temperance, seasons, such as Spring and Summer." Aphthonius offers a model "Praise of Wisdom"; Nicolaus a "Praise of Spring," a "Praise of Winter," and a "Censure of Summer" (*Progym.* 8.2,5; 9.1 in Walz, *Rhetores Graeci* I, 331, 335, 341). Compare Melanchthon, col. 450: "Eodem modo res laudantur, ut artes, Philosophia, Eloquentia, ... Pax."

whom he imitates, while justification could be found in the practical equivalence of hymn and encomium. One can hardly say, however, that the *Hymnes* are planned after the formulae given for encomia. There is indeed a proem which, cast in the form of a dedication to a friend or patron, contrives to introduce the subject; but the poet then plunges directly into a series of *praxeis* or *benefacta,* seldom including other topics of laudation, for example, that of "honorable origins." He invariably ends with a prayer addressed to his "deity," and this feature probably results from Imitation—the ancient "epic" hymns regularly so conclude, and likewise those of Marullo—but imitation might here be reinforced by doctrine concerning encomia.[13]

The *blason,* as reconstructed by Ronsard, being the praises of the Frog, the Ant, the Holly-tree, and so forth, again falls within the sphere of the encomium, which extends to "irrational animals and also plants" (Aphthonius 8). As originally popularized by Marot and his school, the *blason* had been little more than a facetious accumulation of epithets, laudatory or the reverse, as in Marot's well-known *Blason du beau tetin* and *Blason du laid tetin.* In a sense a "description," it was, however, allocated to "praise" or "blame," and this essential feature allows Ronsard to transform it into an encomium, or rather a hymn.[14] He replaces the descriptive epithets with a series of the "deeds" and "fortunes" of the subject, includes a narration or "myth," and invariably ends with a prayer or invoca-

---

[13]See below, p. 304. We may compare Ronsard's *Hymne de la Philosophie* (éd. crit., VIII, 85) with the hints for an "Encomium Philosophiae" given by Melanchthon (*loc. cit.*): "Honestas sumitur ex causis efficientibus, videlicet ab inventoribus, ut Philosophia est donum Dei. Sicut enim divinitus oculis lumen contingit, ita menti veritas, sed verum iudicium divinitus donatum est. Utilitas sumitur ex finibus. Philosophia ostendit praesidia vitae, disciplinam de moribus civilibus, leges, medicinam, numeros, mensuras, quae res omnes in hac vita maxime necessaria sunt." Ronsard's hymn, doubtless *as* a hymn, takes a higher line: Philosophy's *honestas* does not depend on her being a *donum Dei,* she seems to exist eternally and is even described as "osant de Dieu la nature espier." The poet confines his praises to *utilitas,* i.e., *praxeis* or *benefacta,* and here touches on some of Melanchthon's topics—e.g., Philosophy "vint mesurer les grands mers fluctueuses" (127), "la terre arpente" (153), "vint revisiter les villes, / et leur donna des polices civiles, / pour les regir par justice et par loix" (167–69), and among others "le medecin" is indebted to her (178).

[14]Some remarks on Ronsard's treatment of the *blason* will be found in Marcel Raymond, *L'Influence de Ronsard* (Paris, 1927), pp. 153 and 169, and in Laumonier, éd. crit. of Ronsard, VI, 136 n., and VIII, xiii. It is possible that the first steps toward the *hymne blason* were taken by Antoine de Baïf.

tion. Occasionally, as is proper to the encomium (cf. Aphthonius), he uses "comparison,"[15] and in the case of the Holly-tree he details its honorable origins. But Ronsard clearly thinks in terms of the hymn; the whole setting is mythological; the Frog is at once hailed as a goddess: "Nous t'estimons une Déesse, / Chère Grenouille," and the Ants are gods: "Bref, vous estes de petits Dieus." It is only somewhere in the background of the *blason* that we can put the tradition of the "sophistic" encomium, represented by Lucian's *Praise of the Housefly*, which had been resumed in the Renaissance and had inspired Erasmus' *Praise of Folly* and Pirckheimer's *Praise of Gout*.

One or two rhetorical patterns turn up in Ronsard as it were by accident. No school exercise (*progymnasma*) was more favored in late antiquity than *ethopoeia*, the invention of a suitable speech for a given character (commonly either legendary or historical) in a given situation and always presented under the heading, "The words so-and-so might utter upon such-and-such an occasion."[16] Ronsard knew this formula and wrote a poem entitled: "Les Paroles que dist Calypson, ou qu'elle devoit dire, voyant partir Ulysse de son Isle."[17] Is this a conscious rhetorical exercise, or has Ronsard merely borrowed the notion from the numerous verse exercises of this type in the Greek Anthology?[18] Similar is the case of several poems with the rhetorical title *Prosopopée*.[19] By this word Ronsard understands direct address on the part of a dead man who appears to him in a dream.[20] This is not incorrect, though *prosopopoeia* is generally defined more widely, and some authorities— for example, Hermogenes and Aphthonius—have the special term

---

[15]The life of the Frog is compared favorably with that of man (éd. crit., VI, 86); the Ant is gifted beyond all other creatures (VI, 96).

[16]E.g., Aphthonius 11: "The words Niobe might utter when her children lay dead"; many examples in Walz, *Rhetores Graeci*, vol. I.

[17]Published in 1573; éd. crit., XV, 48.

[18]*Anthologia Palatina* IX, 449–80; for example, 458 entitled: "The words Ulysses might utter upon landing in Ithaca." However, the length of Ronsard's poem (266 lines) does not suggest an epigrammatic origin, nor on the other hand does there seem to be any thought of Ovid's *Heroides*. The poem may therefore be a conscious rhetorical exercise.

[19]*Prosopopée de Louis de Ronsard*, the poet's father (éd. crit., V, 40); *Prosopopée de feu François de Lorraine* (XII, 249); *Prosopopée de Beaumont levrier du Roy* (XIV, 114). The *Discours à Jacques Grevin* (Blanchemain, VI, 311) is a *prosopopoeia* of J. du Bellay, and probably there are other examples.

[20]In the case of the greyhound Beaumont, who converses with Charon, the term is extended to something like Lucian's *Dialogues of the Dead*.

eidolopoeia for this form.[21] Ronsard, however, if his knowledge here is not merely lexical, is likely to have picked up the notion from neo-Latin poetry, and specifically from Castiglione's *Prosopopoeia Ludovici Miranduli*, which he imitates in his earliest *prosopopée*.

Thus far any traces of rhetorical form in the poems of Ronsard seem chiefly to rest upon poetical imitation, though some consciousness on his part of rhetorical doctrine is perhaps discernible here and there. It is hardly possible that in the course of his humanist education he should have failed to be initiated into its elementary forms. And he could on occasion produce a Latin prose invective or an academic discourse in French.[22] But in general he remained true to his profession of poet; his *Abrégé de l'art poétique* (1563) contains sections "De l'Invention," "De la Disposition," and "De l'Elocution," but these are pointedly framed for the use of the poet and are as far as possible in content from what the rhetorical headings might lead one to expect. If he aims to include a military harangue in a poem, he turns naturally to the poets for a model. In the *Harangue que fit Monseigneur le Duc de Guise aus soudards de Mez* (1553), the speech turns out to be an imitation of the verses of the Greek poet Tyrtaeus animating the Spartans.[23] And five years later, in his *Exhortation au camp du Roy pour bien combattre le jour de la bataille*, it is again the manner, and to some extent the words, of Tyrtaeus that he adopts.[24]

[21]When distinguished from *ethopoeia* (the ascription of direct speech to a person not present), *prosopopoeia* is commonly defined as the ascription of speech to mute "things," as the city, the sea, or to abstractions (Hermogenes, *Progym.* 9; Aphthonius 11); but the terms are interchanged (Theon 10; Zonaeus in Spengel-Hammer, III, 162; anon., *ibid.*, III, 177); while Quintilian, for example, brings all under *prosopopoeia*—persons not present, gods, the dead, cities, and so forth. (*Inst. Or.* IX, ii, 30–37; cf. III, viii, 49–54); see also *Ad Her.* IV, liii, 66, with Caplan's note. Though theoretically only a part of Style, these forms gained special prominence as a separate school exercise, and probably for this reason appear as separate poems and not only as parts of poems. In mediaeval arts of poetry *prosopopoeia* is much in view (E. Faral, *Les Arts poétiques* [Paris, 1923], pp. 72–73), and indeed Quintilian had noted that as a school exercise *prosopopoeia* would be very useful to future poets and historians. Compare Dante, *Convivio* III, ix, 20: "Usanla molto spesso i poeti." In a full theory of rhetoric, it would sink back to a minor role, as it does in Pierre Fabri, *Le Grand et Vrai Art de pleine rhétorique*, 1522 (A. Heron, ed. [Rouen, 1890], pp. 129, 192) and in Melanchthon's *Elementa Rhetorices* (*Op.* XIII, 490).

[22]The invective against Pierre Paschal, ironically entitled *Petri Paschasii Elogium* (in Pierre de Nolhac, *Ronsard et l'humanisme* [Paris, 1921], pp. 262–70), and two discourses, *Des Vertus intellectuelles et moralles* and *Envie* (*Œuvres*, Marty-Laveaux, ed., VI, 466, 471).

[23]Ed. crit., V, 209.

[24]Ed. crit., IX, 3; IX, 9 n. 1.

But at this point Ronsard, inspired by public events, decides to give us something of a different character. The *Exhortation au camp* was written towards the end of August 1558, when in the vicinity of Amiens the French army under the Duke of Guise was encamped facing some miles away the Spanish forces of Philip II under the Duke of Savoy, Emmanuel Philibert, and one of the decisive battles of European history was daily expected to be joined.[25] Just twelve months before, at Saint-Quentin, the same Emmanuel Philibert had totally destroyed a French army under the Constable Montmorency in one of the greatest disasters ever to befall French arms, and Montmorency himself, Saint-André the Marshal of France, and other notables remained in Spanish hands. No battle, however, took place; instead there sprang up rumors of peace, which in October found substance in negotiations that, though protracted, issued in the next spring in one of the decisive settlements of European history, the Treaty of Cateau-Cambrésis. Presumably in September as the talk of peace was growing, Ronsard composed his *Exhortation pour la Paix*, issued separately as a pamphlet, probably in October when the peace delegates first met. Attached to the French Court, he doubtless knew that Henri II desired peace, and the return of Montmorency, at almost any price; and with obvious tact he addresses his persuasion to neither monarch but to the soldiers on both sides. He had, of course, just been inciting the French army to ruthless slaughter.[26] An oration or declaration in verse is not itself perhaps a very novel concept (though I could not mention many examples), but, as we have gathered, this form is new for Ronsard and rather against his principles; a certain interest may therefore be found in seeing him for once follow "le fil d'une chose" with what seems to be conscious art. For convenience, we resort to a prose summary of the *Exhortation pour la Paix*:

No! Do not fight, be friends, Christians, whom Christ ransomed with his blood, and joined one to another. War is for lions, wolves, tigers, not for Christian men. Lay aside your arms (vv. 1–26). Or if you must fight, there are the Turks, usurpers of the Holy Land and invaders of

[25]Laumonier, éd. crit. of Ronsard, IX, ix.
[26]The repetition of the word "Exhortation" in the title doubtless embodies a passing allusion to a rhetorical *pour et contre*, though it was the turn of events that prompted the poet to "argue both sides of the question" within the space of a few weeks; cf. Laumonier, éd. crit., IX, x. In manner the two poems do not form a pair.

Europe; our internal wars waste thousands of lives to gain or lose a village or a castle, but Asia with all its wealth is a prize that Christian soldiers ought to save from the hands of pagans (27–80). When life is anyway so short, why make it shorter (81–86)? Mother—nay, stepmother—Earth is the cause of war; overburdened with mankind, she induced Jupiter to relieve her by setting in motion the Theban and the Trojan Wars; and subsequent history has left her little reason to complain (87–106). Nature did not make man to be a fighting animal; beasts are born armed with scale and claw, man is born naked and tender; cursed, therefore, be the man who discovered iron and first forged weapons, cursed be Prometheus who brought fire to forge them; cursed the discoverer of gold, without which iron would be harmless (107–46). Happy was the Golden Age of primitive peace; had I lived then I would not see our rivers choked with dead horses and abandoned armor; in war cities are overthrown, laws depraved, altars and churches burnt, justice abandoned, houses sacked, the old slain, maidens violated, the poor laborer despoiled, and vice becomes virtue (147–70). Brave soldiers, instead of committing crimes like these, would you not much rather live surrounded by the delights of domestic peace, far from the hardships of war, letting the spider spin in your helmets and the bee hive in your shields, forging swords into plough-shares or curving them into sickles (171–93)? Peace created the universe out of warring elements, founded cities, developed agriculture, and civilized our wild forebears, bringing them from the woods into settled communities (195–212). Come then, O Peace, crush the wrath of kings, and in the name of the peace that Christ made between his Father and us, banish Discord from among Christian peoples (213–20).

If this composition is susceptible of analysis under the elementary rules of rhetoric, there is a presumption that Ronsard was consciously applying such rules. Accordingly, the following description, simple as it is from a technical point of view, may claim a certain interest; it confronts the *Exhortation* chiefly with Aphthonius' *Progymnasmata* and Melanchthon's *Elementa Rhetorices* as representing elementary knowledge that a sixteenth-century writer may be expected to possess.[27]

The title *Exhortation* gives notice that the poetical speech belongs

[27]Aphthonius in Latin translation and Melanchthon's *Rhetoric* had both been printed several times in Paris before 1558. However, Aphthonius and Melanchthon are used here largely for convenience, and I do not scruple to go beyond them at any point.

to the *genus deliberativum,* which, according to Melanchthon, includes *adhortationes, consolationes,* and *deprecationes.* Though inspired by real events, and perhaps vaguely aimed at some practical effect,[28] it is essentially a literary exercise or Declamation. As such, it is technically either a Thesis or a Hypothesis (*quaestio infinita* or *finita*). A Thesis is a speech on a general question without application to particular persons or circumstances, and, according to Aphthonius, may be either "civil" or "theoretical"—a "civil" thesis, for example, is: "Ought a man to marry?"; a "theoretical" thesis is: "Is there a plurality of worlds?" (Aphthonius 13). A question involving definite persons and circumstances is a Hypothesis: "Ought Cato to marry in his old age?" Melanchthon's examples are much to the point. For Thesis he gives: "Liceatne Christiano bella gerere," while for Hypothesis he suggests: "Sitne bellum movendum adversus Turcas."[29] Ronsard's very themes were in the textbooks. He properly uses the arguments for the "civil" thesis "Liceatne Christianis bella gerere," but his exhortation is strictly a Hypothesis: "Liceatne Christianis *inter se* bellum gerere."

The parts of an oration—*exordium, narratio, propositio, confirmatio, confutatio,* and *peroratio*—normally follow each other in that order, though not all need appear in every speech, and in the deliberative type there commonly is no narration of past events, as, accordingly, there is none here. As for the *exordium,* if the cause is dubious one should use the Subtle Approach (*insinuatio*), but the Direct Approach (*principium*) may be used if the cause is honorable.[30] Secure that his cause is just, Ronsard employs the Direct Opening, beginning even abruptly, as suits an address to soldiers:[31]

> Non, ne combatez pas, vivez en amitié,
> Chretiens, changez vostre ire avecque la pitié,
> Changez à la douceur les rancunes ameres,
> Et ne trampez vos dars dans le sang de vos freres,

[28]A Latin translation by François de Thoor was immediately issued, possibly with the thought of reaching a European public with what was in fact the point of view of the French king (cf. Laumonier, éd crit., IX, x).

[29]Col. 451. Throughout his *Rhetoric,* Melanchthon uses the question of fighting the Turks to illustrate deliberative oratory, and hence "Should a Christian engage in warfare" occurs to him as more general.

[30]Cicero, *De Inventione* I, xv, 20 (tr. by Hubbell, p. 41); *Ad Herennium* I, lv, 6 (tr. by Caplan, p. 13).

[31]And in revocation of his recent *Exhortation . . . pour bien combattre.*

Que Christ le fils de Dieu, abandonnant les cieux,
En terre a rachetez de son sang precieux, [etc.]

The abrupt beginning is intended to secure *attentio;* the immediate indication that the cause is important, by appeal to the mission of Christ on earth, will render the hearers *dociles* (Melanchthon, col. 432). The *exordium* already states the *propositio,* the essence or *summa rei* of any oration—"Christians, cease from fighting among yourselves"—and this is now augmented as if in conformity with Melanchthon's observation (col. 445): "Ac plerumque, ut sit plenior sonus, propositio cum amplificatione recitatur."[32]

The *confirmatio* begins with a topic that, though strictly germane to the proposition *Christians should not fight each other,* has something of a concession about it:

Ou bien si vous avez les ames eschauffées
Du desir de louënge, et du los des trofées, ...
Revestez le harnoys: encore le Turc n'est
Si eslongné de vous, qu'avecques plus de gloire
(Qu' à vous tuer ainsi) vous n'ayez la victoire
De sur tel ennemi, qui usurpe à grand tort
Le lieu où Jesus Christ pour vous receut la mort.

The argument for attacking the Turk proceeds technically from the recommended commonplaces *honestum, utile, facile.* To wrest the sacred places from the infidel is righteous and promises "plus de gloire"; it is *inutile* for you to fight each other ("vos combats qui ne servent de rien," 58) over a "froid village" or a "petit chateau" (51–56) but easy and advantageous to drive the "Saracens" from the Holy Land,

---

[32] Vv. 17-26:

Sus donc, saluez vous d'une amyable voix,
Avecques le courroux depouillez le harnois,
Detachez vos boucliers, et vos piques dressées
Soyent le fer contre bas sur la terre abaissées.
Estuyez au fourreau vos luysans coutelas.
Froissez ainsi qu'un verre en mille et mille esclas
La lance mesprisée, et l'horrible tonnerre
Des malheureux cannons cachez dessoubz la terre
Loing au creux des Enfers, ou au fond de la mer
(Pour plus ne les revoir) faittes les abismer.

Bidden or unbidden, the sixteenth-century poets, armed with *copia verborum,* were only too prompt to "amplify," but it is noteworthy that this piece of pure accumulation occurs precisely where Art required it.

> Où la moindre cité que d'assaut on prendra
> D'un butin abondant tresriches vous rendra.

The argument is fortified by an elaborate *ecphrasis* or *descriptio* of the gorgeous East (63–80):

> Là sont les grans Palais, et les grandes rivieres,
> Qui d'un sablon doré roullent braves·et fieres, [etc.],

which is here not just a digression, but an example of the most moving device of *hypotyposis,* vividly presenting to the cupidity of the soldiers an *imago* of the wealthy East.[33]

With a rather neat transition (77–86) that conceals a logical difficulty, the oration turns from spurring on war against the Turk to a general argument against all war. That is, it returns to the hypothesis "Liceatne Christianis *inter se* bellum gerere" (79) only to pass at once to the most general thesis "Liceatne hominibus bellum gerere" (cf. 107, "Ah malheureux humains"). In itself this use of a general thesis is the correct rhetorical procedure (*transferre hypothesin ad thesin*); it enables the speaker to bring to bear the topics of a general thesis in an *a fortiori* argument upon his hypothesis.[34] If all war is wrong, war is doubly wrong for Christians, and still worse for Christian against Christian. And if in strict logic this voids the preceding argument for war against the Turk (which, after all, was introduced as a concession), sixteenth-century feeling easily missed the irrational element.[35]

---

[33]Melanchthon, col. 454. Quintilian (IX, ii, 44) mentions the vivid description of places as included under this figure by some theorists, whereas others assigned it to *topographia*. That Ronsard's *hypotyposis* is also a digression (*egressio*) accords with the use of digression as described by Quintilian (IV, iii, 12 ff.), who requires it to have some bearing on the case. As it happens, Quintilian mentions "the description of regions" as an example of *egressio*.

[34]Cicero, *Topica* 21; *De Oratore* III, 30; Quintilian III, v, 5–18; Melanchthon, col. 451, and cf. col. 480.

[35]Erasmus was one of the few who had a delicate conscience about war against the Turks, and even he finally wavers and allows it to be just if the Turks attack first (e.g., *Dulce bellum inexpertis* in *Op. Om.,* Clericus, II, 968B). Ronsard has provided for this (vv. 43–45): "Pourquoi jusqu' à la mort hayssez vous leur race, / S'ils ont (sans coup ruer) occupé vostre place? / S'ils ont (sans coup ruer) en Europe passé?" No doubt Laumonier is right (éd. crit., IX, 17) in saying that no crusade was seriously contemplated at this time; but the danger from the Turk was always in the air—a Turkish raid on the Apulian coast in the spring of this very year 1558 had sent a shiver through Europe (Prescott, *Philip II,* bk. 1, ch. 6)—and the impending peace between the two great Christian powers made the thought of turning against the Turk a natural one; the Preamble of the Treaty of Cateau itself speaks of

The defense of the thesis against war finds its *confirmatio* and *confutatio* in a *syncrisis* or *comparatio* of War and Peace, involving a *vituperatio* of the one and an encomium of the other. The druggist of "louanges" can now dispense his familiar wares. Praise and blame proceed from the same commonplaces—in general, *honestum* (*inhonestum*), *utile* (*inutile*), *facile* (*difficile*), and the like. As in praising persons, *honestas* is drawn first from their origin and family, so Melanchthon, for example, says, as noted above, that in praising *artes* (including *Pax*) *honestas* is based on efficient causes, viz., inventors, as Philosophy is the gift of God; *utilitas* is based on purposes and results (*fines*).[36] One should begin with a proem (Aphthonius 8). So Ronsard, in blaming War, begins with a short proem (vv. 81–86) and goes on to the origin of War as the *donum Terrae*. This passage is in the form of a *diegema* or narrative (Aphthonius 2) carried out with the necessary categories *quis, quid factum, ubi, quomodo,* and *cur.* Next, it is *inutile* for men, who lack the natural equipment of wild beasts, to go to war. Further, the remote causes of war—iron and gold—are blamed; and finally, the horrible *facta* or *fines* of war are enumerated (147–70).

Marking the comparison—"N'aymeriez-vous pas mieux..." (171)—Ronsard proceeds to the praise of Peace. This is in two parts: first, what is essentially an *ecphrasis* of Peace (173–94), and secondly, the *facta* or *fines* of Peace (195–212). Since Peace is divine, the "fille de Dieu" (213), no more need be said of her honorable origin.

The confirmation thus finished, the poem ends with a prayer that functions as a peroration:

> Donc, Paix fille de Dieu, vueille toy souvenir,
> Si je t'invoque à gré, maintenant de venir
> Rompre l'ire des Rois, et pour l'honneur de celle
> Que Jesus Christ a faitte au monde universelle

---

employing the fruits of peace for, among other things, "la repulsion des ennemis de la République Chrétienne" (Dumont, *Corps diplom.*, v, 35). At all events, the thought runs through much of the considerable literary output that surrounded the Peace, forming, for example, an argument in Louis Le Roy's prose oration *De Pace* published on this occasion. He introduces the topic much as Ronsard does, since he too defends a general thesis against war, and must then concede: "But if military discipline must not be wholly given up, direct your forces against the Mohammedans," etc.

[36]Above, notes 12 and 13.

> Entre son Pere et nous, respousse de ta main
> Loing des peuples Chretiens le Discord inhumain
> Qui les tient acharnez, et vueilles de ta grace
> A jamais nous aymer, et toute notre race.

This ending is a lucky stroke, but whether prompted by Imitation, Habit, or conscious Art it is hard to decide. Conceivably, as Laumonier thought, Ronsard may have had in view Tibullus 1.10, a peace poem, which ends with a prayer:

> At nobis, Pax alma, veni spicamque teneto,
> Profluat et pomis candidus ante sinus.

But this is hardly likely. Ronsard knew that in the last part of his poem he was writing an encomium or, since Peace is divine, a hymn; and he was in the habit of ending his hymns with a prayer. Probably he had formed this habit in imitation of the Homeric Hymns, Callimachus, and Marullus, but he may have known also that it had the doctrinal support of Aphthonius for the encomium. The *epilogos* of an encomium, according to Aphthonius, should be "rather conformable to a prayer" (εὐχῇ μᾶλλον προσήκοντα), and Renaissance writers of encomia can be shown, sometimes at least, to have heeded this as a demand of Art.[37] In the present poem, Ronsard's apparent care for rhetoric makes this not too remote a possi-

---

[37]In Lorich's popular Latin Aphthonius (1542, and many later edd.), combining the translations of Agricola and Cataneus, the sentence runs: "Postremo epilogo, qui precationi similior sit, concludes," and the injunction reappears in the verse summary:

> *Dispositio Laudis, tetrasticho comprehensa*
> Principium sequitur genus, ut gens, natio, patres,
>   Vita micans studiis, legibus atque bonis.
> Res gestas animus, corpus, fortuna ministrant;
>   Comparat in maius, votaque finis habet.

Doxapatres, commenting on Aphthonius (Walz, *Rhet. Graec.* II, 434), is somewhat embarrassed, remarking that the word μᾶλλον shows that the rule need not always be followed, and noting that Aphthonius' model encomia that follow lack this feature. However, Menander's prescriptions for the encomium of a king (βασιλικὸς λόγος) include, apparently as a matter of course, a prayer at the end: "ἐπὶ τούτοις εὐχὴν ἐρεῖς..." (Spengel-Hammer, III, 377). Claudian's *Panegyricus Probrini et Olybrii* so ends. Lucian's *Encomium of Demosthenes* ends with an invocation. Among Renaissance encomia ending with a prayer, I note Henri Estienne, *Francofordiensis emporii encomium;* J. A. Holtheuser, *Encomium musicae* (Erfort, 1551), in which each division—*exordium*, etc.—is labeled; Wilibald Pirckheimer, *Urbs Norimberga;* Melanchthon, *Oratio in laudem novae scholae.*

bility. But whether born of imitation, habit, or technical knowledge, or somehow of all three, the prayer serves the poem as a *peroratio;* in content it certainly owes nothing to Tibullus, but, as a peroration should do, it "repeats the *propositio*" and does so in an emotional tone.[38] Thus with luck or with conscious art the poet has contrived to end with what is at once the technical close of his encomium of peace and the technical close of his whole *exhortatio.*

Fulfilling the role of "poète français du roi," Ronsard followed the developments of Cateau-Cambrésis through the months with a series of poetical pamphlets, eight in all, registering the emotions of at least the government party: a *Bienvenue* for the returning Montmorency, a *Hymne* for the Cardinal of Lorraine (it ends with a prayer), a poem on the treaty, *La Paix, au Roy,* when it was signed in April. The Treaty of Cateau-Cambrésis was the occasion of celebrations throughout France, and the poets hailed it with more verses probably than any such event had ever before inspired; but an important share of opinion from the first regarded the settlement as on the whole a defeat for the French monarchy. Ronsard's poem *La Paix* is not an outburst of joy but a speech of advice to the king urging him to abide by the Peace that he has accepted. The Introduction is skillfully "drawn from the person of the hearer."[39] Since the poet thinks, or affects to think, that the king may feel that there is something discreditable in such unheroic counsel, there is here a trace of the Subtle Approach (*insinuatio*) in contrast with the Direct Approach of the *Exhortation.*[40] The *exordium* is long and elaborate: The king has been for years a great military leader bent on extending the boundaries of France, and his various successes are enumerated; yet another note is heard from the start— "Meintenant le veinqueur, meintenant le veincu" (v. 8)—and comes out dominant at the end of the proem (35–42):

> Bref vous estes le Roy, . . .
>
> qui plus avez tenté
> Le hazard de Fortune: . . .

[38]Melanchthon, col. 435: "[Peroratio], in qua repetitur propositio principalis," and "Omnis peroratio constat duobus rebus, partim repetitione propositionis et potissimorum argumentorum, partim affectibus."

[39]Cf., e.g., *Ad Her.* III, vi, 11.

[40]On the two approaches, see *Ad Her.* I, iii, 5–vii, 11 (tr. Caplan, pp. 11–23, with notes); the Subtle Approach to be used if the cause is discreditable (I, iv, 6) and applicable to deliberative as well as to judicial causes (III, iv, 7).

Elle vous a montré que peuvent les combas:
Aucunesfois en haut, aucunesfois en bas
Elle vous a tourné: pour exemple, qu'au monde
Un Roy, tant soit il grand, d'infortunes abonde.[41]

The *propositio* then follows in set terms (43–48): Keep the peace
now agreed upon, for God regards those kings who keep the peace
and not those who continually steep their hands in human blood.
As confirmation, we have first a long *encomium pacis* ("D'une si belle
Paix je veux chanter merveille," 49), repeating in different language some of the commonplaces of the *Exhortation* and including,
as an encomium should (Aphthonius 8), a *comparatio* of Peace and
Discord, which ends explicitly (201–202):

Or' voilà donc combien la Paix est trop plus belle
Et meilleure aux humains que n'est pas la querelle.

This greatly amplified encomium is followed by a briefer and more
pointed argumentation (203–36): Sire, be content; France is large
enough, war is *inutile;* it would be *inhonestum* to drag another Christian king through Paris in chains; it would be better, also *facile,* at
your age to live a domestic life with the queen, "Ou bâtir vostre
Louvre, ou lire dans un livre," than "tant vous travailler, / Et pour
un peu de bien si long temps vous batailler" (*inutile*). The conclusion (237–46) is a brief recapitulation repeating the *propositio*—for
example, verse 240, "gardez la [paix] tousjours bien," repeats verse
45, "il faut bien qu'on la garde." But this is not emotional enough
for an epilogue, and Ronsard raises his voice by adding—without
the technical justification of the *Exhortation,* and surely from mere
habit—a rather long prayer to Peace (247–80), including a curse on
those who might break the treaty and a blessing on those who
would keep it, and ending, so as to give the poem the familiar
"ring-form," with the petition that the king may love "science" and
flourish therewith in peace "autant qu'il fist en guerre en force et
en pouvoir."

Sixteenth-century statesmen seeking guarantees for their treaties
were prone to avail themselves of such royal marriages as they

[41]Ronsard's use of the *prooemium* might well have formed part of the present
paper, but may be left for special study. Throughout his career he evidently expended a good deal of care and art on these initial addresses to the great.

might arrange—a shift deplored by Erasmus in his study; but politics must employ the elements of power and interest it finds at hand. In this respect Cateau-Cambrésis made a brilliant finish. Philip II, having lost Mary Tudor in the course of the negotiations and having made fruitless overtures to her successor, now accepted the hand of another Elizabeth, the daughter of the king of France, while to his formidable captain, the Duke of Savoy, was given the king's sister Marguerite, Ronsard's chief protector at Court. The marriages were planned for the beginning of July, but the mirth suddenly was changed into mourning by the fatal accident during the festivities that cost the life of King Henry. Early in June, Ronsard had prepared two poems for the marriage of Emmanuel Philibert and Marguerite, a *Discours* for the Duke of Savoy and a naturally much warmer *Chant pastoral* for the new duchess, publication of which was somewhat delayed by the king's death. Only the *Discours* here concerns us, as evidence that nearly a year after the *Exhortation pour la Paix* the poet's rhetorical fit was still upon him. The *Discours* is a sermon. Its text is Romans 9.21: "Hath not the potter power over the clay, of the same lump to make one vessel unto honour, and another unto dishonour"—

> Qui oseroit accuser un potier,
> De n'estre expert en l'art de son mestier,
> Pour avoir faict d'une masse semblable
> Un pot d'honneur, l'autre moins honorable?—

which forms the *propositio:* God deals with his creatures as He will, "les pots sont siens, le seigneur il en est" (vv. 16–26). For proof, "il ne fault point pour ma *cause* approuver / Un *tesmoignage* és histoires trouver" (41–42), since the fortunes and misfortunes of the Duke of Savoy are sufficient evidence in themselves. The long narration of these vicissitudes (53–272) is thus the preacher's *exemplum* that serves as confirmation of his text.[42] The peroration (273–80) briefly repeats the *propositio:* "Voilá comment ... Dieu ... t'a faict voir qu'il est le Toutpuissant, / Qui va le prince et haussant et baissant [compare verse 9, 'Qui seul va l'homme et haussant et bais-

---

[42]Moreover Ronsard need not supply historical *exempla*, since he has *domestica exempla* to bring the sermon home to the duke. The turn is so natural that no knowledge of doctrine need be supposed; see, however, Anaximenes, *Rhetorica ad Alexandrum* 32, and cf. Longinus, *De Sublimitate* 16.

sant'], . . . et fait, quand il nous taste, / De nous *ainsi qu'un potier de sa paste.*" Very well so far, but this is a marriage sermon;[43] it ends, therefore, with what is unusual in a sermon, a long and well-formed epithalamium. This ending, however, is still artistic, for the marriage of Savoy to the sister of the king of France is represented as the supreme "haussement" of his career and is part of the argument; by throwing it after the technical "peroration" the poet ends his sermon on the festive note required by the occasion.

These poetical declamations of 1558–1559 were something new in Ronsard's literary practice, and in the care with which the rhetorical pattern of oration or sermon is carried out they remained unique, though occasions for similar poems of oratorical intent were by no means lacking in the poet's subsequent career. The Treaty of Cateau-Cambrésis marks an epoch in French history because, unhappily, in putting an end to foreign wars it released the forces of internal conflict on the religious issue; and the Civil Wars, from 1563, raged throughout the remainder of the poet's life. As *poète du roi* and a convinced adherent of the Catholic cause, he found occasion enough for *Discours* and *Expostulations* and *Responses,* but these later poems, however rhetorical in style and animated by a spirit of debate, follow no rhetorical scheme; topic follows topic without necessary sequence, and the poet begins and ends where he happens to be. So far, at least, his Calvinist critic, who may have admired the poetical declamations of 1558–1559, had observed correctly. The shadow of a sermon perhaps lies on the famous *Discours des misères de ce tems* (1562); it begins with a consideration of sin and virtue, contains an apologue (concerning Opinion, the offspring of Jupiter and Presumption), and ends with a prayer to God; but it has no true rhetorical pattern.[44] At first sight, a more certain exception is the whimsical (but seriously intended) *Procès* against the Cardinal of Lorraine, published in 1565. With an *exordium* (perhaps *insinuatio*) drawn from the person of the prince addressed, it states the case—that he has not kept his promise of rewarding the poet—and proceeds to a "narration" of Ron-

---

[43]Addressed in the opening lines to the congregation: "Vous Empereurs, vous Princes, et vous Roys," and brought round to the Duke in verse 45: "Toy, Philibert, Duc des Savoisiens."

[44]It is against the *Misères* that the Calvinist attack is specifically directed, and it presumably prompted the taunt "jadis poète, et maintenant prebstre" (above, note 3).

sard's services to him and to his family. But Laumonier has found good reason for thinking that the *Procès,* the last poem ever addressed by Ronsard to the cardinal, was written in 1560 or at the latest early in 1561, thus putting it back to a time when we may suppose that this piece of "judicial" pleading was the final effort of the poet's rhetorical vein that began in the autumn of 1558.[45] The whimsical tone may be significant. An element of the *tour de force* in all these poems fashioned on a rhetorical *taxis* sorts with the cheerful, not too serious, mood of the time when war was unexpectedly being turned into peace, and Ronsard himself was at last in full career as the accepted poet of the Court. At this moment it pleased him to come forward as *poète-orateur.*[46] His later discourses in verse are of too earnest a temper for such ingenuities; their *genus* is satire. Besides, a few poems in the line of "l'art misérable," following the "fil d'une chose," no doubt were enough for a poet who shrank from being classed with orators and preachers.

[45]Laumonier, éd, crit., XIII, Introd., pp. v–vi.

[46]The declamation perhaps also offered a ready formula for poems that were really "occasional" and produced on short notice.

Gilles Corrozet, François Sagon, et la *Resjouissance de la Paix* de 1559

Deux notes en supplément aux excellentes *Recherches sur Gilles Corrozet* de Mlle S. M. Bouchereaux:[1] Mlle Bouchereaux signale la première édition du *Retour de la Paix* (1544) publiée par Corrozet à l'occasion de la Paix de Crépy, d'une part, et de l'autre, une édition parue chez Benoît Rigaud, à Lyon (1577), probablement à l'occasion de la Paix de Bergerac.[2] Il est utile sans doute de préciser à cet égard que cette seconde édition est en réalité la troisième en date, puisqu'il existe une première donnée par Benoît Rigaud, en 1570, pour saluer, semble-t-il, la Pacification de Saint-Germain. Le catalogue peut donc s'établir comme suit: (*a*) *Retour de la Paix* (1544), édition de Corrozet: (*b*) édition publiée par Rigaud, en 1570; (*c*) édition chez le même, mais datée de 1577.[3] Les deux éditions (*b*) et (*c*) sont anonymes. Corrozet n'a signé l'édition originale que de sa devise *Plus que moins* à la fin du livre, et cette devise n'est pas conservée par Rigaud. Il est à remarquer aussi que dans les éditions de Rigaud les derniers vers qui font allusion à ce qui se passe en 1544 manquent. Ils ne convenaient plus aux circonstances.[4]

From *Bulletin du Bibliophile* (1961) no. 1, 5-17.

[1]*Bull. du Bibl.* mars 1948 à avril 1949; 1954, p. 260, à 1955. p. 20.

[2]*Bull. du Bibl.* 1949, pp. 94-95.

[3]Voici les titres des trois éditions; on voit que celui de l'édition de 1570 est excentrique: (*a*) *Le Retour de la paix en France* [*sic*]. (écu de France sous couronne fermée), (Paris: Corrozet, 22 sept. 1544) [B.N. Rés. Ye. 1108]; (*b*) *Le Retour de la paix, et du fruict provenant du benefice d'icelle. Œuvre tres-utile & digne de ce temps* (La Paix en char triomphal, légende), (Lyon: B. Rigaud, 1570) [Lyon: Bibliothèque munic. 314340]; (*c*) *Le Retour de la paix en France* (La Paix en char triomphal), (Lyon: B. Rigaud, 1577) [B. N. Rés. Ye. 4712]. Dans l'édition de 1570 le poème de Corrozet est précédé de deux quatrains sur la paix; cfr. n. 9 *infra*. Cette édition de 1570 est catalogué par Baudrier, *Bibliographie lyonnaise* III. 269.489, comme anonyme et sans attribution à Corrozet.

[4]Dans le texte de 1570 on a supprimé seize vers à la fin du poème: voir citation

Le second supplément que nous pouvons faire au catalogue de
Mlle Bouchereaux, toujours au sujet du *Retour de la Paix*, est peut-
être un peu plus intéressant; mais avant de l'aborder il faut jeter un
coup d'œil sur ce poème dans l'édition originale de 1544. Il con-
vient de signaler tout d'abord que la coutume de publier de tels
poèmes pour les paix successives du seizième siècle pose un prob-
lème aux imprimeurs: il faut obtenir et imprimer un poème de
circonstance très peu de jours après la conclusion de la paix. On ne
trouve pas facilement le poème utile dans les circonstances don-
nées, le moment venu. Très souvent on se contente donc de réim-
primer un poème déjà existant. Au besoin on recourt à des re-
maniements hâtifs. Corrozet, qui était à la fois poète et imprimeur,
se trouvait dans une position unique. Il n'y a pas lieu de douter qu'il
écrit son *Retour de la Paix*, qu'il publie le 22 septembre, dans les trois
jours après la conclusion de la Paix (le 18 septembre). Ce poème,
qui comprend 143 vers décasyllabes, groupés en strophes de lon-
gueurs variées, développe non sans entrain des considérations
générales sur la paix. Il débute ainsi:

> Tant plus ung bien est longuement caché,
> Plus est requis, attendu & cerché.
> Et quand il vient apres longueur de temps,
> Il rend les gens plus aises & contens . . .
>   Qui est ce bien si longuement perdu? . . .
> C'est le grand bien dont procède tout bien . . .
> Un don du ciel, lequel sans noz merites
> Dieu a transmis cy bas en ces limites . . .
>   Iadis la paix en la terre où nous sommes
> Feit sa demeure avecques tous les hommes . . .
> Avecques elle estoient Foy & Iustice.
> Concorde, Amour, Verité & Police.

Alors on pouvait voyager sans contrainte à l'étranger; jamais le
bruit des armes ne venait vous alarmer; il n'y avait ni procès ni
juges ni avocats; tout le monde vivait en amitié, besoin n'était de
bastions ni murailles.[5] Mais quand le péché né de la malice vint à

---

ci-après: de l'édition de 1577, que je n'ai pas vue, Mlle Bouchereaux dit: «On a
amputé le texte de Corrozet de la dernière strophe.» S'agit-il ici des dix derniers vers
seulement?

[5]Développement inspiré d'Ovide, *Mét.* 1.96–99 (l'âge d'or): e.g., «nondum praeci-
pites cingebant oppida fossae».

vomir partout le vice, la Paix, fille de Dieu, retira au ciel, et Dieu pour nous punir fit monter des enfers la Guerre ayant fer et feu en ses mains. Pourtant aujourd'hui Dieu a eu pitié de nous, et *"en muant noz hélas / en chantz ioieux"* nous a envoyé *"Paix liberalle et franche / tenant en main la belle olive blanche."* Et pour finir:

> O toy mortel si bien tu consideres
> Que c'est que Paix, elle n'est point donnée
> Pour demener vie desordonnée,
> Ny pour servir à peché ny à vice,
> Mais seulement à Vertu & Iustice.
>   O combien sont tous les Princes heureux,
> Qui banissant le temps si rigoureux,
> Ont introduict la Paix en leurs royaulmes,
> Laissans rouiller armeures & heaulmes,
> Sinon au temps qu'oubliant tous debatz
> On faict tournois, & paisibles esbatz.
>   Doncques François, Espaignolz & Germains,
> Rendez à Dieu graces à ioinctes mains,
> Qui les deux cueurs de voz princes assemble:
> Dequoy la terre & le hault Ciel ensemble
> Sont resiouyz. Rendez à Dieu la gloire
> Pour ceste Paix, qui vault mieulx que victoire.
> Faictes les feux, remplissez l'aer de ioye,
> Sonnez Clairons si hault que lon vous oye,
> Et publiez la Paix de bonne foy
> Des deux Amis, l'Empereur & le Roy.

C'est ainsi que le poème se termine dans l'édition originale. Dans l'édition de 1570 il s'arrête au vers, *Mais seulement à Vertu et Iustice,* lequel vers a subi d'ailleurs une légère modification (influence des guerres religieuses?) en devient: *Mais à Vertu, Pieté et Iustice.*

Mais avant que Benoît Rigaud s'en soit servi pour célébrer les traités de Saint-Germain et de Bergerac, le *Retour* de Corrozet a déjà servi en 1559 à saluer la Paix de Cateau-Cambrésis. A cette occasion paraît une brochure anonyme, dont voici le signalement:

La Resiovyssance du traicté de la Paix en France, publiée le septiesme d'Apuril 1559, Paris, Olivier de Harsy, 1559; petit in 8° de 10 ff. n. ch., sign. A-C; privilège du 8 avril de la même année: à la fin: «Nouvellement imprimé à Paris le dixiesme Avril».[6]

[6]B.N. Lb[31].89.

313

Cette *Resjouissance* se présente sous la forme d'un poème continu de 415 vers. En réalité, c'est une fusion du *Retour de la Paix* de Corrozet et du *Chant de la Paix* de François Sagon.

Arrêtons-nous un moment à ce *Chant* de Sagon. A en croire Du Verdier, il a paru en 1538, c'est-à-dire à l'occasion de la trève d'Aigues-Mortes, ce qui paraît ne pas laisser de place au doute, mais la plus ancienne édition aujourd'hui connue est précisément de 1544, publiée comme le *Retour* de Corrozet pour célébrer la Paix de Crépy: *Le Chant de la Paix de France, chanté par les troys estatz,* Paris, Jean André: et à la fin: «Nouvellement imprimé à Paris [samedi] le vingtième iour de Septembre 1544».[7] L'auteur n'est pas mentionné dans le titre, mais au troisième vers le poème porte une *sphragis* («la muse Sagontine»), et à la fin de la brochure, après le «rondeau final», se trouve la devise de Sagon, *Vela de quoy.*

Ce *Chant de la Paix,* comparé au simple impromptu qui est le *Retour* de Corrozet, est une ambitieuse composition de près de 400 vers, à la manière des Rhétoriqueurs avec «Proposition», «Narration», et l'intervention, de temps à autre, de l'«acteur».

Proposition

Paix? Que diray ie apres tant de latins?
Que dira lon, quand ung de ces matins
Chascun orra la muse Sagontine
Chanter de Paix? (Invocation poeticque)
O fontaine argentine,
Lieu de Phœbus, & des Muses repos,
Descouure moy ta source à ce propos,
Car en plongeant dedens ma rude vene,
Mon chant de PAIX sera doulx & amoene.

Narration

Le ciel haultain, de la paix amoureux
Chassant de Mars le regne rigoreux
Et monstrant bien de ce monde avoir cure,
En ces bas lieux a lasché son Mercure
(Douce planette en sa cause & effectz)
Pour annoncer le regne de la paix . . .

---

[7]B.N. Rés Ye. 3701. («Samedi» est conjectural: mot illisible, dans le microfilm, sous le sceau de la Bibliothèque Royale). Sur le titre, écu de France sous couronne comme au titre du *Retour* de Corrozet 1544, mais assez grossièrement exécuté. Pour

L'«acteur» appelle successivement l'Eglise, la Noblesse et le «Labeur», qui prennent la parole pour exprimer chacun à leur tour la joie de la paix retrouvée. Les trois états prononcent même à la vérité de longues harangues, plus ou moins lyriques, et de mètres variés. Cela ne manque pas d'un certain mouvement en d'une certaine couleur. Ainsi l'Eglise, par exemple:

> Les Anges ont bien (soubz grace)
> Pris l'audace,
> Chanter paix quand Dieu fut né.
> Chantons donc en terre basse
> Nostre espace,
> Du bien à nous adonné.

Et le Tiers Etat:

> Chantez oyseaux en vostre chant ramage,
> Vollez en l'air par villes & par champs,
> Et y semez voz degoys & voz chantz.
> Mieulx ne povez à la paix faire hommaige.

L'Eglise compte entre ses raisons de se réjouir le fait qu'on pourra célébrer régulièrement la messe. La Noblesse affirme que le roi écoutera à nouveau les plaintes de son peuple. Les seigneurs eux-mêmes protégeront les voyageurs, les enfants seront mieux élevés et instruits. Quant au Tiers Etat, il se réjouit: «pillerye est estaincte».[8] Enfin l'«acteur» conclue son propos en dix vers. Vient le «rondeau final» ensuite et la devise de l'auteur. L'édition de 1544 se termine par un dizain et deux quatrains sur la paix.[9]

Le *Chant de la Paix* de Sagon semble avoir recueilli un certain

---

l'édition de 1538 voir Du Verdier, *Bibliothèque françoise*, Rigoley de Juvigny, éd. iii, 676: «Le Chant de la paix de France, chanté par les trois Etats, imprimé à Paris, in-8. par Denys Janot. 1538.» L'édition de 1544 ne pourrait être la première, puisque Sagon est mort probablement «avant le 19 août 1544» (F. Bouquet cité par Paul Bonnefon RHL 1 [1894], 285). En tout cas, le poème est trop long et trop soigné pour être écrit dans la seule journée entre la proclamation de la Paix de Crépy (le 18 sept.) et l'«achevé d'imprimer» (20 sept.).

[8]Dans quelques motifs de ce poème—e.g., développements sur David et Salomon—on peut apercevoir l'influence du *Dulce bellum inexpertis* d'Erasme.

[9]Ces deux quatrains— (*a*) *Qui veult avoir apres guerre allegeance.... et (b) Paix est doulceur qui faict vivre en raison . . .*—qui se trouvent en 1544 à la fin du *Chant* de Sagon, sont passés en 1570 au front du *Retour* de Corrozet (voir n. 3, *supra*).

succès.[10] Deux ans plus tard, on l'a réimprimé, au moins partielle-
ment, à Rouen, sans nom d'auteur, à la fin d'une plaquette célé-
brant le traité d'Ardres entre François I et Henri VIII
d'Angleterre: *La Publication du traicté de la paix faicte et accordée entre
Françoys, roy de France et Henry, roy d'Angleterre. Publié à Rouen, le
dimanche treiziesme jour de juin 1546. Avec le chant de la paix de France
chanté par les troys Estatz.* Rouen, Nic. Le Roux pour Robert Dugort,
15446.[11] En 1550, le *Chant* de Sagon paraît de nouveau à Paris à
l'occasion du traité signé entre Henri II et Edouard VI
d'Angleterre qui est l'occasion pour Ronsard d'écrire sa célèbre *Ode
de la Paix.* Cette fois, c'est un petit in-8° illustré par dix attrayantes
vignettes. On a adapté le titre du poème aux circonstances: *Le
Chant de la Paix de France, et d'Angleterre, chãté par les trois estatz,
composé par l'indigent de sapience. Publié à Paris le samedy vingteufiesme
iour de Mars, mil cinq cens quaranteneuf auant Pasques* [1550 n.s.].
Imprimé à Paris par Nicolas Buffet. A part l'orthographe, le texte de
1550 est celui de 1544; mais les strophes, indiquées en 1544 par des
astérisques seulement, le sont ici par l'espacement ordinaire. La
devise de Sagon fait défaut après le rondeau final, mais le titre
porte au lieu du nom de l'auteur: «l'indigent de sapience».[12]

Retournons à la *Resjouissance de la paix* de 1559. Le texte, comme
nous l'avons dit, débute par le *Retour de la Paix* de Corrozet:

> Tant plus un bien est longuement caché . . .

Et puisque la Paix de Cateau-Cambrésis entre Henri II et Philippe
II a permis l'emploi d'expressions semblables à celles qu'évoquait la

---

[10]Je crois pouvoir retrouver écho de ce poème dans la poésie «pacifiste» du
temps. Par exemple, l'appel aux oiseaux à prendre part aux réjouissances paraît être
imité par un certain F. G. dans son *Hymne sur le triomphe de la paix*, [La Rochelle?],
1568, sign. D [B.N. Rés. Ye. 1025], et par Thomas Guiet, *La Resioussance de la paix,
presentée aux quatre Estatz,* (Paris: J. Coqueret, 1588), pp. 15–16 [B.N. Rés. Ye. 4117].

[11]Je n'ai pas vu ce petit ouvrage dit «rarissime» par Ap. B. (Apollin Briquet) dans
le présent *Bulletin* ([1860], p. 1316). Briquet, sans reconnaître l'auteur du poème, en
cite quatre vers qui garantissent suffisamment que c'est bien l'œuvre de Sagon. Il
semble apparaître de ses remarques rapides que les parties du poème antérieures au
«Chant de l'Église» ont été supprimées dans cette version. Cfr. n. 16, *infra.*

[12]Trompés par l'emploi ici du pseudonyme « l'Indigent de sapience», quelques
bibliographes ont attribué le poème à Corrozet, qui en effet s'est approprié parfois
ce pseudonyme. Ainsi dans le *Catalogue général des livres imprimés* de la B.N., le *Chant
de la paix* se trouve au tome 32 (p. 711) à l'article «Corrozet» et apres—correctement
et avec des éclaircissements—au tome 160 (p. 76), article «Sagon». Dans l'intervalle,
la première notice a trompé R. Brun. *Le Livre illustré en France au XVIe siècle* (Paris:
Alcan. 1930), p. 177.

Paix de Crépy entre François I et Charles-Quint, le *Retour*, dans son texte intégral, comprend les derniers vers supprimés dans l'édition de 1570. Seulement au vers final (f. B¹) il fallait une petite modification, pour lire:

> Des deux amis, Philippe & Henry Roy.

Suit immédiatement l'en-tête «Narration», et le texte reprend avec le *Chant de la Paix* de Sagon à partir du neuvième vers:

> Le ciel haultain de la paix amoureux...

C'est-à-dire que le rédacteur, laissant de côté la «Proposition» de Sagon, a rattaché la «Narration» directement à la fin du poème de Corrozet. Le *Chant de la Paix* (Naturellement les titres originaux manquent dans cette fabrication) continue sans interruption jusqu'à f. Ciii¹, où le «Chant de Labeur», bien que dûment annoncé, est omis. Il manque donc 118 vers du poème original. L'«autheur» brusquement «conclud son propos» en dix vers, et s'ensuivent le rondeau, la devise *Vela de quoy*, le dizain et les deux quatrains.

Dans la *Resjouissance* le texte du *Retour* de Corrozet doit nécessairement avoir été pris dans l'édition de 1554, la seule existante. Mais à part les modifications orthographiques et quelques fautes d'impression, nous y trouvons trois remplacements volontaires de mots: *félicité* pour *bienheurté* (v. 29), *vive foy* pour *saine foy* (121) et, comme nous l'avons remarqué, *Philippe & Henry Roy* au lieu de *l'Empereur & le Roy* de 1544.[13] Quant au *Chant* de Sagon, la *Resjouissance* ignore l'édition de Buffet, 1550, et reproduit le texte de 1544 (ou de 1538?), puisque la devise de Sagon, omise par Buffet, se trouve à sa place ici.[14]

Certes, cette mise bout à bout est assez maladroite. On a sûrement pensé que le *Retour* de Corrozet, plus court, plus général dans sa louange de la paix, pouvait servir de «proposition» au *Chant* de Sagon, plus étendu et qui s'adresse plus particulièrement aux trois Etats. Quoi qu'il en soit, le lecteur peut être surpris par l'apparition de l'«autheur» pour la première fois seulement au f. Biii³.

---

[13]Le *Retour* de 1570 ignore la *Resjouissance* et suit l'édition de 1554: v. par exemple les vers 29 et 121.

[14]On peut supposer que ces publications de 1544 pour la Paix de Crépy existaient côte à côte dans mainte collection de livres: de là la possibilité de la facture de la *Resjouissance*, et aussi du transfèrement des deux quatrains du *Chant* au *Retour* de 1570 (n. 9, *supra*).

La *Resjouissance de la Paix* a été victime de l'incompréhension des bibliographes. Aucun en effet ne paraît en avoir saisi le caractère. Il y a cent ans au juste, Apollin Briquet, décrivant un exemplaire dans ce même *Bulletin,* admirait la fécondité du «poète» qui pouvait écrire 357 [*sic*] vers français en trois jours, c'est-à-dire entre le 4 avril (annonce à Paris de la conclusion du traité) et le 8 avril (date du privilège).[15] Selon lui, l'auteur aurait divisé son poème en onze sections, dont la seconde «est intitulée *Narration,* nous ne savons trop pourquoi».[16] Puisque Briquet n'a reconnu ni l'œuvre de Corrozet ni celle de Sagon, il n'avait pas motif évidemment de s'interroger à leur sujet. En effet, La Croix du Maine attribue la *Resjouissance* à Sagon.[17] Il l'a fait sans doute parce qu'il a remarqué la devise à la fin du livre. Mais La Croix du Maine n'a pas vu que ce livre commençait par un poème de Corrozet. Il est peu probable d'ailleurs que Sagon ait fait un ouvrage où la première place fût donnée au poème de Corrozet et en sacrifiant une bonne part de son propre poème. En tout cas, il paraît à peu près établi qu'en 1559 Sagon n'était plus vivant.[18] L'abbé Goujet, il est vrai, déduit de la notice de La Croix du Maine que Sagon vivait encore en 1559; mais telle déduction paraît sans valeur.[19] Personne n'attribue la *Resjouissance* à Corrozet, qui vécut jusqu'à 1568. Bien que son poème tienne la première place et soit reproduit intégralement, avec des modifications qu'on pourrait supposer de l'auteur lui-même, il serait imprudent, croyons-nous, de lui attribuer cet ouvrage, dont nous estimerions bien plutôt qu'il a été fabriqué à la hâte dans l'atelier d'Olivier de Harsy.[20]

[15]*Bull. du Bibl.* (1860), p. 1005; cfr. Brunet, *Manuel* v, 1202.

[16]Il est assez piquant de constater que Briquet, qui a manié la *Resjouissance* en février 1860, n'a pas reconnu en juillet de la même année une grande partie de la même matière dans *La Publication du traicté . . .* de Rouen (n. 11, *supra*).

[17]*Bibliothèque françoise*, Rigoley de Juvigny, éd. 1, 237: «Il [Fr. Sagon] a écrit le Chant de la Paix. fait [*sic*] entre le Roi Henri II et Philippe Roi d'Espagne. imprimé à Paris par Barbe Regnault; la Réjouissance du Traité de Paix en France, publiée l'an 1559, imprimée à Paris par Olivier de Harsy, audit an 1559.» (Nous ne possédons pas d'exemplaire du *Chant* de Sagon dans l'édition de Barbe Regnault.)

[18]Cfr. n. 7, *supra.*

[19]*Bibliothèque françoise* XI, 102. L'avis de Goujet est cité avec approbation par l'éditeur de La Croix du Maine (éd. cit. 1, 238).

[20]C'est un devoir très agréable de remercier cordialement mon collègue, M. Michel Chrestien, d'avoir bien voulu revoir le texte de cet article.

John Leland's *Laudatio Pacis*

John Leland's *Encomium of Peace* was published in August, 1546, to celebrate the Peace of Campe or Ardres concluded on June 8 of that year between Henry VIII of England and Francis I of France.[1] The last of the longer occasional poems written by Leland, it has struck those who have examined it as remarkable among his verses for its religious and philosophical tone.[2] Yet even this tonality in large measure belongs to the literary tradition he followed, and considered within the tradition of peace poetry, the *Encomium* may prove to be chiefly remarkable for the author's obedience to rhetorical precept in arrangement and for the complacency with which he borrowed materials to fill out the latter half of the poem. A number of oddities in this latter part suggest that though at least two

From *Studies in Philology* 58 (1961) 616-26, © 1961 The University of North Carolina Press. Reprinted by permission of the publisher.

[1] Ἐγκώμιον τῆς Εἰρήνης, *Laudatio Pacis, Ioanne Lelando Antiquario autore. Ad Ingenuos pacis cultores* [epigram]. Londini anno M. D. xlvi (at the end: Apud Reynerum Wolfium . . . anno M.D. xlvi mense Augusto). I have used a copy of this first edition in the New York Public Library, and also a microfilm of one of the British Museum copies [B.M. 1075.m.16 (3)]. The poem is reproduced by Thomas Hearne in *Joannis Lelandi antiquarii . . . Collectanea*, 2d ed. (London, 1770), 5.69-78. In three places where the text of 1546 is defective, it is amended in Hearne's edition: v.155, Nymphae omnes comites venerantur ovantem *1546*: summe venerantur *Hearne* (where *summe* clearly is a stop-gap); v.188, Pacem commendat doctique *1546: doctique omitted by Hearne* (see n. 15 below); v.213, Duxit ad aratros *1546*: Duxit araturos *Hearne* (with texts of Tibullus). These corrections, however, are made in manuscript, apparently in a sixteenth-century hand, in the British Museum copy cited above, and Hearne presumably had them from this or a like source; otherwise he might not have risked *summe* in v.155. (They are made in a modern hand, presumably from Hearne, in the copy in the New York Public Library.) In return, several misprints are introduced by Hearne, two of which might cause trouble: v.24, subique *for* sibique *1546*; v. 87, sua suävia, *where omit* sua *with 1546*. Hearne failed to correct *canet* to *canit* in v.38, and *Attiacis* to *Actiacis* in v.202.

[2] Leicester Bradner, *Musae Anglicanae* (New York: MLA, 1940), pp. 27-28, Wolfgang Mann, *Lateinische Dichtung in England* (Halle: Niemeyer, 1939), pp. 121-23.

months elapsed between the signing of the treaty and the date of publication, Leland may in the end have felt pressed for time, as happens to those who write for an occasion.

We should note that in publishing such a poem on such an occasion, Leland followed a continental rather than an English custom. On the continent, and particularly in France, nearly every peace settlement of the sixteenth century was marked by the publication of poetical brochures of this kind, the printers often reissuing an old poem if no poet was at hand to compose a new one on short notice. Thus the Truce of Aigues-Mortes (1538) between Charles V and Francis I had occasioned Clément Marot's *Cantique de la Chrestienté,* an elaborate *Chant de la Paix* by François Sagon, and a still more elaborate *Pacis Descriptio* by the Flemish Latin poet Corneille de Schryver; the Peace of Crépy (1544) between the same two monarchs brought forth, among other poems, a *Retour de la Paix* by Gilles Corrozet and a reissue of Sagon's *Chant;* Sagon's *Chant de la Paix* appeared again in an illustrated edition for the peace of 1550 between France and England, which was also the occasion of Jean-Antoine de Baïf's first notable poem, *Sur la Paix avec les Anglois,* and of Ronsard's great *Ode de la Paix.* As many as thirty new poems and several old ones greeted the important Peace of Cateau-Cambrésis in 1559.

The Peace of Campe, however, seems not to have been much noticed by the French poets. I can mention only a rare pamphlet published at Rouen to mark the event, at the end of which Sagon's useful *Chant de la Paix* was reproduced at least in part.[3] The treaty was in fact unfavorable to France. The English, who in 1545 had been simultaneously threatened with invasion by the French fleet, which made a landing on the Isle of Wight, and with invasion by the Scots on the north, had in the end gained the upper hand, and the chief provision of the treaty was the promise of payment by Francis of an enormous sum of money to the English crown.[4] Though Leland alone appears to have followed the continental custom of publishing a poetical pamphlet on the occasion, it seems

[3] *La Publication du traicté de la paix faicte et accordée entre Françoys, roy de France et Henry, roy d'Angleterre . . . Avec le Chant de la paix de France, chanté par les troys Estatz* (Rouen: N. le Roux, 1546). I have not seen this pamphlet, which is described in the *Bull. du Bibl.* (1860), p. 1316.

[4] Some two million crowns in gold over a period of eight years; when it was paid, Francis was to have possession of Boulogne. However, both Francis I and Henry VIII died early in the next year.

likely that Walter Haddon's verses *De Triumpho propter pacem sus-cepto* were also written for the Peace of Campe, though not published until later.[5]

The poems of this tradition, though displaying a great variety of invention, nearly always contrive to include a number of conventional themes; for example, the cosmic theme that the universe is a peaceful arrangement of mutually hostile elements, and hence a lesson to man; the religious theme that peace was the message of Christ and the Apostles; that Christians should not fight against Christians, but should join together against the Turk. There is likely to be a description of the peaceful state of the world in the Golden Age, and almost certain to be a set contrast between the horrors of war and the blessings of peace, among the latter especially agricultural prosperity and freedom of commerce. On the whole, though again the poems differ, there is more in them of these general topics than of allusion to the events that called them forth; and hence the possibility of reissuing the same poem on successive occasions. They do of course usually include a compliment to the "peace-hero" of the moment. The small amount of nationalistic sentiment in Leland's *Encomium,* which has been commented upon, and the paucity of reference to the treaty of Campe are therefore normal.

As the title indicates, the poem is essentially an encomium of peace; but the encomium proper (vv. 122–290) is preceded by an introductory section of almost equal length (1–121). This Introduction is correctly formed, consisting of the "proposition" followed by a "narration." In the first eleven lines, the "proposition" states the poet's intention—

> Martia bella canant alii gladiosque cruentos:
> Me iuvat eximiae felicia numina Pacis
> Carmine conspicuo vel ad astra extollere pura—

and invokes the inspiration of heaven and the favor of Henry VIII. The "narration" that follows gives the setting, both the ultimate

[5]Haddon, *Poemata* with the *Lucubrationes* of 1567, pp. 56–60; *Poematum libri duo* (1576), in Book II (no pagination). Haddon's poem alludes both to the French and to the Scots, and lauds Henry VIII. It is immediately followed by a shorter poem *De Pace Britannica anno primo Edouardi sexti* (i.e., 1547).

cause and the immediate occasion, of the encomium.[6] First there is an account of the creation of the world (with special mention, among the animals, of the dolphin for the Dauphin's sake), ending with God's promise of peace to such as keep his commandments: let us then be grateful for his present mercy.[7] And since Peace has come, driving Mars away, she should be adorned with all the insignia of a triumph. So at least the poet would wish to picture her; but he lacks the painter's skill, in fact he lacks even the power to praise her adequately in verse as Ovid or Pontano might have done.[8] Yet he has the will to perform this duty, and so ventures to entrust his little boat (*carinula*) to the breeze.[9]

There follows the *encomium Pacis*. Indispensable to an encomium, as every Renaissance schoolboy knew, are an account of the honorable origin or birth (*genus*) of the subject and an account of the subject's good deeds (*benefacta* or *commoda*), to which the handbooks recommended adding a comparison of the person or thing praised with some other person or thing. Leland begins in form (122–23):

> Principio referam genus immortale beatae
> Pacis, & insignem spectatumque illius ortum.

[6]In Sagon's often-reprinted poem, the proposition and narration are labeled as such, and introduce the songs of the three Estates of France as Leland here introduces his *Encomium Pacis*. Sagon's "proposition" also ends with an appeal for inspiration (from the Castalian fount); his "narration" relates that Heaven, caring for mankind, has sent Mercury to announce the reign of peace: let us therefore rejoice.

[7]The topic of cosmic creation occurred to Leland, I believe, because it is traditional in peace poetry. But it is usually employed either to set the example of the peaceful functioning of the universe, or to lead up to the peaceful existence of man in the Golden Age. Leland gives it quite another turn. Though his train of thought is none too clear, he seems to say: the beauty of the world thus created is meant to remind man to obey God's will, and still more so is God's gift to him of a rational soul; the reward of obedience is peace; since He has given us the present peace [despite our disobedience], we should praise His mercy (*clementia*).

[8]A notable example of "affected modesty," on which see E. R. Curtius, *Europäische Literatur und Lateinisches Mittelalter*, p. 91 (Eng. tr., p. 83).

[9]Though this first part of the poem seems to represent free composition on Leland's part, a few borrowings may be noted. The description of the dolphin (43–64), "puerorum notus amator," etc., depends on the Elder Pliny, *NH* 9.8.26 (not on the similar tale in the Younger Pliny, Epist. 9.33); "pax optima rerum" (84) is a common tag from Silius Italicus, *Punica* 2.592 (see below); the contrast between the poet's feeble powers and his intention, "Ut desint iustae vires, tamen ipsa voluntas / Me iubet" (113–14), echoes Ovid, *Epist. ex Pont.* 3.4.79: "Ut desint vires, tamen est laudanda voluntas," a passage which Leland probably read in Mirandula's *Flores Illustrium Poetarum* (heading, "De Voluntate"). For his further dependence on this florilegium, see below.

Peace is in fact the Daughter of God: "summus Coeli Rector . . . progenuit . . . Pacem." The parentage thus assigned to Peace most likely reflects the French tradition of peace poetry, where the designation *fille de Dieu* is seldom omitted while elsewhere the notion is rare; presumably it is a remnant of the medieval theme of the Four Daughters of God—Peace, Justice, Mercy, and Truth.[10] Once born, Peace enters her chariot, ready to descend to earth together with her "companions." The scene is traditional, and the list of *comites* as usual is founded upon those commonly named by the Roman poets.[11] Among them, Astraea is singled out for an extended notice (133-41) which is borrowed from Aratus, as Leland makes plain—"Cuius concinuit laudes hoc carmen Arati"— and we may excuse him from a further confession that vv. 135-36 and 140-41 are taken over intact from the Latin version of Aratus by Germanicus.[12]

God enjoined peace through the Law and the Prophets; Christ came to bring peace; the Apostles and Paul cherished it. Leland is making a transition to the "good deeds" of Peace. This topic he treats in a somewhat novel manner, and one that made the task easy for him. He cites witnesses, or rather quotes texts. This procedure has an advantage over merely enumerating the *benefacta* of Peace inasmuch as the citing of witnesses is also a form of "confir-

[10]On this theme (founded on Ps. 84:11) see Hope Traver, *The Four Daughters of God* (Bryn Mawr College Monographs 6 [1907]), with references; for the decline of the theme, Raymond Lebègue, *Le Mystère des Actes des Apôtres* (Paris: E. Droz, 1929), p. 173. The designation of Peace as the *fille de Dieu* is continuous from the fifteenth century, appearing for example in Alain Chartier, Jean Molinet, Jean Marot, Cl. Marot, Du Bellay, Ronsard, etc. Occasionally in the sixteenth century it is assimilated to the Hesiodic notion of Eirene as the daughter of Zeus.

[11]The descent of Peace from Heaven is common, her descent in a chariot less so, but it is found in De Schryver, *Pacis Descriptio*, in Guillaume des Autels, *La Paix venue du ciel* (1559), and in some later poems. The Lyons printer Rigaud placed a vignette of Peace in her chariot on the titlepage of several publications (Corrozet's *Retour de la paix* [1570 and 1577]; Philibert Bugnyon's *De la Paix* [1577]. In these cases the underlying idea is probably the *triumph* of peace. Pax seems not to be represented with a chariot in any ancient source, literary or graphic, but the Renaissance iconographer, Piero Valeriano, assigns the chariot to all the gods as a symbol of divine majesty (*Hieroglyphica*, s. v. "currus").

For the *comites* of Peace, see e.g., Horace, *Carm. saec.* 57-60: Fides, Honor, Pudor, Virtus, Copia. Renaissance variations are endless; Leland gives: Astraea, Concordia, Quies, Pietas, Probitas, Clementia, Modestia, Charis, Amicitia, Amor, Nymphae; Joannes Secundus, *De Pace Cameraci facta*: Astraea, Fides, Musae, Mercurius, Plutus, Amor. Associates form a regular topic in encomia; compare the *comites* of Folly in Erasmus *Moriae encomium*.

[12]Germanicus Caesar, *Aratea* 112-13, 138-39; cf. Aratus, *Phaenomena* 108-109, 136.

mation." To pass over Scripture, he says, there are many Greek writers who celebrate the "pia munera" of Peace (177–92):

> Euripides, tragicae qui gloria prima Camoenae,
> Pacem describens, opulentam, tumque beatam
> Nominat, haec addens: "Inter pulcherrima Divas."
> Atque alibi: "Quantum bello potiorque serena
> "Sit pax, in primis quae Musas promovet almas,
> "Luctibus ac adversatur, sobolisque suävi
> "Dexteritate, hinc atque opibus congaudet opimis."
> Huius Aristophanes quoque vates comprobat omne
> Iudicium, laudes Pacis praedivitis augens.
> Bacchylides cecinit sacer in Poeanibus ista:
> "Maxima quaeque refert mortalibus aurea Pacis
> "Progenies." Pacem commendat Musa Philonis,
> Haec et commemorat: "Nunc id quod perplacet, ipsa
> "Inveni. Confer quae sunt tua munera large,
> "Nuptiolas, prolem, cognatos, divitiasque,
> "Corporis & sani vires, vinumque suäve."

Let us not be too much impressed by Leland's learning. This passage is only a résumé of Stobaeus, *Florilegium*, Chap. 55 (xiv Wachsmuth-Hense), "De Pace," where Stobaeus has assembled from various Greek poets nine excerpts on peace, most of which are otherwise unknown—passages from Euripides' *Cresphontes,* Aristophanes' *Farmers,* a paean of Bacchylides, Euripides' *Erechtheus,* Philemon's *Pyrrhus,* Euripides' *Suppliants* (481–93), Aristophanes' *Islands* and *Peace* (520–21), and an uncertain play of Menander. Leland may at least be commended for finding out this delightful chapter of Stobaeus, which escaped the notice of most writers on peace in the Renaissance.[13]

It is clear that Leland used the Greek text.[14] He takes only a sentence or a phrase, sometimes only a single word, from the poets he names. Thus from Euripides' *Cresphontes* he borrows the word

---

[13]It did not, however, escape the notice of Girolamo Vida, whose hymn to Peace, simply entitled *Paci,* is likewise a conflation of the passages in Stobaeus, *Flor.* 55, with additions. Needless to say, it is a finer performance than Leland's. (Vida, *Poemata,* J. A. and C. Volpi, eds. [Padua, 1731], 2.150).

[14]The only Latin translation in print was that of Conrad Gesner, (Zürich, 1543); a comparison shows that Leland does not depend on it. The earlier *Apophthegmata* extracted from Stobaeus by Varinus Favorinus Camers (Camerti) (Rome, 1517), omits the excerpts on peace. The Greek text of Stobaeus was published by V. Trincavelli (Venice, 1536).

βαθύπλουτος, "opulentam," and the phrase καλλίστα μακάρων θεῶν, "inter pulcherrima Divas," with "beatam" presumably from μακάρων. In "Quantum bello potiorque," etc. he translates four lines of the *Suppliants* (488–91). He cannot use the homely details of Aristophanes' *Farmers*, but correctly reports that Aristophanes like Euripides calls Peace βαθύπλουτος, "praedives." From the Bacchylides fragment he takes only the first line: τίκτει δέ τε θνατοῖσιν εἰράνα μεγάλα. For Philemon, Leland's "Musa Philonis" obviously will not do; conceivably he let his work go to the printer forgetting that he had not solved a problem here.[15] He freely translates lines 6–7 and 9–10 of the *Pyrrhus fragment:* τήν τε γῆν σκάπτων ἐγώ / νῦν εὗρον [τὸ ἀγαθόν]... γάμους ἑορτὰς συγγενεῖς παῖδας φίλους / πλοῦτον ὑγίειαν σῖτον οἶνον ἡδονήν / αὕτη [εἰρήνη] δίδωσι. Leland makes "Musa" (his own word) the speaker (*ipsa*). Note that he seems to take ἡδονήν as if ἡδύν with οἶνον ("vinumque suäve").

Such is the witness of the Greek poets to the benefits of peace. The Latin poets will follow (193–221):

> Hactenus Aonii celebrarunt carmine Pacem
> Sideream vates. Succedent moxque Latini. . . .
> Sulmonense decus Naso . . .
> Haec cecinit plane dignissima carmina cedro
> Illic, tersa dies ubi fastos Musa celebrat:
> "Frondibus Actiacis comptos redimita capillos
>   "Pax ades, & toto mitis in orbe mane.
> "Dum desunt hostes, desit quoque causa triumphi:
>   "Tu ducibus bello gloria maior eris."

We need not go on with these quotations. Leland follows the two distichs from Ovid's *Fasti* (1.711–14) with a third (*Fasti* 1.703-4), after which he gives a single line from the *Ars Amatoria* (3.502), three distichs from Tibullus (1.10.45-50), and four lines from Silius Italicus (*Punica* 2.592-95). All he has done, however, is unblushingly to lift the whole chapter "De Pace" from the popular schoolbook *Flores Illustrium Poetarum* of Octavianus Mirandula, omitting only a brief quotation from Seneca. The intrusion of elegiac couplets into his hexameter poem seems an especially dubious procedure.

---

[15]Could the superfluous *doctique* of the 1546 text (above, n. 1) be the remains of an attempt at *doctique Philemonis?*

After the poets come the orators, but there are only two of these. Isocrates represents the Greeks (224–29):

> Isocrates rhetor, cum dulcis, tum bonus, acri
> Concussit bellum sceleratum fulmine linguae.
> Causa quidem nota est. Pacis fuit ille patronus
> Innocuae, didicit plus & servire clienti,
> Quam sic a teneris dilexit gratior annis,
> Virginis ut coleret praesentia numina divae.

The reference presumably is to the oration of Isocrates commonly called *On the Peace*, while for the rest, Leland is perhaps improvising.[16] At all events, Isocrates is a natural choice as a Greek orator who constantly advocated peace. As a Roman orator, Cicero might easily have come to mind; his definition, "Pax est tranquilla libertas" (*Philippic* 2.44, 113), for example, had been a keynote in the discussion of peace since the time of St. Augustine. But Leland's Latin orator is anonymous (230–35):

> Alter & orator scripsit, fuit ille Latinus,
> Talia, vir *totus prudens,* de pace togata:
> "Parvae res crescunt, modo sit concordia praesens,
> "Dissipat infelix discordia maxima quaeque,"
> Nil aliud verbis docuit concordibus istis,
> Munera quam Pacis mediis complectitur ulnis.

Leland has versified a well-known tag, "concordia parvae res crescunt, discordia maximae dilabuntur," and faked a setting for it. The words originally come from Sallust, *Jugurtha* 10.6, where they occur in an insincere speech addressed to Jugurtha by Micipsa the king of Numidia, no Latin orator declaiming "de pace togata." But they had long been handed about by writers of peace propaganda, and their origin was sometimes lost sight of. Erasmus, for example, runs them into his description of peace (quoted in part below) without quotation marks.[17] Yet somehow Leland correctly refers

[16]At least the claim in "Quam a teneris dilexit annis" seems not to be founded on anything that Isocrates himself says.

[17]The *sententia* is quoted by Seneca, *Epist.* 94.46, who relates that Marcus Agrippa found in it a useful guide to life; but Leland clearly does not know this passage. Among writers on peace, it is quoted by Marsilio of Padua, *Defensor Pacis* 1.2; Jean Gerson, sermon on "Pax vobis" (*Opera,* Ellies du Pin, ed., 3.1204); Erasmus, *Bellum* (*Opera* [Leiden], II, 957E).

these winged words to an "orator." I can only suggest, without complete confidence, that this may have been an inference from a passage in Richard Pace's *Oratio in pace,* where Pace touches on the orators' praise of peace, and includes this familiar aphorism in close proximity to Isocrates' oration *On the Peace:*

> Pacis autem fructus tam amplus est & copiosus, ut nullus unquam tam disertus & eloquens repertus sit orator, qui pacis bona dignis laudibus prosequi potuerit. Unde illud vulgatum quidem est sed *prudentissime* scriptum, Discordia res magnas dilabi, concordia vero, id est pace, parvas crescere.... Non temere itaque Isocrates (non minus bonus philosophus quam facundus orator) de pace ad populum Atheniensem orationem habiturus dixit statim in initio, se de re maxima & omni humano generi utilissima verba facturum. Cui astipulatus Silius, Ethnicus & ipse, in hunc scribit modum, Pax optima rerum, quas homini natura dedit.[18]

Having given assurance of the "pia munera" of Peace through these authorities, Leland adds the *comparatio* that one expects in an encomium. Inevitably it is a contrast of peace and war such as nearly every "laudatio pacis" contains. Perhaps Leland's comparison differs from most in slighting the description of war; but by expanding on peace he supplements the list of *benefacta* which his witnesses had given him (241–79):

> Bellum tristis hyems, sit fas mihi dicere verum,
> Omnia corrumpit, veluti populator iniquus.
> Nec sperare sinit quicquam, quod dulce futurum
> Utile quodve siet, tanta indignatio crevit.
> Veris at effigies Pax est ipissima laeti,
> Ac sperare iubet felix felicia semper,
> Rebus & humanis affulget ut Hesperus illa.

[18]The *Oratio Richardi Pacei in pace nuperrime composita,* [etc.], was published in 1518 by R. Pynson in London and by J. Gourmont in Paris, and Gourmont at the same time issued a French version, *Oraison en la louenge de la paix,* [etc.]. The oration was delivered by Pace in St. Paul's on the occasion of the treaty of October 1518 between Henry VIII and Francis I. There is every likelihood that Leland knew this work. Pace depends heavily on Erasmus for the topics of his oration—the quotation from Silius with the incorrect *natura dedit* is from Erasmus' *Querela Pacis*—and he may have taken the Sallust quotation from Erasmus' *Bellum* where it is used without mention of the source. (The French translation of Pace's oration adds the references wanting in the Latin: "une chose qui est escripte tres prudemment en lhystoire de Saluste.")

Cultores repetunt agros, hortique renident
Floribus eximie pictis. Pecudes & opime
Pascuntur. Villae passim aedificantur in agris.
Oppida mox instaurantur collapsa, suisque
Hinc exstructa locis ornantur, & aucta profuse
Insolitum ostentant per lumina clara nitorem,
Visque salutiferae legis viget undique tota.
Cognitione valens vera respublica floret,
Relligioque suis innititur alta columnis. . . .
Pacatusque maris reflui furor improbus ille
Mercatoris opes domino sua foenera reddet.
Denique sedulitas studiorum clara bonorum,
Eloquiique decus fama super aethera notum,
Ingenium quotquot felix ostendit & artes.

As we expect, the passage is borrowed. The description of peace—
"Veris at effigies," etc.—is a verse-paraphrase of a cumulative passage ("frequentatio") in Erasmus' *Dulce bellum inexpertis:*[19]

Pacis tempore, non secus ac si novum quoddam ver rebus humanis
adfulserit: coluntur agri, vernant horti, pascuntur laetae pecudes,
aedificantur villae, exstruuntur oppida, instaurantur collapsa, ornantur et augentur exstructa, crescunt opes, aluntur voluptates, vigent
leges, floret reipublicae disciplina, fervet religio, . . . efflorescunt
honestissimarum disciplinarum studia.[20]

According to Aphthonius, an encomium should end "with a
prayer or something of the sort."[21] Leland follows the rule:

Haec ego concinui divinae Pacis amator,
Qualiacunque mei commonstrans gaudia cordis.

---

[19]*Adagia* 4.1.1 (*Opera* II, 957E); *Dulce bellum inexpertis*, Yvonne Remy and René
Dunil-Marquebreucq, eds. (Collection Latomus 8, Berchem-Brussels, 1953), p. 44.

[20]Leland has suppressed one item of Erasmus' description, namely "aluntur voluptates" (compare his treatment of ἡδονή in Philemon, above?). At the end, he has
added two points to those of Erasmus, the resumption of trade, "pacatusque maris,"
etc., and the reparation of the lost generation: "Amissus iuvenum bello grex re-
stituetur. . . . Et numerosa cohors reparabit damna cadentum." It is hard to see how
Erasmus failed to include the first of these points, which is made in nearly all such
lists in the fifteenth and sixteenth centuries; Vida (n. 13 above) inevitably adds it to
his Greek originals where it is also missing. The second point is also traditional,
occurring already in Cassiodorus in a "frequentatio" on peace (*Varia* 1.1): "Haec
[tranquillitas] est enim bonarum artium decora mater, *haec mortalium genus reparabili
successione multiplicans* facultates protendit, mores excolit," [etc.].

[21]Aphthonius, *Progymnasmata* 8.

Leland's *Laudatio Pacis*

Te Superi faciles conservent, maxime Regum
Henrice, Eduardumque tuum. Flos inclytus ille
Nobilium decus & puerorum gloria prima.
Conservent etiam Dii magni foedera longum
Pacis oliviferae, ut tu, clarissime Victor,
In terris vigeas Francisco iunctus amico,
Gallorum Domino summo Regique potenti.
Sic utriusque suis florebit fama nitelis,
Laetus & applausum populus dabit ore canoro.

We have seen Leland busy among his books in the summer of
1546. If the metrical oration he produced from them is not very
much above the level of schoolwork, it is at least firmly based on
sound rules of composition. The "proposition" gives the author's
purpose. The "narration" sets the concept of peace within God's
plan for the world and indicates that the peace newly concluded is a
sign of His mercy. With due expressions of modesty, the author
introduces the encomium proper, in which he follows the pattern
set for this form by the *Progymnasmata* and fills it up by the imitation of approved authors. If these authors have been rather too
easily come by, Leland deserves some credit at least for ingenuity in
adapting them to his rhetorical scheme. No one else mixed this
particular brew. Apart from the intrusion of elegiac quotations into
a hexameter poem, a departure which can hardly be condoned, the
style is agreeable and sufficiently correct. Yet in point of style, as in
other qualities, one must agree with the critic who finds the earlier
and less derivative parts of the poem superior to the rest.[22] We can
hardly escape the conclusion that Leland started ambitiously and
ended in haste.

[22]Leicester Bradner, *op. cit.,* p. 28.

A Speculation on Two Passages in
the Latin Poems of Thomas More

Poem 125 in More's *Epigrammata*, the longest of his poems in number of lines, is placed near the center of the book in the first edition (1518) and exactly in the center in the second (1520).[1] No doubt this was done for the sake of balance, but the structure and content of the poem, its style and verse-form, and perhaps its occasion and destination combine to give it a singular interest.

In form Poem 125 is an address to an imaginary "Candidus" on the theme "Qualis uxor deligenda," a common enough theme of school rhetoric, and is developed according to rule as a *suasoria*. The occasion is stated (it is time for Candidus to marry and marriage is a duty for one of his high station in life); the *propositio* follows: One should not choose a wife for her personal beauty or for a rich dowry; and after discounting the value of beauty and wealth, More proceeds to describe the qualities a good wife should have, prominent among which is the possession of a classical education; he confirms his proof with a series of *exempla;* and concludes with a recapitulation of his argument that neither beauty nor a rich dowry is a proper basis of choice. The presentation is didactic and objective; we do not learn, for example, whether the speaker is himself married.[2] The style is colloquial, but based on imitation,

---

[1] *The Latin Poems of Thomas More*, edited with translation and notes by Leicester Bradner and Charles Arthur Lynch (Chicago: The University of Chicago Press, 1953), pp. 57–64. There is a French translation by Martha Ravoze in *Moreana* 26 (1970) 18–32.

[2] The one passage that seems to inform us on this point is in fact equivocal. This is the asseveration with which the peroration begins (vv. 213–14):

> Sic nunc me amet mea
> Ut nil ego tibi
> Amice, mentiar.

(Now, so love me my (wife) I shall tell you no lies, my friend.) The words *me amet mea*, "May my wife love me" may refer to a future wife rather than a present one; cf. the phrase, *Ita di me ament*. The adverb *nunc* is transitional here, not temporal.

and particularly in the frequent use of diminutives—*tenellula, puellula, ocellulis,* etc.—recalls Catullus 61, an epithalamium. The meter (see the excerpt below) is unique among More's Latin poems, and is correctly described in the title of the piece as iambic dimeter brachycatalectic. That is, it consists of three iambic feet, more familiarly called iambic trimeter in English metrics. This meter is not found in any classical Latin author, but is quickly recognizable as similar in effect to the short lines—what Saintsbury calls "linekins"—that are characteristic of English poetry in More's time, and especially of songs associated with the Court.[3]

Poem 125 is thus rather close to the schools in concept and close to vernacular poetry in metrical form. Its rapid pace and urgent beat admirably suit the content, which centers in the description of a perfect wife—one not too forward in manner nor too backward, not too talkative nor too silent; one who from the best of ancient books draws moral principles that enable her to bear life's vicissitudes and to be the teacher of her children and grand children; with her music and conversation making her home more attractive to her husband than the society of men; able to quiet you when you are too exalted and to raise you up when you are depressed, her discourse combining *eloquentia* with a serious understanding of the world of affairs.[4]

This description is followed by the confirming examples, and it is to these that I wish to call attention. They are examples of young women remarkable for their education and culture. The first is Eurydice—"Orpheus never would have gone to Hades to bring back an uneducated girl (*rusticam*)"; the second is Perilla, the (supposed) daughter of Ovid, "equal to her father as a poet"; next Tullia, the daughter of Cicero, "beloved by a supremely learned

---

[3]George Saintsbury, *A History of English Prosody* (London, 1906), p. 243; cf. William Nelson, *John Skelton Laureate* (New York, 1939), p. 88. Much of Skelton's *Philip Sparrow* is in trimeters, as is almost the whole of his *Ware Hawk.* More's English poem *A Mery Gest* is also in "linekins," i.e., two dimeters and a trimeter, which is the meter of the much admired *Nut Brown Maid.* John M. Berdan, *Early Tudor Poetry 1485-1547* (New York: Macmillan, 1920; reprint, Hamden, Conn., 1961), ch. 3, is surely on firm ground in referring these poems in various types of versicles to the theory and practice of accentual Latin poetry in the late middle ages. More's poem to Candidus could be described as written in a six-syllable line with more than a few traces of rime (though these were perhaps not intentional). It is strictly classical quantitative meter.

[4]There is no mention of religious instruction and the reading of pious authors, though these are regularly emphasized in the humanistic treatises on the education of women. See the forthcoming article by Rita Guerlac, "Vives and the School for Wives."

father"; next Cornelia, the mother of the Gracchi, "her sons'
teacher as well as their parent"; and finally an unnamed modern
example who far surpasses all the rest. To her is devoted an expansion of twenty-one lines. Led up to by a list of ancient women, and
coming at the end of More's whole argument, this unmarried girl
(*virgo*) may even be the raison d'être of the poem.

> Quid prisca secula
> Tandem revolvimus?
> Utcumque rusticum
> 180 Unam tamen tenet
> Nostrumque virginem
> Tenet sed unicam
> Ac sit ut unicam
> Plerisque praeferat
> 185 Cuique conferat
> Ex his, fuisse quae
> Narrantur omnibus
> Tot retro seculis
> Quae nunc et ultimam
> 190 Monet Britanniam
> Perlata pennulis
> Famae volucribus
> Laus atque gloria
> Orbis puellula
> 195 Totius unica
> Ac non modo suae
> Cassandra patriae

But why do I turn back to ancient times? Our own age also, rude
though it is, possesses one such maiden, but possesses only one; yet
even so would prefer its only one to most, and would compare her
with any of those who are reported to have lived in all the ages past.
She now gives warning even to remotest Britain, borne upon the swift
wings of Report, a peerless girl, the praise and the glory of the whole
world, and not the Cassandra only of her native land.

Who is this well-educated girl (*puellula*),[5] unique in More's time
and comparable with any cultured woman of the past? She is not in
England, but comes by report with a warning for the distant Bri-

---

[5]The diminutive *puellula* is repeatedly used by Catullus in reference to the high-
born bride of Catul. 61 (vv. 57, 182, 188).

tons. The "praise and the glory of the whole world" can only be someone of public note, and More's rhapsodical, yet rather indefinite, language suggests that he is speaking of royalty. The present essay will proceed upon the hypothesis that the unique maiden is the youthful Catherine of Aragon, whose humanistic education was famous and admired.[6] It would in fact be an awkward coincidence if More had used terms and tones befitting Catherine and had yet had someone else in mind. If Catherine of Aragon is meant, the poem must have been written before she came to England in the autumn of 1501, but not long before, perhaps in 1499 or 1500. It would thus be among the earliest of the poems in More's collection. However, recognition of Catherine here must remain tentative so long as no Cassandra-like warning by her is known to us. This reported warning (vv. 189–97) is the conclusion and culmination of the whole passage. It shows that, no doubt together with *eloquentia,* the maiden possesses "a serious understanding of affairs." There would be no impropriety in attributing such understanding to Catherine of Aragon at the age of fifteen.[7] Catullus's *ultimam Britanniam* might be intended as a quasi-quotation from her message.

[6] All the biographers of Catherine of Aragon dwell upon her classical education and her learning, which was celebrated by Erasmus and Vives; see, for example, Garrett Mattingly, *Catherine of Aragon* (London, 1942), p. 17.

In the translation of More's verses given above, the familiar tag *ultimam Britanniam* (see Catullus 11,11; 29,4; Horace, *Carm.* 1.35,29) is assumed to have its usual meaning, "far distant Britain," and thus to place the unnamed girl outside the British Isles. Bradner and Lynch, however, followed by the French translator (n. 1 above) have slanted their translation to allow the *puellula* to be someone in England: "Borne high upon the soaring wings of fame, she is now heeded even in the remotest parts of Britain" (a possible interpretation of *ultimam,* but unlikely in this tag). The late R. S. Sylvester, in annotating their translation at this point, nevertheless thought of Catherine of Aragon: "Henry VIII's sisters Margaret and Mary have been suggested . . . and Catherine of Aragon might be added to the list" (St. Thomas More, *The History of King Richard III and Selections from the English and Latin Poems,* Sylvester, ed. [New Haven and London: Yale University Press, 1976], p. 145, n.6). But Sylvester did not press his suggestion, and so far as the bias of the Bradner-Lynch translation favors someone present in England it thereby excludes Catherine, since to call Catherine *virginem* after her arrival in England and her marriage to Prince Arthur would be taking sides prematurely on a question that was to rock the whole of Christendom. An early draft of this paper had the approval of Professor Sylvester.

[7] In a letter dated June 9, 1501 (*Epist.* 221) while Catherine was awaiting favorable winds to carry her to England, Peter Martyr writes of her that though brought up at Court, "pollet tamen animo pro viribus femineis; viget ingenio et prudentia, Matrem praeter ceteras sorores aemuletur."

Since neither the identity of the world-famous girl nor the content of her warning is revealed, the poem presumably was intended for readers who knew these things and would approve More's discretion in avoiding explicitness. Such readers would most likely be found at Court, and a Latin poem destined for the Court would no doubt in the first place be designed for the royal pupils and their tutors. An edifying poem, rhetorically fashioned and on a rhetorical theme, free of sensual allusion, and written in Latin that is almost English, might make agreeable collateral reading. It is hardly conceivable that this poem could have been the product of More's pen (nescio quid scriptorum) that he presented to Prince Henry on the occasion when, with Erasmus and Arnold, he visited the royal children at Eltham Palace in the autumn of 1499.[8] A poem written in a kind of Latin skeltonics might have interested Henry's tutor, John Skelton; but instruction on the choice of a wife would seem grossly inappropriate for presentation to an eight-year-old child, even if that child was going to be Henry VIII. Such verses might, however, have been offered with propriety to Prince Arthur on a similar occasion (he was not present at Eltham), suggesting that a young Englishman, Candidus, would be well advised to choose a wife resembling the princess who was to be his queen. This certainly is speculative, but it is hard to believe that a poem of this description could have been written by More for his desk.

The poem may, however, have a point of contact with More's personal history that may make our hypothesis difficult to sustain.

---

[8]Erasmus, *Opus Epistolarum*, P. S. and H. M. Allen, eds., I, 6. Erasmus' offhand description of More's offering quoted above leaves it doubtful whether a poem or something in prose is meant. That it was a poem, however, may perhaps be inferred from the fact that Erasmus himself immediately wrote a poem for presentation to Henry. This *Prosopopoeia Britanniae* (Reedijk, pp. 248–53) is also composed on a rhetorical model, and evidently was intended to be read by the prince under the eye of his tutor, since Erasmus takes care to include in it a handsome compliment to Skelton in this capacity. As a suitable gift for Henry at Eltham, we might think of More's *Epig.* 5 (Bradner and Lynch p. 24), a short poem in twelve lines on the union of the red rose and the white rose. Erasmus also develops this theme (*Prosop.* vv. 75–87) but vaguely and in fact incorrectly (red roses and white roses grow on the same stem); was he hastily borrowing from More without understanding? More appended his epigram to the poems presented to King Henry in 1509 (n. 13 below) following two poems inscribed *ad regem*, but not itself so designated. It would apply to any one of the children of Henry VII and Queen Margaret.

The cultural attainments to be expected of an eligible bride are introduced by the following lines (vv. 99–102):

> Sit illa vel modo
> Instructa literis,
> Vel talis ut modo
> Sit apta literis.

Let her possess a literary education or be capable of receiving one.

Young women possessing a literary (humanist) education would not be numerous in Candidus's environment, and the alternative "or capable of receiving one" might occur to anyone writing on More's theme, but when said by More the words inevitably recall his actual experience. Jane Colt, whom More married when she was seventeen, was without this culture and More undertook to educate her in "letters and music," which are also the fields of competence recommended for the bride of Poem 125.[9] The accepted date of their marriage is "not later than about January 1505,"[10] so that, if the alternative *sit talis* etc. is taken to reflect the education of Jane, our hypothesis, which requires the poem to have been written before 1501, must be abandoned. Just possibly it may express an idea that More later found himself able to make into a reality when he married Jane. At the age of twenty-one or twenty-two (1499–1500) he might already have been contemplating marriage. However, the four years he spent with the Carthusians presumably fall within the years 1501 and 1504, and it is likely to have been toward the end of this period that, according to Erasmus, he pondered the alternatives of joining a religious order on the one hand or marriage on the other, deciding finally on marriage.

More's devotion to Catherine of Aragon is a fact of importance in his life; beginning on the November day in 1501 when he witnessed her first entry into London and hoped for the best from her marriage to Arthur, and extending to the day when he faced the judges who condemned him and said to them that it was his loyalty to her

---

[9] Erasmus, *Epist.* Allen, IV, 18: "Hanc et literis instituendam curavit et omni musicae genere doctam reddidit."

[10] Allen, *ibid.* Their eldest child, Margaret, was born in or about October 1505.

that had brought him to this pass.[11] It would be interesting if this devotion began even before she came to England. If she could be recognized as the *puellula* of the poem, More would already compare her with any of the cultured women of the past, but in the end he actually compares the *puellula*—in fact identifies her—with the tragic Cassandra, a princess whose prophetic warnings went unheeded—as though under this name she completed his list of ancient *exempla*. Comparison with Cassandra strikes an unhappy note. If Catherine could have foreseen the disasters, beginning with the death of Arthur, that awaited her in England, she would indeed have deserved every syllable of the name.[12]

The only certain appearance of Catherine of Aragon in More's Latin poems is likewise in a context of joyfulness and happy expectation. After the death of Arthur, Catherine had waited in London, often in great uncertainty, for seven years until—rather unexpectedly at the last—she found herself married to the youthful King Henry in the spring of 1509. More's panegyric on the coronation of the new sovereigns, which took place on Midsummer's Day—the poem placed at the beginning of his *Epigrammata*—is again a demonstration of his rhetorical skill, this time in applying the rules for an encomium.[13] Catherine (not even here mentioned by name) is introduced by the same rhetorical device as that employed in Poem 125, that is, by a catalogue of ancient women, each of whom she is said to surpass in some special virtue (*comparatio* is an *encomium* topic): She excels the Sabine women in *pietas;* demigoddesses in

[11]More, letter to John Holt in R. W. Chambers, *Thomas More* (London, 1935), p. 81 (speech to his judges).

[12]According to a report known to Polydore Vergil she did in fact foresee the death of Prince Arthur: "Puella Catarina longe ante tristem huius matrimonii exitum praesigivisse fertur," recognizing as an evil portent the massive Atlantic storm that, when she sailed for England, drove her vessels back to Spain with the loss of one of them (*Anglia Historia,* Book 24 [26], Denys Hay, ed. [London, 1950], pp. 112, 128.) Catherine is also reported to have said that her marriage to Prince Arthur was doomed in advance as made in blood, referring to the execution (1500) of the Earl of Warwick, who was put to death, perhaps at Ferdinand's behest, to remove a possible claimant to the English throne. Biographers of Catherine assume that she learned of this event only after her arrival in England (Mattingly, *op. cit.,* p. 294).

[13]The presentation copy survives (Brit. Lib. Cotton, Titus D. iv), having in its margins annotations, said to be in a later hand, which indicate at the proper places the encomium topics that More had handled: *Laus a corporis dotibus—laus ab animi virtutibus—laus a rebus gestis—laus a litteris—laus reginae* (Bradner and Lynch, p. 22). One may perhaps guess that these marginalia reflect the tutorial instruction of some later prince or princess.

majesty; Alcestis in chaste love; Tanaquil in readiness of judgment; Cornelia (once more) in *eloquium;* and Penelope in loyalty to her husband.

With this mainly legendary list—Cornelia alone is a fully historical person—More's aim is to sketch a portrait of Catherine in symbols. Devoted both to her Spanish father and her English husband, she will work to unite two peoples, as did the Sabine women. Her queenly presence is above any human standard, yet not too far above. Like Alcestis, she is ready to lay down her life for her husband. Her judgment is such that she will give the king wise counsel such as Tanaquil gave to Tarquinius Priscus, and with Cornelia's *eloquentia* she will present her views convincingly and play an active role as a Renaissance sovereign. Finally, her loyalty to her husband has already been shown by her long years of waiting for him.

This passage clearly has something in common with Poem 125. The catalogue of famous women whose virtues Catherine is said to surpass is, to be sure, a common device of *encomium,* but at least it is employed by More only in these two poems, and we see that it is especially appropriate for women of public eminence, and that it occurs to More to apply it when he comes to praise Catherine of Aragon. The women listed in 125 are (except Cornelia) regarded as youthful (two are "daughters"), since they lead up to the glorious *virgo.* In the coronation poem (which is also in part an epithalamium), all are married and are seen in relation to their husbands, and of the named individuals all (except Cornelia) are queens. In both cases *decorum* governs the choices, yet in a device that More uses only on two occasions the contrast might be conscious. So too his praise of the foreign maiden is for the most part vague, but his praise of Queen Catherine, whom he has come to know, is more definite and detailed. At beginning, middle, and end of the list are placed the qualities—devotion, love, and loyalty—that will endear her to her husband. Interwoven with them are her qualities as an individual, her queenly presence, and the intellectual qualities of a ready (and sound) judgment and *eloquentia.* In the last two we recognize the unusual abilities required of a perfect wife in 125, consummate *eloquentia* together with a serious understanding of the world of affairs. And the word *eloquium (eloquentia)* alludes to Catherine's humanist training, since *eloquentia* was the principal goal of such an education.

A final point calls for attention in this list of famous women.

Having said that Catherine surpasses Penelope in loyalty to her husband (*maritali fide*), More elaborates on this last parallel with some lines on Catherine's years of anxious waiting for Henry. The king is addressed:

> Illa tibi, Princeps, multos devota per annos
> Sola tui longa mansit amore mora.
> Non illam germana soror, nec patria flexit,
> Non potuit mater, non revocare pater.
> Unum te matri, te praetulit illa sorori,
> Te patriae et caro praetulit illa patri.

Without doubt the educated reader is expected to catch the allusion in these last four lines, which are an adaptation of Catullus 64.117–20. Ariadne is leaving home to follow Theseus:

> Commemorem, ut linquens genitoris filia vultum,
> Ut consanguineae [sister's] complexum, ut denique matris,
> Quae misera in gnata deperdita laetabatur,
> Omnibus his Thesei dulcem praeopterit amorem.

Little modification was needed to adjust Ariadne's departure from home to fit Catherine's refusal to return; and no matter if the facts are somewhat colored for the occasion—if ever Ferdinand called Catherine home, it was a diplomatic feint. But again More's classical parallel makes us feel uneasy. He seldom works classical passages into his original poems in this way, and this rare example seems unfortunate. The well-educated queen might well recognize the allusion, perhaps with a passing shiver at the omen. Would this Ariadne also be abandoned by her Theseus? She would indeed.

Thus in our reading a small cloud passes fleetingly over each of two cheerful poems. Behind the tragic Cassandra, the unseen Catalina; behind the proud young queen, the unseen Ariadne. Very likely More was unaware of this effect; a warning princess is a Cassandra, a princess who leaves home to follow a foreign prince recalls Ariadne, and that is all. But it seems odd all the same that on both occasions More should have been led to evoke a parallel so ominous in the event.

Review: The Classical Tradition

In this substantial, warmly written, and easily read book, Professor Highet conducts us through the centuries of European literature from *Beowulf* to Anouilh and Cocteau, presenting the broad sweep of classical influence, and yet keeping us always or mainly in the presence of concrete literary works and their authors. The volume is primarily a handbook for students, but this basic character is crossed with a strong literary and critical, and propagandist, purpose that gives it a life and an ethos well beyond the nature of a handbook. As a handbook it presents, with conventional periodization, an imposing array of information, generally based (if one reviewer may judge of that) upon the best modern authorities, and set down with a remarkable degree of accuracy. On its important subject no other book exists that is at once so broad in scope and so full of detail; and surely no one can read it without learning much, and learning delightfully. Where Highet's other purposes enter in, in some measure shaping this material, we cannot but have certain reservations; and the book is sometimes too evidently written down to the supposed level of the American undergraduate or college alumnus to whom it seems primarily to be addressed; but the main point is that it unquestionably succeeds in imparting both solid information and legitimate enthusiasm to minds beyond the contracting circle of classical scholars.

The underlying concept is the just and inevitable one that the classical tradition in literature is vital only in works that are vital themselves. With this limiting principle there goes, perhaps not exactly as a deduction, the idea that from the first only works written

A review of Gilbert Highet, *The Classical Tradition: Greek and Roman Influences on Western Literature* (Oxford University Press, 1949). From the *American Journal of Philology* 73 (1952) 79–87. Copyright © 1952 by The Johns Hopkins University Press.

in the vernacular languages are really alive; classical culture comes home to our business and bosoms only when naturalized in our mother tongue. Accordingly, the whole Latin culture of the Middle Ages and the Renaissance is left out of direct account, and the early Middle Ages are represented only by Old English literature, with mention of the Carolingian revival in a parenthesis, and the later Middle Ages only by the French romances and Dante. That saves space; does it also imply that, before Dante, the heights and depths of the European spirit were fully reflected in the vernacular literatures? The same principle again saves space by allowing Highet to bring Germany into the picture only with the mid-eighteenth century, and to deny that country any earlier Renaissance. "The sixteenth-century Renaissance did not affect Germany," the Table of Contents roundly states (p. xxix); in Germany there came forward no great vernacular writers but "instead, we find nothing except a few [!] humanists writing Latin—the most distinguished being Ulrich von Hutten [?]"—and some poor vernacular writers, the reason being that "the cultural level of the ordinary public was too low" and "the class-distinctions of German society kept a gulf fixed between the Latin-reading and writing university men and the outside world" (p. 368). Literature is vital in so far as it keeps in touch with the common people, and an excess of classical culture is as injurious as too little. "Classical culture always produces its finest effects in the modern world when it penetrates to the ordinary people and encourages a Rabelais to teach himself Greek, puts Chapman's Homer in the hands of Keats, or makes Shakespeare enthusiastic over Plutarch" (*ibid.*). In this spirit, an entire chapter is given to Shakespeare's knowledge of the classics, while Milton is parceled out under Pastoral, Epic, and Drama, and seldom treated with much sympathy; and classical French tragedy, with "baroque" tragedy in general, is "a comparative failure," largely because addressed to a narrow aristocratic audience. A less extreme view is taken in agreement with Du Bellay (p. 232):

"Nationalism narrows culture; extreme classicism desiccates it. To enrich a national culture by bringing into it the strength of a continent-wide and centuries-ripe culture to which it belongs is the best way to make it eternally great. This can be proved both positively and negatively in the Renaissance. It was this synthesis of national and classical elements that produced, in England, Shakespeare's tragedies and the epics of Spenser and Milton. It was the same synthesis in France that, after a period of experiment, produced the lyrics of Ronsard, the satires of Boileau, the dramas not only of Racine and Corneille but of Molière. It was the failure to complete such a synthesis that kept the Germans . . . from producing any great works of literature during the sixteenth century."

In this juster view, Milton and the French tragic writers inevitably revert to their natural eminence, or nearly; for surely Milton and Racine, with more complete assimilation of classical culture, produced finer effects than Keats or Rabelais at least. And the association (here significantly due to Du Bellay) of the growth of Renaissance literature with the rise of national consciousness probably is more historical—though less attractive to the present-day reader—than explanations assuming that French society was more democratic than German in the sixteenth century.

The recognition of a synthesis defines the spirit, but not altogether the method, of the book. Himself seeking to interest a more popular class of readers, Highet does not adhere with rigor to this principle nor develop its implications. To define the classical tradition in literature as a synthesis is one thing, to define the terms of the synthesis and to carry the ideas so defined through the long dialectic of European intellectual history as reflected in literature is quite another, and not the author's purpose. Otherwise, for example, it would be necessary to include the Latin culture of the Middle Ages and of the Renaissance as the matrix of the major ideas and intentions carried over into the vernaculars. It would be necessary to follow the successive literary movements, in France for example, and ask what normative value the classics had for, say, the Rhétoriqueurs, the school of Marot, the Pléiade, and the school of Malherbe. The history of literary theory would have to be taken into account; also the impact of education. It would be necessary, especially for the sixteenth century, to find a means of measuring the relative value of popular and humanistic elements, and necessary to note which of the classics were assimilable in different climates of sensibility, and to what extent. Both sides of the synthesis are compounded and variable. The understanding of antiquity and of individual authors shifts, indeed advances, from age to age, and the literary world follows but seldom is abreast of the advance. Ficino's Plato is not the Plato of Schleiermacher, and even the Platonism of Ficino tends to be reduced by the Renaissance poets to "Platonic love" under the pressure of the courtly love of an older tradition—which itself owed something to an older apprehension of Platonism. Indirect influence and a sort of digestive process, in which the whole "republic of letters" is involved, are essential to assimilation. Doubtless the basic studies are lacking for a firm and connected treatment of some of these essential topics, and to raise the abstract content would very likely lower the concrete content of the book. The author's tact envisages a class of readers who will be more content with a long series of interesting facts and of discussions of individual writers, punctuated by broad and rather unverifiable generalizations about successive historical epochs—social, political, moral, even military in character—from which supposedly the literary phenomena are to be immediately deduced. The intermediate realm of operative causes and occasions—of literary aims, discussions, and schools—is generally passed over; we are presented with results rather than processes, and the material influence of ancient literature is more in evidence than the dynamic influence.

Highet writes less as a scientific historian (of whose attitude he is diffident) or a modern literary critic than as a humanist. That is to say, he allows his authors a considerable degree of freedom from historical and psychological necessity and brings into prominence their personal choices; and he is frequently occupied with the moral content of literature. The stirring Conclusion, though several times promising to return to literary matters, is throughout a sermon on life and conduct. The message of antiquity is, What shall it profit a man if he shall gain the whole world and lose his own soul?—a text which, however, sounds somehow different as paraphrased in Highet's final sentence: "The real duty of man is not to extend his power or multiply his wealth beyond his needs, but to enrich and enjoy his only imperishable possession: his soul." The echo of the Catechism uncomfortably reminds us that neither the Westminster divines nor Plato would have left the real duty of man at that. Nor would Matthew Arnold, "unwilling, pro-pagan Christian" though he be (p. 93)—whose *Hellenism and Hebraism,* as a statement of the "synthesis" upon the moral plane, might well have found mention somewhere in this book. For indeed classical culture has represented a high standard of broad humanity that has guarded religion itself against a narrow and harsh fanaticism, that has fortified the conscience of the West against tyrannies of all kinds, that has upheld the primacy of the intellect and of scientific thought, while providing an antidote to extreme intellectualism by its pervading moral sense; and it has taught literature to rise above the trivialities of the folksongs and romances of ordinary people to embrace deeper issues in disciplined forms adequate to the responses of a mature civilization. If Western culture is to retain its values, the classics can never be just one subject among many or the concern only of specialists—yet that is about where we are. Whatever we may miss in this book in the way of historical nuances, the firm apprehension of this salient point is something to be grateful for.

The limitations of the method, though at the risk of excluding essentials of the subject, enable the author to handle a still enormous material with control and perspicuity. After an Introduction outlining the growth of civilization through the Middle Ages and the Renaissance, the chapter-headings are as follows: The Dark Ages: English Literature; The Middle Ages: French Literature; Dante; Towards the Renaissance: Petrarch, Boccaccio, Chaucer; The Renaissance: Translation;—Drama;—Epic;—Pastoral and Romance; Rabelais and Montaigne; Shakespeare's Classics; The Renaissance and Afterwards: Lyric Poetry; Transition; The Battle of the Books; A Note on Baroque; Baroque Tragedy; Satire; Baroque Prose; The Time of Revolution; Parnassus and Antichrist; A Century of Scholarship; The Symbolist Poets and James Joyce; The Reinterpretation of the Myths; Conclusion. The main lines are: slow growth ending in the "outburst" of the Renaissance; this outburst checked by the Counter-Reformation and various disturbances, leading to the Baroque period, which is marked by a crisis in the attitude to the classics (the Battle of the Books), but continues to the revolutionary period; the nineteenth century notable for its knowledge of antiquity, but ending in a decline of classical education; twentieth-century use of the classic myths as symbols for twentieth-century problems.

Though the Battle of the Books is treated as a kind of symbol under which to gather up all opposition at any time to the classics, there is perhaps a loss of perspective in placing it before the chapters on the baroque authors, inasmuch as, in France, the success of the seventeenth-century writers was the occasion for the Battle and a chief strength of the "moderns." One may wonder whether the term "baroque" has not been stretched well beyond usefulness in recent literary history. Here it is carried pretty far and results in some dubious classifications. Perhaps Calderón (1600–81) is a Renaissance dramatist, while Corneille (1606–84) is a baroque dramatist, but apparently Milton wrote Renaissance epic poems and a baroque tragedy, while Titian somehow goes hand in hand with Tiepolo as a typical baroque painter (pp. 178, 291). There is some chronological confusion also in the account of the "conflicts . . . erupting throughout the early Renaissance" (pp. 178–81), where, among witnesses for the early Renaissance, Tasso, Shakespeare, Donne, Galileo, and Cyrano de Bergerac are clearly misplaced. In a book in which choice must be severe, one finds little to complain of in the omission of authors; and very properly Highet raises his requirements in the most recent period, where he does well to single out "the reinterpretation of the myths" for central attention—especially since with it goes the influence of Greek drama. He keeps close to imaginative literature. Yet one might wish that a little space could have been found for continental travel literature after Chateaubriand (Maurice Barrès, *Voyage de Sparte;* Thibaudet, *Les Heures de l'Acropole;* Hauptmann, *Griechischer Frühling*) as a significant expression of the *rêve grec.* There are unacknowledged, though necessary, geographical limitations; yet Holberg and Ibsen, for example, might have found a small niche somewhere. The Preface promises to show how Greek and Latin influence has "moulded the literature of Western Europe and America," but, not to think of Latin America, very few American authors are considered; absent from the Index are Emerson, Lowell, Bryant, Hawthorne (though Lew Wallace gets in), E. A. Robinson, and Edgar Lee Masters. (Suggestions here might have been found in John Paul Pritchard's *Return to the Fountains.*) Such omissions are, however, relatively unimportant or can be justified; our one legitimate complaint on this score is the absence of a discussion of Molière and the modern comedy of manners. The unfavorable view of baroque tragedy in Chapter 16 seems preparatory to a favorable view of comedy, and the last sentences of the chapter announce the subject. Has a section been excised? The amputation, if such it be, leaves a scar; for of all writers, Molière perhaps best represents the author's ideal of a happy balance between classical influences and the native spirit. La Fontaine too should probably have been included.

In a book on the classical tradition the Renaissance naturally demands a central position. Highet makes it the culmination of his introductory sketch, placing there his remarks on the Revival of Learning, and in the body of the book treats it in a series of chapters on authors and literary species. There is little attempt to understand the Renaissance as an epoch in intellectual history; and from the text of the Introduction and from the references it appears that the author knows of nothing on this subject since J. A. Symonds. Even so, among the topics touched on, humanist education and the humanists themselves need not have been omitted. Indeed, if the decline of classical influence is to be accounted for later on in chapters on the Battle of the Books and a Century of Scholarship, the "outburst" of the Renaissance deserves a chapter on, say, a Century of Humanism to introduce it; and if the failure of latter-day humanist education is emphasized, perspective would be gained by some mention of the success of the "new learning" in the schools of the Renaissance. By such omissions half the meaning of the classicizing movement in the vernacular literatures of the sixteenth century is lost. The *questione della lingua* as a historical actuality does not appear (Bembo, for example, is not mentioned), and except by implication we are not made to see Renaissance literature in its process as a *fond* of older "mediaeval" literary directions yielding to or resisting the conscious efforts at "illustration" by a new classical ideal. The penalty of the handbook method is to make the chapters on authors and literary species exclusive and static. Thus there is no place for the literary dialogue, certainly a chief prose-form of Renaissance literature, and Castiglione, for example, finds no mention. No place is found for Renaissance Platonism (not even Spenser's *Fower Hymns* are noticed), and Platonism as a topic emerges only with Wordsworth and Shelley. The object seems to be to treat literature so far as possible apart from the history of ideas; but this can hardly justify the neglect of Renaissance literary theory, both rhetoric and poetics, which is at the heart of the classical revival. A rapid glance at the Unities (pp. 142–43) is not enough. The neglect is little short of disastrous in the chapter on the Renaissance epic poem—the department in which tension between the popular and the classical tradition came to an open crisis in European letters on the question of the *romanzi*, amid which Tasso's *Gerusalemme* was born, and reborn. Instead of entering into this historical situation, so significant for the classical tradition, the author arranges the material on a scheme of his own, rather in the manner of a college essay; differences among the poems apparently reflect only the impulses of the several poets, and the only difference noted between Ariosto and Tasso, for example, is that Tasso introduces Christian doctrine and the Christian supernatural. Even that point had occupied the critics, and had implications. This is certainly not to say that the details of this chapter lack interest; and the descriptive method itself is legitimate and suits the aims of a handbook; but can historical material even be properly seen and described without adequate historical perspective?

It is time to return to the terms of our first paragraph. Such reservations as we have are almost entirely concerned with matters of historical interpretation in the earlier periods. If Highet has sacrificed a certain depth on the side of historical objectivity, he has gained in what is important for his purpose, namely in personal apprehension. He has read widely indeed, and with sensitivity and discrimination; and the judicious control of so much material is the sign of no ordinary mental energy. There are many excellent observations and many excellent pages. I have marked, among others, the passage on Shakespearean and Senecan pessimism (p. 207); that on classical culture as the common ground of Western culture (p. 292); the interesting association of the "curt" or Tacitean style with unorthodoxy and revolt (p. 326); the suggestion that what Byron and Keats lack as poets is what they might have gained from a better knowledge of the classics (pp. 414, 417); the speculations on why Mommsen did not finish his *History*—more convincing than the suggestions of Collingwood and Toynbee on this topic; the observation of Sir G. Greenwood, which was new to me, that the opening of Keats's *Ode to a Nightingale* is a direct echo of Horace, *Epod.*, 14, 1–4 (p. 637); and the pages that invite one to read the poems of Carl Spitteler (pp. 528–31).

Reviewers' gleanings are notably small in a book that, though large, shows an admirable control of detail and is cleanly proofread. A few points, however, seem to call for comment:

P. 1. Modern medicine and music hardly stand apart from the classical tradition in the same degree as do industry and applied science; cf. p. 180. P. 3 (and pp. 11 and 353). The word "savages" gives a false impression of the barbarian invaders of Italy. P. 6. The division of the Empire no doubt ultimately accounts for the line dividing Poland from Russia, but has lived more directly and as fatally (if at the moment less topically) in the line between

Catholic Croatia and Orthodox Serbia. P. 16. Barlaam was no "secret agent" of the Eastern Empire; the phrase may represent a hasty reading of Gibbon's "subtle agent." The paragraph on the recovery of Greek manuscrips should be replaced; Aurispa and Guarino should be mentioned, and Sabbadini, not Gibbon [!] used as authority. P. 17. "Lascaris ... visited the remote monastery of Mount Athos": read "monasteries." How can one touch even lightly upon the recovery of Greek without mentioning Chrysoloras? Coluccio Salutati rather than de' Salutati (also p. 83). Why give space to Byzantine contractions in Greek typography and make no mention of the far more significant humanist Latin script or of *antiqua* type? P. 21. Admirers of the cathedrals may not agree that in the Middle Ages "the sense of beauty" was "hampered and misdirected," to be recovered only in the Renaissance. P. 89. "The characters of the *Decameron* frequently imply contempt for the Christian church": for "church" read "clergy." P. 113. It is hardly correct to say that "almost as rapidly as unknown classical authors were discovered, they ... were revealed to the public ... by vernacular translations"; generally speaking, the time-lag was considerable, and significant. P. 114. "Never blotted a line": read "blotted out line." P. 117. The remarks on Amyot are flat, probably because Sturel's masterwork was not consulted. P. 119. French versions of Plutarch's *Moralia* before Amyot are more numerous and more important than the English versions, which alone are cited; Blignières' old but unsuperseded *Essai sur Amyot et les traducteurs français* should have been looked up. P. 151. As often in Milton, there is more in *PL*, II, 3 than immediately meets the eye; God's oath is not merely classical but Biblical also (see M. Y. Hughes's ed. *ad loc.*), and the plural "gods" not merely a simple-minded echo of the classical Olympus. P. 155. The paragraph on the invocation of the Muse by modern poets could be bettered; see now E. R. Curtius, *Europäische Literatur*, pp. 233–50. P. 160. The participial titles of Renaissance epic poems, *Orlando innamorato, Paradise Lost,* etc., may be not merely *ab-urbe-condita* Latinisms, but borrowed from ancient drama (e.g., *Prometheus Bound*); at least, it is agreed that in continuing the *Innamorato* with *Orlando Furioso* Ariosto took his title from *Hercules Furens*. P. 187. Mlle de Gournay was not literally Montaigne's "adopted daughter." P. 192. The statement that the Theophrastan character-sketch "grew into the modern novel" needs some qualification; cf. p. 340. P. 220. For "My love is like a red red rose / That's sweetly blown in June" read "O, my luve's like a red red rose / That's newly sprung in June." P. 256. The influence of "the public" requires to be more clearly defined throughout a book that by its intentional limitations constantly raises sociological questions; perhaps Schücking's well-known essay would have been suggestive. If the twentieth-century "public" prefers detective novels to the poetic drama, so, it may be countered, the corresponding "public," in the Renaissance preferred Spanish prose-romances to classicizing tragedies. Pp. 294–95. What is said of Milton's *Samson Agonistes* may be true, but is unsympathetic and one-sided; no doubt "there is a subtlety in Sophocles which Milton could scarcely achieve," but the impression is left that Milton lacks subtlety, whereas it is one of his chief qualities. Is there not a subtlety in Milton that Sophocles could scarcely achieve? P. 395. "Charlotte Corday, before she assassinated Marat, spent the day reading Plutarch." There seems to be no contemporary evidence for this unlikely statement, and the police records are detailed. Certainly the grandniece of Corneille dramatized herself as a female Brutus, and had read Plutarch, but what she had most in mind, and quotes from in her *Adresse,* was Voltaire's *Mort de César,* then playing to large audiences. P. 397. "In his letter of surrender, Napoleon wrote: 'I throw myself, like Themistocles, upon the mercy of the British people': for Themistocles ... had ... thrown himself when exiled upon the mercy of Persia." Napoleon's letter to the Prince Regent was hardly his letter of surrender; he wrote: "Je viens, comme Themistocle, m'asseoir au foyer du peuple britannique"; and this is generally taken to allude to the well-known story (Thuc., I, 136; Plut., *Them.,* 24) of Themistocles as suppliant at the hearth of Admetus king of the Molossians. To compare the British with the Persians would hardly have been tactful—or of good omen for Napoleon himself. P. 400. Virgil, not Vergil, is the name of a village in New York State, and the title of Tennyson's poem (p. 446) is not *To Vergil.* Pp. 489–500. Housman expending intellectual energy upon the text of Juvenal is contrasted unfavorably with Housman on the verge of tears over a poem of Horace. There is doubtless much truth in what is said in these pages about the decline in classical education, and unquestionably more books of an attractive quality, popular in a good sense, should be written on classical subjects; but the whole seems out of focus. Once more, if the rise of humanist education, and its relation to society from the beginning,

348

had been considered, the developments of the last hundred years would have been better understood. It is doubtful if interest in research has been a chief cause of the decline, or if the transplanting to America of continental methods of scholarship, instead of those of Oxford, has been a bad thing. For a different view of the ogrish continental professor of p. 495, "whose lectures were unintelligible or repulsive to all but his best students," it would be fair to read Professor Spitzer's recent remarks on Meyer-Lübke in *PMLA* 66 (1951) 39–48. (The missionary zeal of foreign scholars is always interesting, and may be helpful, to Americans.) It should be considered whether, given the intellectual climate of recent times, the decline might not have been more rapid if the classics had taken their stand merely on the aesthetic and moral grounds that Highet stresses, and had not offered able intellects an area for discoveries, great and small, in the early periods of our culture. The evil influence of the natural sciences upon literary scholarship is an unexamined commonplace and probably much exaggerated; it has hardly "been responsible for the fragmentation of classical study" (p. 499), since classical study has advanced on the feet of limited special dissertations since the time of Poliziano and Budé. "Meanwhile, those looking in from outside see no cathedral arising"—the metaphor is hard to interpret. What is required is, if possible, to re–establish a relationship between the classics and the basic motivations of our age—a relationship that on the whole existed up to the French Revolution. P. 556. The generous Notes (150 pages) begin here, and are, save perhaps for Chapter 19, conveniently arranged for ready reference. Why do publishers so seldom solve this easy problem? Possibly the student would be better served if the bibliographical references were somewhat increased, with some curtailment of the use of the Notes as an overflow from the text; one would welcome a note bringing together the principal works on Milton and the classics as is done for Spenser and for Shakespeare. It is doubtful if the student will grasp much of the "point of view of modern scholarship" on Homer from the books listed for the purpose on p. 669. Two old friends, Egger's *Hellénisme en France* and Zielinski's *Our Debt to Antiquity*, seem nowhere to be mentioned. On the value of Cicero and Tacitus to the French revolutionaries (p. 672), it would be well to go beyond the somewhat sketchy remarks of Zielinski's *Cicero* to Aulard's *Eloquence parlementaire pendant la Rév. fr.* Foscolo's line, *Non son che fui; perì di noi gran parte* (p. 680), evidently echoes Horace, *Carm,* iii, 30, 6, as well as iv, 1, 3. G. B. Vico deserves mention in note 6, p. 690; historiography is hardly considered before Bossuet; yet the concept of history distinguishes the heirs of the Greeks from most of the rest of mankind, and until recently historical writing was thought of as literature. Professor M. F. Fisch's Introduction to Vico's *Autobiography* would be suggestive here.

Review: The Poems of Erasmus

The poems of Erasmus have not hitherto been published in a separate edition, though all save a minor epigram discovered by Reedijk have long since been printed either in the Leiden *Opera* or in Professor Ferguson's *Erasmi opuscula* of 1933. The present edition, from the hand of a reliable bibliographer, is therefore welcome. We see Erasmus' poetical activity as a whole, and since the poems are arranged chronologically and supplied with historical introductions, we see them related to successive moments of his life. Perhaps we know Erasmus a little better from dwelling for once on this side of his work. However, his poetry belongs chiefly to his youth, and especially to the years he spent in the monastery of Steyn; instead of increasing in the environment of the Paris humanists, his writing of verse rather abruptly fell off, and though he still could be styled "*poeta*" on his first visit to England in 1499, his production thereafter declined to one or two epigrams or inscriptions a year. Exceptions are the *Carmen de Senectute* of 1506 and the *Carmen votivum* to St. Genevieve published in 1532—two good poems that show what the mature Erasmus might have done. As it is, the early poems fill out our idea of the young Erasmus; we know, for example, how he occupied himself at Steyn. His youth was a struggle to fulfill himself as a humanist. From the start he had embraced the whole humanist program of writing—*epistolae, orationes, dialogi, poemata*—but, as he later told Botzheim, it was to *poemata* that his enthusiasm was chiefly given. His efforts were ambitious, from a full-blown eclogue written when he was fourteen to a Sapphic ode to the Virgin in 101 stanzas and an epyllion of over

A review of Cornelis Reedijk, ed., *The Poems of Desiderius Erasmus* (Leiden, 1956), reprinted by permission from *Erasmus, Speculum Scientiarum*, XI (Darmstadt, 1958), cols. 31–34.

351

350 lines on the Harrowing of Hell, both probably written when he was hardly twenty. He attained a skill in the handling of a variety of meters such as few of his Italian contemporaries could boast. And he had no sooner attained it than his interest in poetry waned. At the time he may not have realized this himself, and Reedijk is probably right in seeking the reason in outward circumstances. But Erasmus maintained his technical skill, which stood him in good stead in his translations from the Greek—two plays of Euripides and numerous passages from other Greek poets included in the *Adagia* and other works—which outmeasure his original verse after 1500. Most humanists would have included such translations among their published poems, and I am not sure that Reedijk has done right in excluding them, though I see the difficulties they present.

One must admire the energy that the editor has brought to his task, especially since he writes in a language not his own. Possibly he has attempted too much. The text of the poems is preceded by a general Introduction in four chapters, of which the last two are distinctly the best. The first chapter, a rather helter-skelter survey of neo-Latin poetry throughout Europe, is intermittently relevant as "background" for Erasmus, but suffers from the faults of improvisation. Reedijk will get a surprise when he turns up the verse of Aeneas Silvius Piccolomini (Pius II), which he thinks is "religious and moralizing poetry" (p. 4), while on the other hand it seems too bad to single out M. A. Flaminio as one who "unconcernedly . . . makes play with his pagan motifs" (p. 6), since Flaminio was celebrated for the sanctity of his life, and his sacred poems and Psalm-paraphrases went through many editions. And what is Clément Marot doing in this galley as a leading Latin poet of the time (p. 10)? Later on (p. 101) Erasmus is apparently taken to task for speaking ill of the poetry of Poggio, though Poggio wrote no verse to speak of, and Erasmus is not talking about verse. One misses any reference to such indispensable books as Rossi's *Quattrocento,* Renaudet's *Préréforme et humanisme à Paris,* and Weiss's *Humanism in England during the Fifteenth Century.* The last, for example, might have saved Reedijk the trouble of looking up the manuscript of Carmigliano's *De Vere,* and would have given him more light on Stefano Surigone. The second chapter needlessly asks why the humanists wrote Latin and why they wrote verse, without getting either question very well into focus. But with the third chapter we are in quite a different atmosphere. Erasmus' association with poets and his own practice of poetry throughout his life are combined into an essay that may well be definitive on these subjects. The last chapter again is an interesting collection of materials: Erasmus' pronouncements on poetry and poets; an account of his metrical tricks and translations not included in this edition; and opinions on his poetry, ending with a judicious estimate by Reedijk. A misconception may be noted. Reedijk observes (p. 102) that eighteen translations by Erasmus appear in the *Selecta Epigrammata Graeca* published by Bebel in 1529, and says that he has been able to trace only a few of them to the *Adagia*. All, however, were in the *Adagia* by 1526, most of them already in 1508; and it is not Bebel's book that should be cited but the second edition of J. Soter's *Epigrammata Graeca* (Cologne 1528), the contents of which, including Erasmus's translations, were taken over in the 1529 volume.

What we chiefly desire from such an edition is an expert presentation of the text, and on this cardinal point Reedijk gives a high degree of satisfaction; indeed he has made an important contribution to Erasmian studies. Following the method of Allen's edition of the *Opus Epistolarum,* he has prefixed to each poem a special introduction embodying whatever historical and bibliographical information bears upon it. He has been tireless in gathering this material, which includes a number of new facts, and judicious in sifting it. Thus it is important to know what authority the Gouda manuscript, and the manuscript of Scriverius have, since these are the only sources for most of the early poems, and Reedijk has convincingly settled the provenience of the first and given a very probable account of the second of the manuscripts. He reasonably assumes that in Scriverius' manuscript the poems appear in the order of composition, and on this and other grounds assigns them approximate dates. Equally interesting for Erasmus' biography is the proposed dating of *Carmina* 34–37 on Michael and the other angels to the first months after Erasmus' arrival in Paris in 1495 instead of to an earlier period (c. 1489, Allen). This would extend the full vein of his poetry by several years and place an unusual burst of composition in the autumn of 1495. The argument for this date is unfortunately not decisive, but it will merit attention. Reedijk's perfect command of the early editions enables him to give a complete account of the poems published in Erasmus' lifetime, and to choose the most authentic reading. The result is a text altogether supersed-

ing that of the faulty Leiden *Opera* on which we have hitherto had
to depend. (There are very few misprints in the text; I note *omne*
for *omnem* in *Carm.* 5, 32 and again in 8, 7; *Atque* for *Atqui* in 83,
144; and *Niteat* for *Niteatque* in 83, 238.) There is a brief commentary identifying the classical tags, which are numerous in the early
poems, and offering explanations of the text where needed. Inevitably tags have here and there been missed (e.g., 4, 7, *Videam ar-
gumenta senectae,* cf. Seneca, *Epist.* 12.1; 24, 33, *tenueis rapitur ceu
fumus in auras,* cf. Virgil, *Aen.* 5, 740; 39, 33, *solus neque solus,* cf.
Cicero, *De Off.* 3.1.1) and, less excusably, some of Erasmus' named
references have been left bare (e.g., 14, 121–24, Biblical; 83,53,
Aristotle; 83, 135, Homer), but on the whole this necessary labor
has been well performed. Various obscure allusions are made
plain: for example, Reedijk is doubtless right in identifying the
germanos Druidas of 131, 41 with the doctors of the Sorbonne. I
have noticed two lapses. On 39, 59–60, where Erasmus mentions
Gallus, Varus, and Pollio as the persons honored by Virgil in *Ecl.*
10, 6, and 4, this point is missed, Gallus goes unrecognized (cf.
Index also), and the note on P. Alfenius (*sic*) Varus is garbled. On
83, 148, *Et Cynthiae volucres / Et rapidas Phoebi sisti figique quadrigas,*
the words *Cynthiae volucres* are glossed "Pleiads" (*sic*), with a reference to Athenaeus, whereas Erasmus surely means only the moon
and the sun (*volucres* adj. with *quadrigas*).

The text is followed by an admirably complete survey of the
manuscripts and printed editions that contain the poems or any
part of them; a list of *initia;* six Appendices, including, with other
matter, poems that have been doubtfully ascribed to Erasmus; an
Index; a general list of books. No doubt it serves a purpose to have
all that concerns Erasmus and the subject of poetry brought between two covers, but in the effort to do so the *ultima manus* has
been unequally applied, especially as between the Introduction and
the text. That is the more regrettable, since the text and the bibliographical work that supports it are sound and will make the book
indispensable to all students of Erasmus.

Review: Ronsard and the Greek Epic

Professor Silver's work in completing Paul Laumonier's critical edition of Ronsard, his numerous articles in periodical publications, and now the first volume of his study of Ronsard's Hellenism establish him as the leading *ronsardisant* of the day, in the line of Laumonier and Henri Chamard. In undertaking to study the whole of Ronsard's Hellenic heritage (the present volume on Ronsard and the Greek epic will be followed by one on Ronsard and the other Greek poets and one on Ronsard and Greek thought), he has obviously chosen a topic of the first importance which has not hitherto been properly isolated and treated comprehensively. Silver is interested not only in the extent of Ronsard's substantial debt to the Greeks but, more important, in the use he made of his borrowings, the limits of his understanding and the degree to which he was able to assimilate what he took over. With complete control of modern views on the Greeks and Greek poetry on his own part, he examines in this volume Ronsard's debt to Homer, Hesiod, and Apollonius of Rhodes in a long series of passages from the poems and in a special study of the *Franciade,* beginning therefore with a most important aspect of Ronsard's Hellenism in view of the poet's labors in preparing to write his own epic poem. That it is not the whole story, nor altogether the happiest part of it, leaves us to await with lively anticipation the further volumes of Silver's work.

The book, which is divided like an *Iliad* into twenty-four chapters, opens with a survey of the Homeric knowledge of Ronsard's predecessors beginning with Jean Lemaire de Belges and an exam-

A review of Isidore Silver, *Ronsard and the Hellenic Renaissance in France:* I, *Ronsard and the Greek Epic* (St. Louis: Washington University, 1961). From *The Romanic Review* LIV, 4 (December 1963).

ination of the translations by Salel, Peletier, and Jamyn. Remarks on Jean Dorat as a teacher and on Ronsard's own testimony regarding his Greek studies introduce the vital question whether the poet knew Greek. Answering affirmatively, Silver proceeds to demonstrate Ronsard's independence of the existing translations of the epic writers. Three chapters are devoted to Ronsard's relative evaluation of Homer and Virgil and to his concept of the epic poem. There follow nine chapters on the influence of Homer, Religion and the Gods, the last topic leading naturally to the *Theogony* of Hesiod and thence to the *Erga.* The influence of Apollonius of Rhodes is traced first in the *Hymnes* and then in the *Franciade,* and we are thus brought back in the last three chapters of the book to a very interesting discussion of the failure of Ronsard's epic poem in the light of what he might have learned from Homer. The brief Conclusion restores the balance by recalling the positive magnitude of Ronsard's Hellenic legacy and its importance for subsequent French literature.

We must confine our comments to a few salient points. Among the most interesting is Silver's defense of the position that Ronsard knew Greek and knew it well. In itself the taking of this position by one who has dwelt for many years on Ronsard's use of Greek materials and has found it the only possible working hypothesis must have considerable weight. Yet Paul Laumonier at the end of a lifetime devoted to Ronsard could still express uncertainty on this matter, and his authority has encouraged doubt in others. Laumonier apparently was skeptical even of Ronsard's explicit statement: "disciple je vins estre, / A Paris, de Daurat qui cinq ans fut mon maistre / En Grec et en Latin," since it occurs in an epistle to Pierre de Paschal from whom Ronsard at the time was expecting a panegyric (p. 47, n. 1). Silver's book will surely put an end to such skepticism. Much cumulative evidence, including passages of Greek written in Ronsard's hand, confirms the *a priori* probability that the pupil of Dorat knew Greek. That he knew it well follows from Silver's examination of his copy of Nicander in the Morgan Library. With Ronsard's signature, the volume has interlinear translation and marginal glosses in Greek and Latin, all written, in the view of Laumonier, in the hand of Ronsard. But the ascription of one textual correction to Dorat ("sic Auratus") was enough to make Laumonier decide "presque à coup sûr que les autres annotations, ainsi que la traduction latine interlignée, ont la même origine et furent écrites par Ronsard sous la parole de son maître." If this means that Dorat dictated this extensive material to Ronsard either in class or privately, Silver pertinently asks why Dorat and Ronsard went through this elaborate process if it is possible to say of the latter, as Laumonier does: "Je ne suis pas sûr du tout qu' [il] ait su le grec." Silver concludes that the work is Ronsard's own and indicates considerable competence in Greek. It is supposed to have been done several years after his formal studies under Dorat were ended. I do not know what inconveniences would arise, if, withdrawing slightly from Silver's high estimate of Ronsard's scholarship, we were to conjecture that translation and annotations may have been transcribed by Ronsard from a (hypothetical) copy of the same edition belonging to Dorat and perhaps used by him for his lectures. We would still have to acknowledge considerable zeal and competence on the part of Ronsard with regard to an out-of-the-way Greek author. That Ronsard read the Greek texts for himself is also the only natural conclusion from Silver's demonstration of his independence of the Latin and French translations of the epic writers.

It must not be thought unfortunate that this first volume on Ronsard's Hellenism has to deal so largely with Ronsard's disastrous epic poem. The unfinished *Franciade* is a failure, but the study of it is a success in marking the limitations of Ronsard's Hellenism, or rather Ronsard's limitations *tout court*. Silver traces the failure of the poem in every respect, including the inferior choice of meter in which Ronsard deferred to the wishes of Charles IX, to the fact that the court poet conceived his poem upon a dynastic principle (praise of the Valois) and not on a national principle like the *Aeneid* or a dramatic principle like the *Iliad*. The chapters in which this criticism is developed (22–24) are convincing and highly enlightening. At first glance, it may seem unfair to compare the *Franciade* exclusively with the *Iliad*. The author, while showing that Ronsard differed from common Renaissance opinion in his high estimate of Homer in relation to Virgil, has nevertheless rightly decided (p. 119) that in the *Franciade* "the Virgilian debt was the preponderant one in every respect." The *Franciade* might come off better if compared with the *Aeneid,* which is something of a dynastic as well as a national epic. But Silver's subject is Ronsard's Hellenism, and the contrast with the *Iliad* shows clearly what Ronsard failed to learn from the Greeks. The point has already been well put on p. 142: Ronsard was deeply impressed by the wrath of Achilles as such, but "had [he] truly, that is to say, inwardly and poetically, understood

357

that the moving force in the *Iliad* is the wrath of Achilles, some reflection of this would have appeared in his theoretical remarks on epic poetry, and the character of his epic hero and of all those who necessarily take their pace from him would have been inwardly transformed." One wonders if Ronsard could read, let alone write, a long poem. He might have learned from Ariosto, who contrives to unite, or at least to interweave, a dynastic theme (Bradamante-Ruggiero) with a dramatic one (the wrath of Orlando-complete with anagnorisis, peripety, and dénouement). In reading Silver's chapter on Ronsard's theory of epic poetry, we get the impression that even in the latest prefaces to the *Franciade* he advanced little beyond the view of the *long poème français* set forth in Du Bellay's *Deffence;* he came to know something of Aristotle's *Poetics* and there are scattered echoes of Italian epic theory in his critical writings, but clearly principles derived from Aristotle directly or through the Italians did not penetrate his thought on the subject very deeply. It was to the ferment of the *romanzi* controversy that Tasso's *Gerusalemme* owed its structural merits. Yet we must not oversimplify Ronsard's problem. Could one make a satisfactory national, or dynastic, epic turn on a tragic flaw in the national hero, even if like Achilles or Orlando he were psychologically transformed in the end? Italian critics themselves had generally decided that the hero of an epic poem should be "perfect," like the pious Aeneas; accordingly Tasso's Goffredo is "perfect," while the tension and movement of the poem depend on the faulty Rinaldo. Ronsard may have thought the problems through, since he chose to follow the *Aeneid*; but Silver is on solid grounds in affirming that if he had had any sense of dramatic construction he would have given a hint of it somewhere. Our allusions to the Italians only reinforce the point.

The dramatic plot involving an appropriate concept of character no doubt is the great lesson that Western literature has learned from the Greeks. But it is possible to learn it, once the idea is abroad, without otherwise being deeply imbued with the Greek spirit, and it is possible to imbibe a good deal of this spirit without having a sense of the dramatic. Perhaps we should think of Racine and Molière as the great Hellenists, but when the word is used we tend rather to think of André Chénier, Leconte de Lisle, or Heredia. Ronsard is of this company, and the first of them. Throughout his literary life, he constantly shows how strongly he was drawn to the Greeks. Silver's ample pages impress us with the vast amount of detail that he derived from the Greek epic writers alone; it is a case of quantity passing into quality and affecting the style of the man. But the quality further depends on the fact that these traits come in large measure directly from the Greek texts and bring an echo of their original tonality with them.

By laying out his Homeric materials under topics (chs. 8–19), Silver invites us to consider what Ronsard was able to assimilate and what not, though he judiciously warns us that in literary borrowing chance plays a part. Under "Nature," Ronsard is shown to have taken only a few passages of direct description from Homer, which is not surprising, but considerably more references to nature reach him in the form of imagery, notably such images as are already symbolic in Homer, for example the generations of men compared with falling leaves, or such as easily become symbolic, as the migratory cranes or the smoke rising from the chimney of a distant home. The modern poet wishes to infuse everything with sentiment and meaning. It is also on the whole in forms of symbolic imagery that Ronsard can use passages reflecting Homeric ethics and religion, though clearly Homeric ethics (Achilles' anger, the duties of hospitality, heroism) is more accessible to him than Homeric religion (sacrifices, dreams, ideas of death). Ronsard does not altogether avoid conventionality. The comparison of his own resentment against Saint-Gelais with the wrath of Achilles is saved from absurdity by conventionality, and from conventionality by a naive and learned reflection of Homeric language; meanwhile the comparison raises the moment compared into the serenity of an ideal world: Achilles' anger is an immortal idea in which Ronsard's sheds its mortal pettiness and pain. In this sense, as ethical symbols, the whole array of Homeric heroes and heroines visit Ronsard's pages and lend their immortality to all whom he wishes to honor, from Cassandre and Hélène to Montmorency and Catherine de Medici. (In reference to p. 206, it may be noted that the ascription of Aristotelian *megalopsychia* to Achilles need not be inferential, since Aristotle himself cites Achilles as an example of this quality in *Anal. Post.* 97^{b}18 and derives his "wrath" from it.) Traits of Homeric religion generally appear either in poems of a playful character or in poems of antique setting, primarily the *Franciade*. The gods, however, are ubiquitous, and Silver has taken care to bring out passages in which they are clearly Homeric or Hesiodic gods and not just the conventional gods of "mythology," that is, usually, passages in which there is a reflection of epic language. But the sixteenth-century poet can seldom recreate the mingled awe and familiarity felt by the epic writers for the gods: "The danger of falling into frigid artificialities was almost unavoidable, and it was only when the poet forgot his erudition and was caught up in the natural vision to which a particular divinity owed its being, that he was able to write verses that were truly Hellenic" (p. 311). That this happened to Ronsard chiefly in the case of the Muses is not difficult to explain.

Though Homer gave Ronsard a great number of details in comparisons, allusions, and adaptations, it was from Hesiod and Apollonius, less obvious and hence fresher sources, that he drew, together with many details, the basic substance of three poems which are among the most successful he ever wrote. Silver brings out well the wedding of Hesiodic content (Muses and Titanomachy) and Pindaric form in the Ode à Michel de l'Hospital; a true example of assimilation, since the enclosing thought, the renaissance of poetry, had a personal meaning for the poet. As for Apollonius of Rhodes, Silver firmly rejects the suggestion of Vianey that the whole plan of the Franciade was founded on the Argonautica, but notes that Ronsard studied that poem closely in preparation for his own epic and from these studies producted two fine epyllia, the Hymne de Calais et de Zetes and the Hymne de Pollux et de Castor, both of 1556. He analyzes these hymns in detail, showing how Ronsard developed the originals by expansion and contraction and by the insertion of materials from other sources to secure the proportions and the effect he desired. The interest of these pages prompts one to think that the pupil of Dorat was often especially happy in the Hellenistic part of his Hellenic heritage.

Perhaps it is not too much to say that the Greek epic and the Greek poets in general pervaded Ronsard's work with a serener, saner, and more cheerful strain than would otherwise have existed in a poet in whom melancholy often seems to be the most personal note—melancholy, a lack of which in the Greeks would lead Mme de Staël to dismiss them in a single gesture as incapable of feeling or expressing the still, sad music of humanity. Neither the Renaissance nor the Romantic spirit had a chance of coming to terms with Greek tragedy which seems all-important to the post-Nietzschean generations. However, it is Chénier's Hellenism that is elegiac, not

Ronsard's. To bring the world of Homer, Hesiod, Pindar, and the Alexandrians abundantly into French poetry, often with an authentic Hellenic tonality, was something new and great and at once raised modern literature to a higher plane. Silver's book gives to this important aspect of Ronsard's literary personality the high relief it deserves, and does so the more effectively since it is written with a restrained enthusiasm that makes the reader feel that in associating at once with Ronsard and the Greeks he is moving in high places where it is good for him to be.

Review: Hellenistic Epigrams

This monumental work of classical scholarship on a high level may well be worth the price of five ordinary nine-dollar books; at less than five cents a page, it may even be a bargain. The title indicates its scope. From the mingled mass of the Greek Anthology, more than 4000 epigrams, Gow and Page have extracted 815, those written between 323 B.C. and about 100 B.C., and have arranged them by author, adding forty epigrams by the same authors preserved in other places. Thus they have not made a corpus of all known Hellenistic epigrams, but have in effect brought out from the Anthology the remains of Meleager's *Stephanos* minus the pre-Hellenistic epigrams that Meleager included. This is feasible because Cephalas' collection, chiefly represented for us by the Palatine manuscript, stands so close to its principal sources in Meleager, Philippus, and Agathias that epigrams from these earlier collections tend to appear in more or less solid groups; where this test fails, the editors have proceeded with tact and candor. Hellenistic literature thus regains, so to speak, a central book—its epigrams as known to the literary tradition—to stand beside Theocritus, Callimachus, and the rest. It will be welcomed alike by students of that literature and by students of the Latin poets who were influenced by the Hellenistic epigram. The foreword informs us that, apart from the epigrams of Meleager, which were the responsibility of Page, the work is fundamentally by Gow, but that both editors have scrutinized and generally endorse the whole. Mechanically, the work attains something like perfection; the consecutive numbering of the lines throughout, for instance, makes cross-

A review of *The Greek Anthology, Hellenistic Epigrams*, A. S. F. Gow and D. L. Page, eds., 2 vols. (Cambridge University Press, 1965). From *The Classical Journal* 63 (January 1967) 175-78.

reference simple and in itself enables the large work to function as a whole with ease.

To assemble the Hellenistic epigrams of the Anthology means bringing together about as perplexing a series of texts as can be found in Greek literature. Amateurs of the Anthology who use Paton, Waltz, or Beckby, who had to form translatable text, may hardly realize how shaky the ground beneath their feet really is. Here we have a scholarly text bristling with daggers. The apparatus is spare, limited to the manuscript testimonies and the emendations of which the editors approve; but in the commentary we see the remarkable critical energy of the editors at work squeezing the comprehensive apparatus of Stadtmüller into the austere one presented here. Alas that the sharp and informed apprehension of a problem so often ends necessarily in no solution; emendation of the Greek epigrams is notoriously difficult and uncertain. But the editors (mostly Gow; the ms. text of Meleager is relatively good) rise to meet this challenge. They offer over a hundred conjectures of their own, most of them to be sure only presented "for consideration" in the commentary, but about thirty promoted to the apparatus and over twenty printed in the text. These last are a somewhat mixed bag. The correction of Antipater 17, *AP* 7.30(278–79), too complicated to be quoted here, seems to me to be forced; that of Theaetetus 1, *AP* 6.357(3342), τίνες γένος ἐστέ for τίνος γένος ἐστέ seems to solve one difficulty (γένος, here "offspring," repeated later in the sense of "race" or "nation" (only to create another— upon meeting two children, to say "Bless you, children, what is your nationality?" seems strange, and the children answer very explicitly about their parents as though the natural question had been asked, one of them, it is true, adding κεῖμὶ γένος Μακεδών. But it seems rash to efface the very question they mostly answer. At need, I suppose, one could think of τίνες τίνος ἐστέ, comparing Leonidas 70, *AP* 7.163(2395), τίς τίνος εὖσα, γύναι and Simonides, *AP* 16.23, τίς τίνος ἐσσί. On the other hand, there are a number of attractive conjectures; for example, ἄγερθεν (324), Λυκόρτας (478), and εὔφυλλον (2245) thought bold are convincing, as is also Page's ἐκεῖνον in *AP* 12.106 (4548).

What gives this work its great and permanent value is the commentary, which deals with much more than textual problems. It is the first full commentary on a large portion of the Anthology since Dübner, or perhaps one should say since Jacobs. Among its conspicuous merits is the exhaustive discussion of words, especially words for things, a matter of prime importance for the epigrammatists, who revel in strange diction. Throughout one meets freshness of approach, tight thinking, and precision of language that can express fine shades of criticism. Examples are easily cited, from the explanation of Diotimus 5, *AP* 7.475(1739), where what has been taken to mean the gates of a town is persuasively understood to mean the gates of Hades; through the historical analysis that identifies the persons of Antipater 46, *AP* 6.111 (478), and the formidable learning made to serve criticism on Theodoridas 15, *AP* 13.21(3569); to a definitive note on lap dogs on Tymnes 5, *AP* 7.211(3613).

In what amounts to 855 commentaries, for no epigram is left bare, the reader will inevitably find some comments against which he sets a question mark. Here follow a few of those that I have queried.

Antipater of Sidon 65, *AP* 12.97(632–37), is a rather odd epigram that has embarrassed earlier commentators and which our editors leave in confusion:

Εὐπάλαμος ξανθὸν μὲν ἐρεύθεται ἴσον Ἔρωτι
μέσφα ποτὶ Κρητῶν ποιμένα Μηριόνην,
ἐκ δέ νυ Μηριόνεω Ποδαλείριον οὐκέτ' ἐς Ἠώ
νεῖται· ἴδ' ὡς φθονερὰ παγγενέτειρα φύσις.
εἰ γὰρ τῷ τά τ' ἔνερθε τὰ θ' ὑψόθεν ἴσα πέλοιτο
ἦν ἂν Ἀχιλλῆος φέρτερος Αἰακίδεω.

Everyone sees that the epic heroes Meriones and Podaleirios mean "thigh" (μηρός) and "foot" or "lily-foot" respectively, and at the end Boissonade thought of "swift-footed" Achilles and our editor more vaguely suggest "godlike" Achilles. Boissonade thought Eupalamos was a cripple; they think only complexion is meant, ruddy above the thighs, pale below. Line 3 gives trouble. Like Paton the editors favor Toup's nominative Ποδαλείριος, with which Paton incredibly translates: "but from Meriones onwards Podaleirius no longer goes back to the Dawn," and they extract: "as he is lily-footed he [can] no longer (as he could above the hips) attain to (or equal) Eos, who is . . . ῥοδοδάκτυλος." Surely the simple remedy is to keep the ms. accusative Ποδαλείριον and read nominative Ἠώς: "but from Meriones to Podalierios (from thigh to foot) the (rosy) Dawn no longer advances." The long antistrophe of ἐς (kept intelligible by balancing ἐϰ) will not trouble readers of Antipater who have just accepted μυρία τοι, Πτολεμαῖε, πατὴρ ἔπι (i.e., ἐπί τοι) in 338 and ἧς ἔπι ϰαλὸν ἄμυξε ϰάτα ῥέθος (ϰατάμυξε) in 330. What the verses lack in substance they gain in ingenuity. In v. 2 a little enigma is set by solemnly calling Meriones "shepherd of the Cretans" and at once resolved in 3 by the forcible juxtaposition of Μηριόνεω and Ποδαλείριον at the cost of a violent antistrophe. The conceit turns only on complexion, but the pallor of the boy's lower extremities, whatever it implies, is regarded as a natural (cf. φύσις) defect, and this defect is the subject of the epigram and the source of its point. There need be no doubt about the point—if Eupalamos, who is certainly εὐπάλαμος, "handy," "clever of hand," had also been εὔπους, he would have been one up on Achilles, who is only πόδας ὠϰύς. The epigram, though complimentary, seems hardhearted in drawing an elaborate conceit from a personal misfortune, but we do not know the circumstances. In ἴδ' ὡς (v. 4) it perhaps bears Antipater's signature. Setti seems clearly right in claiming the recurrence of this locution in Antipatrian epigrams as a mannerism of the Sidonian, not the later Thessalonian Antipater (Kaibel), though he oddly rejects the present epigram without understanding it. Anyone may say "See how," but Antipater is hardly able to refrain from saying it as he approaches the point of an epigram:

> AP 6.219 (630): ἴδ' ὡς ἐδίδαξεν ἀνάγϰα
> 7.172 (318): ἴδ' ὡς τὰ ϰατ' αἰθέρα λεύσσων
> 7.210 (606): ἴδ' ὡς Ἥφαιστος ἀμύντορ
> 7.498 (546): ἴδ' ὡς λιμένα γλυϰὺν ἄλλοις
> 7.743 : ἴδ' ὡς νίϰημι διϰαίως
> 12.97 (653): ἴδ' ὡς φθονερά

Except for *AP* 12.97, the expression always begins the last half of a hexameter, and this "oral" procedure cannot fail to remind us that Cicero knew of Antipater as a famous *improvvisatore* ("solitus est versus hexametros ... fundere ex tempore," Introd. p. xv). The method of the present edition, unfortunately I think, does not favor much comment on the literary and rhetorical procedures of the several poets (unless on Meleager), but this point perhaps should have found mention as something sufficiently objective and interesting. I think it might have tipped the scales in favor of admitting *AP* 7.743 (though hardly, I suppose, *AP* 1.143: ... ἴδ' ὡς τὸ μὲν εἰς χόλον αἴρει, which Planudes gives to Antipater of Macedon), but this is not a point I would press; the editors have done well enough with the vexed question of Antipatrian attributions. A new and startling interpretation is proposed for the well-known epigram of the Locrian poetess Nossis, *AP* 5.170 (2791-4):

> Ἅδιον οὐδὲν ἔρωτος, ἃ δ᾽ ὄλβια δεύτερα πάντα
> ἐστίν· ἀπὸ στόματος δ᾽ ἔπτυσα καὶ τὸ μέλι.
> τοῦτο λέγει Νοσσίς· τίνα δ᾽ ἃ Κύπρις οὐκ ἐφίλασεν
> οὐκ οἶδεν †κῆνα τ᾽† ἄνθεα ποῖα ῥόδα.

As the editors say, corrections divide between κῆνα referring to the antecedent of the relative τίνα and κήνας referring to Κύπρις— either "whom Cypris does not love, that woman does not know . . ." or "one whom Cypris does not love does not know (the flowers / roses) of Cypris." Finding neither course free from objection, the editors suggest a third, "namely that κήνας is right, but refers not to Aphrodite but to Nossis herself ('the man untouched by love knows not what blooms her roses are,' i.e. what a lover she is)." "If so," they continue, "N. was presumably a hetaera like Polyarchis" (*AP* 9.332, a dedication written by Nossis for a hetaera). We could bear to think of Nossis as a hetaera and perhaps, though with more difficulty, of her poem as a bit of self-advertisement, but it is hard to believe in the validity of the sentence in parentheses. If it means "only a lover will know what a lover she is," the thought seems hardly worth committing to deathless verse. Of the other possibilities, κῆνα, however saved (κῆνα γ᾽ Reitzenstein), is open to the objection that τίνα as relative pronoun seems deliberately chosen to avoid committing the generalization to either sex and a belated revelation in κῆνα that τίνα was really feminine would be irritating. (Bentley's τάν for τίνα recognizes this, and is not so unnecessary, if κῆνα is read, as the editors think.) I see nothing better than to read κήνας τἄνθεα with Meineke, who is followed by Waltz, and to translate: "One whom Cypris does not love does not know what roses Cypris' blooms are." One could drop the definite article with Reiske and understand κήνας ἄνθεα ποῖα ῥόδα to mean "what flowers her roses are," but a material point about this poem is that its insistent music is played out on labials and dentals, to which the definite article contributes; alliteration is also partly responsible for ἐστίν, which the editors find unexpected. The point is not tautological if it

Hellenistic Epigrams

is assumed that the rose is the supreme flower. It might help this
reading if we could think of τὰ τῆς Κύπριδος ἄνθεα as a recognized
and accepted metaphor, and perhaps we can: it is possible, or even
likely, that there ran in Nossis' mind (she is a bookish poet) a verse
of Pindar: κόρον δ᾽ ἔχει καὶ μέλι καὶ τὰ τέρπν᾽ ἄνθε᾽ ᾿Αφροδίσια (N
7.52-3), where the metaphor is sufficiently explicit. Ὄλβια also is
one of Pindar's words.

When careful reasoning leads to an absurdity the editors are
sometimes content to leave it at that rather than to adopt a "sensi-
ble" meaning against the evidence. This does not apply, however,
to Menecrates 1, AP 9.390 (2589-94), where a mother who has lost
three children puts the fourth on the fire at birth:

«οὐ θρέψω,» λέξασα, «τί γὰρ πλέον; Ἄιδι, μαστοί,
κάμνετε· κερδήσω πένθος ἀμοχθότερον.»

"You are only working for Hades, my breasts" seems plain enough,
but the editors prefer to take κάμνετε as imperative and translate
"death to my children!" apparently overlooking μαστοί. An absurdity in Phanias 3, AP 6.295 (2978-85), seems consciously accepted.
Among the objects a clerk dedicates to the Muses is a sponge: ὅν τ᾽
ἐπὶ μισθῷ σπόγγον ἔχεν καλάμων ψαίστορ᾽ ἀπὸ Κνιδίων. Gow and
Page insist that ἐπὶ μισθῷ "must mean (however improbably) that
he had to hire a sponge." But it is too improbable that he should
dedicate a sponge that did not belong to him, and, though the
phrase may be a bit odd, there is less strain in understanding "the
sponge which he had earned (had for pay) from the exercise of his
pens." One is similarly baffled by the explanation of Phalaecus 4,
AP 13.27 (2954-61), verses for a cenotaph, beginning:

Φῶκος ἐπί ξείνῃ μὲν ἀπόφθιτο, κῦμα γὰρ μέλαινα
νεῦς οὐχ ὑπεξήνεικεν οὐδ᾽ ἐδέξατο
ἀλλὰ κατ᾽ Αἰγαίοιο πολὺν βυθὸν ᾤχετο πόντου
βίῃ Νότου πρήσαντος ἐσχάτην ἅλα· ...

Various conjectures aimed at replacing ἐδέξατο have been made,
and Paton left a blank in his translation when he came to this word.
Our editors think that ὑπεκφέρω may mean "cast [the billow] overboard," but consider also a meaning "escape" attributed to Aristar-
chus. They think the text possibly sound—"neither cast overboard
(or escaped), nor shipped, but sank." They parallel ἐδέξατο,

"shipped water," with Aeschylus *Sept.* 795, πόλις ... ἄντλον οὐκ ἐδέξατο, and conclude: "The meaning would then be that the ship was not overwhelmed in the storm, but sank, perhaps from a leak." That certainly is a surprise ending. One would rather expect the two negatives to carry verbs of parallel meaning contrasted (ἀλλά) with a third, and consideration at least might have been given to the common meaning of δέχομαι, *sustineo irruentem* (*Thesaurus*), exemplified by its use when troops "receive" and withstand an enemy's onset (e.g., Thuc. 4.126): "When a violent storm had arisen, the black ship neither eluded nor yet stood up to the seas, but went to the bottom."

In the commentary on Theodoridas 2, *AP* 6.156 (3512–15), Wilamowitz, Waltz, and Beckby are rebuked for disregard of grammar. They may deserve rebuke, but not for that reason. This text is given:

Καλῶ σὺν τέττιγι †Χαρισθένεοϛ† τρίχα τήνδε
κουρόσυνον κούραις θῆκ᾽ Ἀμαρυνθιάσι
σὺν βοὶ χερνιφθέντι· πάις δ᾽ ἴσον ἀστέρι λάμπει
πωλικὸν ὡς ἵππος χνοῦν ἀποσεισάμενος.

Since Χαρισθένεος is in the genitive case, there is no subject for the verb, and hence Wilamowitz (*Hell. Dicht.* 1.138), perhaps after καλλῶ of the Schol. Bern., replaced the vapid καλῷ with a feminine Καλλώ to play this role. Waltz and Beckby follow suit, taking Καλλώ, as Wilamowitz presumably did, to be a mother who dedicates "the hair of Charisthenes" her son; for them the subject changes in 3 to the boy himself. But the editors comment: "Wilamowitz ... without pausing to consider that the τέττιξ is a male adornment and ἀποσεισάμενος masc., said *die Weihende* Καλλώ *heisst;* Waltz and Beckby, similarly indifferent to the sex of *die Weihende*, printed Καλλώ and left the part. masc." "It could," they note, "if necessary agree with ἵππος but if the dedicator is a girl ἵππος also might be expected to be fem." I have tried to understand this as elaborate fooling intended to hint that no one in his right mind would take Καλλὼ Χαρισθένεος for anything but "Callo the daughter of Charisthenes." Certainly there is good sense under the confusion. Even if we could endure "the hair of Charisthenes," the introduction of the boy's name without sign of relationship is intolerably abrupt. But the editors' own solution is not very attractive—to invent a name Χαρισθένιος, wholly unknown, they admit, to Greek nomenclature. And if "Charisthenios" makes his own dedication, it is fair to ask who utters the striking praises of him in the latter part of the epigram. They would ill become the boy himself and would seem to come with better grace from his mother. That, however, is no problem if we orient ourselves properly to the epigram. The verses profess to be a real dedication, as τήνδε shows, and in real life such dedications of a boy's hair most naturally would be made by his parents; thus a father dedicates his son's hair in an inscription from Paros cited on an earlier epigram (1801). Theodoridas 1, *AP* 6.155 (3506), is closely parallel to Theodoridas 2; in it four-year-old Crobylus the son of Hegesidicus is represented, also in the third person, as having made the dedication, but the parent's voice comes through clearly in the prayer at the end: "Grant, Apollo, that Crobylus come to manhood and protect his property." This prayer exactly matches the praise of the boy in Theodoridas 2. The whole of our epigram, then, is an inscription dictated by a parent, and as the father of Crobylus reveals himself in the words παῖς Ἡγησιδίκου there is some expectation that a father similarly reveals himself in Χαρισθένεος. If that is right, the masculine name Κάλλων for the boy would meet the requirements—banish the inert καλῷ, preserve the better-protected form Χαρισθένεος and make with it an expected relation ship, "Callon son of Charisthenes" (for the word-order, cf. 2057: Ἀλκάνδρῳ τοῦτο τί Καλλιτέλευς), and have the advantage of being a real, indeed a quite common, Greek name (see 2976 and the note on 2811).

Index

Index

Index

Index

Index

Index

Library of Congress Cataloging in Publication Data

Hutton, James, 1902–
    Essays on Renaissance poetry.

    Includes index.
    1.   European poetry—Renaissance, 1450-1600—History and criticism—
Addresses, essays, lectures. I. Guerlac, Rita. II. Title.
PN1181.H88   809.1′03   80-66898
ISBN 0-8014-1253-6